Women's Activism and Globalization

Women's Activism and Globalization

Linking Local Struggles and Transnational Politics

Edited by

Nancy A. Naples & Manisha Desai

Published in 2002 by

Routledge
29 West 35th Street
New York, NY 10001

Published in Great Britain by

Routledge
11 New Fetter Lane
London EC4P 4EE

Routledge is an imprint of the Taylor & Francis Group.

Printed on acid-free, 250-year-life paper.
Manufactured in the United States of America.

10 9 8 7 6 5 4 3 2 1

Library of Congress Cataloging-in-Publication Data
Women's activism and globalization : linking local struggles and transnational politics / edited by Nancy A. Naples and Manisha Desai.
p. cm.
Includes bibliographical references and index.
ISBN 0-415-93144-4--ISBN 0-415-93145-2 (pbk.)
1. Women social reformers. 2. Women political activists. 3. Globalization. I. Naples, Nancy A. II. Desai, Manisha.

HQ1236 .W596 2002
303.48'4--dc21 2001045728

Contents

Preface

THIS COLLECTION IS A RESULT OF COLLABORATION AMONG MANY SCHOLARS INTERested in documenting the diverse ways women in different parts of the world creatively and heroically face the challenges posed by the global economic and political changes associated with "globalization." We include case studies of community-based, cross-national, regional, and transnational organizing to highlight the multiple sites in which women confront the oppressive features of the global expansion of capitalism and the neoliberal policies that support it. In choosing the chapters, we were primarily interested in identifying cases that demonstrate the intersection of the local, regional, and global dimensions of restructuring and resistance strategies. We take as our starting point the fact that globalization is a result of particular actions taken by identifiable actors, and that it lands in particular places. Rather than view globalization as something that occurs "out there" and that is therefore distant from the everyday lives and activities of particular actors, we seek to demonstrate how global economic and political change are manifest in the daily lives and struggles of women and other members of communities in different parts of the world in ways that are often hidden from view in analyses of globalization that start from the perspective of multinational corporations, transnational organizations, and international political institutions.

Our goal in this collection is to render visible the limits and possibilities of women's organizing in the context of globalization. Women in communities all around the world are fighting the negative effects of globalization and are using the transnational political stage to press for social, economic, environmental, and political justice. This collection documents effective organizing efforts in all of these realms. It also highlights the dilemmas of feminist praxis in the context of globalization. In this regard, it builds on coeditor Nancy Naples's collection *Community Activism and Feminist Politics: Organizing across Race, Class, and Gender* (1998), which emphasized women's community-based organizing in the United States with particular concern for cross-class and cross-race coalition-building efforts. This new collection is designed to reach beyond a specific national border and demonstrate how most local organizing campaigns are, in many ways, responses to broader social, economic, and political changes.

Space constraints prohibit us from including all of the case studies we have identified in the course of putting this book together. We would like to thank those authors who worked with us over the past two years, including those whose work we could not incorporate here. Our thanks also go out to University of California,

Irvine, graduate student Trish Erwin for her editorial assistance. Our special thanks to Bandana Purkayastha, Mangala Subramaniam, Mary Bernstein, and Nicole Bennett who helped us think through an organization of the book. Nancy would also like to express her special thanks to students in her graduate seminar "Postcolonial, Transnational Feminism, and Community Activism" for their comments on earlier drafts of each of the chapters. We are grateful to Jill Bystydzienski and an anonymous reviewer for their helpful comments on an early draft of the book. Our special thanks to Kimberly Guinta for her valuable editorial assistance. We are most appreciative of the support given us by Ilene Kalish, our editor at Routledge, for all her work to make this collection a reality.

1
Introduction

1

Changing the Terms

Community Activism, Globalization, and the Dilemmas of Transnational Feminist Praxis

Nancy A. Naples

COMMUNITY-BASED SOCIAL CHANGE EFFORTS SEEM ALL TOO LIMITED WHEN PLACED up against the structures of inequality that shape the wider political and economic context. Global processes of economic restructuring are undermining unionization, job security, sustainability of communities and the environment, and social supports, especially those provided through the so-called welfare state.[1] However, political activism designed to challenge the expansion of global inequality has generated worldwide attention, as evident in protests against the World Trade Organization, the World Bank, and the International Monetary Fund in Seattle; Washington, D.C.; Toronto, and many non-Western locales that receive little if any media attention. Furthermore, community actions on behalf of progressive agendas remain salient features of local encounters with the state, with corporations, with employers, and with racist and sexist forces pervading many spheres of social life. This book seeks to make visible the relationship between local organizing efforts and global economic restructuring as well to highlight the contradictions of transnational feminist politics.

Much of the literature on globalization concentrates on the broader economic, social, and political dimensions of contemporary global changes and neglects the ways in which these changes reshape the everyday lives of women in different parts of the world, except to highlight the increased participation of women in the labor force and the feminization of poverty among other dimensions of women's economic oppression. The case studies presented in this book demonstrate the diverse ways women respond to these powerful forces as well as how their activism can pose challenges to the "scattered hegemonies" (Grewal and Kaplan 1994) associated with the global expansion of capitalism. While transnational organizing has a long feminist history that the contemporary emphasis on globalization might obscure,[2] processes associated with globalization are "changing the terms of feminist politics"

(Krause 1996, 225). As Mary Meyer and Elisabeth Prügl (1999) observe in the introduction to their edited collection *Gender Politics in Global Governance*, "international economic and political crises destabilize entrenched institutions, including institutions of gender, thus opening up opportunities for emancipatory politics" (16).

Our collection makes salient the contradictions of transnational feminist organizing for locality-based women's movements and feminist organizing more broadly. As we work toward sustainable transnational feminist movements, many dimensions of power and inequalities of access and resources must be recognized and addressed. For example, many feminist global studies scholars note that "women's groups based in the North or whose members are primarily white, middle-class, well-educated women have usually held a leading role" in national as well as international feminist organizations (Krause 1996, 233).[3] Furthermore, as Manisha Desai (personal communication) points out, "while not necessarily elite organizations, certain Third World NGOs [nongovernmental organizations] such as the Grammen Bank in Bangladesh receive sustained attention and support from the West, while others that have more grassroots connections such as SEWA [Self-Employed Women's Association], which was founded by labour activist Ella Bhatt, who pioneered the microcredit movement in India" are marginalized on the international political stage.

The call to reaffirm the grassroots as a site from which more claims take on a more genuine logic runs through much of the feminist literature on women's movements and political organizing. However, this privileging of the so-called grassroots can also lead to a romanticization of this site of struggle as well as a tendency to "other" women said to be of the grassroots (see, e.g., Grewal 1999; Mindry forthcoming). Transnational feminist practice is further complicated by the problem of translation. For example, while I have used the term grassroots to a great extent in my own work on women's community-based activism in the United States, the term may not travel well as we attempt to explore women's community organizing in other contexts. For example, Nawal Ammar and Leila Lababidy (1999) point out in "Women's Grassroots Movements and Democratization in Egypt" that *the grassroots* "has no literal Arabic translation" (151).[4]

In this chapter, I discuss what I term "the politics of naming" including the diverse ways feminists are conceptualizing transnational feminist organizing and globalization. I highlight these issues with reference to the chapters in this collection. In the following chapter, Manisha Desai details the political economy of globalization and the neoliberal policies that support the global expansion of capitalism. In the last chapter in this introductory section we outline the organization of the book and the key issues addressed by each of the authors.

Transnational Organizing and the Politics of Naming

How we explicate and frame our approach to the intersection of global and local organizing says a great deal about our political orientation, disciplinary assumptions, and cross-cultural sensibility. The terms *global, transnational, international,* and "the" grassroots remain hotly contested among postcolonial, Third World, and international feminist scholars. The terms *Third World* and *postcolonial* are themselves contested constructs. The former became popular in the 1980s and was used by scholars in the fields of international relations, development studies, and the political economy of the world system to describe the uneven development and inequalities among nation-states primarily located in the southern region of the globe. So-called *First World* nations included North America and Western Europe. Although less frequently used, the Second World referred to the former communist nations. Those nation-states considered Third World were defined as underdeveloped or developing nations that were economically disadvantaged and therefore dependent on First World nations for financial, scientific, and technical assistance. This use of "Third World" has been strongly criticized by postcolonial scholars who argue that it discursively justifies the construction of the First World countries as dominant and more advanced (e.g., Mohanty 1991b). "Postcolonial" is typically applied to nations like India where a former colonial power has been removed. Some scholars who object to this term emphasize that it may mask continuing colonial relations that shape the lives of people in these nations. Both terms—*postcolonial* and *Third World*—are used to describe specific geographic and regional locations and nation-states as well as specific inhabitants of these regions. As identity categories, they also have been used to refer to former inhabitants of these regions. This use of the term has also been hotly debated by scholars who argue that this identity construction contributes to "othering" women from non-Western countries. In the context of feminist scholarship, "Third World" has been broadened to include women of color born in the so-called First World. These terms have also been taken up as theoretical frameworks to describe scholarship that focuses on the concerns or perspectives of Third World and postcolonial women. The authors in this collection use the terms *Third World* and *postcolonial* in multiple ways with a sensitivity to the contestations surrounding their usage and an awareness of how "relations of ruling" (D. Smith 1987) infuses all attempts to represent diverse women's lives and diverse locations with a singular categorization.

Feminist scholars interested in analyzing women's agency in a globalizing context also prefer the term *transnational* to other conceptualizations like *international women's movement* or *global feminism*. For example, Inderpal Grewal and Caren Kaplan (1994) use the term *transnational* in their work on feminist practices and critique the use of the term *global feminism* because, they argue, it "has elided the diversity of women's agency in favor of a universalized Western model of women's liberation that celebrates individuality and modernity" (17). Jacqui Alexander and Chandra Mohanty (1997b), who argue for analyses that intertwine "the global and the local," also use the term *transnational feminism* as a corrective to the notion of "global sisterhood," which, they argue, evokes the "'center/periphery' or 'first-world/Third-World model'" of feminist organizing (xxi). Along with Alexander and Mohanty (1997b), Grewal and Kaplan want to avoid the "the old sisterhood model of missionary work, of intervention and salvation that is clearly tied to older models of center-periphery relations" (1994, 19; see Enloe 1990).

Anne Sisson Runyan (1994) uses the term *inter-national,* inserting the hyphen to acknowledge the continued significance of national borders. In contrast, feminist scholars in dialogue with the international relations tradition of political science prefer the term *global* (Stearns 1998). Meyer and Prügl (1999), who are working to insert a feminist presence in the field of international relations, use the term *global governance* because, they argue, it "signals a movement beyond the narrow study of international organizations" (4). Gillian Youngs, coeditor of the new *International Feminist Journal of Politics* (Youngs, Jones, and Pettman 1999), also views *international* as a problematic term because it "has itself contributed to the power/knowledge hierarchies that structure dominant understandings of the world" (7).[5]

In a 1998 article in *Feminist Studies*, sociologist Karen Booth explains why she too prefers the term *global* to *international.* The latter, she argues, "undergirded the Western powers' founding vision of the UN, which was to be the manager of a collaboration of sovereign and equal nations." The internationalism of the United Nations was used to define it as "a politically neutral space for the representatives of these nations to discuss and debate issues of common concern" (119). In contrast, for Booth, "globalism" is a more radical construct.

> Global actors reject the sovereignty, at times even the relevance, of the nation state and the significance of the citizen identity. Instead, they behave as if the political and economic relations forged across geographical boundaries—in multinational enterprises, conferences, and organizations, devoted to specific issues [such] as the environment or AIDS, in immigrant enclaves, over the internet, and so on—were the most relevant sites of decision making and identity formation.

Booth uses the term *transnational* to refer to "any actor, organization, or issue that could be either international or global in orientation" (120).[6] As scholars debate the terms best suited to describe transnational feminist practices, we remain relatively uninformed about which strategies might be most effective in inserting so-called grassroots women's interests in national, international, and global organizing efforts (also see Bystydzienski and Sekhon 1999).

Many feminist geographers and Third World feminist scholars argue that a more effective approach to globalization is to address "the manifestations of the global in [our particular] local" (Eschle 1999, 328 in her review of Miles 1996).[7] Other global studies scholars interested in differentiating the capitalist form of globalization from a more grassroots or socially just approach distinguish between globalization from above and globalization from below or transnational grassroots politics. In her contribution to Michael Peter Smith and Luis Eduardo Guarnizo's (1998) collection, Sarah Mahler defines "transnationalism from above" as "multinational corporations, media, commoditization . . . and other macro-level structures and processes that transcend two or more states are not produced and projected equally in all areas, but are controlled by powerful elites who seek, although do not necessarily find, political, economic and social dominance in the world" (66–67). In contrast, Mahler explains:

> "[T]ransnationalism from below" generates multiple and counter-hegemonic powers among nonelites. Moreover, transnationalism from below describes "the ways that the *everyday practices of ordinary people*, their feelings and understandings of their conditions of existence, often modify those very conditions and thereby shape rather than merely reflect new modes of urban culture." (Mahler 1988, 67, quoting M. P. Smith 1992: 493–94; emphasis added by Mahler)

Mahler recognizes limits to the terms *transnational from below* and *grassroots*. She asks "*who* is deemed grassroots: traditionally disenfranchised groups, anyone who does not represent state or corporate interests, perhaps elites who take counter-hegemonic positions, or even coalitions that include diverse members?" (69–70; emphasis in original). She references Sikkink's (1993, 439) observation that "[t]he idea of a social movement . . . with its emphasis on bottom-up citizen protest, fails to portray accurately the range of actors involved in human rights issues, including foundations and international and regional organizations" (70). For example, in her study of South African NGOs, Mindry (2001) describes how the term "grass roots" was used by white and middle-class women to refer to black and rural women. Mindry argues, "It is important that we begin to examine the ways in which moralizing discourses such as those concerning the 'grassroots' and 'poor, black, rural women' as targets of intervention structure relationships among women working in NGOs in ways that are remarkably hierarchal.

This construction of the "grassroots" fails to capture the politics of accountability and the extent to which so-called grassroots groups are inclusive and encourage participatory democratic practices. For example, left unanswered are the following: Who gets to define issues to be brought to the transnational political stage, who gets to participate in this form of activism, and whose voices are left out of the dialogue? Mahler fears that the bipolar construction "transnationalism from above" and "transnationalism from below" privileges formal organizations. This distinction also masks the complex ways resistance operates on multiple levels simultaneously and the relations of ruling that may shape so-called grassroots or local organizing efforts. In fact, as Guarnizo and Smith (1998) argue, transnational organizing takes place in multiple sites and at multiple levels:

> [T]ransnational political spaces should be treated as the resultant of separate, sometimes parallel, sometimes competing projects at all levels of the global system—from the "global government" agenda of international organizations and multinational corporations to the most local "survival strategies," by which transnational migrant networks are socially constructed. (6)

Guarnizo and Smith use the term *transnational social formation* to emphasize how "transnational practices, while connecting collectivities located in more than one national territory, are embodied in specific social relations established between specific people, situated in . . . localities, at historically determined times" (11).

In a similar vein, using the plural *globalizations* Jane Jenson and Boaventura de Sousa Santos (2000) argue for an approach that views globalizations "as the extension of particular localisms" (12). By highlighting the links between diverse locales and processes associated with globalization, our collection further contextualizes globalizations. This collection demonstrates how globalization must be understood as a process generated from the everyday activities and negotiations of diverse individuals, communities, governmental bodies, and transnational coalitions. In the next section of this chapter, I further clarify the debates over terminology and the politics of location in order to explicate the dynamics of globalization and resistance.

Globalization and Resistance: Defining the Terms of Debate

The term *globalization* is sometimes used as a synonym for *global economic restructuring* of capitalism. It is also used to discuss the movement of peoples, information, and consumer culture. In the first usage it often refers to "a single, though heterogenizing system tightening its grip on the world's remotest localities and enclaves" (Buell 1998, 550). In the second usage, it is used to refer to "a complex system becoming still more decentered." Consequently, as Fredrick Buell (1998) points out, "Thought about globalization has thus been deeply uncertain and schizophrenic: it is centering and decentering, catastrophic and creative all at once" (550).

Feminist scholars offer insights into the contradictions associated with globalization by exploring how gender, sexuality, racialization, and region are mobilized to reinscribe differences through market relations. For example, as ethnic studies scholar Lisa Lowe (1996) argues, "One of the distinct features of the global restructuring of capital is its ability to profit not through homogenization but through the differentiation of specific resources and markets that permit the exploitation of gendered and racialized labor within regional and national sites." Ironically, "the very processes that produce a racialized feminized proletariat . . . displace traditional and national patriarchies," thus generating "new possibilities precisely because they have led to a breakdown and a reformulation of the categories of nation, race, class, and gender" (161–62; also see Kelly, Bayes, Hawkesworth, and Young 2001). As Lowe points out, the contradictory processes associated with globalization reshape the possibilities for political action to "the interstitial sites of the social formation in which the national intersects with the international" (172).

Globalization processes lead many observers to assert that borders between nation-states are becoming "markedly less relevant to everyday behaviour in the various dimensions of economy, information, ecology, technology, cross-cultural conflict and civil society" (Beck 2000, 20). Immigration scholars, however, stress that while capital and goods travel more easily across borders, immigrants do not move as freely, despite their centrality within global economic processes. Saskia Sassen (1998) notes how U.S. domestic policies contribute to displacement of peoples from different regions who then seek emigration to the United States. For example, when the U.S. government provided $3 billion to ensure a steady price for U.S. sugar producers, an estimated 400,000 workers lost their jobs in the Dominican Republic because producers in the Caribbean Basin countries could not compete. Sassen contends that this domestic policy resulted in the emigration of large numbers of Dominicans to the United States. Yet, U.S. immigration policy, with its focus on limiting entry to the United States, "is increasingly at odds with other major policy frameworks in the international system and with the growth of global economic integration" (60).

Guarnizo and Smith (1998) describe how a number of "historically specific factors" that converged to produce a highly complex form of transnationalism: "the globalization of capitalism with its destabilizing effects on less industrialized countries"; "the technological revolution in the means of transportation and communication"; "global political transformations such as decolonization and the universalization of human rights"; and "the expansion of social networks that facilitate the reproduction of transnational migration, economic organization, and politics"

(8). Each chapter of this book highlights one or more of these dimensions from the point of view of women's local, regional and transnational struggles for social, political, and economic justice.

Shifting from the local to a regional site of organizing, Sharon Navarro analyzes how women's geographic location along the U.S.-Mexico border affects the structure and content of their sociopolitical identities. Navarro's case study illustrates the ways in which gender, class, race, language, and geographic location intersect to form individual and collective sociopolitical identities and how these constructions of identity shape political activism. Political scientist Rachel Cichowski examines how activists have used the European Union to expand women's rights in member nations.

Moving to examine the interaction between international nongovernmental and financial institutions and local communities, Winifred Poster and Zakia Salime demonstrate how the discourse of microcredit and microenterprise promoted by the United States Agency for International Development (USAID) and the Work Bank limits transnational feminist efforts to ensure women's economic and social empowerment in the United States and Morocco. They examine how the microcredit projects sponsored by the USAID and the World Bank provide livelihoods limited to the informal sector that, rather than move women out of poverty, exacerbate gender dynamics at the household level. As in this case, international agencies and some NGOs can reproduce inequalities between Northern experts/donors and Southern recipients of aid. Alexandra Hrycak provides further evidence for this process in her study of a U.S. NGO's efforts to support women's political participation in Russia. On the one hand, resources provided by Northern or Western NGOs to women's groups in other parts of the world that emphasize international conferencing and transnational networks can also serve to divert activist attention from local issues, as Elisabeth Friedman (1999) illustrates in her study of Venezuela's women's movement.[8] On the other hand, activists have taken the vision of a "global civil society" to infuse local community organizing efforts with new strategies for linking community-based economic development and consumption practices with a sensitivity to the interdependence of the local and global dimensions of social life. By situating analyses of globalization in women's community-based efforts and in local feminist praxis, these essays help to deepen our understanding of the limits and possibilities of counter-hegemonic alternatives to oppressive forms of globalization, especially those associated with global economic restructuring.

The global economy has been undergoing a process of restructuring since the early 1970s. Some trace this restructuring to the 1973 oil crisis, "when big companies in the West resorted to international subcontracting to survive" (Stearns 1998, 134). As international relations scholar Jill Stearns notes, transnational corporations forged a geographic division of labor that had far-reaching repercussions. The knowledge-intensive aspects of the production process remained lodged in the West, but those that were labor intensive shifted

> to developing countries where cheap female labour was abundant. In the 1980s as big business emphasized the importance of managerial flexibility and decentralized production, corporate strategies in the West sought a more flexible workforce to undermine the power of traditional unions. (134–35)

Features of global economic restructuring include a decline in organized labor and formal labor contracts; increasing internationalization of capital; growth in informal and part-time employment; loss of local economic and natural resources; cutbacks in social provisioning associated with the so-called welfare state; restructuring of women's work; and a growing disparity between classes. For example, in Bangladesh, young women sewing clothes for Walmart earn up to 20 cents an hour. In 1998, Walmart CEO David Glass took $40 million in pay, options, and bonuses: compensation equal to almost $20,000 an hour for a 40-hour work week. Walmart is the largest private-sector employer in the U.S. United States workers earn an average of $6.10 an hour. One half of these workers qualify for federal food stamps (National Labor Committee 1999).

Poor women, who are disproportionately women of color, bear an unequal burden of the economic and social dislocation resulting from these gendered, racialized, and internationalized processes. The consequences for women in terms of their social citizenship, health, work burden, education, and their access to employment, credit, and income have been well documented (see, for example, Charlton, Everett, and Staudt 1989; Goldberg and Kremen 1990; Peterson and Runyan 1993; Staudt 1990; and Vickers 1991). Jill Stearns (1998) reports: "Where women are encouraged to take up roles in the paid sector—and women now make up some 41 per cent of paid workers in developed countries and 34 per cent worldwide—it is still the case that on average they earn 30–40 per cent less than men for comparable work." In addition, structural adjustment programs and neoliberal policies promoted by national governments, whether consciously or unconsciously, assume that women will continue to expand their unpaid labor in the home and communities to compensate for the increase in poverty and loss of local resources. In response to increased economic, social, and environment pressures, women are organizing within their communities, across national borders, and challenging neoliberal policies as well as oppressive labor demands (e.g., see Mendez, Navarro, and Weber in this volume).

The process of global economic restructuring has been hastened by the *structural adjustment policies* enforced by the International Monetary Fund (IMF) and the World Bank in return for loans Third World or so-called developing countries (see Desai in this volume). The goal of structural adjustment policies has been to liberalize economies around the world. Structural adjustment and related neoliberal policies emphasize privatization and production for export over domestic consumption practices. Neoliberal policies also enhance women's unpaid household and caretaking labor as a direct consequence of the decline in public provisioning or welfare supports.

The complex mix of ongoing economic inequalities and new economic restructuring are woven in and through community and household survival strategies that themselves are embedded in cultural practices, local patterns of inequality, and contextualized responses to the economic changes (Jameson and Miyoshi 1999; Ong 1999; Rajan 1993). As Aihwa Ong (1999) emphasizes in her study of the "flexible citizenship" of Asian immigrants, analyses of global economic restructuring should incorporate both "the economic rationalities of globalization and the cultural dynamics that shape human and political responses." Furthermore, she argues,

> When an approach to cultural globalization seeks merely to sketch out universalizing trends rather than deal with actually existing structures of power and situated cultural processes, the analysis cries out for a sense of political economy and situated ethnography. What are the mechanisms of power that enable the mobility, as well as the localization and disciplining, of diverse populations within these transnational systems? How are cultural flows and human imagination conditioned and shaped within these new relations of global inequalities? (5)

Our collection seeks to provide such a resource, one that includes richly contextualized ethnographic case studies of individual and organizational efforts to negotiate the political economy that shapes their everyday lives. We also offer an interdisciplinary feminist exploration that highlights the diversity of women's activist responses to globalization. The intersectional, interdisciplinary, and ethnographic case studies presented in *Women's Activism and Globalization* demonstrate the complex material, political, economic, historical, and discursive processes by which global economic restructuring proceeds while illustrating how women and other marginalized actors can resist what Jeremy Brecher and Tim Costello (1994) term "downward leveling" (4) associated with the globalization of capitalism.

Conclusion

Our collection is designed to show the myriad ways women are organizing against the gendered, racialized, and regionalized processes of global capital expansion.

Women activists are also challenging militarization, as Yoko Fukumura and Martha Matsuoka illustrate; organizing against regional trade agreements that do not protect workers, as is evident in Sharon Navarro's and Jennifer Mendez's studies of cross-border and regional organizing; fighting for sustainable agriculture, as Betty Wells demonstrates; and using international human rights discourse and international conferences to enhance women's rights, as Susanna Wing documents. Finally, as Bandana Purkayastha demonstrates, women around the world are also helping to empower the next generation of women activists who will build on the valuable foundation laid by the foremothers.

Notes

1. According to a 1999 Human Development Report, the percentage of the population who live on less than $1 a day in the following countries is: Mexico, 14; Chile, 15; Phillipines, 28; Bangladesh, 29; Brazil, 29; China, 29; Guatemala, 53.

2. For example, as a consequence of transnational organizing on behalf of women's suffrage, women activists from both sides of the Atlantic met in Washington, D.C., in 1888 and established the "first lasting multipurpose transnational women's organization, the International Council of Women" (Rupp 1997, 15). The international council was slow to foster the formation of national councils in countries other than the United States and Canada. However, under the leadership of Lady Aberdeen and through the international organizing efforts of Teresa Wilson, national councils were developed in Australia, Germany, Great Britain, Sweden, and the Netherlands. Historian Leila Rupp reports that, by 1939, 36 councils were affiliated with the international council.

3. And, as Deborah Stienstra (1999) points out, "Gender, race/ethnicity, class, and colonization also shape the internal relations within movements" (264).

4. Ammar and Lababidy (1999) note:

> The issues of democracy, grassroots movements, and women's rights are not alien to the Egyptian culture, which have a historical heritage of the *shoura* principle, but are hindered by a global economic calculus and a local elite that perceives such issues to be threatening to their power and status. In Arabic the word "democracy" has been adopted from English and arabicized to read *demoqratiah.* The word is often used in a revolutionary/violent context and, therefore, is never connected to the local democratic practice of *shoura*, which literally means public opinion as well as embodying the notion of consensus, and is part of the overall Arab-Islamic political heritage. Hence, connecting terms such as "grassroots" or "empowerment for women" to the term *demoqratiah* in the Egyptian context would give them a negative connotation. (151)

Those working in the 1960s and 1970s to challenge elite rule in Arab societies "assumed a Marxist vision of the populace as a base, *al-qa'ida*. Thus the term translated within the cultural and historical context comes loaded with issues that render it suspect or negative."

5. Anthropologist Aihwa Ong (1999) retains the term *globalization* when discussing "new corporate strategies" but prefers the term *transnationalism* when referring "to the cultural specificities of global processes" (4). In a similar vein, immigration scholars Linda Basch, Nina Glick Schiller, and Cristina Szanton Blanc (1994) define transnationalism as "the processes by which immigrants forge and sustain multi-stranded social relations that link together their societies of origin and settlement" (7).

6. However, Booth (1998) explains, for the most part, UN femocrats working for the World Health Organization draw on the "internationalist constructions of women's needs" because the WHO "derives its legitimacy from member states' perceptions of it as an apolitical agency" (119).

7. Jacqui Alexander and Chandra Mohanty (1997) emphasize the need to explore, as one reviewer said, "located subjectivities . . . against the backdrop of globalising capitalism and the complex, diffuse ways it builds upon and retrenches colonial relationships" (Eschle 1999, 329 in her review of their edited collection *Feminist Genealogies, Colonial Legacies, Democratic Futures*).

8. Elisabeth Friedman (1999) notes that the U.S. Agency for International Development (USAID) was the primary sponsor of the Latin American regional process that links local NGOs to the UN conference planning process. Friedman reports: "Women's movements throughout the region debated whether or not to accept money from an agency with a history of promoting US interests to the detriment of those of Third World nations" (362). Furthermore, "Argentine feminists found the influence of the dominant Argentine political party so pervasive at the Latin American NGO regional preparatory conference [for Beijing] that they set up an alternative forum at the September 1994 meeting in Mar de Plata" (363). Although Venezuela's women's movement benefited greatly from participation in the Nairobi conference in 1985, NGOs and women's movement organizations did not receive similar benefits from the 1995 fourth world conference in Beijing.

2

Transnational Solidarity

Women's Agency, Structural Adjustment, and Globalization

Manisha Desai

In this chapter I examine how global capital, structural adjustment programs and international institutions such as the United Nations have shaped women's agency around the world. In particular, I focus on two important features of women's agency in the global era. First, just as global capital is fluid and exists simultaneously in multiple spaces, resulting in "scattered hegemonies" (Grewal and Kaplan 1994), so is women's agency evident in multiple spaces from the local grassroots movements and community-based nongovernmental organizations (NGOs) to national and transnational feminist networks. Second, women from around the world have been forging transnational feminist solidarities via networks, regional meetings, and world conferences. At these sites, the flow of ideas and activism is no longer unidirectional, from the North to the South, but multidirectional. The ideas and activism are dispersed into varied local sites where they are picked up and refashioned as they resonate in contextualized ways.

While globalization has been variously defined (for example, Wachtel [2001] has collected 450 definitions), many analysts associate globalization with the homogenizing impact of global capital (e.g., Giddens 1990). This occurs via increasing economic integration resulting in one world market. Transnational corporations (TNCs) and international financial institutions shape this market through global production, consumption, and capital flows facilitated by the revolution in information and communication technologies. By contrast, analysts who focus on the global flows of people, ideas, and images emphasize the hybridity, or the heterogeneity that results as people from different parts of the world interact and creatively combine their own patterns of meaning making with those that derive from other cultures (Appadurai 1990; Hall 1991).

These two apparently contrasting views appear not so contradictory when one recognizes that each view tends to focus on only one aspect of globalization—the political-economic dimensions in the case of the "homogenizers," and cultural practices in the case of the "heterogenizers." Moreover, neither specifically looks at how women are responding to the global political economy through innovative political, economic, and cultural strategies. When one shifts the focus to women's agency in the global political economy, we see a complex set of relations that are built on preexisting patriarchal, racial, and ethnic practices. One also sees women creating new sites for action at the local, national, and transnational levels in which to enact new political, economic, and cultural practices. In this way, women activists offer alternatives to the seemingly inevitable course of global capital. Consequently, women's agency in this era of globalization challenges the dominant framing of globalization and opens up new directions for both feminist theorizing and activism.

The Gendered Effects of Structural Adjustment Programs

Structural adjustment programs (SAPs) are the primary mechanism through which globalization has affected women's daily lives in the South. In the North, similar effects result from economic restructuring of manufacturing and neoliberal policies that emphasize privatization in all aspects of the political economy. SAPs were first engineered by the International Monetary Fund (IMF) and the World Bank. Sean Riain (2000) argues that globalization has imposed the dominant Anglo-American neoliberal model of the relationship between state and transnational capital on neoliberal, socialist, and postcolonial states. Hence, most states have adopted a package that share some variant of the following features:

> (1) cutbacks in public spending to balance government budgets and service debts; (2) monetary policies designed to fight inflation by restricting the money supply (and incomes); (3) the selling of government enterprises (privatization) in an attempt to balance government budgets and improve business production efficiency; and (4) the shift of manufacturing and agricultural sectors toward production for export instead of the domestic market, in order to improve international balances. (Wiegersma 1997, 258)

The basic argument scholars have made about the impact of SAPs on women worldwide is that "adjustment intensifies the trade-off between women's producer and non-producer roles, or, in stronger terms, that the 'crisis of social disinvestment (under adjustment) is financed from a "social fund" provided by the superhuman efforts of poor women' (UNICEF 1989)" (Baden 1997, 38).

These policies have had four major effects on women. First, there has been a contradictory impact on women's paid work. There has been a feminization of the global labor force and an increase in women's employment in the low-paid service sector (Fuentes and Ehrenreich 1983; also see Nash and Fernandez-Kelly 1983; Ward 1990). This is evident in the increasing rate of women's share of paid economic activity all over the South particularly in export processing zones in the North. In 2000, women constituted 36 percent of the total global workforce. In the global trade policy literature this is known as the "employment effect" of international trade. Women are now 33 percent of the Asian labor force as compared to 25 percent in 1970; women are 28 percent of the labor force in Latin American and the Caribbean compared to 20 percent in 1970; women comprise 42 percent of the European labor force compared to 35 percent in 1970, and in North America, women are 30 percent of the labor force compared to 24 percent in 1970 (Neft and Levine 1997). In Sub-Saharan Africa, where agriculture is still the predominant means of support, women have not become a large part of the industrial labor force; rather, they contribute, in large measure, to export-oriented agriculture, and through their unpaid labor in the home (Fontana, Joekes, and Masika 1998).

Second, there has been an increase in women's employment in the informal sector, where workers receive no protections from unemployment, no benefits, and wages below poverty level. Third, women's share of unpaid labor in the home has increased as public funding for health, education, and other social services has declined. Finally, as more and more land is appropriated for global production, land for cultivation and local sustenance diminishes, and environmental damage escalates. Women in the South, who depend on their environments more directly for material and cultural resources, face great survival difficulties while women in the North, particularly those living in poor neighborhoods, find their communities becoming dumping grounds for toxic and other waste generated in an economy that hardly benefits them. Women in the North and South have responded to each of these challenges in multiple ways leading to what is best called scattered resistance.

The Gendered Restructuring of Labor and Women's Resistances

Global capital has a contradictory impact on women's daily lives. Along with the selective increase in women's work there is also evidence of increasing unemployment. For example, in Ghana, 20 percent of women in the traditional trading markets lost their jobs as SAPs provided credits to large-scale trading enterprises controlled by men (Manuh 1997). Small trading markets were made obsolete by these changes. In eastern European countries, where women had high rates of labor force participation compared to the rest of the world, the picture has changed dramatically since 1989. Many of these countries have undergone the transition from a planned economy to a free-market economy. As a result, female labor force activity has declined in 10 of the 14 eastern European countries. An estimated 26 million jobs were lost in the region from 1990 to 1995, and 14 million of those jobs were women's (Moner Project 1999).

While overt unionizing was, and still, remains difficult in the export processing zones (EPZs), feminist analyses focused on various political as well as cultural resistance of women at the local level. For example, anthropologist Aihwa Ong (1987) discusses the claims of spirit possessions, which require time-consuming rituals to free women workers and/or their machines from these spirits, as among a very resourceful resistance to increased demands and new tasks. These have led to work stoppages as well as garnering certain benefits such as breaks. Similarly, analysts of women in the maquiladoras along the U.S./Mexico border note how women workers engage in work stoppages for cultural celebrations and use religious and other traditional practices to organize workers (e.g., Fernandez-Kelly 1983; Tiano 1994).

Transnational solidarity networks have also grown to post a significant challenge to SAPs and other neoliberal policies. These networks include unions, movements, NGOs of local women working in the EPZs as well as middle-class activists from the country and transnational NGOs and movements (see, for example, Mendez and Navarro in this volume). Alvarez notes the increasing NGO-ization of women's movements with its attendant decline in radical critique and an increasing role in serving as experts and implementers of government and international donors' programs. Some NGOs are no more than fronts for the government, while others Alvarez calls "hybrid NGOs" maintain links with movements and try to work both within and outside the system. These NGOs simultaneously provide a critique of government agencies and actions as well as mobilize to gain resources for empowering women.

Activist networks are often supported by public consciousness-raising efforts that are mainly located in the Northern countries and whose focus is educating Northern consumers. Many NGOs include consumer education as part of their advocacy work on behalf of maquiladora workers and other low-wage workers in the "global assembly line." For example, Women Working Worldwide in the United Kingdom is an international coalition that highlights the effects of trade liberalization on women workers in Bangladesh, India, Korea, Mexico, Peru, South Korea, Thailand, and the United Kingdom through networking and public education. The Clean Clothes Campaign, based in the Netherlands, supports the struggles of women workers in garment-producing units, sweatshops, factories, and home-based industry for improved working conditions in the South and North by making the European public aware of the situation. Label Behind the Label is a similar effort based in the United Kingdom to promote the rights and working conditions of women workers in the garment industries around the world.

In addition to activist networks, many academic and policy-oriented international groups work together with NGOs around the world to contextualize the oppressive features of global economic restructuring. Groups like DAWN (Development Alternatives with Women for a New Era) and the Women's Alternative Economic Summit focus on research and policy through developing regional centers in Latin America, Asia, and Africa. While the local and transnational networks focus on women in the global economy, most women find themselves in the so-called informal sector where the struggle is to assert a right to work.

Asserting a Right to Work

Over the globe, 71 percent of women work in the less visible informal sector where they prepare products for sale in the market, domestic service, and work in their homes to produce goods for subcontractors (e.g., Benería and Feldman 1992; SEWA 1998; Ward 1990). Although such work is unregulated, poorly paid, and involves long hours, it plays a crucial role in maintaining a modicum of livelihood for most poor women in a post–structural adjustment world. In fact, the World Bank and other development agencies like the U.S. Agency for International Development (USAID) have celebrated and supported the microcredit movement, as Poster and Salime detail in their chapter in this volume. These writers emphasize how the discourse of microcredit and microenterprise prioritizes the market rather than women's economic and social empowerment.

Women have been at the forefront of detailing the relationship of their informal work and unpaid household labor to the formal economy. The Self-Employed Women's Association (SEWA) in India was one of the first organizations to define the various informal activities of women, such as vegetable vending, ragpicking, and producing goods at home for sale *as work.* Established in 1972, SEWA successfully unionized informal women workers who had been prevented from organizing unions because trade union laws in India did not recognize them as workers. In addition to unionizing, women in India have formed cooperatives based on their various economic activities in order to market effectively, share resources, and form support networks. Most important, SEWA has trained community health workers and set up a SEWA university to train women not just in production and managerial skills but to be leaders and organizers who can participate in decisions that affect their lives. SEWA now has close to two million members in cities throughout India as well as in rural areas in Gujarat. SEWA has had the dual focus on "union" and "development" from the start but over time it has become more defined and elaborate. In the process of unionizing, SEWA also fosters a critical understanding about the economy and social inequalities and uses that knowledge to address these inequalities—particularily the impace of religious violence among Hindus and Muslims.

Similarly, women working in the informal economies in Tanzania, Ghana, Zimbabwe, Ecuador, Peru, and other countries have formed networks to pool resources, start savings and credit associations and form solidarities for survival (e.g., Bose and Acosta-Belén 1995; Nash and Safa 1985; Osirim 1996; Rowbotham and Mitter 1994). In addition to local networks, self-employed women, like their counterparts in the EPZs, have also formed transnational networks such as GROOTS (Grassroots Organizations Operating Together in Sisterhood) International, primarily to learn new ideas, share best practices, and influence local and international policy making around informal sector issues. Marina Karides's chapter demonstrates such transnational activism and unionizing efforts of another major sector of the informal economy, namely domestic work. She shows how Trinidad's National Union of Domestic Employees (NUDE) has worked for the rights of domestic workers, who are primarily women, by using the global rhetoric and international agreements signed by Trinidad to make the government accountable at home.

In the North, the informal activity is primarily concentrated among women of color, mostly immigrant women of color, who provide services that cannot be shifted to the South, such as domestic help and low-wage jobs in the food and health services. Sassen (1999) calls this the "de-valorized" sector of the economy as opposed to the valorized, information technology sector, which employs only a small, highly educated segment. White, upper-class women's increased presence in professional sectors of the North has influenced the incorporation of immigrant women of color into what Hochschild (2000) calls "global care chains," a "series of personal links between people across the globe based on the paid or unpaid work of caring" (131). Hochschild takes a critical modernist perspective on the global care chain, recognizing the global inequalities of resources as well as care, and does not see it as simply an inevitable part of globalization. At the same time she avoids a "primordialist stance" that mothers should care for their own children and kin and not migrate to care for others' children. She advocates not only better pay and working conditions for the immigrant caregivers but immigration policies that would allow children access to their mothers who have migrated North.

Struggling for a Better Quality of Life

Another major effect of global economic restructuring has been the increase in women's unpaid labor at home. Even before SAPs, women did 70 percent of the world's unpaid work. Now women all over the world are engaged in providing more care for children, elderly parents, and other family members, in addition to their poorly paid work either in the formal or informal sector of the economy. Women thus bear additional emotional stress arising from the "belt-tightening" demanded by economic restructuring (Kirmani and Munyakho 1996; Nzomo 1994).

As the price of goods—especially food—has increased in all parts of the world, women have become even more vulnerable to malnutrition as they eat last after providing for their children and family members. This has led women's groups in India, Zimbabwe, and other countries to demand the continuance and growth of the public distribution system, which in the case of India provides subsidized food to the urban and rural poor. Women's groups are also working with the World Food Program to ensure that women and children are able to get at least the minimum food required to sustain them. As Blank (1997), Naples (1998c), and other scholars have demonstrated, so-called welfare reforms in the United States have also disproportionately affected women-headed households.

The absence from national statistics of women's unpaid work and informal labor continues to be a concern for feminist activists. The Beijing Declaration and Platform for Action that arose out of the Women's World Conference in 1995 affirmed the need to count women's work in the home and remunerate women for that work, but most countries have not taken any serious steps in that direction. To highlight this noncompliance, women in Ireland called a women's strike on March 8, 1999, demanding an end to the devaluation of women's waged and unwaged labor. Since then the strike has become global as women from 64 countries observed it in 2000. It has also been taken up by the International Wages for Housework Campaign and the International Women Count Network.

In addition to such international challenges, a myriad of local challenges are addressing the "public provision" effect of SAPs. Many local and international NGOs have taken up the task of providing women with education, health services, and political empowerment. For example, programs like Mahila Samakhya in India, partly funded by the state, is a program of education for empowering women based on a process of consciousness-raising, organizing, and broadening the awareness and skills of poor rural women in order to take control of their lives. This program exists in six states in India and is run in collaboration with women's-movement groups, which oversee both the content as well as the process of educating women for empowerment (IAWS 1995).

Other women's groups have organized in urban and rural areas to provide and demand health services from the state. However, many of these services are being dismantled or privatized. Women and children are the main users of health services, and women are the primary providers of health care. If health is taken to mean, in accordance with the World Health Organization (WHO), a "state of complete physical, mental, and social well-being" then women's health has deteriorated in all respects in the contemporary era of global trade.

Starting in the early 1980s, the World Bank promoted a series of health-related initiatives to pressure Third World governments to control population growth. It recommended universal measures for reform that did not take into consideration

Third World women's economic, social, or cultural realities. These initiatives emphasized privatization of health care to be understood as introduction of user charges in state health clinics and hospitals, especially for consumer drugs and curative care (the rationale was that the rich would be made to pay, thus leaving the government free to pay for community services and public health for the poor); promotion of third-party insurance such as sickness funds and social security; promotion of hospitals, nursing homes, and clinics; and decentralization of planning, budgeting, and purchasing for government health services (Turshen 1994). Such privatization recommendations are especially problematic in countries where the people already assume a greater share of health care burden than in First World countries. In the latter, especially Scandinavian countries, governments assume more than 90 percent of health expenditure. By contrast, in Sub-Saharan Africa and Asia, governments contribute only about 52 to 57 percent of the total health budget.

One of the consequences of privatization of health care in Third World countries has been a cut in public health services, particularly primary care, and the increased use of nongovernmental and private voluntary organizations to deliver services (Turshen 1994). In Africa, NGOs provide between 25 and 94 percent of health services. For example, 25 percent of hospital care in Ghana is private; in Zimbabwe 94 percent of services for the elderly are private; and in Uganda and Malawi 40 percent of all health services are private. Privatization has greatly reduced government-funded primary care, thus limiting the access of poor people, particularly women, to health care. In some cases, health care is completely inaccessible to poor women. When poor women have to pay for health care from their meager earnings, they do so for their children but not for themselves (Butegwa 1998).

In the United States the linking of health care to employment has meant that women who are unemployed or work part-time have no health care. The introduction of managed care in the United States and the crisis in socialized medicine in western and northern Europe has meant a decline in the availability of health care for many women and their families. Women are expected to make up the cuts in public services by providing unpaid care at home and by buying it in the marketplace. One of the sharpest measures of women's deteriorating health can be seen in eastern European countries undergoing transition. The UNICEF-sponsored Moner Report found that in 16 of the 23 countries in the region, life expectancy has declined. In Russia, women have lost 3.2 years since 1989.

Women have responded to declining health services by developing community-based health projects, making demands on the state to be more accountable, and linking with groups in their country and around the world to influence national and international policies. In India groups like the Centre for Enquiry into Health and Allied Themes (CEHAT, which also means "health" in several Indian languages) are at the forefront of providing services to women and of researching and providing critiques of the impact of SAPS on women's health. Studies by CEHAT reveal that the state has never committed more than 3.5 percent of its gross national product to the health sector. This small percentage has further eroded since the 1970s and reached a low of 2.6 percent in 1994–1995, at the peak of the liberalization effort. The public health expenditure's share in the national income since SAPs is less than 1 percent. Most of the health budget comes from the state and not the national government. At the individual level, the CEHAT studies found that given the paucity of public health availability, 80 percent of health care costs come out of people's own pockets.

In addition to conducting research, CEHAT has a number of activists who live in urban and rural poor communities and develop health education and primary health care projects alongside the people in the communities. Many CEHAT members are founders of the second wave of the women's movement in India. Through their effort, they have incorporated a feminist perspective into the health debates and have added a concern for health to the women's movement agenda. CEHAT's assumption is that equitable and appropriate health care can be possible only in a context of economic and social equality. Hence, CEHAT has worked with local women to form village-level women's health teams, to establish a bank run by women, and to provide training for health work.

In addition to community-based work, a national network has emerged through CEHAT's efforts. Called HealthWatch: A Network for Action and Research on Women's Health, its major objective is to increase the attention paid to women's health needs and concerns in public debates and national policy. HealthWatch has begun a dialogue with the government at various levels. For example, in 1998 it brought together activists from the western region in India to discuss a new government initiative known as a "target-free" approach to population policy. This initiative provides for a more woman-centered approach to reproduction and eliminated the quotas that local health practitioners had to meet for population control.

CEHAT is also part of international networks such as the International Network of Health and Human Rights Organizations, ISIS-International, the Women's Global Network on Reproductive Rights, and the International Women's Tribune Center. It was the mobilizing efforts initiated by such international networks that led to the presence of many women's health NGOs like CEHAT at the Cairo Population Conference in 1994. The declaration from the population conference in Cairo, which emphasized the need to empower women and protect their human rights as the best strategy of population control, was an important victory for the international women's movement.

Nurturing Nature

Whether it is the destruction of the rainforest in Latin America, the felling of trees in the Himalayan Mountains in India, desertification in Africa, or toxic dumping in the United States, the environmental desecration caused by global economic policies have led to increasing material and cultural hardships for women (Mies and Shiva 1993). For women in the Third World, destruction of the environment means that women have to spend more time every day to gather wood for fuel, fodder for cattle, and fetch drinking water. Many women have been at the forefront of environmental movement (e.g., Agarwal 1997; Braidotti et al. 1997; Kaplan 1997; Shiva 1987; Westra and Wenz 1995). While the efforts of women in the Chipko movement in India may be familiar to many, there are numerous other women's groups in India and elsewhere that focus on the material and cultural relationships of women and nature. For example, in India, women in the Stree Mukti Sangharsh (Women's Liberation Struggle) were at the forefront of building an ecologically sound small dam, despite much government resistance, to address the issues of recurrent droughts in the area. In the process of building the dam women also organized to gain land rights and water rights for women and landless community members (Desai 1995). Other women's groups in India have been active in gaining fallow common land and experimenting with organic farming to produce food for local consumption.

In Latin America many of the environmental organizations focus on environmentally appropriate technologies, forming extracting reserves for the indigenous tribes' cultural and material survival, calling for the ecological use of the rainforest, and more recently focusing on the issue of intellectual property and biological diversity in the region. For example, in Ecuador the Fundacion Ecuatoriana de Tecnologia Appropriada works on biogas, rural housing, and small hydraulic turbines. SAEMTA in Bolivia focuses on organic potato farming, biological pesticides, medicinal plants, and small-scale irrigation. CENDA in Bolivia, which is a bilingual (Spanish and Quechua) grassroots support organization, takes action in the poor isolated areas of the Andes on reforestation (Fisher 1993). In Kenya, activists in Greenbelt focused their attention on reforestation and sustainable rural development. In the United States, women of color have been at the forefront of the environmental justice movement (e.g., Faber 1998; T. Kaplan 1997).

In all cases cited, environmental activists attempt to develop sustainable alternatives to the industrial development model that reduces food available for local consumption, destroys the local ecology, and produces toxic byproducts. The struggle against all these environmental ills has been strengthened by the emergence of transnational feminist solidarities. In some cases, the UN and its various world conferences have helped to create such solidarities and have brought them public visibility; however, as Alvarez (2000) and Basu (2000a) note, such solidarities are not top-down orchestrations but have emerged from specific political and social local movement contexts.

The UN and Transnational Feminist Solidarities

International women's networks and transnational organizing date back to the middle of the nineteenth century, when women from the United States and Europe came together around antislavery efforts (Rupp 1997). At the turn of the twentieth century, women from Europe, the United States, and India joined to fight colonization. In the early part of the twentieth century, women from Europe and the United States lobbied the newly formed League of Nations and the Pan American Organization to lay the groundwork for what was to become the UN Charter and the Universal Declaration of Human Rights. One of the major differences between earlier transnational activism and current activism is their scope and the variety of actors engaged in them.

The UN's efforts for women have evolved in four phases (UN 1997). In the first phase (1945–1962) the UN worked to secure women's legal equality. In 1946 the Commission on the Status of Women (CSW) and the Commission on Human Rights (CHR) were established. In 1948 the Universal Declaration of Human Rights was adopted and became the foundation for establishing the legal basis for equal rights for women. The early focus of CSW was a worldwide survey of laws that affected women, compiling data related to women, gathering public opinion on women's issues and organizing a forum to hear from experts and "launch a worldwide campaign to inform the public about women's issues" (UN 1991, 12). Both CSW and CHR agreed that while they would hear violations of women's rights they had no legal authority to take action. In 1952, the UN adopted the Convention on the Political Rights of Women, which became the first international instrument to recognize and protect women's political rights. During this phase the UN also worked on equality for women in work and education as well as legal equality for married women and gathered data on traditional practices and customs around the world that affected women. While there was consensus around the need to abolish practices that harmed women and children, there was little agreement on how to achieve this.

The research of the first phase documented the unequal status of women worldwide and the deteriorating status of women in the newly independent and post-colonial countries of Asia and Africa that, along with Latin American countries, had undertaken the path to development based on the liberal modernization model. These findings shifted the focus of the UN in the second phase, 1963–1975, from legal rights to the economic and social context within which legal rights can be meaningful. The continuing poverty in the world also challenged the development efforts of the UN, resulting in its move away from the modernization approach of the 1950s and 1960s to the basic needs approach in the 1970s, and then sustainable development and empowerment approach in the 1980s and the 1990s.

Troubled by women's economic and social inequalities, the UN first embarked on integrating women into development, without recognizing that perhaps it was the very process of development that was leading to some of these inequalities. The focus of UN development efforts for women in this period concentrated on their role as economic agents whose economic potential should be enhanced by providing them income-generation schemes and birth-control information. The UN's efforts also initiated the emergence of the field of "women and international development," which began questioning the inadequacy of the UN's efforts and developed a critique of its role in promoting a form of development that ignored the needs of women (see Benería and Sen 1982; Boserup 1970; Elson and Pearson 1981; Tinker 1990). They began to articulate a people-centered approach to development that became a precursor to the sustainable development and globalization discourses of the late 1980s and 1990s.

During the second phase, the consolidation of the Cold War led to challenges of the Universal Declaration of Human Rights from the Soviet Union that insisted that human rights should not be defined as just civil and political rights but should also include economic, social, and cultural rights. As a result, the United Nations International Covenant on Economic, Social, and Cultural Rights was passed in 1966 to augment the International Covenant on Civil and Political Rights proposed by the West. The latter covenant has often been referred to as the "first generation of rights" while the former is often called the "second generation." Historically the West has supported the enforcement of the civil and political rights, for which member states have legal obligations, while the former Soviet Union and the Third World countries have been promoters of the economic and social rights for which there is very limited enforcement. It is these latter rights that have been used in the 1990s by the transnational women's movements to forge solidarities and demand accountability from their governments (e.g., Bunch and Reilly 1994; J. Kerr 1993; Peters and Wolper 1995).

In order to enhance efforts on behalf of women's economic and social equality, the UN adopted the Declaration on the Elimination of Discrimination against Women, which brought together the issues of legal equality and economic development. Following this declaration, the UN made resources available to gather women's NGOs from around the world to discuss how they could collaborate to advance women's social, economic, and political rights. In 1970 the UN General Assembly passed a resolution titled "Programme of Concerted International Action for the Advancement of Women." The resolution was targeted for all UN agencies to address the objectives of the program and make resources available for them. Given these commitments, CSW recommended that the UN declare an International Women's Year to "remind the international community that discrimination against women, entrenched in law and deeply rooted cultural beliefs, was a persistent problem in much of the world—and that governments, NGOs, and individuals needed to increase their efforts not only to promote equality between men and women, but to acknowledge women's vital role in national and international development efforts" (UN 1997, 33).

In 1975 the UN declared International Women's Year with a focus on equality, development, and peace. The last focus was added by the delegations of Greece and Guatemala, which contended that women's role in peace and disarmament should be recognized and furthered. That year was highlighted by the First Women's World Conference in Mexico City. Two thousand delegates from 133 countries (women headed 113 of these delegations) attended the conference. Around 6,000 women and men from NGOs attended the parallel International Women's Year Tribune, which had been organized following similar gatherings of NGOs at the 1972 World Conference on the Human Environment and the 1974 Bucharest Population Conference. The Mexico City's Tribune was unique in its scope and intensity. Women gathered from around the world for what was dubbed "history's largest consciousness raising session" (UN 1997). For many of the participants, the discovery of their common and divergent issues was a transformative experience. This level of engagement was possible because of the emergence of a second wave of women's movements in many countries of the North and South.

The conference adopted a World Plan of Action on the Equality of Women and their Contribution to Development and Peace, and regional follow-up meetings were held throughout Africa, Asia, and the Pacific regions. The UN subsequently declared 1975–1985 the International Women's Decade and scheduled international conferences for 1980 in Copenhagen and for 1985 in Nairobi. The International Women's Decade, the third phase of the UN's efforts for women, promoted and legitimized the already growing international women's movement and marked the beginning of the transnational feminist solidarities that have come to characterize women's agency in the global era.

In this third phase of the UN's efforts the big shift in focus was on recognizing that there could be no equality, development, or peace without women's full participation. It was during this phase that the UN committed resources for women's advancement and created institutions that were to become an important part of transnational feminist solidarities. The two main institutions were the International Research and Training Institute for the Advancement of Women (INSTRAW), the main purpose of which was to conduct research and training in issues related to women and development, and the United Nations Development Fund for Women (also known as UNIFEM), formalized in 1984, which was to fund specific projects for women around the world. Despite the institutional establishment of INSTRAW and UNIFEM, the resources committed to them were limited. For example, during the International Women's Decade UNIFEM funded only 400 projects around the world for a total cost, in U.S. dollars, of $24 million. In addition to establishing these institutions, the UN also finally adopted in 1979 the Convention on the Elimination of All Forms of Discrimination against Women, which had been formulated as a nonbinding declaration in 1967. However, many countries, including the United States, did not ratify it, and those that did sign it had reservations about so many issues that for all practical purposes it was meaningless.

The most enduring accomplishment of the decade was its creation of transnational solidarities. Prior to each world conference there were local, national, and regional meetings that led to the formation of many local and national grassroots groups as well as international NGOs that wanted to participate. Though the world conferences were limited to formal governmental delegations from each country, the NGO forums, which were organized parallel to each world conference, provided the opportunity for women from around the world to meet and discuss women's issues. Approximately 6,000 women met at the Mexico Tribune in 1975, 15,000 women attended the Nairobi conference in 1985, and at least 30,000 women convened in Beijing in 1995.

These world conferences and their accompanying NGO forums, however, were highly contentious occasions. For example, most Third World women's groups and governments were still influenced by the nationalist rhetoric that had informed their freedom struggles. The decolonization of most countries in Africa and Asia following World War II, together with the Cold War between the United States and the Soviet Union, shaped the sensibilities of governments as well as women's groups. The postcolonial states were defined in opposition to the Western colonial empire. In this context, women were constituted as the bearers of tradition and posed against the modernizing influence of the colonial powers. Such self-understanding was further consolidated as Western women cast Third World women as "the oppressed other" of their more liberated self (Mohanty 1991b; G. C. Spivak 1987; Trinh 1989). Therefore, early encounters between so-called First World and Third World women were strained.

The conferences in Mexico City and Copenhagen were particularly volatile (Basu 2000; Desai 1995; Peters and Wolpert 1995). Women from India, Brazil, Palestine, and other Third World countries, based on their own anticolonial struggles and assumptions of the role of the West, challenged First World feminists' claims that women were universally oppressed because of their gender and that sisterhood was global. They countered that for women in the Third World, class, nationality, race/ethnicity, and religion intersected with gender in both oppressing them and providing spaces for liberation. Some of the differences among women at these world conferences also reflected the geopolitical tensions of the time. For example, two of the most heated issues were, first, whether Israel was racist in its relationship to Palestinians, and, second, the role of the West in perpetuating neocolonial strategies.

Such critical confrontations were resolved not by the force of the better argument but by the reciprocal recognition, fueled by women's grassroots organizing around the various issues, of the validity of various claims. The breakthrough for transnational solidarities came at the Nairobi conference in 1985, which, because of its location, drew many women from Africa and Asia. The timing of the conference, at the end of the International Decade, when women from all parts of the world had a chance to interact for ten years, contributed to the recognition that women's issues vary by society and require multiple strategies of liberation. In addition, Third World women were able to show First World women their own privilege and complicity in the oppression of women in the Third World. Learning about the common goals of freedom, justice, and equality variously defined, and of apparently different women's movements around the world inspired, reflective solidarity among women who otherwise were on different sides of the East/West, North/South, left/liberal, white/black, lesbian/straight, feminist/nonfeminist divide.

The breakthrough in women's transnational solidarities at Nairobi, and later in Beijing, was also a result of other social forces playing out in their respective locales (Desai 1995). For example, in the United States and United Kingdom, women of color were challenging the white feminist understanding of the category "women" and introducing race, class, and sexuality as among the factors destabilizing "sisterhood." In the Third World countries, the postcolonial governments based on constitutional equality for women were still defining women in circumscribed roles in nation building. The rise of religious fundamentalism, which defined women as only culture bearers, further sharpened women's feminist consciousness. Such larger social forces as well as the ongoing encounters among women enabled them to create solidarities based not on preconceived identities but on historically specific circumstances of the global economy that were constraining the lives of women around the world. This mutual understanding was further consolidated in Beijing in 1995 because the collapse of the Soviet Union and the consolidation of the global economy had enabled a framing of issues in terms other than the nationalist, First World/Third World terms of earlier decades. It was at this conference that human rights discourse became the language for demanding women's rights. Thus, the third phase of the UN's efforts helped catapult transnational women's networks and brought women into the center stage of world politics. The networks established during the decade became the basis for solidarity and action in the current phase of the UN's work, from 1986 to present. It was very clear to everyone at the end of the International Decade that despite the energy and optimism it had aroused, it had failed to achieve the goals of sustained progress for a majority of women. The 1990s posed a further challenge to women's equality as capitalist expansion and political displacement further interfered with women's social, economic, and political empowerment. In response, the UN called a series of world conferences in the 1990s that were to measure the success of its various efforts in the previous decades, particularly those efforts devoted to women's rights, human rights, population, development, and environment.

This last phase demonstrates the power of women's transnational solidarities. The World Environmental Conference in 1992 in Rio, the World Human Rights Conference in 1993, the Population Conference in Cairo in 1994, the World Summit for Social Development in 1995, and the World Women's Conference in Beijing in 1995 all capitalized on the networks women had established during the previous decades. Women's NGOs were at the forefront of these world conferences. For example, in preparation for Vienna in 1993, the Center for Women's Global Leadership, based at Rutgers University, helped to coordinate a Global Campaign for Women's Human Rights. In 1991, the center organized a leadership institute at which women from all over the world explored the relationship between human rights, women's rights, and violence against women. Women organized on both Human Rights Day and the International Day against Violence against Women to generate a petition drive calling on the World Human Rights Conference to "comprehensively address women's human rights at every level of its proceedings" and to recognize gender-based violence as a "violation of human rights requiring immediate action." The petition garnered 300,000 signatures from 50 countries and had been signed by 800 organizations when it was delivered to the world conference.

At the World Human Rights Conference, women's groups were the most organized and vocal. They held more than 60 workshops, seminars, and lectures at the forum on women's human rights. They also coined the now famous slogan "Human Rights Are Women's Rights and Women's Rights Are Human Rights" popularized by Hillary Rodham Clinton at Beijing in 1995. Similarly, the international conferences at Rio de Janeiro, Copenhagen, and Cairo were occasions for women's transnational networks to influence the agenda and policies of the UN and its member states. They also provided additional opportunities for women's groups from around the world to network and forge more strategies for action. According to Alvarez (2000), this activism embodies the "transnational IGO (Intergovernmental Organizations)-advocacy logic," which focuses on influencing policy. Since these transnational IGOs are dominated by Northern feminist nongovernmental organizations, they have a contradictory impact at the local level (Friedman 1999; Sandberg 1998). However, most women who participated at the NGO forums of these conferences were more interested in what Alvarez (2000) has described as "international identity-solidarity logic." Women's NGOs at the world conferences adopted two different strategies (see Clark, Friedman, and Hochstetler 1998). The more prominent national and international groups tended to caucus to influence the agenda setting of the world conferences and the UN bodies, while the vast majority of the NGOs focused on sharing information and experiences and networking for collaborative action in the future.

It is this last phase of the UN's efforts for women that has helped cement the nature of women's agency in the global era. Women's networks have now taken over the review processes following the world conferences, namely the Beijing Plus 5, Copenhagen Plus 5, and Cairo Plus 5, to assess what has been achieved and to make their governments accountable for their international agreements. Women's groups have learned to negotiate the national and international arenas, as shown by many chapters in this volume (see, for example, Cichowski, Karides, Mendez, Weber, Wells, and Wing). However, as Basu (2000a) argues, transnational activism for women's political and civil rights is much more likely to succeed than similar activism for economic rights. As I have indicated earlier, this stems in great measure from the dominance of these forms of rights claims in the West as opposed to the second generation of rights.

While transnational solidarities among women have grown, they are not without problems. As Nancy Naples and others discuss in this volume, these solidarities often reproduce existing inequalities. For example, women from the North and educated women from the South are more dominant in the international networks and NGOs than are grassroots women. Of the 30,000 women present at Beijing, more than 8,000 were from the United States alone. Furthermore, as Basu (2000a) argues, transnational activism creates divisions at the national level between the elites who belong to such networks and the vast majority of grassroots women who don't.

Another problematic aspect of the transnational solidarities is the continuing reliance of women and NGOs of the South on Northern donors and funders. The Ford Foundation, in particular, has been responsible for supporting a great deal of such transnational activism (Alvarez 1999; Basu 2000a). As Weber's chapter in this book shows, however, many Northern groups are aware of this and have made attempts to make their Southern partners more independent by enabling them to look for sustainable alternatives. In addition, other Northern NGOs are actively engaged in understanding and publicizing the ways in which Northern women's consumerism implicates them in global inequalities; the Label behind the Label and the Clean Clothes Campaign are two examples of activists' efforts.

Transnational solidarities have also been accompanied by an increasing NGO-ization of the women's movements, with its attendant decline in radical critique and an increasing role in serving as experts and implementers of government and international donors' programs. But as Alvarez (1999) shows for the women's movement in Latin America, NGO-ization is extremely complex and different in each country. Some NGOs are no more than fronts for the government; others, which Alvarez calls "hybrid" NGOs, maintain links with movements and try to work both within and outside the system. These NGOs simultaneously provide a critique as well as mobilize resources to empower women.

Alvarez (2000) has identified yet another problem with transnational solidarities, in the contradictions between the two different kinds of transnational logics: the internationalist identity-solidarity logic and the transnational IGO-advocacy logic. She sees the first logic as guided by identity, reciprocity, affinity, complementarily, and substitutionism (33), and as having very benign effects on local progressive politics. Transnational IGO advocacy, by contrast, is guided by experts with special skills shaping international gender policy. Though Alvarez acknowledges that these two logics can work in tandem, the contradictions concern her. I think that as with all binaries, this one overstates the differences and selectively highlights contradictions of one logic while understating those of the other logic.

The Prospects of Women's Agency in This Era of Globalization

Research by academics, policymakers, and various UN agencies overwhelmingly shows that women and children have suffered disproportionately as a result of global economic restructuring (e.g., Afshar and Dennis 1992; Blank 1997; Naples 1998c, Visvanathan et al. 1997). Policies associated with economic restructuring use existing patriarchal assumptions about women's labor and endurance abilities, and therefore reproduce inequalities. Furthermore, women are considered only as economic agents rather than central political actors on the global stage. Globalization has reduced the ability of women around the world to find paid work that offers security and dignity. The UN's perspective is that the harm caused by the policies is short term. There is also a gendered division in the implementation policies of international institutions. The IMF and the World Bank institute structural adjustment policies while UN agencies promote legal and cultural changes that would allow women access to the new market forces. The flaw in this analysis is that it misses the gendered nature of most economic policies.

Women have organized in response to the hegemonies of global capital. Their new political presence has been defined alternately as "global civil society" (Waterman 1998) or "globalization from below" (Falk 1993). While some analysts see these scattered counterhegemonies as ineffective against the hegemonizing presence of global capital (e.g., Sklair 1991), others celebrate the new global solidarities (e.g., Brecher, Costello, and Smith 2000). As I have shown, however, the important point is that global capital is not unchallenged. Many resistance strategies embody a radical critique not just of global capital but also of preexisting social inequalities based on race, class, gender, sexuality, and nationality. Many activist women's efforts focus, to varying degrees and in various ways, on developing concrete economic alternatives based on sustainable development, social equality, and participatory processes, though such economic initiatives have not been as successful at the transnational level (Basu 2000a). These counterhegemonies have succeeded in transforming the daily lives of many women at the local level. This, in my view, is what gives women's agency immense potential. Similarly, the transnational feminist solidarities, while they reproduce existing inequalities, are forged not on preconceived identities and experiences but in the context of struggle and as such are more reflexive about these inequalities. To what extent can these fluid, multiple, reflexive transnational feminist solidarities change the shape of the global political economy? We offer this collection of case studies as an indication of the limits and possibilities of transnational feminist organizing to improve the lives of women in diverse locales around the world.

3

Women's Local and Translocal Responses

An Introduction to the Chapters

Nancy A. Naples and Manisha Desai

THE ORGANIZATION OF CHAPTERS IN *WOMEN'S ACTIVISM AND GLOBALIZATION* IS designed to highlight the multiple sites in and through which women are organizing in response to global economic and political restructuring. We begin at the site of the "local"—where grassroots organizers work in a community based setting or in tandem with transnational activists to effect changes in specific communities and in particular national and regional contexts (part 2 of the collection). We shift attention in part 3 to the work of transnational advocacy networks to explore how these "sites" link global politics with local struggles. We also show how national women's movements and transnational networks draw on global discourses of human rights and economic justice to advance their organizing efforts. The case studies in part 4 examine how community activists and national women's movement organizations draw on UN conferences and the transnational governmental organizations and economic institutions to improve the quality of life and press for social and political justice in local communities and national contexts.

Organizing across Borders

In part 2 we focus on the work of individual activists and community-based organizations that collaborate with activists and advocacy organizations based in other national or international contexts. A major theme addressed by the authors in this section of the book is the extent to which organizing across borders reproduces or challenges regional and class inequalities. Many feminist activists and scholars note the difficulty faced by organizers in the Third World who must rely on resources from First World organizations that do not necessarily share their priorities or political framework. Inequalities based on class, education, and access to transnational political forums further inscribe hierarchies of privilege and economic dependencies that are difficult to interrupt and contest. The selections in this section illustrate four different approaches to these imbalances; first, self-conscious attempts to work against the structural inequalities in order to develop more egalitarian cross-national alliances (as illustrated by Clare Weber in chapter 4); second, failure to adequately reflect on the different priorities of First World activists leading to a mismatch between the assistance given and empowerment of local activists (as discussed by Alexandra Hrycak in chapter 5); third, transnational organizing across national borders by women who are more similarly situated in terms of class and race (as Sharon Ann Navarro demonstrates in chapter 6); and fourth, through the individual efforts of "alien insiders" and center women, and activist mothers who help build alliances across cultural, race, and class differences, facilitate the development of counterhegemonic networks, and generate cross-national links among activists (as Bandana Purkayastha demonstrates in chapter 7; also see Naples 1998a and 1998b; Sacks 1988).

Clare Weber's chapter, "Women to Women: Dissident Citizen Diplomacy in Nicaragua," shows how a progressive organization in the United States, the Wisconsin Coordinating Council on Nicaragua (WCCN), changed its original focus to better reflect the changing needs of women in Nicaragua. WCCN was originally formed to actively protest the United States' interventionist foreign policy in Nicaragua through the 1980s. But after the U.S. strategy to install the counterrevolutionary Contra government was successful, it changed its emphasis from peace and justice to justice in the context of economic restructuring. The WCCN developed a relationship with a women's nongovernmental organization (NGO) in Managua, the March 8 Inter-collective, and the two organizations exchanged strategies and information around issues of violence against women and then the economic violence of structural adjustment.

Through the Women's Empowerment Project and the Nicaraguan Loan Fund they developed alternatives based on Nicaraguan women's definition of their needs and strategies for political mobilization. Weber terms the work of the U.S.-based advocates "dissident citizen diplomacy" and demonstrates how these advocates created an association with Nicaraguan activists through which they could share their political analyses, born through revolutionary practice, with U.S. women' groups. Weber shows how international and national political environments influence transnational networks. By framing the needs of Nicaraguan women in a way that persuaded people in the United States to support them through socially responsible investing and community loan funds, WCCN was successful in raising funds to support the work of Nicaraguan women's community-based initiatives. Through dialogue and commitment to work through differences, Nicaraguan activists and U.S. advocates self-reflexively negotiated power differences and diverse political perspectives to generate a more egalitarian cross-national relationship.

In chapter 5, Alexandra Hrycak chronicles how a U.S.-based NGO helped to reshape women's political activism in Russia. Hrycak notes: "When glasnost freedoms first allowed women community activists to engage in independent collective action, they used the discourse of motherhood to elaborate a 'maternalist' activism against the state." In the liberalization of Russia, the mechanisms used to link women with the political sphere were disbanded. The new groups had few resources and limited ability to coordinate beyond the local level and therefore were unable to achieve effective representation in, and recognition by, the Russian state. The Unites States and other Western governments tried to develop or strengthen ties with Russian organizations, and one result was the founding of a group that has had significant influence on women's political organizing, the Women's Consortium. The consortium was developed, Hrycak says, after the U.S. Agency for International Development (USAID) issued an invitation to the Winrock International Institute for Agricultural Development, an Arkansas-based nonprofit, to expand its field area to Russia. Winrock had never worked in the Soviet Union before Elise Smith, an organizer from Winrock, joined a USAID-funded trip to several former Soviet cities to explore the possibilities of developing a USAID partnership program. She met with a small number of new women's organizations before returning to the United States to raise money for programs to develop leadership among women. But the consortium had little respect for the maternalist politics of many Russian women's organizations. And because the consortium targeted professional women in its efforts to develop women's leadership it failed to involve grassroots community activists in the training project. Hrycak shows that transnational activism may sometimes divide local activists. In the Russian case, the U.S.-based activists did not want to work with older Soviet-style women's community groups but rather sought to indoctrinate new groups in Western feminist ideologies and strategies. Hrycak suggests local NGOs in Russia might be better able to empower women than Western NGOs working in Russia.

In chapter 6, political scientist Sharon Navarro focuses on the cross-border organizing of women workers who have lost jobs as a result of restructuring under the North American Free Trade Agreement (NAFTA). She explores the coalition politics and construction of sociopolitical identity among Mexican-American women at the border who participate in the nongovernmental organization La Mujer Obrera (The Working Woman). The goal of this organization, as a working-class grassroots organization, is to organize, empower, and fight for the rights of low-income workers, particularly the single mother, head-of-household, immigrant women who are the center women of the group. Members of the organization fear, like the Zapatistas in southern Mexico, that NAFTA will eliminate them from an economy that was built with their labor and their resources. The organization provides women with economic and social avenues that differ from the limited opportunities available to them in the free trade zones that surround the U.S./Mexican border.

Bandana Purkayastha's case study of two community activists focuses on how as "alien insiders" they serve as catalysts for building activist and advocacy networks. As a mother and daughter with different histories and living in different national and community contexts, they share the experience of alien insiders and a commitment to social justice that informs their community-based activism. Their liminal position provides some advantages as they are able to negotiate across differences and to challenge the boundaries within and across communities. However, as alien insiders, they remain marginalized from the sites of power within the communities in which they reside. Purkayastha's chapter stresses the ways transnational mobility restructures relationships in ways that are not bound by nation-states.

Localizing Global Politics

The four chapters in part 3 focus on the impact of transnational activism, transnational agreements, and global human rights discourse on local communities and individual nation-states. In chapters 8 and 9, the authors highlight the significance of transnational advocacy and activist networks for improving the lives of individual women and communities. In chapters 10 and 11, the authors emphasize the significance of transnational human rights discourse for mobilizing on behalf of women and their communities in specific national contexts. All four chapters emphasize the empowerment of women in local communities that result from their activist engagement in transnational networks and local community actions.

In the first chapter in this section, sociologist Jennifer Mendez describes the organizing efforts of a transnational network of Central-American women's organizations that is working for maquila workers' rights. Mendez details the strategies developed by members of this network to resist the negative effects of neoliberal political-economic policies. Women workers in the network document their working conditions and gather detailed information about how fast they work, what they produce, for which corporations, and their relationships with supervisors and others in managerial positions. This information is used for local unionizing efforts and is communicated through network NGOs to groups in the North to enable them to undertake public consciousness-raising. Mendez argues that although some people have described the network's engagement with state agents, factory owners, and public opinion campaigns as self-limited radicalism, it makes more sense to see it in terms of its transformative potential for women at the local level. According to the author, the major success of the maquila women's political activism is the democratic and feminist vision the women have articulated, which has enabled them to challenge hegemonic definitions that affect their daily lives, such as the gender division of labor and decision making in the home.

In "Context, Strategy, Ground: Rural Women Organizing to Confront

Local/Global Economic Issues," Betty Wells describes the work of the Women, Food, and Agriculture Network (WFAN). The network, which comprises women growers and consumers, focuses on resisting the global expansion of industrial agriculture and is anchored in specific places where members live and work. WFAN engages women landowners, farmers, and food consumers in participatory research to document how industrial agriculture exhausts the land, diminishes the quality of food produced, and threatens the economic stability of farm families and agriculturally dependent communities. The strength of the network lies in interpersonal communication and support among members of the network. Despite the diverse urban and rural locales represented by women in the network, their collective commitment to the protection and expansion of sustainable agriculture and food provides a shared vision that further strengthens the network. WFAN supports local farmers' cooperatives as well as small-scale food enterprises engaged in community-supported agriculture. It also offers an informed critique of industrialization and corporate control of agriculture and trade liberalization. Through small group meetings, workshops, Internet communication, and a newsletter, WFAN educates members about the consequences of biotechnology and trade based on profit rather than sustainability.

In chapter 10, Marina Karides describes how Trinidad's National Union of Domestic Employers (NUDE), a registered trade union of Trinidad and Tobago, attempts to link the struggles of domestic and low-wage workers with international efforts toward ending women's exploitation. Karides highlights, as do many other authors, the significance of international conferences for providing the context through which women workers' organizations around the world can identify their mutual interests and develop effective transnational organizing strategies. NUDE's president general, Clotil Walcott, views her attendance at international conferences as a way to highlight the needs of grassroots women in Trinidad and Tobago to the international community. Members of NUDE also use the human rights frame to organize domestic employees and to influence state policy on women workers. NUDE participates in the International Wages for Housework campaign and uses UN policy statements, such as "Forward Looking Strategies," which focuses on ending the discrimination of women, to internationalize their grassroots efforts.

In chapter 11, Susanna Wing documents how the women in the Sahelian state of Mali have used the international discourse on women's rights to increase women's activism on behalf of their constitutional rights and their political representation. Wing notes that since 1991, when Mali began to pursue political liberalization, the proportion of legislative seats occupied by women went from 2 percent to 13 percent in one round of elections. Wing shows that women's groups who were trying to bring home the Beijing platform found that the best way to do so was acting on concrete initiatives relating to political participation without referring to

Beijing because it was seen as an elite conference that did not address the realities of women in Mali. Women's groups localized the message of Beijing by articulating it in local terms of new democracy and the role of women in nation building. The women's groups are creating a foundation based on local values and local networks. Though such activism has changed women's daily lives to some extent, restrictions still remain.

Activism in and against the Transnational State

Part 4 explores how community-based and national women's movement activists mobilize through transnational political sites—the UN and transnational NGOs—to gain resources for local and national organizing efforts against transnational governmental organizations and institutions to increase their safety and economic security. The United Nations served as the focus of women's solidarity efforts even before the International Women's Decade (1975–1985). The UN's commitment to women's rights dates back to its founding. For example, Eleanor Roosevelt, as the U.S. representative, read an open letter to the General Assembly that emphasized how World War II "was won through the joint efforts of men and women working for the common ideals of human freedom at a time when need for united effort broke down barriers of race, creed and sex" (quoted in UN 1997, 11, and cited in Otto 1996). The UN included a commitment to the rights of men and women in its original charter, declaring that "the organization must be conducted without distinction as to race, sex, language or religion" (UN 1997, 3, and cited in Otto 1997). It also encouraged governments around the world to encourage women to take an active role in national and international affairs. Although there was no self-enforcement of this equality, the UN took a progressive stance when most countries, even in the West, did not have equality under the law for women. However, power imbalances and difference in access to the UN NGO forums and its associated organizations, conferences, and declarations, lead to contradictory effects on women's community-based activism and national women's movements.

While some community-based and national women's movement NGOs were able to gain access to official UN agencies through external funding and international conference participation, external funding often narrowly defined who could represent national women's movements and diverse women in different regions within each nation-state. Furthermore, national governments exert various pressures on local NGOs and further constrain who gets to participate in transnational political events (see Friedman 1999). Winifred Poster and Zakia Salime highlight the detrimental impact of the international ideological frameworks that originate in the First World and get rearticulated through NGOs globally. They also argue that international policies influenced by international donors impede grassroots activism and international alliances, just as the larger NGOs restrict the access of grassroots groups to transnational feminist organizing.

The expansion of transnational governance has provided a context through which transnational activists have been able to insert some feminist agendas. For example, in her examination of the European Union, Rachel Cichowski demonstrates how activists have used this new international political entity to expand women's rights. Key to the progressive potential of the EU is its "social dimension." Recognizing that companies would rush to the poorest regions of a united Europe, the architects of the EU included a social dimension that imposed minimum labor standards and provided "structural funds" to compensate poorer member states for the costs they might incur in meeting EU standards (Brecher and Costello 1994, 138–39). Although the progressive intent of the measure was compromised by the UN's decision to waive the labor standards in Britain's case and by the top-down decision-making process, the social dimension provides a frame through which progressive activists can press for greater protections for workers.

In her discussion of the Equal Pay Principle (Article 119 of the 1957 Treaty of Rome) first incorporated into the EU in 1957, Cichowski demonstrates how feminist activists successfully used it to advance women's economic equality. The Equal Pay Principle was first inserted at the insistence of the French delegation. At the time, France was the only country to have equal-pay laws, and French employers feared that they would not be able to compete with member states who did not have such legislation. Cichowski stresses the significance of feminist organizing in France during the 1940s for the incorporation of the Equal Pay Principle. Her analysis highlights how the dual history of the Equal Pay Principle—linked both to elite concerns about competition and feminist activism—"led to a set of both intended and unintended policy outcomes." Cichowski's analysis reveals the significance of historical perspectives on the development and consequences of transnational feminist organizing. It illuminates the need to trace the origins and outcomes of such policy innovations in both directions—from the local to the international and transnational and back. For example, what are the effects of transnational policies like the Equal Pay Principle on different women's economic lives in different member states? How have women in different member states used the Equal Pay Principle to achieve greater economic equality?

In the last chapter in this section, Yoko Fukumura and Martha Matsuoka analyze Okinawa women's resistance to U.S. militarism. Most of the literature on globalization fails to point out the extent to which militarism accompanies global capitalist expansion. We chose to end with this chapter to draw attention to the "framework of alternative security" developed by women who are negotiating the continued presence of the U.S. military in their communities. Referring to John Feffer's (2001) argument that "[a] true multilaterialism—independent of the

United States, economically equitable and accountable to the citizens of the region—cannot be solely created by government officials," Fukumura and Matsuoka analyze the organizing strategies developed by Okinawa women who are fighting the legacy of colonialism and the continued militarism of the United States in Okinawa. Their chapter reminds us that any effort to resist the oppressive effects of globalization must include creating a vision for an "alternative security framework," one that seeks "the transformation of our society that is permeated with weapons and violation, into a community built on mutual trust and partnership" (Okinawa Women Act against Military Violence 1998).

This collection offers strong evidence for the possibilities of women's resistance and their contributions to a social democratic vision for what Elise Boulding (1988) terms "global civic culture." The term is used by activist scholars in the transnational peace studies networks that Boulding has worked over the past 40 years. She explains that participants in these networks "refused to accept subject matter categorizations that separated the civic issues of the economy, governance, and security from the civic issues of the environment and human rights" (xxv). In this framework, transnational activists work to link counterhegemonic struggles and develop connections between social, political, economic, and environmental issues and diverse coalitions. The case studies in this collection provide only a small illustration of the extent to which women in communities around the globe are generating alternatives to the oppressive features of globalization.

II

Organizing across Borders

4

Women to Women

Dissident Citizen Diplomacy in Nicaragua

Clare Weber

THE WISCONSIN COORDINATING COUNCIL ON NICARAGUA (WCCN) WAS PART OF an historic social movement in the United States that aimed to end U.S. military intervention in Central America and, in particular, Nicaragua. In the 1990s, the organization shifted its transnational activist strategies to challenge the gendered and racialized effects of global economic restructuring in Nicaragua. To this end, the WCCN worked with the Nicaraguan March 8 Women's Inter-collective on projects to end violence against women and with the Coalition of Protestant Churches for Aid and Development (CEPAD) to establish a loan fund. Viewing this reconfiguration from a multicultural, multiracial feminist standpoint, I explore how the WCCN developed a series of projects with Nicaraguan nongovernmental organizations (NGOs) that aimed to address the social and economic injustices of global economic restructuring in Nicaragua. The study demonstrates that, even as the WCCN worked to reverse the North-to-South flow of ideas and development strategies, the organization and its Nicaraguan counterparts were circumscribed in locally specific ways by the very power imbalances they were attempting to undo.

Third World feminist scholars have criticized First World feminist scholarship and activist strategies for viewing Third World women through a Westernized lens, assuming that individuality and modernity would be liberating forces for Third World women (Grewal and Kaplan 1994; C. Kaplan 1997; Mohanty 1991b). Women, viewed through this hegemonic lens, lose agency. International conferences and United Nations–sponsored projects have both perpetuated and challenged this hegemonic form of global feminism (Meyer and Prügl 1999). In their work on transnational activist networks, Margaret Keck and Kathryn Sikkink state that contemporary transnational activism does not always fit the much-criticized North-to-South pattern of international nongovernmental organizations transmitting liberal Western values to less powerful activists in the South. Rather, "many networks have been sites of cultural and political negotiation rather than mere enactors of dominant Western norms" (1998a). Keck and Sikkink do not offer a specific gendered analysis of transnational activist networks. Newer research in this area, as exemplified in this book, examines women's activist challenges to globalization in a transnational context.

Building on U.S. Third World feminist scholarship (Hurtado 1996; Sandoval 1991; Zinn and Dill 1996), Nancy Naples and Marnie Dobson (2000) view feminist praxis as "a grassroots strategy and an ongoing achievement based in the philosophy and practice of participatory democracy and situated knowledges" (3). I use this definition of feminist praxis to illustrate how a predominantly Euro-American progressive organization, a Nicaraguan feminist NGO, and a Nicaraguan church-based development organization advanced a strategy of exchange and activism aimed at challenging the gendered and racialized effects of global economic restructuring in Nicaragua.

The WCCN emerged as a left progressive organization opposed to the U.S. policies toward the socialist government of the Nicaraguan Sandinista Party. The WCCN referred to its activist strategies, which I discuss below, as citizen diplomacy. Drawing on the work of Holloway Sparks (1997), I refer to this idea of citizen diplomacy as *dissident* citizen diplomacy. While Sparks's work focuses on marginalized activist women in the United States, her concept of dissident citizenship is appropriate for the purposes of this study in that it highlights the "noninstitutionalized practices that augment or replace institutionalized channels of democratic opposition when those channels are inadequate or unavailable" (83). Dissident citizen diplomacy and multicultural feminist praxis enabled the WCCN to challenge, in gendered ways, the hegemonic powers that first waged a counterrevolutionary war against Nicaragua's socialist government and then imposed neoliberal economic policies favorable to international capital.

Nicaraguan Revolutionary Activism

Nicaragua underwent tremendous social, political, and economic transformations in the latter part of the twentieth century. It received intense international scrutiny, as well as support, when the Sandinista guerrilla movement overthrew the Somoza dictatorship on July 17, 1979. The Sandinistas, in the early years of their government, established a form of participatory democracy that gave formal power to a myriad of grassroots organizations (Hoyt 1997; Quandt 1995; Ramée and Polakoff 1997). The government implemented social programs to decrease poverty, expand social security, and increase access to land, housing, health care, education, and basic provisions. As part of a mixed economy, the majority of production stayed in private hands. Nevertheless, peasant farmers had greater access to land in the form of state farms, cooperatives, and some individual titles. Food production for domestic consumption increased significantly.

Nicaraguan women had the most to gain from the improved social conditions of the revolution, given their disproportionate responsibility for household and for community caretaking. Additionally, the government, at the urging of the Sandinista-affiliated Nicaraguan women's association Luisa Amanda Espinoza, passed laws in favor of women's rights, such as the right to have wages garnered for child support. However, the government also pushed women into the formal labor market and encouraged them to participate in the party, grassroots organizations, and cooperatives. In effect, this increased women's work adding onto their responsibilities as mothers, housewives, and single heads of households. Furthermore, feminist concerns of patriarchy and male privilege within the household were overlooked by the Sandinista Party (Chinchilla 1995; Molyneux 1986; Randall 1992).

Nicaraguan women's attempts to advance a feminist agenda were further thwarted when Ronald Reagan, elected U.S. president in 1980, made it his personal cause to overthrow the Sandinista government. The Reagan administration gave military support to counterrevolutionary forces living in exile, pressured the World Bank and the Inter-American Development Bank to cut off all economic aid and loans and began an impressive propaganda campaign to internationally discredit the Sandinistas (Burns 1987; Walker 1997). Applying many of the lessons learned from the Vietnam War, the CIA recruited, trained, and supported counterrevolutionary forces in a strategy of low-intensity warfare designed to wage war without the use of U.S. troops. By the end of the Contra War, 30,000 of Nicaragua's total population of 4 million had been killed, and more than $12 billion in damage had been done (Kornbluh 1987; Prevost 1997).

Because the low-intensity warfare strategy avoided the use of U.S. troops, it also avoided an anti-interventionist movement like that which emerged during the Vietnam War (Kornbluh 1987). Despite attempts by the U.S. government to avoid popular opposition to its involvement with the war in Nicaragua, an anti-intervention movement did emerge to mobilize public opinion against the war. The movement pressured the U.S. Congress to end military support for the Contras, but the Reagan administration simply resorted to illegal means to fund them. While not stopping the Contra War, movement activists generally concur that they successfully prevented an outright invasion of Nicaragua by U.S. troops.

While Nicaragua successfully garnered international support against U.S. policy, the Reagan administration effectively undermined many of the aims of the revolution. The last five years of the Sandinista government saw deterioration in an economy that had previously been growing. The power granted the grassroots organizations was diminished by a transition to electoral representation and the use of these organizations to carry out top-down Sandinista policies in the face of a worsening economy and the shifting of resources from social welfare to war (Walker 1997). Popular support for the Sandinistas, after nearly 10 years of war, had diminished. In 1990, the Sandinistas were voted out of office and replaced by the U.S.-supported United Nicaraguan Opposition (UNO).

Nicaragua–U.S. Relations in the 1990s

The 1990 electoral victory of UNO paved the way for the United States to direct Nicaragua's economic policies. The White House had a ruling party that would willingly restructure Nicaragua's government and economy to serve the interests of international capital. While the Sandinistas fell short of the revolutionary goal of undoing gender inequality, the Chamorro government actively targeted women's issues from a conservative agenda (Metoyer 1997).

The UNO government's imposition of neoliberal economic policies, as dictated by the U.S. State Department, the World Bank, and the International Monetary Fund (IMF), began undermining the social and economic gains of the Nicaraguan revolution. These policies continued after the Liberal Party won elections in 1996. The neoliberal economic policies now in place in Nicaragua and many other countries and regions of the world shift the burden of social services away from the state and onto women, relying on their unpaid labor as mothers, homemakers, or single heads of households (Benería 1996).

In 1990s Nicaragua, neoliberal policies in the form of structural adjustment programs (see Desai in this volume) compromised food security, increased unemployment, threatened land tenure for poor rural and urban Nicaraguans, limited access to credit for small producers, and cut state support for health care and education. International peace and justice organizations like the WCCN faced a worsening economic situation in Nicaragua and a government that was anything but friendly. In addition, U.S. grassroots support for work in Nicaragua waned once the war ended. Nevertheless, 10 years of revolutionary government left a legacy of a politically mobilized population and a network of international solidarity. Both would play key roles in shaping activist challenges to global economic restructuring.

U.S.–Nicaragua Activist Allies

The WCCN was created in 1984 by the citizens of Wisconsin in response to a disagreement with the Wisconsin Partners of the Americas regarding its sister city relationship with Nicaragua.[1] Left progressive citizens of Wisconsin disagreed with the Partners position of not opposing President Reagan's policies toward the Sandinista government. Friends in Deed (Chilsen and Rampton 1988), a how-to of sister city projects published by the WCCN, developed the notion of citizen-to-citizen diplomacy from an activist manual titled "Having International Affairs Your Way: A Five Step Briefing Manual for Citizen Diplomats":

> So, you want to become a diplomat? Welcome aboard! You're about to join the ranks of thousands of Americans who've decided that diplomacy is too important to be left to the diplomats. It's a big step, a step that may well change your life. But it's also a step that will enrich your life and the lives of many others. Diplomacy is essentially the art of helping the world. (Shuman and Williams 1986, 3)

Motivated by ideals of social and economic justice, Wisconsin citizens effectively used the model of Partners of the Americas to establish an alternative foreign policy merging activist challenges in the United States and development aid in the form of nationwide sister city projects. The projects supported Nicaraguan communities' efforts to build schools and housing, dig wells, and take on other social and economic projects in agreement with the aims of the revolution.

In Nicaragua, many Sandinista activists who were once part of the revolutionary government organized grassroots NGOs to challenge the neoliberal economic policies of the UNO and, later, Liberal Party governments. These organizations drew on members' 10 years of experience in revolutionary organizing and grassroots participation to challenge the neoliberal government's attempts to dismantle the social, material, and political gains of the revolution. In addition, these grassroots NGOs drew on international contacts and networks formed during the war years when international solidarity with Nicaragua was strong.

The Nicaraguan women's movement is particularly significant to the growth of NGOs and community activism in Nicaragua. Many women working within the Sandinista Party and government formed NGOs independent of the party with the aim of addressing women's issues regardless of the Sandinista Party's policies on any given women's issue. The women's movement incorporated a broad spectrum of concerns, such as violence against women and legal, health, labor, and abortion rights. The woman-headed household as an economic unit positioned women as ultimately responsible for meeting the needs of the family (Benería 1996). This economic responsibility, coupled with the collective experience of feminist activism during the revolution, led many women to organize on behalf of their communities (Aguilar et al. 1997).

In the 1990s, the WCCN would connect with the March 8 Women's Inter-collective and CEPAD, one of the oldest and largest NGOs in Nicaragua. The process and the emergence of the WCCN's activist strategies are grounded not only in the organization's history, but by a multicultural feminist praxis. This approach was represented in the organization's goal of equal exchange of ideas and, potentially, resources. The development and issues of the WCCN's Women's Empowerment Project and the Nicaraguan Loan Fund represent transnational activist responses to economic restructuring in Nicaragua that are worked out in a local context, often contested and almost always dynamic.

In the postwar 1990s, the WCCN offered alternatives to the neoliberal economic policies meted out by the government. A WCCN activist said of the organization's economic initiatives,

> It's a way of coming to terms with the market system. If things are going in the direction of the victory of big-time capitalism or maybe small-time capitalism, we'll be a help. Maybe there's a way for this idealism and this desire for justice to work itself out in this quite different political circumstance once the Sandinistas were beat in the election.

When the Sandinistas lost power in Nicaragua, many U.S. activists involved in the anti-intervention strategies saw the electoral defeat as a victory for international capital. Activists then had to grapple with how to address U.S. policy in its newest form. Building on the relationships of international solidarity and activist experiences in Nicaragua, the WCCN continued challenging global economic restructuring in local and grassroots ways.

Maintaining a commitment to social justice in Nicaragua meant that the WCCN had to transform itself. The WCCN was one of a number of organizations that worked to understand the significance of global economic restructuring in a grounded and contextualized manner; it asked itself how this restructuring affected people's daily lives in Nicaragua. Through feminist praxis, the WCCN not only critiqued the harsh gendered and racialized effects of neoliberal economic policies, but developed strategies that responded to needs in Nicaragua while continuing financial and political support for the organization in the United States. A member of the WCCN's Women's Empowerment Committee said,

> Now we're focused on different economic models-both through the loan fund and through the Women's Empowerment Project. So it's focused on alternatives to what already exists. You know, it attracts people who want to live some of those alternatives.

The Women's Empowerment Project

In this section I demonstrate how the WCCN, through multicultural feminist praxis, centered women's issues in 1990s Nicaragua, effectively inserting a feminist agenda into dissident citizen diplomacy. Prior to the Women's Empowerment Project, dissident citizen diplomacy served as a tool to organize against U.S. military and economic aggression in Nicaragua. The 1990s emphasis on women's issues signified a shift from the antiwar politics of the 1980s. Dissident citizen diplomacy represented a feminist, proactive strategy intended to serve as an alternative model to U.S. economic and political hegemony in Nicaragua. However, this does not mean that the WCCN did not pursue political actions of opposition in the United States.

From the outset the WCCN women who formed the Women's Empowerment Project engaged in a grassroots strategy of participatory and democratic decision making, all the while trying to educate themselves on the situated and lived realities of Nicaraguan activist women. They were clear that they wanted an exchange of information and as equal a relationship as possible. One member of the Women's Empowerment Project gave the account of the group's early days:

> One of the things that was initially really important in really making things happen was getting a core group of women together and saying, "We need to really think about what the objectives are, we need to think about what the mission is, we need to think about what it is that we can do, how we can share information, how we can continue to communicate in a way that's egalitarian in which both parties are learning a lot."

The challenge for the Women's Empowerment Project would be to realize this commitment to a multicultural feminist praxis given the dependency of Nicaraguan grassroots organizations on financial support from sources outside of Nicaragua.

Taking its cue from Nicaraguan feminists who formed NGOs independent of the Sandinista Party, the WCCN established a working relationship with the Managua-based March 8 Inter-collective. The feminist praxis of dialogue and exchange led to a unique project that grew out of the WCCN's sister city project and linked women activists in the United States and Nicaragua.[2] During the 1980s, the WCCN coordinated a sister city relationship between Madison, Wisconsin, and Managua, Nicaragua. However, Arnoldo Alemán, the conservative who was elected mayor of Managua in 1990 and became president in 1996, politically opposed the aims of the WCCN's sister city relationship. The alternative for the organization was to affiliate with grassroots NGOs in Managua. This coincided with the growth of Nicaraguan feminist NGOs (Aguilar et al. 1997; CAPRI 1997).

Nicaraguan feminists, concerned about the insufficient attention given to women's health and domestic violence, formed barrio-specific centers and organizations, and later formed the March 8 Inter-collective. The Managua-based Inter-collective consists of three women's centers: the Ocho de Marzo, Itzá, and Xochitl. The organizations provide programs for poor women in Managua that include legal support, women's health, family planning, intervention in abuse cases, prenatal care, and workshops in self-esteem and sexuality. The Inter-collective uses popular education methods and grassroots political organizing to end violence against women.

In 1990, Ellen Jones, a WCCN organizer, visited several women's NGOs in Managua, including the March 8 Women's Inter-collective. With the hope of supporting women's organizing in Nicaragua, WCCN met with women activists to assess the needs and interests in a collaborative project. As a result of these meetings WCCN developed, in effect, a sister organization project to support the first women's shelter in Nicaragua. Jones spoke of her visit with one of the leaders:

> I said, "Look, you know, we'd really like to organize another delegation and come down and share information. What sort of things do you think we should talk about? What sort of things should we focus on? What should our itinerary look like?" She seemed very excited, and said that one of these things that they were really focusing on, as a collective, working with some of the other women's centers as well, was the chauvinistic violence. And I thought great, okay, we'll go back to the U.S., we'll get a group together who has experience working on these issues, and particularly they were interested in getting all of the information that it could about setting up a shelter—at the time there was no women's shelter in Nicaragua.

The formation of the first women's shelter in Nicaragua illustrates the way activist women in the United States and Nicaragua negotiated notions of North to South domination in a local context. The Nicaraguan feminists wanted knowledge about the formation and management of women's shelters. They, not the WCCN representatives, generated the topic of exchange. The March 8 Inter-collective functioned democratically, complementing the aims of WCCN's intended relationship with the NGO and making the goal of equal exchange attainable.

One Nicaraguan activist who worked with the Inter-collective said that the WCCN's Women's Empowerment Project, with its emphasis on the exchange of strategies to counter violence against women, had effectively shattered some Latin American impressions of North Americans:

> It's important to understand that here in Latin America there is a strong rejection of North American policies toward Latin America. So, it's moralizing to know that there are others that are also working on these issues. For that reason we're here. We feel a true connection. In a world where there is so much discrimination, it's a fight, and I feel the connection of an international fight. At least we're communicating.

This communication and sense of solidarity, coupled with an understanding of the historical tendency for the United States to discriminate and dominate, later led to a critique of state-run U.S. women's shelters.

The specific activities of the Women's Empowerment Project included annual delegations of North American majority women who were interested in women's issues in Nicaragua, a tour of the United States by a Nicaraguan theater group, a visual art display about violence against women that was exhibited in both countries, and a delegation of Nicaraguan women activists studying the shelter system in the United States. The delegations of North American women, with some men participating, focused on different themes—for example, health care issues and violence, men's participation in the movement to end violence against women, strategies for connecting professional and grassroots activists, and recovery and shelter programs. These grassroots-to-grassroots exchanges enabled North American and Nicaraguan women to learn from each other. One WCCN woman delegate from Wisconsin said that the high level of competence she had observed in the Nicaraguan feminists made her optimistic about the future of women in that country:

> I left Nicaragua with an incredible feeling of hopefulness for change. The women in these collectives have an incredible skill in organizing, women doing it about women. When I asked how they got so skilled in this, the answer I got was, "Well, we had a revolution." They accomplished things in that revolution, and you can't take that back.

By acknowledging that there were experiences and organizing models to be learned from in Nicaragua, the delegate not only recognized similarities across many boundaries, but also subverted the hegemonic notion that Euro-American, middle-class women could supply the answers to working-class women in Nicaragua.

In 1995, the WCCN women's rights activists from Nicaragua began making annual visits to the United States to examine programs addressing violence against women. Included in the itinerary were visits with Native American women, Latinas, and African-American women. The WCCN supported shelter "experts" from the United States to work in Nicaragua with the collective as it established the first women's shelter there. Xiumara Herrera toured the United States to study its shelter programs and came away with the strong impression that a basic misconception guided the shelters treatment of their charges:

> The movement had, in that time [the 1970s], the image of a very strong political movement. I feel that now this part of the movement is no longer a political movement, it has remained as professionally run shelters. The woman is professionally viewed as an individual and is not socially located in

> a society where gender inequalities exist, where discrimination exists. The impression that I have of the shelters is the individualization of the problem. It is risky when the state gets involved in a movement and makes changes. The cases are seen as a woman's psychological problem, as a true pathology, and it shouldn't be like this. Here, we are trying to work on the issue as a political fight of raising awareness in the community. The indigenous communities [in the United States] were very interesting to me. I felt that they were not only working to support the women, but they were thinking about how to educate their community about the problem.

The work on violence against women in Nicaragua has historically been a political struggle; the violence is approached not as a psychological problem with the individual victim, but as a function of societal structures that enable men to be violent (Kendrick 1998). The Inter-collective's grassroots efforts to end violence against women include popular defenders who raise awareness in the communities, often going door to door. The popular defenders publicly confront men who are violent and offer legal support and accompaniment to women. Commenting on the work of the popular defenders, a WCCN activist said,

> The popular defenders are a very decentralized way of working on that [violence against women]. And the women are incredible organizers, too. I mean, there's a lot of really talented organizers there who we think could teach women here a whole lot. So there are a lot of possibilities we see for true technical exchanges, for us to learn from them.

Upon completion of a tour in the United States, a popular defender quoted in a WCCN report (1995) said that the work of the Inter-collective was not only unique and appropriate to her work in Nicaragua but offered lessons to North Americans as well.

The Inter-collective's grassroots efforts included other forms of popular education—for example, art therapy and theater. In an effort to raise funds for the women's shelter in Nicaragua, the Inter-collective brought its theater performances to the United States. One actor and activist of the Inter-collective stated,

> I like the theater because it is a way of helping to transform values of women. It is different, it is unusual. It makes me feel good to see how women feel reflected in what they see us do—they see themselves in this space. You can tell that seeing us helps them to see themselves. (WCCN report of theater group)

As a result of these types of technical exchanges, the activists of the Inter-collective developed a sense of international leadership. However, while the theater group's performances in the United States were part of a shared exchange of strategies and popular education, the fund-raising aspect highlights the unequal access to financial resources that exists between the WCCN and the Inter-collective.

While the exchange of information was at the forefront of the work between WCCN and the Inter-collective, financial support from the WCCN was a necessary component. Originally, the March 8 Inter-collective requested funds from WCCN to support the women's shelter in Managua. The WCCN limited its contribution and requested that the Inter-collective send a group to the United States to raise money. Negotiating this agreement was difficult—the WCCN had limited resources, and the Inter-collective assumed otherwise. After much dialogue both organizations arrived at an understanding on the issue of financial support. No matter the commitment to equal exchange, the WCCN was still in the position to help financially, and the March 8 Inter-collective, like most women's NGOs in Nicaragua, was dependent on external funding for its work.

The WCCN's activist works in the United States needed to appeal to left progressives if the organization was to survive. Activists in the United States supported the issues regarding violence against women, but it was not the project that kept the organization's doors open. The WCCN would have to appeal to more popular issues among the progressive left.

In 1997, the Women's Empowerment Project began to explore issues of labor rights in Nicaragua. This coincided with activist opposition to the North American Free Trade Agreement (NAFTA) and the postwar growth of maquiladoras in Managua, Nicaragua (Klein 2000). The WCCN's 1998 U.S. women's delegation was titled Women's Work Is Never Done. The strong interest in offshore sweatshop labor by activists in the United States would draw new activists into the Women's Empowerment Project. One WCCN activist became involved in issues of violence against women through her interest in labor issues. She stated,

> I'm more interested in sort of the economic justice issues. And I guess through my experience with the Women's Empowerment Project I got to see more of how they were connected. You know, see, like, domestic violence and women's economic conditions are really linked together there. Companies can pick up here and move to Nicaragua, and the workers in Nicaragua, who are mainly women, don't have adequate working conditions or wages. The workers here, obviously, have lost out. The only ones that are winning are the owners of these companies. I mean, in that sense, I think it's very, very much in the mission of what we're doing. And I think if you're looking

> at violence against women, too, I mean, this is another form of violence. And if women can't support themselves in a situation where they're experiencing domestic violence as well, I mean, it's like a double-edged sword. They're forced to stay in that situation because of the economic context.

Dissident citizen diplomacy, with its emphasis on grassroots-to-grassroots exchange, created the space for activists to learn from the women's movement in Nicaragua and place women's issues in the context of a global economy. By addressing women's labor issues in the maquiladoras, the Women's Empowerment Project engaged in grassroots actions directly challenging U.S. policy, recognizing the gendered ways that Third World labor is exploited.[3]

The Nicaraguan Community Development Loan Fund

In the 1990s, the WCCN not only reconfigured dissident citizen diplomacy to include women's issues; the organization also addressed the politics of economic development. The WCCN developed the Nicaraguan Community Development Loan Fund to address the economic hardships brought about by structural adjustment policies. However, the strategy was not just a response to activists in Nicaragua. The organization had a pragmatic need to develop programs that would attract the financial suport of progressive activists in the United States. The way in which the Nicaraguan Community Development Loan Fund developed made the goal of equal exchange and inclusion of gender issues a challenge for WCCN.

A 1989 WCCN document discusses the future of the WCCN and the importance of working on issues of alternative development:

> [The board should] associate WCCN with a vision of what political and economic policies toward the Third World ought to look like, demonstrating "what's wrong with current government policies and why they hurt the United States." Why people-oriented change, sustainable development, and Third World self-determination are in our interests. What makes WCCN important is "citizen diplomacy that respects self-determination." Our projects have a big opportunity to demonstrate that this approach to development is better than AID's [Agency for International Development]. Specific projects of this type can attract foundation support. U.S. foreign policy has no answers to human misery. Nicaragua offers a constructive, alternative answer to all sorts of problems we're going to see in Latin America.

During the Contra War, the WCCN's sister city projects offered an alternative to the bellicose policies of the U.S. government. The proactive strategy of the

Nicaraguan Community Development Loan Fund continued that approach in a manner that would, the WCCN hoped, provide enough money for it to continue its work. The Nicaraguan Community Development Loan Fund would tap into a growing movement of U.S. citizens interested in socially responsible investments. Discussing the beginnings of the Nicaraguan Community Development Loan Fund, a WCCN activist stated,

> We went and recruited people who were involved in socially responsible trade, and we said, "Look, Nicaragua has a lot to offer, it's opening up, the trade embargo is no longer there, it's in tremendous need of development, it's in tremendous need of social and economic justice, and we want you to come with us to explore." And it's funny because at the same time, the U.S. State Department was organizing trade delegations at high levels, corporate people, and here we are trying to get together with these groups of alternative traders.

The Nicaraguan Community Development Loan Fund in collaboration with CEPAD continued WCCN's dissident citizen diplomacy by maintaining grassroots-to-grassroots challenges to the hegemonic economic model of neoliberalism.

CEPAD began in 1972 as a coalition of Protestant churches that organized emergency medical relief after the Managua earthquake that year. It then grew to offer numerous social and material aid programs. While Protestants are a minority religious group in Nicaragua, CEPAD had a broader social and political influence. CEPAD supported many of the Sandinistas' revolutionary programs of social justice (Macdonald 1997) and played a key role in the peace and reconciliation process between the Contras and Sandinistas (Weber 1992). The work of CEPAD also included direct material aid, a small loan fund supported largely by donations, and a women's project. These programs changed in the 1990s in response to the Nicaraguan women's movement, economic issues, and political interests of church activists in the United States and Western Europe.

In 1992, the WCCN agreed to work with CEPAD to form the Nicaraguan Community Development Loan Fund. The WCCN would recruit investors and manage the portfolios, and CEPAD would manage the loans. While the need for the loans was great in Nicaragua, convincing U.S. investors of the viabililty of such a loan fund was a difficult endeavor. One of the founders of the loan fund, a U.S. citizen working in Nicaragua, said,

> [T]hat first year was a hard sell. People would say, "What?! I'm gonna do what with my savings?! You gotta be kidding! I've been to Nicaragua! It's impossible for those people to pay back! They're poor!" You know. And this was

> a period of time at which microcredit was just beginning to be known in this country [United States].

The WCCN successfully drew upon an emerging grassroots movement in the United States and in the Third World that supported alternative forms of credit to poor communities.

The target groups for the loans would be the sectors most excluded from the economic plan of the Nicaraguan government and multilateral lending institutions. They included the organized poor (the cooperatives), lending to women and to small and medium producers. A CEPAD worker said,

> We've really focused a lot of our loans to small farmers. And they're the most excluded, you could say, in the neoliberal model now. Now, we sort of run against that grain a little bit, in lending to those agricultural areas, small farms, because that's the social priority—recognizing that there's a risk in agricultural loans to small farmers because, again, the agro-export model does not favor them.

The support of small farmers who produced for domestic consumption matched the WCCN's concerns about neoliberal economic policies that favored large agro-exports. In addition, it met the criteria for socially responsible investment. One WCCN activist discussed the appeal of the loan fund:

> [It] makes you feel good about what you're doing and what you're involved with. And really, that's where it starts, one person at a time. I mean, I don't think that we can solve all the ills of the country. There's a long history for why things are the way they are in Nicaragua. But I think you have to start a person at a time. That's what the loan fund does.

In a postwar context, many U.S. activists were unsure what to do once the politically and economically conservative Chamorro government took power in 1990. The loan fund was a proactive strategy that could help individuals and counter, to a small degree, global economic policies.

The fund also represented a step forward for CEPAD. The neoliberal economic politics of the 1990s forced CEPAD to reexamine its development programs that were originally intended to compliment those of the Sandinista government. Under the Chomorro government, CEPAD could no longer rely on the government to address the basic economic needs of the Nicaraguan people. Subsequently, the organization shifted its emphasis from programs of emergency material aid to development aid. This change took place at a time when CEPAD's international donors were cutting funds. European churches accounted for a large amount of CEPAD's financial support, but with the end of the war and the defeat of the revolutionary government, international solidarity groups closed their doors, feeling defeated or left without a clear mission. Nevertheless, CEPAD mined the contacts it had with international solidarity and church groups sufficiently to solve its own problems. CEPAD sought out a Northern partner that could channel investments to CEPAD's loan fund. This coincided with a growing number of people in the United States involved in socially responsible investing and community loan funds. One of the CEPAD founders of the loan fund was himself a North American who had worked in the area of community economic development in the United States, and it was he who persuaded the leaders of CEPAD to try this model in Nicaragua. This blurred distinctions between the North and the South. Though the North American worked for CEPAD, he was, nevertheless, an outsider. The fact that he designed the initial Nicaraguan Community Development Loan Fund program lessened CEPAD's sense of ownership over the program.

The original idea of the loan fund, as envisioned by CEPAD, did not prioritize loans to women. Nevertheless, women within CEPAD supported the WCCN's interest in seeing that money and technical support got to women in Nicaragua.

Despite worldwide analysis that poor women are good credit risks (Buvinic, Gwin, and Bates 1996), some members of CEPAD were wary of lending money to women. A woman who was a leader of the loan fund stated,

> The best thing is that it's not the institution that is driving this project. It's the people in the rural area. They are deciding who they are going to loan to and who they are not. They set the rules of the game. And they have demonstrated the capacity to pay. I once argued with Jorge because he was one of the men that said, "Why do we need a women's bank if there is already a bank?"

Maintaining a multicultural feminist praxis proved difficult for the WCCN and CEPAD. Unlike the Women's Empowerment Project, which primarily worked with women's organizations in Nicaragua, the loan fund project included men as staff, with men brokering more power than women. The structure was more hierarchical than that of the March 8 Inter-collective. In addition, the basis of the relationship was centered on money being channeled from the North. Implying a sort of "flavor of the month" approach, one male leader of CEPAD said, "This year the popular issue for international funding is gender, before that it was the environment, and before that it was indigenous issues." In essence, the focus on financial resources that the loan fund necessitated created more of a dependent relationship between CEPAD and the WCCN, giving WCCN more leverage in prioritizing loans to women.

It would be inaccurate to say that the men of CEPAD were not concerned with women's issues. The goal of helping women *was* a commitment for CEPAD, but within a Marxist frame of social justice that meant helping the poor as a class of people with particular relations to the means of production and the state. This class-based approach to antipoverty and development programs fails to incorporate the intersectionality of class and gender and the contributing role of patriarchy to women's impoverishment (Sen and Grown 1987). Lending to women also met with structural legal barriers in Nicaragua because agricultural production, be it through a cooperative or a family farm, is largely controlled by men. The WCCN and CEPAD's Department of Gender worked to ensure that loans were given to women, but even when a woman did receive an agricultural loan, there was no guarantee that she would maintain control over it, given the structure of patriarchy. One woman informed me that she took out a loan for the family farm and then gave the money to her husband, relinquishing all control. Additionally, women were given smaller loans than men and, usually, in areas socially designated as women's work. A member of CEPAD's Department of Gender expressed a prevalent attitude of the women working at CEPAD:

> If a man is unemployed, he's not the type that will go and look for work. If the woman is unemployed she'll sell tamales or sweets, do laundry, iron or do something in the house. Therefore, I say, perhaps too graphically, but it's true that women and children maintain Nicaragua because even the children work. Therefore, it's the women that worry about social problems because she's involved in infant cafeterias, she's involved in projects of violence against women. Women are involved in projects of visiting the sick, the jails. I was surprised one day because a group of men came to me looking for help for a project to rescue delinquent children. I congratulated them that men would care about such things.

While supporting women through loans, the loan fund did not directly address the gendered division of responsibilities for child rearing and social reproduction.

In some instances women not only received loans, but also managed them through the Rural Women's Bank (Banco Campesina). Ana Nuñez, a member of CEPAD's Department of Gender, said,

> Here, the women's pastoral met, and we did some planning. We had a brainstorm of ideas to see how we could develop social and economic products. One of the women said, "Why don't we have a small bank like a credit cooperative, and each one can have a thousand Cordobas. And that's how we

> started. There was always the question of why we don't give to men. But the truth is that the experience that we have lived is that men get more support. Therefore, the women decided to prioritize women mainly in businesses, small industries, and services such as beauty salons, restaurants, things that offer services.

While the Rural Women's Bank reinforced certain gendered divisions of labor and child-rearing responsibilities, they also supported women in ways that helped the women meet their immediate needs. The WCCN supported this approach by prioritizing investments to women and encouraging the male leadership of CEPAD to do the same.

Conclusion

The WCCN's reconfiguration in 1990s Nicaragua was a balancing act. The loan fund consumed the organization's time and resources, and the WCCN found itself straining to accomplish its other mission. The tension is best summed up by a WCCN activist:

> As the loan fund began to emerge and grow, it essentially tapped all of our resources. It was this huge project that took up a tremendous amount of time, and the Women's Project, in a lot of ways, was always pushed to the side because it required a lot of attention, but we couldn't give it the attention that it needed. So, the loan fund transformed WCCN in a lot of ways. I think in a lot of very positive ways, but it was still very challenging because, all of a sudden, we didn't have lot of time to do the things that we had historically done.

The organization worked to respond to needs in Nicaragua and survive financially in the United States, which meant creating projects that would garner popular political interests among the progressive U.S. Left. At the same time, the WCCN worked to stay focused on the feminist politics of dissident citizen diplomacy and gendered issues of the global economy.

Although international and national political environments clearly influenced the WCCN's reconfiguration in the 1990s, the reconfiguration was not only a response to global economic processes. Through a multicultural feminist praxis, the WCCN developed grassroots strategies that supported popular movements in Nicaragua and forged transnational alliances. Dissident citizen diplomacy became more than a proactive strategy of addressing U.S. foreign policy—it was a grounded response to needs in Nicaragua that garnered the support of left progressive middle-class activists in the United States by framing issues in ways that appealed to them, specifically through socially responsible investing and community loan funds.

The WCCN inserted a feminist agenda into dissident citizen diplomacy that previously emphasized a gender-neutral, antiwar frame. The Women's Empowerment Project received direction from the Nicaraguan Women's Inter-collective and developed transnational activist strategies on issues of violence against women. In addition, the WCCN supported women's issues within the male-led institution of CEPAD as it responded to women's demands in Nicaragua.

The WCCN, the Nicaraguan Women's Inter-collective, and CEPAD, in this practice of solidarity, are reshaping notions of global and First World feminisms. In "No Basta Teorizar" (It's Not Enough to Theorize), Pfeil (1994) states that solidarity is constructed "through forms of dialogue and struggle that presuppose a common commitment to ending all forms of oppression and exploitation, however organized through the intertwining of race, class, gender, sexual orientation or cultural differences and that work out and work through the differences from there" (225–26).

Building on the solidarity of 10 years of opposing President Reagan, the WCCN, the Women's Inter-collective, and CEPAD developed new transnational strategies that addressed women's issues in Nicaragua. The organizations involved developed specific strategies through a dialogue and a commitment to work through differences. It is not my intention to paint an overly optimistic picture of the work of WCCN, but rather to posit that by studying this transnational network of organizations over time and viewing its reconfiguration from a multicultural, multiracial feminist standpoint, we can see how activists self-consciously work out power differences and issues of domination in geographically and culturally specific contexts.

Notes

1. In the book *Friends in Deed,* authors Liz Chilsen and Sheldon Rampton describe the birth of the sister city project that began with the Wisconsin-Nicaraguan sister state relationship formed in 1964 under the Partners of the Americas program established by President Kennedy. Partners of the Americas promoted the political aims of the Alliance for Progress, whose rhetoric called for implementation of democratic institutions, economic development, and social justice. However, during the Cold War the Alliance for Progress ultimately became more concerned about issues of national security. Though the Alliance for Progress ended in 1969, the sister state and sister city relationships between the United States and Latin America continued.

2. The WCCN continued to support sister city relationships between numerous U.S. and Nicaraguan cities.

3. The WCCN continued to develop relationships with other Nicaraguan women's organizations in an effort to support work in Nicaragua and an exchange of political and organizing strategies in the United States. Areas of Nicaragua suffered great losses after a hurricane in 1998. The Women's Empowerment Project now supports work addressing violence against women in the context of the trauma caused by the devastating Hurricane Mitch. For example, the WCCN supports a U.S. volunteer, trained in techniques of psychological healing, to work in Nicaragua on healing therapies for men and women of the affected communities, with the hope of reducing acts of violence against women. In 1999, the WCCN began working with the Network of Violence against Women, which consists of 170 groups and individuals working nationwide on issues of violence against women.

5

From Mothers' Rights to Equal Rights

Post-Soviet Grassroots Women's Associations

Alexandra Hrycak

SINCE THE COLLAPSE OF THE SOVIET UNION, HUMAN RIGHTS GROUPS HAVE expressed considerable concern about post-Soviet women.[1] Arguably, this is because most glasnost-era discussions of the Soviet Union's democratization paid little attention to its impact on women.[2] But this is not the only reason. Despite considerable effort on the part of international women's rights programs, the region's nongovernmental organizations for women are themselves new, inexperienced, and relatively weak. They are finding it difficult to cope with the demands of the current transition, which has exacerbated previous social, political, and economic problems and created new ones like unemployment, inflation, and homelessness.

It is estimated that post-Soviet women's rights organizations constitute less than one percent of nongovernmental organizations active in the former Soviet Union (Abubikirova et al. 1988, 16). Not only are there too few women's organizations to effectively meet the needs of local women, but those organizations that do exist are small and inexperienced at working together. Lack of coalition building experience has hurt some of the women's movement's biggest campaigns. For instance, many women in Russia and Ukraine were concerned when women lost political representation in Russian and Ukrainian parliaments after the demise of Soviet-era quotas. They formed a variety of women's parties. However, so far, these women's parties have failed to elect any of their candidates and their influence has arguably declined at least in part because of rivalries. In Ukraine, at least four separate women's parties have formed in the last decade, each short-lived and weak.

The current weakness of post-Soviet women's activism is the consequence of preexisting weaknesses that have long been stressed in Western accounts of socialist states' treatment of women: the absence of a Western-style civil society of nongovernmental organizations (NGOs), exacerbated by state paternalism (Kligman 1998; Verdery 1994) and lack of contact with the international women's movement (Browning 1987; Jancar 1978; Lapidus 1978). In order to explore how these factors left post-Soviet women unprepared for community activism, my analysis will focus on how changes in state policy limited Soviet women's access to three sets of crucial collective action resources: nongovernmental women's organizations, collective action frames, and coalition-building opportunities.[3] There are many other factors that influence women's community activism; however, the ability to establish nongovernmental organizations, develop effective collective action frames, and gain experience in coalition building have repeatedly emerged as important dimensions of successful collective action (e.g., Bleyer 1992; W. Gamson 1990; Katzenstein and Mueller 1987; Minkoff 1995 and 1997; Kalzenotein 1995; Staggenborg 1986 and 1991). Thus, a focus on these dimensions constitutes a useful (if imperfect) starting point for making cross-national comparisons about globalization's consequences for post-Soviet women as activists, as well as for assessing how other factors have affected local activists' domestic capacities for collective action.

I begin by discussing women's community activism prior to the introduction of market reforms, or perestroika. Next, I briefly examine the kind of organizations and collective action frames that women community activists developed during the final years of Soviet rule. After this, I turn to analyze the collective action frame that has been encouraged by the NIS-US Women's Consortium, a U.S.-funded organization designed to foster post-Soviet women's leadership through cooperation between U.S. and post-Soviet NGOs. I conclude by suggesting some reasons why the ultimate success of such transnational partnerships depends on whether they promote or impair domestic coalition building between older and newer activist networks.

Women's Community Activism prior to Perestroika

Observers have tended to view the Soviet Union through two opposing perspectives. Party leaders and official Soviet women's activists claimed that the Soviet state had emancipated women from traditional forms of patriarchal exploitation, and enabled women to enter all traditionally male-dominated spheres of society. The Soviet Union's critics saw it as a paternalist one-party state in which both men and women were atomized and powerless, and in which the party monopolized resources for collective action. Both perspectives present a distorted view of Soviet women's capacities for collective action.

Though the Soviet Union *was* one of the first countries to make gender equality and women's rights important political goals, claims that Soviet women had attained full political equality with men are overstated. In reality, their progress was slow. The Soviet leadership carefully recruited women into official organizations such as the Communist Party and other secondary associations, and as the country industrialized, women's access to these and other resources for collective action gradually expanded. As the country became more urban and more industrial, Soviet women and other Soviet citizens also gradually developed a certain degree of political influence, within limits set by the party leadership. Most of these changes occurred during the post–World War II era.

During the early years of Soviet rule, the party strove with little success to integrate Soviet women into state-building projects. Initially, these efforts were coordinated through local branches of "Women's Departments" [*zhenotdely*] of Communist Party organizations coordinated through a Women's Department (or *zhenotdel*) of the Communist Party's Central Committee founded in 1919 at the urging of Aleksandra Kollontai. The Women's Departments trained a cadre of local women activists, recruited local women into the party, and directed community relief work among orphans, wounded soldiers, and the homeless. But Soviet leaders quickly closed Women's Departments when they became channels for local anticollectivization protests. In 1930 the Central Committee abolished the Women's Departments, and merged their branches with local Communist party organizations.[4]

After World War II, the party consistently targeted women in its recruitment drives. In the 1960s and 1970s, Soviet women entered the party in greater numbers, but their role in the party remained relatively limited (Clements 1992, 99–121). The proportion of women party members, which for decades had remained low, very gradually rose to one-quarter by the late 1970s. Official Soviet statistics on party leadership show that by 1980, women had also achieved a certain kind of political influence as party leaders at the local level, where they constituted half of all people's deputies and a majority of judges.[5] Women activists also began advancing through the system of Communist Party and state-controlled secondary associations. There were several reasons for the party's efforts to recruit more women and to pay greater attention to their welfare. One of the most important was declining birthrates and an increasing incidence of one- and two-child families. Party leaders feared that steady declines in the postwar birthrate would, in decades to come, create serious labor shortages. In an effort to reverse this trend, a variety of measures were taken to investigate and formulate solutions to problems that Soviet women faced. Women party members and academics were appointed to state agencies and commissions that investigated issues related to childbearing. These investigations determined that many women would not have more children because they lived for years in overcrowded dormitories or apartments, came home from work to face a stressful "second shift" of household work (unshared with their husbands) made more difficult by chronic shortages in housing and consumer goods. State leaders made some effort to use trade unions to relieve some of the pressure on women workers. Groups called Women's Councils [*zhensovety*] were periodically revived within trade union organizations in order to help women gain access to day care and vacation passes for their children. Because the councils were concerned primarily with using existing trade union resources to help women workers to combine work with childbearing, their contributions to Soviet women's material gains were limited. Women's Councils were politically weak, and there continued to be no women in the Politburo and few women in decision-making bodies.

How did Soviet women fare in terms of their control over indigenous organizations, the development of a collective action frame, and opportunities for coalition building among groups with ideological differences? Soviet women were officially given considerable attention. They were treated as an interest group with a common identity— "working mothers." They were encouraged to have more children. In order to help them to combine work and motherhood, women were mobilized into official women's organizations. To some extent, this allowed women to develop organizational resources through which to articulate grievances within the workplace. However, these organizations were not intended to help women engage in collective action in other realms.

Soldiers' Mothers Committees and "Maternalist" Activism

Soviet women first began to engage in independent, locally based collective action in the late 1980s, during the Soviet Union's brief experiment with market reforms. In the mid-1980s Mikhail Gorbachev introduced perestroika, "restructuring," or market reforms, and glasnost, "openness," or political liberalization. During the first years of reform, Gorbachev gave women's issues considerable attention. Like earlier Soviet reformers, he promised to help women combine motherhood and work (e.g., by creating more part-time positions and alleviating housing shortages). He also pledged to promote more women to positions of authority. More important still, Gorbachev revived the Women's Councils, and placed them under the jurisdiction of the high-profile Soviet Women's Committee, which represented Soviet women internationally and thus had ties to international women's groups from whom the country's activists had been isolated for so long.[6] Gorbachev thus increased women's activists' access to new collective action frames and created opportunities for new international coalitions.

These reforms had some results. Women's Councils expanded their membership rapidly. By April 1988, there were reported to be 236,000 Women's Councils, with a total membership of 2.3 million.[7] Women's Councils formed in workplaces throughout the country, to investigate and discuss solutions to their members' concerns. Contacts with international women's activists also increased, leading to new, more critical treatments of domestic problems. Not only did these developments broaden the realm of public debate to include a variety of formerly taboo issues such as abortion, contraception, and even feminism (which party leaders had long cast as a bourgeois ideology), they also emboldened women activists to engage in collective action outside state- and party-controlled channels.

During 1989, a year when glasnost protest activity began to spill over from state- and party-controlled channels throughout the Soviet Union, women activists formed dozens of direct action protest groups. A handful of women (located primarily in Moscow) experimented with feminism and tried to adapt it to Soviet women's problems. The vast majority of these protest groups was unconcerned with this largely foreign ideology, and brought together local mothers who sought to force state agencies to provide relief and assistance to their children.

Soldiers' Mothers Committees organized and carried out the first such women's protests to capture the support of the public and receive considerable attention from the Soviet leadership. These committees were initially founded in 1989 by mothers of conscripts who had died in peacetime military service as a result of hazing. At that time, Soldiers' Mothers groups staged a series of public demonstrations and hunger strikes through which they sought to draw attention to the system of hazing and to pressure the party leadership to reform military service. These protests achieved sufficient moral authority in the public's eyes that Gorbachev met with its representatives to hear their concerns.

Beginning in 1989, women activists also formed many other new women's direct action groups to force other state agencies to reform their treatment of women and their children. Independently or with the assistance of local Women's Councils, such "maternalist" activists established dozens of new community associations that sought state protection or assistance from Soviet state agencies to mothers of large families, single mothers, mothers of disabled children, disabled mothers, and other categories of needy mothers.

Also in 1989, non-Russian women began to form new national women's associations that embraced a nationalist variant of maternalist activism that sought to recognize the role women played in national identity formation. These groups tended to utilize organizational resources from the system of secondary associations (chiefly, professional unions and academic institutes) that the Soviet state developed to administer areas of education and culture (Dawson 1996). Nationalist women's activism of this type was concentrated in the western Ukraine, the Baltics, and the Caucasus, where national sentiment was rising.

This wave of community activism had complicated effects on women's capacity to use glasnost freedoms to gain greater control over indigenous organizations, successfully develop a collective action frame, and build coalitions among groups with ideological differences. For the present discussion, it is important to note first and foremost that the most effective attempts to seek control over community organizations united local networks of needy women who embraced fairly conservative Soviet definitions of women's rights and pursued fairly short-term goals, principally, increased state assistance to their children. Rarely are such community groups interested in, or able to pursue, coalition building that might increase women's political power. Typically, such groups form self-contained networks or work in relative isolation.

Associations of Mothers of Large Families that began forming in 1989 now exist throughout the Newly Independent States. In Ukraine (which Western women's rights advocates would later claim had only three women's NGOs in 1994), such an organization formed in 1993.[8] As of 1996 (the most recent year in which a comprehensive survey of Ukrainian women's NGOs has been conducted), 25 local chapters of this NGO had united under the auspices of the All-Ukrainian Association of Large Families, based in Kiev. This organization has engaged in a wide variety of activities. It cooperates with a variety of state agencies and advocacy groups for women, children and the disabled, and conducts regular meetings, independent research, conferences, and public service work to bring attention to the rights of children and families.

Similar organizations have also proliferated in Russia, although many outside Moscow and St. Petersburg work in relative isolation from each other (perhaps because of the country's size), and conduct activities primarily in conjunction with local successors to Soviet Women's Councils. In Kalingrad, an organization was established in 1990 that sought to help mothers of large families by providing assistance, advocating the preservation of state benefits, and raising public awareness about large families. It claimed 600 members in 1998. A second such organization is Home (Dom), located in the town of Olenegorsk, Murmansk oblast, established in 1989, with 250 members. A third community group, Women Together, of Novosibirsk, was established in 1994 and claims 300 members. Hundreds of such organizations have formed throughout the NIS by formalizing preexisting informal networks of mothers whose children had received particular types of aid. Only rarely have these mothers' associations merged two welfare constituencies to create a stronger group. One relatively rare example is Orange Tree of Leningrad Oblast, which was established in 1991 with the goal of mutual support of mothers with many children and single mothers. In 1998, it claimed 260 members. As important as these groups may be for needy women, they have limited political goals and capacities, and hence a limited impact on the policy-making process.

Ethnocultural women's associations originally sought to revive women's commitment to national languages and cultures and claimed to have no political goals. However, many were closely affiliated with organized movements for national sovereignty that during the final years of Soviet rule called for independence. These types of groups, in mobilizing support for national sovereignty, enjoyed considerable political influence. In part as the result of the new conditions of independence, some of these groups have been able to form large federated national associations with dozens of local chapters. However, they have achieved their success primarily by building coalitions with nationalist groups that were not focused on women's rights and that have lost vitality since achieving their goal of independence from the Soviet Union.

Although national revival movements have subsided, a number of nationalist women's groups have survived independence. Two examples are the Ukrainian Women's Association (Zhinocha hromada), affiliated closely with the Ukrainian movement for independence (Rukh), and the Ukrainian Women's Union (Souiuz Ukrainok), both of which were established in 1989 to restore national traditions and are run by wives of prominent nationalist leaders. These two organizations have prospered and achieved a sizable mass membership of locally based chapters affiliated through a national association based in the capital. In 1996, the Ukrainian Women's Association claimed 15,000 members, and the Ukrainian Women's Union claimed 11,300 (Women's Information Consultative Center 1996).[9] Both lost some members as new feminist women's NGOs have formed. And neither they nor the new feminist groups have had much success in their attempts to advance women's issues in the political arena. Indeed, the share of women in Ukraine's parliament is lower than it is in Russia's. The success of these groups will depend on their ability to build coalitions. So far, efforts to build such coalitions have foundered.

As these examples suggest, it not true that Soviet-era secondary organizations failed to become channels for Soviet women to engage in collective action. Nonetheless, Soviet-era resources have been insufficient for women to develop political power in their own right. Soviet women activists used both institutional and noninstitutional channels to increase their control over local organizational resources. The strongest protest activity was motivated by maternalist claims, which foreign and domestic observers have often argued had a depoliticizing effect on women. When glasnost first allowed women community activists to engage in independent collective action, they utilized this discourse of motherhood to elaborate a "maternalist" collective action frame to make new political demands. Soviet women thus turned "maternalist" activism against the state. Groups of soldier's mothers, welfare recipients, and non-Russian cultural activists tried to wrest from the party and the state control over areas that had long considered the jurisdiction of women. But opportunities for coalition building have declined as the result of this sudden decentralization of state power. Many new community organizations either don't know of each other's existence or are prevented by ideological differences and new political borders from common initiatives, and this might be seen as an important limiting factor on glasnost-era women's community activism.

In short, when the Soviet state loosened long standing prohibitions on nongovernmental associations, the gains for women community activists were mixed. While Soviet state organizations quickly gave rise to certain kinds of independent women's community activism, nonetheless, the official, federated Soviet women's associational structure created through Women's Councils collapsed, and this organization ceased to be able to coordinate activities that might have translated greater agenda-setting independence into increased political power.[10] As a result, glasnost-era organizations remain nodes of community activism, but their efforts to coordinate women's collective action have been fairly local, and even at the local level, community activists have been seriously hampered by the state's incapacity to make concessions in a time of economic crisis.

Post-Soviet Women's Activism

Perestroika and glasnost were intended to stimulate the USSR's flagging economy and inspire greater confidence in the country's government. Instead, they soon unleashed a dramatic wave of protest against party and state hegemony.[11] In one republic after another, the Soviet state lost control. Separatist movements arose and demanded greater local control over economic and political affairs for the Soviet Union's republics. Those pressures contributed to the Soviet Union's collapse and led to the reconstitution of its far-flung republics as independent states, many of them quite unstable.

Local independence movements stressed the inability of Moscow-based reform to understand and be responsive to conditions in their republics, and advocated that local leaders develop their own policies. However, since independence, the locus of control over post-Soviet economic and political reforms has moved from Moscow even farther abroad. The International Monetary Fund (IMF) now sets the pace and decides the nature of reforms with support from foreign lenders who constitute a major source of funding to post-Soviet states: the World Bank, the European Union (EU), the European Bank for Reconstruction and Development, and the governments of the United States, the United Kingdom, Germany, and Canada. These foreign donors have worked closely with one another to put pressure on local aid recipients to increase the pace of mass privatization and economic restructuring, and of course, to increase foreign trade and investment.

What effects have these macropolitical shifts had on resources for women's community activists? It is important to note that donors have made repeated efforts to stimulate the growth of civil society, and in particular, to empower local women's NGOs. The U.S. Department of State and the U.S. Agency for International Development (USAID) have focused considerable attention on developing a unified strategy for civil society building. In the words of an early report that set the agenda for future Western partnerships in Russia and Ukraine (the largest post-Soviet countries and the first priority for Western assistance), "[f]acilitation of private voluntary action and the strengthening of civil society institutions is necessary to generate a successful transition to democracy" (Lear 1992, ii).

In short, U.S. policy has targeted coalition building between American NGOs and local post-Soviet partners as a policy priority. This approach to democratization has created several unintended problems that have weakened preexisting local women's groups. First, it fails to acknowledge the important role that local state agencies and governmental organizations can play as local nodes of civil society–building activity (thus ignoring the organizations that trained many Soviet women's activists). Second, it gives priority to transnational exchanges between local organizations and U.S. partners, rather than seeking to strengthen domestic ties between the dozens of small women's groups that formed during the Soviet period. Third, in practice, rather than building on well-networked local organizations such as the Women's Councils as nodes of women's community activism, it leads to the creation of new women's groups able to appeal to the particular interests of Western foundations and other intermediaries who act as gatekeepers for Western initiatives. These new women's groups often have little practical knowledge of other local women's organizations or access to the local political process. Their success also subtly shapes the kinds of activities preexisting nongovernmental groups must engage in to win ongoing financial support.

The US-NIS Women's Consortium is an instructive case for understanding some of the reasons why Western aid and Western activists have not, as yet, built effective local foundations for post-Soviet women's community activism. The Women's Consortium is the largest coalition of American and local post-Soviet women's groups to have formed through U.S. civil society partnership programs. As of September 30, 1998, 216 member NGOs and 11 individual advisers belonged to the consortium. Of these, 93 were women's groups from 26 cities across Ukraine, 2 were from Belarus, 4 were from Moldova, 2 were from Armenia, 1 was from Azerbaijan, 1 was from Uzbekistan, 91 were from Russia, and the remainder represented the United States. This is a smaller coalition than the Soviet-era network of Women's Councils, and few of the coalition's initial members originated in older activists networks. As a result, many have not been able to coordinate their activities with these more experienced potential allies.

The Women's Consortium was initially formed in response to a USAID invitation to the Winrock International Institute for Agricultural Development, an Arkansas-based nonprofit with field offices in Brazil, India, and the Philippines. Winrock had received numerous federal grants for development work, but had no prior ties to the Soviet Union and had never established a women's advocacy group. A self-consciously feminist representative of Winrock, Elise Smith, first traveled to several post-Soviet cities on a USAID-funded tour intended to identify local partners for USAID partnership programs. Smith had time only to meet briefly with a small handful of the organizations that had formed during glasnost. On the basis of their promises to join, Winrock successfully applied for two initial grants: a

$95,000 grant from the Eurasia Foundation,[12] and a $750,000 grant from USAID, both intended for leadership training programs for local women.

Few of the consortium's U.S. advisers and staff had ever worked with grassroots community groups, which most proponents of civil society see as the foundations of democratic life. They typically had previously worked in U.S. development agencies or other official Soviet-U.S. exchanges (e.g., Peace Links, Friendship Forces). A few of the consortium's advisers had taken part in official exchanges sponsored by the Soviet Union's official women's organizations. Others had recent experience working full-time either with the U.S. Embassy or federally funded organizations that had only recently established programs or chapters in Moscow (e.g., the Peace Corps), or with American nongovernmental organizations that had received subcontracts from larger federally funded organizations to undertake projects in the region after the Soviet Union's dissolution. Still others had experience working with high-profile, professionally staffed, single-issue U.S.-based organizations like Planned Parenthood that had developed and maintained chapters in developing countries and were being encouraged by the federal government to expand into the former Soviet Union. Conspicuously absent were representatives of the small ethnic or religious community–based women's service organizations that were staffed by local volunteers and relied primarily on face-to-face fundraising and more closely resemble grassroots ideal-types of community activism. Indeed, far from belonging to a face-to-face community group that post-Soviet women's activists might emulate, many of the high-profile activists the consortium enlisted in the project had been participants in large international development projects that had worked primarily with women in developing countries. They found it hard to support the interests and objectives of the glasnost-era welfare rights mother's groups and nationalist women's associations that existed outside Moscow.

The local post-Soviet partners who became active in the consortium were from similarly elite circles. For example, one of the primary Russian figures in the consortium's work in Russia was Elena Ershova, who in the first years of the consortium's existence succeeded an American staff member to become the consortium's Moscow coordinator. A 1950s graduate of Moscow's elite Institute of International Relations (the training ground of the Soviet Union's developers of foreign policy), Ershova worked for the Communist Party organ *Kommunist* from 1957 until 1968. She then wrote a *kandidat* thesis on the American peace movement for the Academy of Social Sciences of the Central Committee. Upon completion of her degree, Ershova left party work for a position as a researcher at the USA-Canada Institute of the Soviet Academy of Sciences, an elite think tank where she and other politically reliable scholars worked on the American New Left and on second-wave feminism—topics that were off-limits to most Soviet citizens. Until glasnost, she was also a consultant to such official organizations as the Soviet Peace Committee and the Soviet Women's Committee. Several other Russian activists prominent in the consortium also held positions at the USA-Canada Institute and were, like Ershova, scholars rather than community activists. They had a knowledge of feminism and could frame their concerns in terms familiar to American activists.

Initially, relatively young, highly placed local women with strong ties to local academic establishments were the only prospective members who expressed interest in the consortium's invitations and were encouraged to join. Few members of local community women's groups founded during glasnost joined the consortium. This was at first surprising and frustrating to the consortium's American employees, who had hoped to mobilize more classically grassroots women's groups in the former Soviet Union. Yet they felt little enthusiasm for the local women representing the Associations of Mothers with Many Children and nationalist women's associations who attended public meetings organized by the consortium and spoke to consortium staff about the political functions of motherhood. These activists' goals seemed to subordinate women and so did not mesh well with the consortium's preexisting agenda to strengthen women's leadership in post-Soviet societies.

As a result, the consortium's local members and partners in the former Soviet Union are mostly new groups that are not typical of the first small autonomous women's protest groups that formed during glasnost. It has helped to fund a series of important local women's ventures modeled on Western women's NGOs. These range from rape crisis centers to business incubators and gender studies centers. All of these are, of course, institutions that did not exist in the Soviet Union, are sorely needed, and without question have made a genuine contribution to post-Soviet women's rights. Nonetheless, with few exceptions, because the consortium's agenda was based on strengthening women's leadership, most of its initiatives have been oriented toward highly educated professional women who might become future leaders.[13] Its programs failed to support more classically grassroots community organizations that formed prior to the consortium.

Local members of the consortium are a select group who have been and remain better positioned to compete for Western funding than to develop local sources of financial support. The consortium teaches a relatively small number of women how to compete for Western grants. These local partners then run campaigns for women's rights that are modeled directly on U.S. or western European styles of activism. Through the consortium's influence, a handful of new post-Soviet women's groups have become integrated into transnational networks. They rarely work cooperatively with preexisting local women's groups, whose solutions are often hostile to feminism and whose focus is on maternalist causes. As a result, deep ideological rifts have formed between a small feminist community and broader networks of community activists.

Invariably, Western funding can undermine local alliances and inhibit badly needed local coalition work. Indeed, one of the greatest current obstacles to domestic coalition building has been the clash between the "maternalist" collective action frame that local post-Soviet activists tend to adopt, and the feminist collective action frame that foreign advocates use and encourage in their post-Soviet partners' funding proposals. International organizations that have established independent programs in the region soon encountered a frustrating dilemma: their mobilizing strategies frequently presuppose a type of women's rights activism that is absent in the region, particularly at the grassroots.

Western conceptions of women's rights that focus on political empowerment and independence were and remain alien to the broader population (Einhorn 1993; Marsh 1996; Pilkington 1996; Posadskaya 1994; Racioppi and O'Sullivan See 1997). They are also far from the collective action frame of women activists who joined glasnost-era associations and who are often unable to identify with international organizations' objectives. Hence many more seasoned activists have had little or no access to new Western resource bases, and their organizations have struggled to exist during the economic crisis that began after the Soviet Union's collapse. Indeed, the new women volunteers and activists who became involved in Western outreach efforts were quite often not the same women who had previously managed organizations created from above by the state, such as Women's Councils and state agencies concerned with maternal and child welfare. Rarely are Western initiatives likely to attract the wives of prominent politicians or political activists who now run nationalist women's associations. Instead, their local partners tend to be small groups of young women in their 20s with close ties to academic and political elites and above-average receptiveness to Western literature—feminist writings in particular. In short, the post-Soviet women's groups formed with the assistance of American partners are distant from many preexisting women's community groups and are also much smaller in size, tending to draw their membership and leadership from a small, relatively elite stratum of women with fairly close ties to Washington and Moscow state-based programs and agencies.

Conclusion

Clearly, civil society as it currently exists in the former Soviet Union has brought little relief to the local women community activists who sought greater state protection for their children. It is also far from having met the objectives of transnational women's activists who arrived to help post-Soviet women develop a capacity for feminist activism. Women's organizations have been particularly hard hit by the institutional rearrangements that the Soviet Union's collapse has entailed, and as I pointed out earlier, women's NGOs now constitute less than 1 percent of all post-Soviet NGOs.

To what can this sad state of affairs be attributed? I began by asking whether the current weakness of post-Soviet women's activism results primarily from globalization (by which I mean recent economic and political programs intended to help integrate the former Soviet Union into the world economy), or if this weakness is primarily the consequence of preexisting weaknesses that have long been stressed in Western accounts of Soviet women. In order to determine an answer, my analysis focused on changes over time in women's access to three sets of resources needed for collective action: control over indigenous women's organizations, the development of a collective action frame, and opportunities for building coalitions among women's groups divided by ideological differences. My analysis suggests that a tentative answer can now be made.

The relative weakness of post-Soviet women's community activism is a byproduct of increased dependence on foreign activists and causes; this is a direct (albeit unintended) outcome of U.S. policy, rather than simply an unintended consequence of a weak local tradition of community activism. The centerpiece of foreign policy on civil society has been to establish transnational partnerships of local and foreign NGOs and to cultivate future leaders. Women's activists' prior dependencies (on the party and state leadership) have been replaced by ties to Western activists and causes that strive to teach local activists Western strategies for conducting community initiatives.[14] Consequently, nearly a decade of Western assistance has taken local civil societies one step forward (increasing possibilities for international coalition building), but two steps back (decreasing local control over women's NGOs and action repertoires).

The weakness of local women's NGOs is not simply a continuation of a long history of powerlessness. An examination of access to three sets of collective action resources suggests that during the Soviet era, women gradually developed control over indigenous women's organizations and elaborated an effective collective action frame based on mothers' rights. Increasing access to these first two sets of resources created a capacity for decentralized collective action that manifested itself in a variety of new forms of women's activism and in a proliferation of new women's NGOs.

However, recent post-Soviet political instability (caused by the Soviet Union's collapse and the impact of subsequent market reforms and globalization) has indeed prevented these new forms of collective action from translating into increased political power. But this is not simply the result of globalization, as the USSR's demise brought an end to preexisting coalitions created through official women's groups. The subsequent shifts in political and economic life have tended to create great challenges for women's community activism. In other words, ironically, Soviet women activists increased their access to certain kinds of collective action resources, but their opportunities for another kind of important collective action declined considerably.

An unintended benefit of globalization has been increased Western support for post-Soviet women's activism, manifested in greater access for women activists to new public and private sources of aid and assistance from Western women's advocacy groups. Unfortunately, increased possibilities for Western coalition building have failed to compensate for the real loss of locally based coalitions. Very few of these ventures have been able to build on the wave of women's community activism that began in 1989. Instead, many Western initiatives have encouraged the formation of new partnerships between U.S. women's groups and local post-Soviet groups. Not only has this coalition-building strategy led to the formation of new, typically feminist groups oriented toward U.S. agendas and dependent on Western public and private support, it has failed to encourage (or at least, has delayed) the formation and strengthening of cooperative ties between these new groups and the older activist networks formed during glasnost.[15] This coalition-building failure can be attributed in part to a mismatch between the collective action repertoires that local "maternalists" adopt and the feminist one that transnational feminists view as legitimate. Thus, Western policies have stressed an approach that creates considerable unintended negative consequences for post-Soviet women's activism.

A number of new Western-funded civil society building initiatives seek to provide continued relief and support to post-Soviet women's NGOs. According to the most comprehensive recent survey of post-Soviet women's groups to date, 63 percent of Russian women's organizations that responded report that they derive financial resources from Western foundations, while just under a third receive support from their government (Abubikirova et al. 1998, 16). This trend has been observed throughout the region, although in the Caucasus and Central Asian regions Western outreach efforts have largely failed to generate women's activism.[16] This suggests that the region's activist networks may become increasingly divided, rather than being strengthened by increased contact with Western women's activists. This cannot fail to prevent women from sustaining local community initiatives, regaining their lost political influence.

In sum, globalization and the policies intended to soften its effect on post-Soviet societies have had complicated effects on women. The Soviet Union's transition from state socialism to free-market capitalism abruptly overturned a corporatist political system within which women's rights activists and organizations were becoming an increasingly important interest group. Even though men monopolized positions of authority and influence, Soviet women were represented politically by activists who were given access to policy makers through institutionalized political channels. Official governmental women's rights activists and glasnost-era maternalist organizations have been fatally weakened by the dissolution of this corporatist system, but nonetheless, it does seem to be the case that they have a stable, perhaps even growing niche, among the region's women. New post-Soviet groups are small, rarely cooperate with one another, and rely heavily on Western sources of short-term support. Increasingly dependent on outsiders, post-Soviet women's rights activists and organizations remain poorly positioned to use the political system to revitalize the local infrastructure of women's organizations that might have helped shield local women from the disastrous effects of globalization.

Western initiatives have introduced complementary approaches to the local activist community. The new women's rights activists differ in composition, size, and primary basis of affiliation from the previous generation of Soviet-era women's activists. Women's groups have become more numerous, more overtly political in their demands, and in fact may now have started to develop a broader membership base (although many membership figures that post-Soviet women's groups claim are suspiciously large and may include lapsed members from the Soviet era). However, the activist community remains divided over ideological issues.

There is obviously one possible way out of this dead end: increased local coalitions between older activists who came of age before or during the glasnost eras, and younger activists who have gravitated to Western initiatives. In the short run, this may not be the strategy taken. U.S. women's activists who work for Western foundations and initiatives are often impatient with the Soviet-style women's advocates who run local successors to Soviet Women's Councils, which they see simply as bureaucratically run, mass-membership organizations that are not responsive to their members' needs and requests. But this characterization is only a half truth that obscures the fact that these organizations were anchored in valuable networks of activists who were familiar with local conditions and integrated into preexisting local and regional associations and organizations.

It is worth considering more explicitly what the costs are to leaving the "maternalists" out of Western initiatives. At least in their network ties, these older activists remain far better suited to working within the local political system than foreign-funded groups tied to international agendas. While Women's Councils were also tied to party agendas, these official Soviet women's organizations represent an enormous resource pool of trained leaders and networks of career activists throughout the Soviet Union. Unfortunately, former party members and former party-controlled organizations bore little or no resemblance to the style of activism Western funders (in particular, women's rights advocates) expected to find. As a result, preexisting activists and organizations instead fell into disfavor with reformers, who provided the building blocks for integrating women activists. Although Western funders and advocates never came to see local Women's Councils and other locally based groups as capable of acting in their behalf, these groups continued to become important bases for community activism during and after glasnost. Thus it seems that the effectiveness of Western initiatives might be greater if they placed priority on building domestic coalitions rather than international partnerships. This is an important point to stress.

Coalition building with external advocates should not be pursued to the exclusion of other strategies for increasing local women's control over other collective action resources. Post-Soviet women who do not fit the leadership profile that Western funders adopt are badly in need of bargaining power to increase their influence over policy making. Prior to glasnost, an absence of democratic freedoms prevented local Soviet women from using official women's associations and local organizational resources to develop the commitments, skills, and resources necessary for effective community activism. Once democratic rights were introduced, these women's groups began to develop new strategies for influencing policy, but they were not far along when the Soviet Union's collapse destroyed a significant share of their previous resource base. Rapid "shock therapy" reforms promoted by the IMF, the World Bank, the EU, and Western governments threaten to undermine existing women's organizations by moving the locus of policy making and funding further beyond their access. As a result, older activists with an understanding of the rules of local politics were at first largely bypassed by Western funders in favor of more radical women's groups of younger activists, many of whom embrace feminism and Western understandings of rights. Although these new women's groups are much easier for Western observers to identify with, they are less effective in mobilizing public support than are older activists. It may be difficult to build bridges between new feminist groups and older networks of Soviet activists, but greater local control over organizational resources and collective action frames will ultimately give local women greater future opportunities for effective and sustained collective action, and this, after all, has long been the objective of Western advocates.

Notes

1. State involvement in and tolerance of overt gender discrimination, and the state's failure to investigate violent crimes against women in post-state socialist countries, are reported in several Helsinki Watch and Women's Rights Project publications (see Human Rights Watch 1992, 1995a, 1995b, and 1997) as well as in the U.S. Department of State's annual human rights reports (see U.S. Department of State 1994, 1997). Governmental responses to global trafficking in women and children from Ukraine and Russia are examined in the United Nations Commission on Crime Prevention and Criminal Justice 1996 and in several RFE/RL reports (see Hyde 1998; Kamerud 1988; Moffet 1997). Public policies toward women and families are examined by annual United Nations and USAID reports (see *United Nations Gender in Development Bureau* 1999; USAID 1998).

2. For the most comprehensive Western discussions of the status of Soviet (primarily

Russian) women prior to glasnost, see Lapidus 1978 and Atkinson, Dallin, and Lapidus 1977. For the most comprehensive discussions of the women's activism during and after glasnost, see Buckley 1989 and 1991; Lapidus 1993; Marsh 1996; Pilkington 1996; Posadskaya 1994; Racioppi and O'Sullivan See 1997; and Sperling 1997.

3. I interviewed or consulted representatives or members of the following North American organizations that work with NGOs in the former Soviet Union: the Alliance of Russian and American Women; the Canada-Ukraine Parliamentary Program; the Center for Safe Energy; Counterpart International; Friends of Rukh of Northern New Jersey; Human Rights Watch; ISAR: Initiative for Social Action and Renewal in Eurasia; the MacArthur Foundation; Magee Womancare International; the NIS-US Women's Consortium; the Peace Corps; Planned Parenthood of New England; the Samuel Rubin Foundation; the Ukrainian Women's Union; the United States Agency for International Development; and the US-Ukraine Relief Committee. During extensive field research conducted during winter and spring 2001, I also interviewed representatives and/or members of more than 60 women's NGOs in three Ukrainian cities.

4. Party leader Lazar Kaganovich justified the organization's dissolution with the claim that it had become too focused on women's issues that were better dealt with by the party as a whole: "In view of the fact that work among women has acquired important significance in the present period, it should be carried out by all departments of the Central Committee and, more specifically, it should be continued under the rubric of the successful mass campaigns which the Party organizes in towns and [the] countryside" (Goldman 1996, 63). Historians have produced a considerable literature on the party's treatment of early Soviet women activists. For an overview of the history of the early Soviet women's movement, see Stites 1978. On the rise and fall of the *zhenotdel,* see Clements 1979 and 1992; Farnsworth 1980; Goldman 1996; and Wood 1997.

5. Some official Soviet reports inflated women's political power, and most were largely silent about their continuing problems. One official report widely available in the West claimed that by 1980, Soviet women deputies occupied 49.5 percent of the seats in the USSR's representative institutions, only 3.8 percent less than the proportion of women in the total population (Council for Mutual Economic Assistance 1985). But this statistic was inflated, for women had achieved this level of representation only on relatively powerless local councils. The report failed to point out that Soviet women were not as well represented at higher levels of government. Nor did it indicate their share of party membership.

6. Women's Councils began to be formed locally in small numbers in the late 1950s, but the party came to use these organizations as transmission belts for party directives. Large numbers of Women's Councils were founded during the Khrushchev thaw in the early 1960s, and then again under Gorbachev in the 1980s during glasnost. But these groups tended to be short-lived and isolated (predominating in rural areas). According to Browning's (1987) study of the Women's Councils, they never developed sufficient au-

tonomy to raise women's political awareness or sufficient power to provide women greater access to formal political posts and formal politics (65, 126–29).

7. Buckley 1989 (21) and Muzyria 1989 both give the same figures.

8. For membership figures and alliance structures, I have relied on the two most recent surveys of Ukrainian and Russian women's NGOs, the Women's Information Consultative Center 1996, and Abubikirova et al. 1998.

9. In the Central Asian republics and among minority populations elsewhere, ethnocultural organizations emerged on a far smaller scale, and in most cases, did not achieve wider popular support. Thus far, Central Asian groups that promote a revival of Moslem traditions such as the League of Moslem Women of Kazakhstan, based in Almaty, and the Fatima-Zakhira Society of Moslem Women in Gyandzha, Azerbaijan, have not achieved a mass membership.

10. U.S. government commissions on women's status, by contrast, did become vehicles through which women articulated further political demands for equal rights (see Ferree and Hess 1994, 59–68).

11. For a fascinating English-language collection of Soviet women's responses to the early stages of perestroika and glasnost, see Buckley's (1989) collection.

12. The Eurasia Foundation was created in 1993 to help the NIS introduce markets and democratic institutions. It is funded by both public and private donors.

13. Hence, in contrast to the unknown women who formed local soldiers' mothers groups, several of the consortium's most prominent board members on the Russian side had been leaders of the official Soviet women's organizations and had considerable experience advising government officials and communicating with the mass media.

14. Thus, for example, international agencies have continued to tolerate gross violations of civil rights in Chechnya, but they pulled out of Belarus only after its government repeatedly failed to implement economic reforms.

15. The Soviet state's collapse has permitted widespread intervention by Western states such as the United States and international institutions such as the World Bank and IMF. As reforms accelerated, so has the flow of Western aid and Western representatives who run various Western organizations. Among those who arrived were a wide variety of Western women involved in official intergovernmental scholarly exchanges such as IREX and Fulbright, or in bilateral offical exchanges through such governmental organizations as Peace Links or the Citizens Democracy Corps. Many of these women, alarmed by what they perceived to be the remarkable political apathy they encountered among Soviet women and their absence from positions of political power and authority, quickly immersed themselves in local feminist activism. Some translated Western feminist works into Russian and arranged for their publication. Others started feminist publications with Russian partners. Most were frustrated with the resistance to feminism among all but a few of the women they encountered.

16. Nijole White (1997) writes that cooperation with Western women's movements is "likely to continue to play a major part in shaping the strategy of the movements in Latvia and Lithuania and also in lending them support, both moral and material." She concludes that "the women in the Baltic and the women in Russia have two major things in common: the Soviet experience which they strive to leave behind, and the Western models of feminism which they strive to emulate to a greater or lesser extent" (215). By contrast, Shirin Akiner (1997) concludes that in Central Asia, development agencies and NGOs' efforts to integrate women into development programs often misfire. "Central Asians, both men and women, deeply resent what they regard as a patronizing attitude of some of the administrators of these programs [whose] schemes have little relevance to local conditions. . . . Another cause of irritation is the implicit, or even explicit, bias that some Western (or Western-trained) staff display against Islam and traditional society." According to Akiner, women who work with Western organizations are seen as opportunists. Women's organizations are also seen as illegitimate in the Caucasus (Dragadze 1997; Dudwick 1997).

6

Las Mujeres Invisibles/The Invisible Women

Sharon Ann Navarro

> NAFTA is a story of violence against women. It is a treaty that created violence against women and their families. There are tremendous implications, the economic implications and the whole impact it has had on women's health, their lives, their future, and their families. It is as violent as any beating, if not more destructive.
>
> —La Mujer Obrera

El Paso, Texas, is a microcosm of the inherent contradictions created by the North American Free Trade Agreement (NAFTA) along the border. On the one hand, NAFTA profoundly shifted the focus of national and international commerce, moving it from an "East-West" emphasis to a "North-South" paradigm. In doing so, El Paso became the gateway to the tremendous economic opportunities available to Mexico and Latin America (Ortega 2000). At the same time, north of the U.S.-Mexican border, NAFTA acted as a catalyst, another force, or another trend, that is steadily squeezing Mexican-American women workers (in the garment industry) to the margins of the economic sector in El Paso. These Mexican-American garment workers are typically low-skilled and low-income women. As the garment industries close down their businesses and move across the border, the Mexican-American women that once worked in these businesses are being left out of the economic restructuring taking place under NAFTA. These women are being marginalized. The type of work that they have done—in some cases for more than twenty, years—is now becoming obsolete and replaced by advanced technology.

Before this study is presented to you, it is important to note that NAFTA is not characterized as *the main factor* for the displacement (or permanent layoffs) of female garment workers in El Paso. NAFTA is instead used by one grassroots nongovernmental women's organization, La Mujer Obrera (LMO), as a symbol of what they face as female workers in a border city, as a tool for political activism and mobilization. The women's organization examined in this study has succeeded in contextualizing NAFTA as a tangible culprit, the *primary cause* of their current struggle for a better quality of life for the displaced workers and their families.

LMO's direct response to globalization, as manifested in NAFTA, should not be interpreted to mean that one organization is simply bashing NAFTA only. Instead, because of the attention given to NAFTA by politicians, various interest groups, and scholars alike, NAFTA has simply become the topic of selection that organizations like LMO use as the source of their struggle. Similar agreements, such as the General Agreement on Tariffs and Trade, the Free Trade Area of the Americas, or the Multilateral Agreement on Investment, could just have easily been targeted.

For the Mexican-American garment workers in El Paso, an entire way of life and standard of living are fast disappearing. These Spanish-speaking, women have worked all of their lives to provide for up to four generations of their families. Now they have lost their livelihood, their health-care insurance, their homes, and their futures. When NAFTA was first introduced in the late 1980s, various organizations with labor interests believed that NAFTA was going to be their opportunity to set labor standards for workers in the three participating countries. However, that was not at all what the crafters of NAFTA intended. Instead, labor interests were left out of NAFTA.

And so NAFTA became an incitement to discourse, an invitation to review the voices whose identities, as Spanish-speaking, female garment workers, are vehicles for political expression. This woman's nongovernmental organization mobilized to express their anxieties about the way NAFTA has affected their economic subsistence, their way of life. The struggle for this grassroots organization is not over the politics of influence, but to transform the terms and nature of the debate; it is a struggle to integrate previously excluded groups, voices, and issues into local and national politics.

Drawing on literature from political science, as well as from a wealth of new data obtained through fieldwork,[1] this study examines LMO's use of central icons, traditions, history, and customs from Mexican culture to mobilize constituents in appeals to U.S. local, state, and federal government institutions. More important, this study explores how one women's organization used the U.S.-Mexico border to highlight its struggle in the post-NAFTA era.

This chapter is divided into three sections. The first focuses on the uniqueness of a border city in the post-NAFTA era. The second offers a gendered look at globalization as manifested in NAFTA. The last section looks at culture as a mobilizing tool for LMO, paying particular attention to the way in which LMO embraces Mexican culture to highlight the displaced workers' struggle.

El Paso: A Border between Two Worlds

The physical designation of a boundary may serve as an observable reminder that the politics, economics, and culture of countries and subnationalities differ (Agnew, Mercer, and Sopher 1984). The uniqueness of El Paso–Ciudad Juarez stems from the fact that a city from the First World shares a border with a developing city from the Third World. Boundaries create cultures and identities that impose order on cities, communities, and individuals by shaping them in a way that embodies the values and beliefs of a society or geographic location. The physical and cultural closeness of the United States and Mexico, as well as the political, social, and economic ties that connect them, creates an intriguing bicultural arrangement that provide a laboratory for studying identity formation and mobilization across borders.

In theory, a border is a line that separates one nation from another or, in the case of internal entities, one province or locality from another. The essential functions of a border are to keep people in their own space and to prevent, control, or regulate interactions among them. For the purposes of this study, the terms *border, borderland,* and *frontera* are used interchangeably. The terms are used to denote an area that is physically distant from the core of the nation; it is a zone of transition, a place where people and institutions are shaped by natural and human forces that are not felt in the core or heartland of the United States or Mexico.

For example, the U.S.-Mexico boundary is the busiest land border in the world, the longest and most dramatic meeting point between a rich and a poor country, and the site of the most intensive interaction between law enforcement and law evasion. Nowhere has the state more aggressively loosened and tightened its territorial border grip at the same time. Nowhere else do the contrasting state practices of market liberalization and criminalization more visibly overlap. The result has been the construction of both a borderless economy (via NAFTA) and a barricaded border. More concretely, the politics of opening the border to legal economic flows is closely connected to the politics of making it appear more closed to illegal flows: illegal drugs and migrant labor.

Oscar Martinez, one of the leading scholars on the U.S.-Mexico border, acknowledges the political, economic, and social cultural significance of the frontera. He proposes that the dynamics of the border create four models of borderland interaction: alienated borderlands, coexistent borderlands, interdependent borderlands, and integrated borderlands. Each model illustrates a different degree of cross-border interaction (Grimes 1998). For example, today interdependence is overwhelmingly dominant in the U.S.-Mexico borderlands, and therefore the most appropriate designation for that binational zone is the interdependent frontera.

That is not to say, however, that elements of alienation, coexistence, and even integration are not part of the zone at a given time. Martinez's findings are nothing new for this border city and its border people. The influence of Ciudad Juarez on El Paso is a natural daily occurrence.

The uniqueness of the U.S.-Mexico border, specifically the border city in question, plays a critical role in the sociopolitical construction of identities. Kimberly Grimes, in her study of migration to the United States from Putla de Guerro, Oaxaca, Mexico, suggests that identities are rooted in geography. Grimes's claim holds the key to understanding the seemingly contradictory strategy of LMO, which on the one hand embraces the Mexican culture—which is suggestive of a "borderless cultural region"—to mobilize its members, but at the same time reemphasizes the U.S.-Mexico border to highlight the struggles of displaced workers. According to Grimes, borders play an important role in distinguishing "us" from "them." Moreover, people's sense of self includes identification with particular geographical spaces. People negotiate constructed political, economic, and social (cultural) borders of self-identification. Identities are grounded in space and time, and they transform as time passes, as people move across spaces, and as national policies and global conditions transform. People react to these changes and constructions by accommodating or challenging and/or resisting them.

Mexican-American Women Workers in El Paso: A Gendered Look at Globalization

For the close to 20,000 displaced workers, NAFTA and ongoing deep economic restructuring have not ushered in the new dawn of prosperity hailed by political leaders. The explosive growth of lower-paid export manufacturing jobs in the maquiladora sector in Mexico has been offset by the immense loss of jobs in the domestic manufacturing sector in the United States and Canada.

The globalization of capital necessary for economic restructuring is being deliberately hastened by most national governments, by international institutions like the International Monetary Fund and the World Bank, and by global corporations themselves. While international trade is nothing new, our system of nation-based economies is rapidly changing toward a "new world economy" (Takaki 1993). At the center of this change lies a sharp increase in capital mobility. Computer, communication, and transportation technologies continue to shorten geographical distances, making possible the coordination of production and commerce on a global scale. Lower tariffs have reduced national frontiers as barriers to commerce, thus encouraging transnational production and distribution. Corporations are becoming global not only to reduce production costs, but also to expand markets, elude taxes, acquire resources, and protect themselves against currency fluctuations and other risks, including the growth of organizations like LMO that would mobilize workers and demand that their interests and voices be heard in the new world economy (see also Brecher and Costello 1994).

Three hundred companies now own an estimated one-quarter of the productive assets of the world (Barnet and Cavanagh 1994, 15). Of the top 100 economies in the world, 47 are corporations—each with more wealth than 130 countries (Harison 1994). International trade and financial institutions like the International Monetary Fund, the World Bank, the European Union (EU), and the new World Trade Organization have cultivated powers formerly reserved for nation-states. Conversely, national governments have become less and less able to control their own economies. This new system, which is controlled by the so-called Corporate Agenda, is not based on the consent of the governed (Brecher, Childs, and Cutler 1993), and it has no institutional mechanism to hold it accountable to those whom its decisions affect.

In general, the effects of capital mobility, which is designed to increase economic efficiency, have been malignant for workers. An unregulated global economy forces workers, communities, and countries to compete with each other in an effort to attract corporate investment. Each tries to reduce labor, social, and environmental costs below the others.[2]

In the debates surrounding NAFTA, globalization and regionalization are often interpreted as homogenizing vehicles, without regard to the fact that women, and in particular women of color, are paying a disproportionate share of the costs of the processes of neoliberalism. Globalization hits especially hard racial/ethnic minorities in the United States and female factory workers in the U.S. (Larudee 1999, 123–63). It has profoundly changed the lives of women in El Paso, Texas, creating inequalities that interact with pre-existing class, ethnic, gender, and regional cleavages (Gabriel and Macdonald 1994, 535–62).

Job losses have been especially substantial in the apparel sector in El Paso and in some small communities that are heavily dependent on factories, which shut down and moved to Mexico. Since NAFTA took effect in 1994, El Paso has lost between 15,000 and 20,000 jobs.[3] Table 6.1 shows the number of job losses from 1994 to 2000. Table 6.2 shows how Texas ranks in comparison to other states with respect to displaced workers. Free trade and the reduction of tariffs made it easier for companies to close plants and move to Mexico only to continue as maquiladoras (Myerson 1998, 1C, 22C).

In December 1998, El Paso's average unemployment rate was almost three times (11 percent) the state unemployment rate of 4.4 percent and the U.S. rate of 4 percent Kolence 1999c, B10). The community of El Paso was for a very long time advertised as a low-wage, low-skill manufacturing paradise. A 1993–94 study conducted by the Greater El Paso Chamber of Commerce Foundation Inc.

Table 6.1: NAFTA Job Losses In El Paso, January 1994–November 2000

YEAR	NUMBER OF DISPLACED WORKERS
1994	1,045
1995	2,193
1996	2,573
1997	3,435
1998	3,641
1999	2,125
2000	1,940
TOTAL	**18, 975**

SOURCE: Texas Workforce Commission.

Table 6.2: NAFTA-TAA Certified Workers, by State as of mid-July 1997

Texas	*	Massachusetts	1,315
North Carolina	*	West Virginia	1,288
Pennsylvania	*	Kansas	1,184
New York	*	Kentucky	1,016
California	7,476	Alaska	780
Georgia	6,186	Louisiana	778
Indiana	5,811	Arizona	684
Tennessee	5,640	Connecticut	631
Arkansas	5,397	Montana	613
New Jersey	4,471	Maine	432
Ohio	4,413	Wyoming	392
Wisconsin	4,405	Vermont	361
Michigan	3,783	Minnesota	336
Washington	3,445	North Dakota	300
Missouri	3,329	Utah	292
Illinois	2,902	New Mexico	242
Florida	2,804	Oklahoma	230
Iowa	2,785	Nebraska	220
Oregon	2,550	New Hampshire	139
South Carolina	2,305	Maryland	86
Virginia	2,166	Idaho	83
Colorado	1,990	Nevada	76
Alabama	1,383	South Dakota	65

*The Department of Labor does not have the total number of displaced workers for the states of Texas, North Carolina, Pennsylvania, and New York, but claim they are the states with the highest numbers.

SOURCE: Department of Labor, NAFTA Trade Adjustment Assistance Office.

NOTE: Certifications are for January 1, 1994 to July 18, 1997.

reported, "[I]f you want to be the low wage paying capital of the world, don't do anything, you're already there" (El Paso Greater Chamber of Commerce 1997, 10). Cheap Mexican labor, in particular, has always been El Paso's strongest selling point (also see Garcia 1981). Roberto Franco, director of the City's Economic Development Agency, articulated this point best when he said, "El Paso was perceived as the jeans and slacks capital of the United States" (Kolence 1999a, 4).

Approximately 80 percent of the garment workers in El Paso's garment and other manufacturing industries were Mexican-American women. Their subordinate social status limits their employment opportunities and makes them vulnerable to exploitation. As a result of NAFTA, however, thousands of Mexican-American workers, many of whom had migrated from Mexico to El Paso in search of a better life, lost their jobs. A total of 97 percent of the displaced Mexican-American workers in El Paso are Hispanic, and 80 percent are women (Gilot 1999, 10B). One-third of these women head single households. Half are between the ages of 30 and 45, while the majority of the other half are older than 45. In addition, most of the affected workers are sustaining up to four generations of their families—themselves, their parents, their children and their grandchildren (La Mujer Obrera 1999a, 1). Using an average figure of four persons per household, the population affected by NAFTA in El Paso can be estimated at 40,000. When taking only into account the number of so-called certified NAFTA displaced workers,[4] the at-risk population is at least 80,000—13 percent of El Paso's population—and the potentially affected population is as large as 200,000. The women's job skills cannot easily be transferred from low-tech to the mid to high-tech manufacturing jobs entering El Paso in record numbers (El Puente CDC/La Mujer Obrera 1999, 6). The testimonies of displaced Mexican-American women workers reveal their immense financial struggles. Typically over 45 years of age, with less than a fourth-grade education in Mexico, they have lost health insurance and other benefits because the businesses they worked for shut down production, and they are typically two to three months past due on rent and utilities.[5] The lead organizer of the Asociacion de Trabjadores Fronterizos (Association of Borderland Workers), Guillermo Glenn (1999), describes the burden globalization has foisted on female Mexican-American displaced woman workers:

> In El Paso, women suffer what is called a *"doble jornada"* (double day's work) because they have two jobs, one at home and one at the factory (or school since there are very few factories open). They suffer all the discrimination. Language discrimination, discrimination because they are Mexican, and discrimination because they are women. . . . There is still a lot of discrimination in terms of their role, in terms of their decision-making, in terms of how they are treated.

LMO has been working for nearly five years to make the conditions of Spanish-speaking, NAFTA-displaced women workers visible locally, regionally, and nationally. The seeds of LMO were planted in 1972, when a campaign to unionize workers in the Farah plant (the biggest jean maker at the time) in El Paso intensified (see Coyle, Hershatter, and Honig 1980, 117–43). LMO was formed because women felt that the Amalgamated Clothing and Textile Workers of America, or for that matter, any union (such as the AFL-CIO), did nothing to address their needs, ignored their rights as *women* workers, and did not respect their membership as *women* members in the union (Flores 1998). This devaluation of women's work is deeply rooted in the history of U.S. labor unions. According to Glenn (1999), the old labor movement of the 1970s—including the one that organized Farah workers—"characterized itself as . . . [a]very macho kind of an organization. We (LMO) feel that the labor unions have not gotten away from that." For example, during the strike against Farah, male organizers in both the Amalgamated Clothing Workers of American and the AFL-CIO ignored women worker's concerns, such as sexual harassment, health care, child care, domestic violence, political education, and verbal abuse by their employers (Flores 1998). Moreover, employers often view the income of the female workers as "extra" or "supplemental" to their husband's income.

In 1981, following the Farah campaign, LMO was legally established as a non-profit community-based organization of women workers in El Paso. LMO has defined itself, first and foremost, as a *woman's* organization (La Mujer Obrera 1993, 3). It combines community organizing, popular education, leadership development and advocacy into a comprehensive struggle for a better quality of life for the women and their families. Like other organizations operating in a resource-poor environment, the organization relies on outside funding (La Mujer Obrera 1999, 1 and 2). The organization turns to national churches, private foundations, the federal government, and local entities for financial support (Arnold 1999a). LMO initially had a yearly budget of $150,000, and in 1998–1999 its budget was between $500,000 and $750,000 (Arnold 1999b). The organization employs a total of six women as full-time organizers. The board of directors is made up of two men and five women, all of whom have been displaced by NAFTA. The support staff consists of a paid secretary and a grant writer as well as various interns and volunteers.

The organization struggles to achieve *siete necesidades basicas* (seven basic goals): decent, stable employment, housing, education, nutrition, health care, peace, and political liberty. One of LMO's principal objectives is to educate workers so that they are able to defend their rights and to take leadership positions in their own communities. Educational programs form the basis for organizing work and raise workers' awareness of their roles as *women* and as economic producers. Like other women's movements, LMO has struggled to integrate previously excluded issues into politics by pushing women's concerns (e.g., child care and health care) (Peterson 1992, 183–206). LMO also serves at a safe place where friendships develop, experiences are shared, and where women become educated not only about their rights as workers, but, perhaps most important, their rights as women, mothers, and spouses. To this end, LMO has established a child care center where displaced workers may leave their children while they attend school, look for work, or go to their jobs.[6]

To achieve institutional changes that will lead to the creation of genuine economic alternatives for workers in the midst of globalization, La Mujer Obrera has also recently reorganized and broadened its structure (La Mujer Obrera 1998, 4). The most critical developments have been the emergence of two new quasi-independent organizations under LMO's corporate umbrella. One is the Asociacion de Trabajadores Fronterizos, which has taken on the worker and community organizing, direct action, and mass mobilization components of LMO's work (5). The association includes Spanish-speaking men and women workers who were employed and laid off from the manufacturing plants in El Paso. Launched during the summer of 1996 with the support of LMO, the association extends beyond LMO's traditional base of women garment workers and incorporates displaced men, workers from electronics, plastics, medical supply manufacturing, and other labor intensive industries. Growing from an initial membership of 20 workers to a current roster of more than 700 active members, the association has built a countywide network with representatives of LMO in seven factories and school committees throughout El Paso (6–7).

Through these networks, the association has the participation of more than 2,000 workers, the majority of whom are women, and a governing board of 14 displaced workers, two elected from and by each of the seven factory and school committees (26). At the same time, LMO began constructing its capacity to develop and operate community economic development programs on behalf of, and with, displaced workers. In December of 1997, LMO established El Puente Community Development Corporation as a vehicle for developing training and education, jobs, self-employment, housing, the development of microenterprises, access to credit and neighborhood revitalization strategies as a means to create jobs, income, and economic self-sufficiency for the workers and the organization. Moving into this arena has required that LMO negotiate and work with local, state, and federal agencies and officials for financial support (26–27).

By creating a space in the political and economic arena, LMO has already produced tangible results for the displaced workers. The organization succeeded in getting a $45 million grant—the largest grant ever given by the U.S. Department of

Labor—to retrain displaced workers. To get this grant, LMO made its concerns known locally and nationally with one act that proved to be a turning point for LMO. On June 1997, several Mexican-American women (all from LMO) blocked the Zaragoza International Port of Entry, which is one of El Paso's busiest commercial bridges with Ciudad Juarez, Mexico, for one hour by stretching a rope across the port. The goal of the protest was to bring the plight of NAFTA-displaced workers to the attention of Secretary Robert Rubin of the Department of the Treasury, which is responsible for a variety of NAFTA programs. But instead of meeting with him, his representative, or other state or local authorities, protesters were arrested and charged with obstructing highway commerce.

The $45 million grant allows LMO to institute alternatives to existing federal and state retraining program. These programs entitle displaced workers to benefits while attending English classes, courses for their general equivalency diploma (GED), and retraining within an 18-month period. Many of these programs, however, are plagued with a variety of problems, especially inadequate buildings and equipment, outdated curricula, incompetent or poorly trained teachers, and administrators who make racial/ethnic slurs and personal insults (Klapmeyer 1998).

In the summer of 1999, Margarita Calderon, a researcher at Johns Hopkins University, tested 60 displaced workers at 12 different schools to see what they had learned. The results were shocking. Only two of the 60 students, some of whom had spent up to five years in various federally subsided training programs, had learned enough to handle an interview in English. Calderon, an expert in bilingual education, found that retraining schools set up for displaced workers had been using rigid teaching techniques long abandoned by better language schools, such as lectures and translation exercises (quoted in Templin 2000, B1 and B4). In addition, there is a perception among case managers, state and local agencies, school administrators, and teachers that "the displaced workers are just there to get paid and don't want to learn" (Klapmeyer 1998). Frustrated with many of the inept retraining schools, LMO opened up its own school for displaced workers on February 1, 1999. It hired a full-time teacher to teach English, the general equivalency examination and microenterprise training. LMO has also established a business incubator that will support the self-employment initiatives of displaced workers. Further, LMO is currently in the process of developing a bilingual adult education curriculum specifically designed for displaced workers in El Paso. This curriculum will be the standard curriculum for every school in El Paso if they are to accept displaced workers in their schools. LMO has also played an instrumental role in helping El Paso win the Empowerment Zone designation that provides federal funds for economic development. As a result, the poorest area of the city—South Central—will receive much needed federal money for revitalization, which would create jobs. LMO plays a role in deciding how that money will be spent.

The Uses of Mexican Culture for Mobilization

For LMO, culture has become a unique dimension in women's activism. In her study of two Chicano struggles in the Southwest, Laura Pulido (1998, 31–60) points out that culture plays a key role in mobilization efforts both by "providing familiar and meaningful guideposts and by facilitating collective identity." The use of symbols, customs, traditions reminds people of who they are, of their share traditions past and present, and of what they can achieve by uniting and acting collectively.

In the 1960s and 1970s Latinos/Chicanos became aware of how their culture not only differed from, but was also maligned by, mainstream Anglo America. Once-shameful cultural icons were reappropriated and turned into symbols of resistance. In the course of building a movement, farmworkers and activists publicly displayed statues and posters of La Virgen de Guadalupe not only as a source of solace and inspiration, but also (and far more consciously at times) as an expression of pride in the Mexican culture and a tool of mobilization. By openly engaging in ritual prayer, they asserted their identity to the larger society (see Herrera-Sobek 1990; Rodriguez 1994). LMO similarly uses La Virgen de Guadalupe as an expression of inspiration and as a vehicle of mobilization and consciousness raising. For the women of LMO, La Virgen de Guadalupe thus not only represents strength, hope, and respect, but "she is also viewed as a woman and a mother who has suffered with the death of her son and, like her, we (displaced workers) are suffering for our families and our children" (Orquiz 1999).[7]

In a study of Mexican-American women in East Los Angeles, Mary Pardo examines how they transform "traditional" networks and resources based on family and culture into political assets to defend the quality of urban life. Here, the women's activism arises out of seemingly "traditional" roles, addresses wider social and political issues, and capitalizes on formal associations sanctioned by the community. Religion, commonly viewed as a conservative force, becomes intertwined with politics. Often, women speak of their communities and their activism as extensions of their family and household responsibility. Women's grassroots struggles center around quality of life and challenge conventional assumptions about the powerlessness of women as well as static definitions of culture and tradition (Pardo 1998).

LMO also identifies with the Mexican culture and its members through its landscape. Outside its building, LMO has corn (maize) stalks growing in place of an assortment of bushes or flowers. As Refugio Arrieta explains, "The maize is symbolic of our Mexican culture. It is a symbol of the resistance too. . . . It is more like the resistance that leads to maintaining the culture here and helping it live and grow here in the U.S. and not simply being forced to abandon the Mexican culture" (Arrieta 1998).

Moreover, LMO also tries to maintain and reinterpret its history and heritage with Mexico in symbolic remembrance of Emiliano Zapata and the Zapatista rebels. Hanging from some of the walls of LMO are portraits and pictures of Emilio Zapata and Zapatista *women* rebels. For LMO, Zapata and the Zapatista rebels represent the struggle of resistance against neoliberalism, specifically NAFTA. They represent in Mexico the voice of people who have been eliminated in Mexico by NAFTA. As one member stated, "We are kindred spirits because of what the U.S. economy is doing to and Mexican-American factory workers what the Mexican economy is doing to the indigenous people of Mexico" (Anonymous 1998). To some extent, LMO believes, like the Zapatistas in southern Mexico, that NAFTA will eliminate them from an economy that was built on their backs.

LMO further uses the Mexican *corrido* as a mobilizing mechanism that reflects their political situation.[8] For example, during Guillermo Glenn's trial on March 17, 1999, after he was arrested for his participation in the blocking of the Zaragoza Bridge, LMO members gathered outside the courthouse in protest. With the news stations there, LMO members began to sing the "Corrido de los Desplazados" (The ballad of the displaced), which they had written themselves:

Ano de 94	In the year of '94
Comenzo la pesadilla	The nightmare started
Se robaron los trabsajos,	They stole the jobs,
Nos dejaron en la orilla	They left us at the edge
Los obreros en El Paso,	The workers in El Paso,
Recuerdan bien ese dia.	Remember well that day.

The "Corrido De Los Desplazados" embraces all displaced workers, raises their level of consciousness, unites them, and inspires them to mobilize. This type of cultural practice also represents the organization's strategy of activism and mobilization. It adds to more conventional forms of political participation, such as voting, in an effort to stress demands for respect, dignity, and justice of the Mexican-American workers and their traditions. Cindy Arnold (1999b), coordinator of El Puente at LMO, summed up the organization's philosophy of political participation as follows: "For us, political involvement is not based on an electoral or party process, but [is seen] in terms of on-going dialogue with political leaders at all the different levels." As a political actor, LMO emphasizes that it has no political affiliation and does not endorse any particular political party or politician. Its legal charter as a community-based organization does not permit it to become involved in electoral politics. Now that half of its members are citizens and thus eligible to vote (a change that became evident in the last city election), it will also encourage its members to vote.

Yet the March 1999 protest in support of Guillermo Glenn also illustrated one of the obstacles to LMO organizing efforts, which stems from the roles typically ascribed to women in Mexican culture. These roles make Mexican women feel uneasy about their political activism—despite the fact that they do not see it as political. As local news cameras panned the crowd of LMO protesters, which included both men and women, some women hid their faces behind the protest signs because their husbands would be angry with them for appearing on television. One woman said, "My husband would be humiliated by his friend if they saw me on television" (Anonymous, 1999; my translation of the original Spanish).

In other instances, LMO activists have been accused by their spouses of neglecting their family obligations when they became involved with the organization (Olvera 1990, A12). Women in leadership roles often reveal that they have strained relationships with their husbands because they refused to adhere to the role of a traditional Mexican wife (I. Montoya 1999). Other women reported that it was okay for them to participate in LMO as long as they also did what was expected of them as mothers, housekeepers, and wives (Reyes 1999; see also Fernandez-Kelly 1990; Garcia 1981). Some women describe the difficulty of getting away from housework and their husbands. Maria Acosta describes the problem she has with her jealous husband: "Every time I get ready to come to the meetings, my husband gives me a hard time. He says that I come to [La] Mujer Obrera because I am either looking for a boyfriend or I come to meet my boyfriend."[9] According to Acosta's husband, there could no other reason for her to come to LMO, despite the fact that it is helping her to get into a retraining program.

Conclusion

LMO's activism in response to global economic restructuring, as manifested in NAFTA, relies on contradictory yet successful mobilization strategy. On the one hand, LMO became visible when its members literally reemphasized the U.S.-Mexico border to highlight NAFTA's disastrous effects on Mexican-American women garment workers. On the other hand, LMO de-emphasized the U.S.-Mexico border culturally by embracing the Mexican culture. This is what makes the border city of El Paso unique. Displaced by NAFTA, the lives of the LMO women have been disrupted and forever changed by the corporate agenda driving NAFTA. Spanish-speaking women, who once migrated to El Paso in search of a better life, have received a rude awakening after dedicating their entire lives to building the city's economy. After having been subject to exploitation and limited employment in El Paso, these women are now being marginalized and slowly eliminated from an increasingly internationalized economy.

To mobilize these women, LMO has focused on Mexican culture as a vehicle that links individual members to the organization. The use of Mexican religious symbols, traditions, histories, and customs has served to reinforce a bond between the organization and its members, as well as to contextualize the plight of the NAFTA-displaced workers. At the same time, its creation of a transnationally shared space of Mexican culture has enabled LMO to become a legitimate economic actor in the city's economic restructuring. Symbols such as the *Virgen de Guadalupe*, the cultivation of corn stalks, pictures of the Zapatistas, and the use of the Mexican *corrido* have served as icons of political resistance against a transnational agreement that has affected their lives. The success of this strategy has manifested itself in the fact that no other organization in the U.S.-Mexico border region has achieved as much as has LMO. It has helped obtain El Paso's designation as an Empowerment Zone, won a $45 million grant for displaced workers, created two umbrella organizations—the Asociacion de Trabajadores and El Puente, opened its own school for displaced workers, is currently developing the first bilingual adult curriculum for displaced workers, and has established a child-care center. All of its achievements serve as a testament to the power of a transnational culture in women's political activism. But, be that as it may, a much larger question looms: Although this essay is about one grassroots globalization movement at the U.S.-Mexico border, are there lessons to be learned from its experiences?

Certainly the first lesson points to the fact that any one specific identity—in this case the Mexican identity—may not necessarily be enough to forge a cross-border alliance. Other principal factors may come into play, such as shared gender, shared experiences, values, beliefs, ideology. For example, a much more useful and broader theme that workers could mobilize around could be the pursuit for social justice among all workers, specifically the push for "living wages." By mobilizing around the theme of social justice, LMO would broaden its support base by being inclusive of other grassroots organizations and perhaps catapult them into the international area where their voices would be much more difficult to stifle. The most recent example of this was seen in the Summit of the Americas meeting on April 20–22, 2001, in Quebec City, where numerous grassroots movements gathered to protest the expansion of economic integration (free trade) at the expense of social justice.

In addition, what becomes evident in this essay is the importance of contextualizing the workers situation under NAFTA. What this case study suggests is that mobilization depends upon the way in which an organization chooses to construct, define, identify, or contextualize itself given a certain set of circumstances. The way in which an organization chooses to identify itself and whether or not that particular identity resonates with its members has bearing on the organization's behavior and the perception external agencies, individuals, and institutions have of that organization. The perception of others outside of the organization may have significant political repercussions. For example, the identity of an organization can affect its access to resources made available only by governmental agencies.

Moreover, this essay also points to the growing participation of women in grassroots mobilization, specifically as leaders, against NAFTA, the Free Trade for the Americas Initiative scheduled for completion in 2005, as it is for the Multilateral Agreement on Investment and other similar agreements. Lisa Montoya and her colleagues correctly point out that political scientists have tended to neglect or discount Latina leadership and participation in electoral and community politics (Montoya, Hardy-Fanta, Garcia 2000, 555–61). A key issue within the debate about gender differences is whether there is an essential divide between the public and private dimensions of politics. For Latina women, much more than men, the boundary between these supposedly distinct spheres of life is blurred, indistinct. With their emphasis on grassroots politics, survival politics, and the politics of everyday life and through their emphasis on the development of political consciousness, Latina women see connections between the problems they face personally and community issues stemming from government policies.

Notes

1. This study is based on 56 face-to-face interviews I conducted from August of 1998 through August 1999 in El Paso, Texas, with active women who have lost their jobs because of NAFTA—that is, businesses moving from El Paso to Mexico. I have defined as "active" those women who dedicate 20 hours to LMO by either attending weekly meetings, belonging to committees within the organization, volunteering their time, or attending and helping in organizing fiestas (parties), rallies, and protests. The interviews were conducted in Spanish (and on occasion in English) at LMO, protest and rally sites, and, when it was convenient for the person interviewed, over the phone. I have also included interviews with the lead organizers of LMO, a former bilingual teacher, who was employed to teach these women English at one of the many schools that offer English classes, a public relations spokesperson from one of the last mammoth garment industries (Levi Strauss) in El Paso, politicians, and various governmental/political officials. Depending on the individual, these interviews lasted between 15 and 75 minutes. In LMO, the women speak only Spanish, range in age from 35 to 72, and more than half have no more than a fourth-grade education in Mexico. At the time of my interviews with the women of LMO, almost all of them were either in school learning English, studying for their high school equivalancy diploma, or in some retraining program.

2. According to Brecher and Costello (1994), "race to the bottom" is the reduction in labor, social, and environmental conditions that results from global competition for jobs and investment.

3. This is the only credible number that I have seen reported.

4. In speaking with John Ownby of the Dislocated Worker Service Unit at the Texas Workforce Commission, I was told that being classified as "certified NAFTA displaced

worker" might not reflect the true number of displaced workers. Businesses that close up shop because of NAFTA are supposed to certify their workers with the Texas Workforce Commission, which simply means that the workers were laid off because the business closed down due solely to NAFTA. Certification by the Texas Workforce Commission ensures that the displaced worker will be eligible for retraining programs. However, the Texas Workforce Commission does not have the manpower to see that businesses due in fact register their workers as certified NAFTA displaced workers. Thus, the number of certified displaced workers may not be a true account of displaced workers. Ownby believes the number to be much higher (Ownby 1999).

5. This information is based on face-to-face interviews and informal discussions with women.

6. The power of culture as a mobilizing force is not a new phenomenon. It has been instrumental in the civil rights movement, the Chicano movement, and the farmworkers movement as well as many others.

7. In both my formal and informal conversations with LMO and staff members, this was the response given by all.

8. A *corrido* is a simple narrative ballad that relates an event of interest only to a small region; it may be a love song or a comment on a political situation.

9. This name has been altered to protect the identity of the woman. The information was revealed in a private informal conversation.

7

Contesting Multiple Margins

Asian Indian Community Activism in the Early and Late Twentieth Century

Bandana Purkayastha

ECONOMIC RESTRUCTURING INVOLVES AT LEAST TWO CONTRADICTORY PROCESSES. First, the dominant global and national processes of restructuring attempt to centralize power by marginalizing and dislocating communities of color. Part of this process involves providing ideological justification for the extension of "benign," "modernizing" influences to "traditional" or "alien" communities. The development of racialized images is central to the process of controlling communities (Mullings 1994). Communities of color also bear the costs of economic restructuring because significant numbers of people are forced to move in search of new economic opportunities. In addition, many are forced to emigrate for espousing political perspectives that are in opposition to the economic (and political) restructuring of their home country. The second contradictory process, then, follows from the first. Since people of color often end up living with others like themselves, in culturally and/or residentially segregated spaces, the presence of "alien insiders" in the community creates a new impetus for resistance and organizing in the community.[1] The meaning of the community, the nature of its boundaries, and the symbols that provide a sense of emotional ties are often reinterpreted by communities to challenge the processes of race/gender oppression and to foster group survival and growth. While such community activism rarely results in outright victories, traces of community resistance survive. These alternative repertoires are available for use in other times and places by other marginalized communities.

The focus of this chapter is on community activism in India and the United States during the early and latter parts of the twentieth century. I explore how community activism keeps alive repertoires of resistance against disruption and dislocation unleashed through economic restructuring. I argue that individuals who may not have "deep roots" in a community, the alien insiders, may nevertheless become active in redefining and promoting a version of community as a way of resisting marginalization. Because of their alien insider status within a local community these individuals are often able to bring together other community members who were fragmented by conflicting religious, caste, or class loyalties. I focus on the alien insiders to look at how contested cultural meanings are used to re-create conscious networks and meanings, and the link between the ability to maintain such alternative meanings and challenging the macropower structure.

Using two biographies, set within specific historical contexts, I am able to trace how alien insiders mobilize the community in which they have settled and reflect on the multiple, interacting levels of power and how activists organize communities to resist marginalization. My mother's biography, gleaned from semistructured interviews with her, supplemented by letters she wrote during the first half of the century as well as archival research, are used here to re-create an activist's experience in the beginning of the twentieth century. My own experience as a "woman of color" in the United States illustrates the continuing history of resistance. These biographies are not unique. They resemble, in many ways, the lives of other alien insiders, who are located at similar intersections of race/class/gender structures. Though both cases focus on activists working for women's empowerment, neither case exemplifies empowerment in the sense of individual mobility. Instead, both cases provide a glimpse of the process through which alternative discourses are maintained in the face of new forms of marginalization.

My focus on the role of alien insiders is based on a particular understanding of community. Although earlier research assumed that communities were based on pregiven characteristics such as geographical co-location, inherited characteristics, or historical memory, more recent work conceptualizes communities as consciously forged (Espiritu 1992; Nagel 1994). I draw on the work of the latter group and think of communities as dynamic entities where groups and organizations play a role in making individuals more conscious of their membership in a larger whole (J. Gamson 1996; Taylor and Whittier 1992). The dominant group often erects boundaries between itself and the marginalized community by ascribing unchanging deviant characteristics to the group. Marginalized communities resist such forces by using cultural symbols to create alternative discourses and by forging community networks and ties in new ways. Alien insiders often play a crucial in creating and keeping alive the discourses of resistance and the ability of the community to rethink its social location within a larger adversarial context.

The chapter is divided into three parts. The first section provides a brief discussion on the link between restructuring and community activism. This is followed by a discussion of the two cases from my own family. Both the context of activism and the work of activists are narrated in this section. I conclude the chapter by comparing the two cases, and by analyzing power relations and transnational community activism.

Restructuring and Community Activism

Over the last several centuries, macroeconomic and political processes have ensured the preeminence of West European and North American societies within a world economic/political system. The spread of industrialization during the first half of the century brought systematic reorganization to the peripheries of the world. Economic and political colonization led to the disruption and destruction of existing economic/political systems, as marginal regions became suppliers of raw materials and services for global colonial empires. This process was accompanied by voluntary and involuntary migration of people whose local opportunities for livelihoods had been disrupted. Economic restructuring also affected the local power balance as the colonizers sought to increasingly centralize power in such a way that the benefits of restructuring accrued primarily to them.

As the global economy restructures at the beginning of the twenty-first century, a similar set of processes appears to be under way. Peripheral parts of the world are becoming sites for training highly skilled workers needed in the core countries and thus shifting the costs of education to those countries. They are also becoming places where lower-tier manufacturing and service jobs are performed. But skilled workers who are recruited for white-collar jobs in the core societies find, upon migration, that they are subject to the negative effects of racial formation in these societies (e.g., Ancheta 1998; Prashad 2000; Woo 2000). As restructuring proceeds, seemingly neutral rules of international economic and political engagement continue to marginalize peripheral societies, limiting access to opportunities, destroying and discrediting local knowledge systems and control over resources (Shiva 2000), and justifying intervention through the rhetoric of structural adjustment (Wignaraja 1993). Such economic reorganization is accompanied by the development of racialized/gendered ideologies that "justify, support and rationalize the interests of those in power: they tell a story of why things are the way they are, setting out a framework by which hierarchy is explained" (Mullings 1994, 266). Experiences and endeavors of marginalized groups are dismissed by many as "traditional" and useless in a modern society, and their cultures are blamed for their "backwardness" and "traditional" customs. Bald (1995, 111) argues that "the colonized learn limits which are both mental and physical. . . . [Once] internalized [they] instinctively know what they can or cannot do. . . . Thus their marginalization maintains the center."

However this process of disruption and marginalization is never complete. At the grassroots level, it is contested by people who try to stem the disruption of their communities. Women, particularly, have been very active in challenging the forces that push "cultural humiliation and destruction, political subordination and economic exploitation to maintain a hierarchy that limits life chances of a people"

(Gilkes 1994, 232). In order to mobilize the community, these activists frequently engage in redefining common sources of solidarity. Assignment of marginalized statuses by outsiders helps to provide the seeds for coming together, but activists also invoke and create cultural commonalties—despite race, caste, class, religious, linguistic, historical memories, and other differences—to establish conscious bonds among people in the community (Barth 1969; Nagel 1994; Swidler 1985). Thus there is an ongoing engagement: the group in power attempts to build up an ideological justification for marginalizing and controlling the subordinate group, while community activists "assign meanings and new interpretations of relevant events and conditions in a way that . . . mobilize[s] potential adherents and constituents . . . and demobilize antagonists" (Snow and Benford 1988, 198).

The biographies described below need to be understood against a backdrop of economic/political restructuring that brings together people of disparate background and creates the context for further development of networks. In the first instance, women's activism is set within the context of British colonialism in India in the early years of the twentieth century. The second biography focuses on experiences in the United States toward the end of the twentieth century. The two accounts of activism are linked by the continuing experience of marginalization within phases of economic restructuring. Both cases illustrate how community networks are created and maintained as a way of dealing with local and macro-level power hierarchies.

Maintaining/Creating Community

The first case looks at community activism during my mother's generation, based in Bengal, India, from the mid-1920s to the early 1940s. My mother, Anjali Sen, grew up in Khulna, a small town in East Bengal (now Bangladesh) where her father worked in the British postal service. Despite of their lower-middle-class position, her parents believed in educating all of their children. Though education was commonplace for Bengali men, educating daughters, especially with the intention of sending them to college, was somewhat unusual for lower-middle-class folk during the early twentieth century.[2] My grandparents' decision was influenced by several factors. First, they belonged to the Baidya caste, primarily a professional group—*Baidya* literally translates to physician in Bengali—and thus had a long tradition of acquiring work-related education. Second, like many others of the urban middle class, my mother's family was influenced by two contemporary Bengali social movements—the Ramakrishna Vivekananda (RKM) movement, which emphasized the "service as spirituality" aspect of Hinduism (Radice 1998), and the Brahmo movement, which emphasized female equality and emancipation (Kopf 1989). Thus my mother's family reflected the ethos of some of the larger movements for social change in Bengal in the ninteenth and twentieth centuries.

As the British consolidated power and exerted increasingly repressive control over the Bengali and Indian politics and economy,[3] a strong nationalist movement developed in Bengal by the late nineteenth century. The British undertook several measures to control this movement.[4] One was the passage of the Rowlatt Act in 1919, which suspended all civil rights and provided the British government with the power to imprison people for indefinite periods of time without trial for acts such as reading "seditious" material or uttering *bandemataram*, the rallying slogan of the Indian freedom fighters. The freedom fighters, or "anarchists" as they were officially known at that time, adopted two tactics for resisting British power. First, they advocated economic and cultural nationalism and organized efforts to carry out this agenda. Second, they organized armed insurgencies.

The political measures adopted by the British were paralleled by the controlling ideologies that justified the British presence and its use of official violence in India. A case in point is the book *Mother India*, by American author Katherine Mayo. Published in 1926, the book argued, in essence, that Indian women were sexual slaves of licentious Indian males, and the withdrawal of the benign and modernizing British presence from India would be disastrous. *Mother India*, with its familiar race/gender images of uncivilized men and helpless women,[5] received wide publicity, and despite a barrage of protests from Indians, remained one of the most quoted treatises on Indian women till the last quarter of the twentieth century (see Sinha 1998). This book, along with many other official literary and missionary publications, kept this ideology alive well into the latter part of the century (Jayawardena 1995; Sharpe 1994).

Among the core principles of the nationalist movement in Bengal was the idea of *swaraj* (economic and social self-sufficiency) and *swadhinata* (political independence). In order to promote cultural nationalism, Bengali women leaders such as Swarnakumari Devi popularized *mahila silpamelas*, fairs where women's crafts were exhibited and sold (Borthwick 1984; Kumar 1993). By the turn of the twentieth century these had become very popular among nationalist women all over India, and as a child my mother accompanied her mother to many of these fairs. Thus, a combination of religious and political influences in Bengal created a keen sense of social obligation and began to breach the private/public divide that had kept women in their homes in earlier times.

By the mid-1920s, my mother's oldest brother and his friends (including my father) became the principal student organizers of the nationalist movement in Khulna. The family house became a gathering place for students reading nationalist treatises, practicing political songs, and honing their public speaking skills. A number of them wrote letters to newspapers to protest Katherine Mayo's diatribe, and there were many discussions about the role of men and women in society and about ways to counter the negative influences of such ideologies.

My maternal uncle's political activities had serious ramifications for the whole family. As a punishment for failure to control his anarchist son, my grandfather was demoted and sent to a remote village to be its postmaster. His salary was slashed, and his responsibilities curtailed dramatically. Though the "anarchist" had earlier left home and gone underground to evade imprisonment under the Rowlatt Act, the rest of the family—urbanized and educated—was forced to move to a place where a mix of animism and orthodoxy governed socioreligious practices, and the nationalist and RKM movements were events of faraway places. In addition, there were no high schools and no provisions for educating females. In fact, when the family arrived by boat singing (nationalist) songs to bolster their sagging spirits, the villagers thought a *jatra dal* (a band of street performers) had arrived because, in their experience, respectable women (*bhadramahila*) never sang in public.

A glimpse of the state of women in rural Bengal is available from accounts of scholars such as Chitra Deb (1984), Nirmala Banerjee (1990), and Samita Sen (1999). Banerjee (1990) reports that toward the end of the nineteenth century Bengal was the most industrialized area of India, and was also remarkable for the high percentage of females who were formally employed (more than 20 percent compared to an average of 15 percent for the rest of the country). Nevertheless, by 1931, these numbers had dwindled significantly as British policies regarding industrial labor drew on existing gender norms ("women did not work," "women work sporadically") and redefined women's jobs as seasonal and temporary, with lower wages and no medical, housing, or other support services (S. Sen 1999). At the same time, reorganization of agriculture to support industrial production, along with an increasing population, imposed severe strains on rural families that had long survived on subsistence economic practices.

By the time the Sen family was sent to the village, more and more of the landless families were becoming female-run households as the young and able men went to seek work in the cities. While some of the lower-caste women had migrated to the cities to work in the jute mills, by the 1930s they had been replaced with male laborers from other states (Banerjee 1990; S. Sen 1999). Some of these laid-off women had returned to their villages, attempting to resume their traditional occupations or find other avenues for supporting their families. Among "women's work" were home-based cotton spinning, caste-specific occupations (lower-caste women worked as part of the household unit at making pottery, weaving, etc.), and production of subsistence crafts (making foodstuffs such as *muri* and *chire* or making leaf plates, baskets, mats, nets, brooms, etc.). However, the reorganization of selected sectors of the economy to support the industrial output in Britain meant that the local crafts were in an unequal competition with cheap, factory-produced foreign goods.

The seeds of community activism were laid unobtrusively. My grandparents appointed a tutor for educating the children, but they also insisted that the children build ties with the local community by going to the local elementary school and learning skills such as fine embroidery. In the process the family established close relationships with some of the local teachers. Over the next few years, the Sen children were also apprentices to my grandmother's efforts to create informal women's religious circles (*pathachakras*) in the tradition of the RKM movement. These meetings were not religious in the conventional sense, but women gathered to sing devotional songs and to listen to socioreligious readings. As educated, non-Brahmin, non-affluent folk, the Sen family was outsider to the established social hierarchy. They did not belong to the local caste-based or land-owning elite who had their own closed circles of family and friends. But they were deemed worthy of respect because they were educated, their son was in the nationalist movement, and the parents were direct disciples of the RKM order. Thus, the very modest home of these "outsiders" was seen as a place where women of different social strata could gather without upsetting the entrenched social order. My grandmother and mother (the oldest child at home) took turns in leading the discussions and singing. Later, several teachers joined in the effort to encourage more and more women to attend these gatherings. The songs that were sung often served a dual purpose. At one level they paid homage to the local female goddesses, but the subtext extolled the motherland *Bharatbarsha*. Nationalist ideas merged with ideals of religion within this primarily female domain and acted as a binding mechanism for the newly created networks. In addition, during *bhai-phota*, a Bengali festival at which sisters traditionally tie bracelets of good fortune on their brothers' hands, my grandmother's oldest son was arrested, which seemed to strengthen the bonds of this female group. Since he was arrested before he could eat his lunch, many of the village women grieved and were angry about this violation of a woman's right to nurture. This incident brought the British-Indian political conflict directly to the remote village.

Through these *pathachakra* networks my mother and her family came to know about the increasingly desperate struggle of local women to support their families. As ardent believers in *swaraj* and the RKM version of social service, the Sen women started instructing their neighbors in the art of informal cooperatives. The women were encouraged to make *achar* (pickles), *moya* (rice cakes), *paposh* (reed mats), and to share and sell some of their products locally, while the Sens organized sending some of the products to fairs organized by female nationalist leaders in large urban areas. Because some of the products were being sent to the cities for the nationalist cause, the near-destitute upper-caste women, whose caste/gender norms forbade them to "work," slowly became involved in craft production.

Though these efforts did not substantially mitigate the financial struggles of these rural families, the themes of cultural nationalism such as *gram udyog* or rural enterprise, *atmashakti* or self-sufficiency, and *desh-seva* or service for the motherland became part of the women's lexicon. There was an increasing sense that, despite being homebound and poor, they were contributing their skills to a larger social cause. And as they participated in the informal cooperatives a new type of community status emerged; those who promulgated the nationalist cause gained new stature in the community. Thus the poverty that decimated many of these families was not able to totally strip them of their dignity or their sense of their place in the larger society.

In 1942, the agricultural policies adopted by the British caused a devastating famine in Bengal (e.g., A. Sen 1999). My mother, who had just graduated from college in Calcutta, went back to organize the relief effort. She had been living with my grandmother, who had moved to Calcutta at the end of the 1930s to be close to her sons, who were in British prisons.[6] My mother chose to go back to "their" village because she knew intimately the devastating effect the famine would have on the economically marginalized community. Her coordination of the relief effort was shared by her village "relatives-by-adoption," women who claimed they were looking after "nieces," "nephews," "brothers," "sisters," "aunts," and "uncles" in an attempt to equitably distribute the pathetically meager food supplies that came their way. In objective terms, such relief efforts were a disastrous failure: more than 3 million people died in the Bengal famine (Rothermund 1993). In human terms, however, a quiet revolution had taken place. Women were now publicly visible in coordinating relief efforts. Despite British attempts to keep alive the image of the enslaved Indian woman, these "mothers of the nation" began to claim their spaces in more public arenas (Kumar 1993).

The efforts of hundreds of women like my mother and grandmother helped over several decades to blur the distinctions between the private home and the public world for the women of India. Women's activism to uphold the community began to be valued, albeit unevenly, within the larger nationalist struggle (e.g., Bulbeck 1998; Forbes 1996; Kumar 1993). For example, Mahatma Gandhi's ability to mobilize hundreds of women for the non-cooperation movement against the British was based upon the prior efforts of community activists who had built bridges between fragmented "community" groups and the nationalist movement. Relatively invisible acts such as creating the space for women of different castes and classes to meet or providing some means of sending handicrafts to the large towns created new networks among the village women and made them aware of the link between their lives and larger political processes. Unobtrusive community activism by the alien insiders had moved the taken-for-granted community to become a part of a larger, abstract, and more consciously created community.

My mother and her family moved to Calcutta when India was partitioned in 1947. She married a former terrorist, raised a family, and pursued a career in that metropolis. My earliest memories of my mother are as an upper-level officer of the West Bengal government. Her fairly high status administrative job was testimony to the way educated, middle-class Indian women had established themselves in the public sphere through their contribution in the Indian independence movement. There had never been any question whether these *khadi* (cotton) sari-clad women belonged in higher administrative positions or whether they had gotten there because of some kind of some biased form of "affirmative action." Their roles and service in the nationalist movement made it seem inevitable that they should continue in leadership positions within the formal work sphere in independent India.[7]

In Search of a Community

Whereas my mother's move to the Bengali village was prompted by political pressures associated with colonialism in India, my migration to the United States from India can be better explained in terms of recent economic restructuring and the attendant political reorganization. The development of a postindustrial economy in the United States created an urgent need to find highly skilled people who could work in professional service and knowledge-production industries such as hospitals, laboratories, engineering, and software industries. This growing need for highly skilled people coincided with the civil rights era and the subsequent dismantling of a number of race-based laws. One law that was dismantled in the mid-1960s was an Asian migration ban that had been in effect since 1917. United States corporations were free, from 1965 on, to recruit highly skilled persons from non-European parts of the world. This recruitment created a new type of migrant: highly educated individuals who were well poised to achieve economic success, but who, as nonwhites, would have to negotiate their racial position in the United States. My migration, as the wife of a highly skilled professional, is typical of the migration pattern from India. Indian males (who dominated in the sciences) were recruited to white-collar occupations, especially medicine and engineering, and they were allowed, for the first time in U.S. history, to sponsor the migration of their nuclear families.

The changes that took place in the United States after the 1960s reflect economic and political restructuring associated with globalization. Two aspects of restructuring are important for understanding the activism described here. First, as the United States moved to a postindustrial phase, newer jobs were increasingly bifurcated into upper-tier professional and lower-tier service occupations. Immigrants filled both types of positions. Under colonialism, which was related to the development of the industrial economies of the west, marginal countries were sources of raw materials. In the postindustrial phase, knowledge and skills are valued commodities (Sassen 1994; Zukin 1995), and countries like India are a major source of highly skilled labor for niche positions in the more developed areas of the world. The second related issue is the growing political restrictions on recent immigrants, who are mostly people of color. One of the primary political changes that affected new immigrants is the move toward making social benefits contingent upon citizenship. During the industrial phase, labor movements had ensured that participation in the formal labor market would yield social benefits such as unemployment, welfare, or retirement support. While permanent residents (legal immigrants who work and pay taxes in the United States but are not citizens) were eligible for such benefits earlier, since the mid-1990s they have had very limited access to these benefits. More important, since the end of the 1980s, highly skilled jobs have been increasingly classified as temporary jobs, under the provisions of the H1-B visas. This visa, which has become the preferred means of recruiting workers from non-European countries, cuts off access to all social benefits. In addition, a number of extra restrictions disproportionately affects the political position of female immigrants in the United States. For instance, since the mid-1980s, spouses have had to prove to the U.S. Immigration and Naturalization Service (INS) that they are still married, after two years, to the person who sponsored them for permanent residency. Thus, till this provision was marginally modified in the 1990s, the spouse's ability to acquire legal immigrant status was based *solely* on the ability to maintain a marriage. The H1-B visas add a higher level of restriction to the "proof-of-marriage" criteria that disproportionately affects female immigrants—the spouses of the highly skilled workers are barred from working in the United States.[8] Thus, although there is a continuing push to get highly skilled labor from non-European parts of the world, political restrictions limit the social benefits and legal protection to which these workers are entitled in the country of work. The "new" immigrants, even those who are highly educated, are caught in a liminal position: despite their economic achievements, they remain socially marginal.

My experience in settling down in the United States exemplifies how people like me are caught between the contradictory economic objective of encouraging highly skilled immigration and the political reality of continuing race/gender restrictions during the current phase of restructuring. When I first came to the United States in 1984 and moved to a mostly white, middle-class suburb in Connecticut, I had expected, as an English-speaking, highly educated woman, to fit right into "the community." My husband had a professional job with a multinational company in this state, and I expected to follow his path of incorporation. As I searched for jobs, I volunteered for a number for local organizations like the library, the Newcomers Club, and an environmental think tank. My daughter was born in 1987, and I joined other mainstream organizations—play groups, parent-teacher organizations, activity groups, and more. Although I developed deep and enriching friendships with a few people, in general I was usually ascribed an outsider status based on the widely held belief among these groups that recent immigrants learn modern ideas and skills only after long contact with U.S. society. Similarly, in the job arena I found that although I could get multiple offers for part-time teaching positions based on my postgraduate degree from one of the top colleges in India, if I applied for full-time positions, my foreign degrees and experience became insurmountable barriers. Unlike my husband, who benefited from the highly skilled worker classification, I had to contend with the sections of the labor market that were not receptive toward immigrants. Later, I realized this was a pattern that affected most women of Asian origin who were steered toward low-tier, part-time, and temporary jobs, based on a presumption about their poorer quality education or low English proficiency, or because people assumed that most Asian women were docile and lacked initiative (see Chow 1994; Espiritu 1997; Fong 1998; Woo 2000). As the laws targeting immigrants changed through the 1980s and 1990s, Asian "wives" found themselves cut off from the labor market (Abraham 2000; U.S. Department of Justice 2000).

Looking for a full-time job raised other structural issues. For immigrant women like me, the search for services that enable white women to work is complicated by our status as women of color. Simple tasks such as arranging child care involved protracted negotiations over the status of the mother vis-à-vis the caregiver (regarding appropriate foods, methods of discipline, and related care work). At the same time, like other mainstream "corporate wives," we were subject to gendered corporate norms that require upper-level managers to work long hours and travel constantly, and thus require that wives be available at home to provide caretaking and support activities (Acker 1990). Overall, then, the fabled equality of opportunity remained elusive in our daily lives.

My involvement with community activism arose from my frustration in trying to find a niche in the United States. Interactions with people in the town where I lived had already made it clear that place of residence and community were not coterminus. Yet I did not automatically gravitate toward the Asian Indian community either. Significant differences in language, religion (and religious practices within Hinduism), food habits, cultural norms, generation, and historical memories meant that there were more differences among "the ethnic community" than similarities. Any sense of community had to be forged through ideas and interactions. Since there are no geographic enclaves of Asian Indians in Connecticut, there were also no opportunities to grow into a community by virtue of shared daily routines (Purkayastha 1999). The other complicating factor in searching for a community was that linguistically and culturally I, as a Bengali, had more in common with immigrants from Bangladesh (the country from which my parents had moved after the Indian subcontinent was partitioned in 1947). In many ways it was easier for me to identify with the pan-ethnic South Asianness than the emerging version of Indianness.

I was also an outsider to the emerging conservative trend within a section of the Indian group. As this group gained political clout, their public rhetoric glorified their economic achievement in the United States as an outcome of a "superior" culture (Shah 1997; Shukla 1999). This cultural emphasis distanced Asian Indians from groups of color that were not as economically successful. And as selected traditions were reinvented and resurrected by this conservative group, the roles and contribution of Asian Indian women became rapidly invisible. In public events such as the celebration of the Indian Independence day, icons such as Gandhi were invoked frequently; female Indian nationalist leaders such as Swarnakumari Devi, Sarojini Naidu, or Aruna Asif Ali (icons from my childhood) were conspicuous in their absence. Having grown up in the RKM and Indian nationalist movement tradition, I was an alien to this version of ethnicity.

The lack of access to jobs and mainstream services, along with the changing immigration laws, continued to marginalize women like myself, but an additional critical factor was the controlling ideology that defined us as subordinate and drained us of our agency (Espiritu 1997). These images arose in several overlapping spheres of life. First, neither fluency in English nor the economic success of first-generation Asian Indians freed them from the expectation demanded of all immigrants: Anglo conformity. As this group negotiated its social status in the mainstream, the symbolic meanings surrounding a sari-clad Asian Indian woman with a *bindi* on her forehead became a point of discursive and physical conflict.[9] The preference of many first-generation Asian Indian women for wearing saris, at least for special events, appeared to substantiate the mainstream's views about the "traditional" or premodern culture of an ethnic group whose women would not embrace modern Western attire. Despite the variety of class, religious, regional, and cultural differences among Asian Indian women, the dominant image in the popular media of "the Indian woman" was one of subjugation and subordination. Stories of wife burnings, dowry deaths, abandoned widows, and domestic violence (in India) remained the main fare about Asian Indian women in the popular press.

Second, along with the popular images, the absence of accounts of Asian Indian women in academic literature contributed to the image of "the Indian woman" who lacked agency. Though academic work on mainstream women challenged many of the popular myths about women's essential nature, much of the focus was on the experiences of white, middle-class women. There was very little recognition of women's movements in other parts of the world and alternative thinking about gender. This absence of academic engagement with other epistemological frameworks, along with the work of some prominent researchers who wrote on the basis of ahistorical assumptions (e.g., Daly 1978; Okin 1998) kept alive the racialized image of the subjugated Asian Indian woman. Critiques by "scholars of color" such as Mohanty (1987) or Narayan (1997) often did not have the reach or stature of the work by white scholars. Work by Indian scholars was rarely featured in the U.S. journals, a fact that contributed further to the invisibility. To bring the histories and activism of Asian Indian (and other immigrant) women into the mainstream, accounts of interacting race/gender/class on a global scale would have to be developed.

My involvement in community activism can be summarized as trying to find ways to create multiple overlapping communities that transcend political boundaries of ethnicity, national origin, race, and religion in order to address the new forms of marginalization emerging within global restructuring. This activism is based on the development of discursive elements that create a different consciousness about community and women's roles in it (Katzenstein 1995). Focusing on discursive politics does not suggest that this form of community activism consists of developing ideas alone. A crucial piece of these politics involve building multiple partnerships based on common interest in specific issues. The networks (which increase the numbers of people involved in selected issues) are invaluable for addressing discriminatory laws or bureaucratic practices that marginalize people.

I have worked with several people and groups in creating multiple overlapping community networks and generating discursive alternatives to challenge what Leith Mullings (1994) describes as controlling ideologies. Part of my activism is linked with the Connecticut-based women's network Sneha, where I work on issues of empowerment of women. Sneha's multifaceted activities—which are carried out by a remarkable network of academics, corporate executives, homemakers, other professionals, students, and retirees—are narrated elsewhere (e.g., Purkayastha, Raman, and Bhide 1997), but a recent program described below illustrates the nature of discursive community activism. I also work with other people in the United States and India to merge women's achievements in the subcontinent with those of women in the United States in ways that create transnational links and communities.

The recent program developed at Sneha, in which I have been centrally involved, illustrates how the multiple structures of hierarchy are challenged. A few years ago while we were discussing how to get more members into our women's group, a Sneha activist, Kshiteeja Bhide, suggested organizing an event at which women could wear their best saris. Other activists, lead by Shyamala Raman, developed a rich exposition on saris as textiles and as syncretic cultural forms.[10] My task was to link women's empowerment with saris, so that we could challenge the mainstream representations of sari-wearing women as premodern, and create new thinking about saris among the women who wore them. I focused on several themes. First, I pointed out the economic implications of buying saris, linking the personal choices of South Asian women and the viability of an entire *local* industry.

Second, I used vignettes of women's history such as the khadi-clad women of the Indian independence movement, the nineteenth-century women who devised new ways of wearing saris so that it was easier to move around in public, and the nationalist women who worked to revive the handloom industry that was almost destroyed by the British. I found second-generation South Asians to present these histories, so that both they and their parents became aware of these histories, which were becoming invisible in the ethnic group. Third, I described the implications of continuing to wear saris in the United States, the personal costs as well as the empowering possibilities. Since saris are worn in several countries in South Asia, this was also an opportunity to work jointly with women from different countries to create a South Asian forum. This program, which has been presented by Sneha several times to mainstream and ethnic audiences, has generated excitement among a cross-section of South Asian women who might otherwise be reluctant to be part of a "feminist" group. Many women told me that my speeches gave them a good reason for buying saris because no one could dismiss their buying practices as "female frivolities" (e.g., Roy 1999); others felt a new sense of commitment to wearing saris to many "formal" work and social events in the mainstream. The use of saris as a theme also provided us with political leverage to ask for inclusion in "Indian" programs. And as the mainstream press reported the program, there was an attempt to move away from the "traditional immigrant" ideology. Thus the careful presentation of a well-known cultural symbol helped Sneha to create new networks and circulate a sophisticated, transnational political message linking ethnic "tools" with race/gender issues in our contemporary lives.

A different aspect of my community activism has involved challenging the invisibility of South Asian women in academia. Very often South Asians, who do not easily fit the black/white racial scheme of the United States, are left out of discussions about people of color. Some people are also reluctant to include a relatively affluent group under the category of *minority.* With the help of friends in various universities, Shona Ramaya and I have obtained several grants to organize a yearlong series on South Asian women. We brought in female academics, corporate executives, film critics, and activists to discuss the diasporic experiences of South Asians. We called the series "Amba."[11] Amba's story contests the idea that women can be treated as spoils of war, and that they are passive subjects of patriarchal bargains. The story illustrates agency, strength, and the possibilities and difficulties of creating one's own history within a discriminatory system. Like Sneha's sari-katha program, I explained the story and symbolism of Amba, linking her story with current women/human rights themes to academic and community audiences. The program served as a way of bringing together discursive elements and histories from India, Bangladesh, and the United States to illustrate how women continue to challenge discriminatory structures emerging in specific locales. The main program, showcasing the achievements of speakers, who were all immigrants from India and Bangladesh, also added to the effort of building pan-ethnic communities.

Along with my South Asian friends in academia, I have used other strategies to address the invisibility of South Asians in academia. We have organized sessions at local women's studies and teachers' conferences to present gender issues from the perspective of South Asian women. Often my friends and I have taken up popular stereotypes attending such practices as arranged marriages and placed them in contexts of racialized images. We have presented papers theoretically examining transnational models of gender, emphasizing the experiences of South Asian women in both the United States and South Asia. We have also tried to fight the institutional biases against "foreign degrees" and have argued for the recognition and inclusion of South Asian/Asian-American experiences in the "multicultural" and "diversity" curriculum across institutions of learning. We have begun, with other progressive groups, to challenge the restrictive provisions of the H1-B visas. We continue to create networks with other groups to address issues that affect people of color.

Like the community activism my grandmother and mother engaged in, my/our efforts are successful in very limited ways. We have been able to put Asian Indian women "on the map" within some of the local progressive networks in Connecticut. We have been able to draw in people from multiple Asian Indian and Bangladeshi cultures to work on "women's issues" and work toward collective empowerment. We have also been able to persuade a few key Indian community organizations to include information about South Asian women in their publications and invite us to speak at their events. Despite a reputation for not being "typical" Indian women in some sections of the Asian Indian community, in other sections we are recognized as people who work for positive social change. We have drawn many women into this "unobtrusive" activism, and many have felt empowered by the process. And by creatively combining aspects of women's activism in India with activism in the United States, we have created a different model of activism, one that better reflects our lives in the current phase of global restructuring.

There are many groups and individuals in the United States who work on similar issues, but our position here has remained marginal. Despite the increasing acceptance of multiculturalism in the United States the reality is that whose cultures count, how these cultures are represented, and who reaps the benefit of representing different cultures remain a very contested process. In everyday interactions, the "Asian immigrant woman" stereotypes structure many interactions: people are still surprised we speak English and those of us in the labor force continue to encounter lower glass ceilings than Anglo-American women. Moreover, as the political climate of the mainstream and the ethnic communities change—both exhibit a distinct drift toward religious fundamentalism among some sections of the populace—the factors affecting women's position demand new strategies of engagement.

Another Look at Community Activism

The two cases described above share some features. In both instances, activists have tried to help women in a concrete way combining material help with attempts to resist and contest the ideologies and material conditions that marginalize them. Both cases illustrate how migration associated with economic/political restructuring brings together diverse people and how community relations are renegotiated. Some alien insiders, at least those individuals who are politically aware, play the role of catalysts for negotiating networks within the community. These efforts affect, in limited ways, both the "community" and the "society." Both cases illustrate how community activism keep alive repertoires of resistance that challenge entrenched power relations in society.

One issue that is evident from these cases is the need to rethink the definition of communities. The long history of community researchers' focus on local ties—those based on geographical proximity—have had the unintended consequence of equating community membership with long residence in one geographical locale (Wellman and Leighton 1979). Here, by emphasizing the role of alien insiders, those with shallow roots in the community, three aspects of community are evident. First, people with shallow geographical roots are often able to mobilize networks in the community. Thus my mother, who had been tied to the nationalist and RKM movement through her family networks, was able to use the cultural symbols of those movements to breach the public/private divide in the rural community to which my family moved. I have used some "South Asian" cultural tools to craft a transnational women's discourse to challenge the race/gender marginalization of Indian women in the United States. Second, the focus on alien insiders illustrates the dynamic nature of the community and the networks within it. Individuals who begin as alien insiders may become "center people"—that is, they are able to mobilize networks within the community even if they do not always have a public leadership role (Sacks 1988). Marginalized in multiple ways, alien insiders often create bridges among their different networks as a way of extending the power and influence of the networks they mobilize. My mother was able to build bridges between her village networks and the nationalist effort in large urban areas. I have been able to mobilize some of my academic networks in India and the United States to challenge the marginalizing rhetoric about Indian women and push toward a transnational conception of community. Third, the liminal position of the alien insider has some advantages. Since they are outsiders to the local community hierarchies, alien insiders are able to create a neutral space for a variety of people to meet. The outsider status of my mother's family made it possible for their home to be used as a meeting place for diverse women in the community. My migration status as a younger member among first-generation migrants, along with my activist family background and the fact that I am one of the few South Asian women with a full-time job in academia in Connecticut, provides me with a similar outsider/insider status in the ethnic community. These three facets illustrate that neither long residence in one place nor ongoing geographic proximity is a prerequisite for community activism. Instead, the circulation of people and ideas are often the catalysts for linking communities through activism.

However, the cases described above also illustrate the partial nature of the "victories" vis-à-vis entrenched power structures. At the level of the community, activists may succeed in creating a space for women's issues and in gaining control of the myths, symbols, and language that shape people's concerns. For many women who have been drawn into these movements, the experience has been transforming.[12] The effects of interacting race/gender structures are less open to change. That the two groups—separated by half a century and thousand of miles—were subject to the same controlling ideologies based on the images of subjugated Asian Indian women indicates that there has been little change in the racial hierarchy. Some of the protests that occurred after the publication of Katherine Mayo's book (archived in Sinha 1998) sound remarkably similar to the language of protest my co-activists and I use at the turn of the century. "How ideologies—used here in the sense of production of meaning—are generated, maintained, and deployed is intimately related to the distribution of power" (Mullings 1994, 266). The current configuration of power has simply generated new structural and ideological forms of control. Thus "new" community activism continues in multiple sites across the globe to address this "new" phase of restructuring.

The cases described here reflect a more deterritorialized form of activism. During my mother's life this meant moving from a community defined by the geographic locale to an abstract idea of a nation that was yet to gain its independence. At the turn of the century, my friends and I work toward a community that is not bounded by the structures of the nation-state. Although we focus on race/gender structures within the contemporary United States, we have extended the range of our thinking and activism to link colonialism in earlier times and marginalization of people of color in the current phase of restructuring as parts of one continuing process. While this latest phase of economic restructuring is seen as a "new" process in the contemporary Western world, for those of us with roots in former colonies, the effects on communities of color seem to be all too familiar. Restructuring breaks up families, cuts off social support systems, simultaneously devalues and co-opts our experiences and knowledge bases, restricts our civil rights and access to social benefits, and forces us to remain "the perpetual other" (Nandy 1995). The deterritorialized activism, described here, creatively weaves together past legacies and present realities through a historically grounded process of resisting marginalization at multiple levels in a global world.

The activism described here is not unique. It bears striking resemblance to the community activism among lower-class African-American women and Latinas (see Bookman and Morgan 1988; Naples 1998a; Pardo 1995; Baca Zinn and Thornton Dill 1994). Contradictory institutional structures in the West—the economic incentive to get cheaper workers versus the political imperative to maintain white hegemony—clearly determines the social location within which such activism occurs. Asian Indian women, like African-American women and Latinas, engage in activism that is "focused on internal development and external change, and create(s) ideas enabling people to think about change" (Gilkes 1994, 231). These acts of challenge, within a context of disruption and dislocation caused by economic restructuring, connect facets of community life and contribute to the survival and empowerment of groups. Such activism remains the primary way in which people of color, throughout the world, contend with ongoing, multiple marginalities.

Notes

1. The term *alien insider* is similar to Patricia Hill Collins's (1991) concept of *outsider within.* However, alien insiders are considered by the majority to be insiders to the community because they share some aspect of the community's dominant status. To the community members they may be alien because of their education or religion or lifestyle. The alien insider concept also overlaps with Karen Sacks's (1988) *center people.* Alien insiders become center people, but it is a position and relationship they cultivate.

2. From the middle of the 1910s there had been bitter debates among the Bengali middle class about the need, objectives, and content of women's education (Chanana 1994). Though some elite women had acquired college degrees by the turn of the century, it was still not common to send women to colleges.

3. The British conquered Bengal in 1757, so this state had been under British rule the longest and had been subject to various phases of economic restructuring—the forcible conversion of subsistence agricultural land to plantations followed by the destruction of local industry as the British started their enterprises in and around Bengal. The history of British rule in other Indian states varied, as did the trajectory of the Indian nationalist movement. Since this case is situated in Bengal I will refer primarily to the Bengali movement.

4. The colonial powers often resorted to violence. In 1919, they fired on an unarmed gathering of people in Punjab, killing several hundred people, and then clamped down on all news from the area to prevent the news of the massacre from spreading (Kumar 1993).

5. Similar controlling imagery has been used against many other marginalized groups—blacks, Asians, and Chicanos (see Espiritu 1997; E. Glenn 2000; Mullings 1994).

6. My grandmother's move to Calcutta with only her children while her husband re-

mained near his work in East Bengal was a courageous act for a woman at a time when few middle-class women attempted to live by themselves.

7. Though many middle-class women achieved educational and occupational equality, by the 1970s it became apparent that such conditions had not reached the greater number of women. The literature on women's movements in India indicates the causes of continuing inequality (e.g., Kumar 1993; Menon 1999; Ray 1998).

8. The H1-B visas classify all incoming workers as temporary. Because the primary worker is classified as temporary, the social benefits of this worker (retirement, unemployment, social security etc.) remain the responsibility of the country of origin. Family members are seen as part of the private sphere and therefore not the responsibility of the United States. Thus, by instituting the H1-B visas, the United States has been able to control the total number and costs of "foreign workers" in two ways: spouses are not allowed to work, nor are they eligible for any benefits in their own right. The presence of the primary worker and his family is dependent on the needs of the U.S. economy.

9. The rise of gangs calling themselves "Dotbusters" in parts of the United States, and the rise in the incidence of hate crimes is testimony to physical violence against Asian Indians (Chowdhury-Sethi 1994).

10. Sneha members who were centrally involved in the research and preparation of the program were Shyamala Raman, Dipa Roy, Shanthi Rao, Madhu Chandra, and Lalitha Mehta.

11. Amba is a mythological figure from the 3,500-year-old Indian epic the *Mahabharata.* She was forcibly abducted by a prince, Vishma, who was looking for "suitable" brides for his brothers. Amba protested strongly and was allowed to return to her home. But on her return she was rejected by her fiancé, who felt that Vishma, by virtue of abducting Amba, had acquired the right to fashion her destiny. Rejected and angry, Amba vowed to kill Vishma, even though she knew he had been granted a boon by the gods that he would never die unless he so wished. She lived in many (human and nonhuman) forms acquiring skills and expertise to fulfill her vow. She also practiced severe austerities and penances to please the gods, who agreed that she could become a critical factor in ensuring Vishma's death (even though, because of his boon, he could not be killed by her). During a destructive war when all warriors failed to defeat Vishma and bring an end to the fighting, Amba achieved her objective by acting as a human shield for other warriors. Then she knocked Vishma off his chariot and threw him onto the ground and into a bed of arrows. Vishma willed his own death shortly after.

12. In many conversations, activist Shanthi Rao has indicated how her involvement with Sneha has empowered her to re-create a different life for herself in the United States. Correspondence between my mother and my cousins indicates similiar feelings of empowerment and a desire to change many of the contemporary social conditions.

III
Localizing Global Politics

Creating Alternatives from a Gender Perspective

Transnational Organizing for Maquila Workers' Rights in Central America

Jennifer Bickham Mendez

The merengue music blasted as the six of us danced around the line of five chairs in a "Central-American style" game of musical chairs. When the music stopped, each of us scrambled to find her own seat, so as not to be the one left standing. In the free-for-all that ensued, high heels went careening into the larger group of workshop participants who were cheering us on. By the time the majority of us had been eliminated, and the two remaining finalists competed for the last chair, the room was in an uproar. The game, however, did not end because Ana, a cooperante from Canada, used her hips to bump the very petite Rosa Maria from Guatemala from the last chair. "Now we're going to change the rules and play again," the workshop leader explained. When the music started this time the new object of the game would be for everyone to find a place to sit as fast as possible. No one would be eliminated though chairs would continue to be removed. Each dancer had to find a way to sit down regardless of whether or not she had a whole chair to herself. The rest of the workshop participants howled with laughter as the first few rounds ended with larger women sprawled on the laps of women significantly smaller than them. By the last round, however, we had organized, and when the music stopped Marta from Nicaragua stepped forward to quickly direct us so that the six of us fit on the last chair. As Ana balanced the whole stack of us on her lap, and we swung Rosa Maria to the top of the pile, the women observing jumped to their feet in an emotional standing ovation.

SUCH WAS THE SCENE AT A TWO-DAY WORKSHOP AT A MEETING OF THE CENTRAL American Network of Women in Solidarity with Maquila Workers (hereafter: the Network). This Network is made up of autonomous women's organizations from Guatemala, Honduras, Nicaragua, and El Salvador. All the organizations work within local communities, offering programs to improve the lives and working conditions of women garment assembly workers, or *maquilas*.[1] Organizers realized soon after they formed the Network that their struggle had to occur not only in local communities, but at the regional and, indeed, transnational levels.

The exercise described above was part of a workshop on negotiation and lobbying techniques. More than a fun, group-bonding activity, the message communicated by the exercise was clear: globalization has meant a change in "the rules of the game" for oppositional groups, particularly in the context of Central America. "Before"—that is, in the war-torn 1970s and 1980s—oppositional groups such as labor unions used confrontational tactics like strikes, marches, and demonstrations to achieve their goals. In the current context of globalization, however, the "new" rules of the game often require cooperation and compromise. Negotiation, lobbying, and mediation tactics have become the winning instruments in the current moment.

Analysts of contemporary social movements have differentiated them from the class-based struggles of the 1970s and 1980s. In a context that includes the fall of the Soviet bloc and a deep crisis of the New Left, participants in the so-called New Social Movements (NSMs) develop and enact practices in the realm of civil society, as opposed to the traditional political arena. Turning away from the totalizing narratives of class-based movements and political parties, contemporary movements "abandon revolutionary dreams in favor of radical reform that is not necessarily and primarily oriented to the state" (Cohen and Arato 1992, 493). Researchers have heralded the NSMs as creating alternative ways of "doing politics" and expanding the public spaces for discourse.

In a similar vein, various researchers treating Latin-American social movements have begun to turn their attention to the "internationalization" of political mobilization (see Alvarez, Dagnino, and Escobar 1998a; Keck and Sikkink 1998a; Melucci 1989 and 1995; Sikkink 1993; Slater 1998). These scholars have built on NSM theory to analyze transnational social movement networks or "webs," examining "the intricacy and precariousness of the manifold imbrications of and ties established among movement organizations, individual participants, and other actors in civil and political society and the state" (Alvarez, Dagnino, and Escobar 1998b, 15). These networks operate within an increasingly global world in which for the first time the core activities of the world's dominant institutions work in real time as a unit and in which global economic restructuring has repositioned states, making them more dependent on foreign investment (Castells 1993; Guarnizo and Smith 1998). At the same time, increased transmigration and the promotion of emigration by some sending states have forged "transnational subjects" as well as the reinvention of states' role in the "new world order" (Guarnizo and M. P. Smith 1998, 8).

The globalization of capitalism and transnational capital accumulation strategies have resulted in the establishment of free trade zones (FTZs)[2] in regions throughout the world. Conditions in the assembly factories of these zones are extremely harsh, and a largely female labor force labors long hours, frequently earning less than subsistence wages. The growth of the "sweatshop industry" has prompted new organized resistance initiatives on the part of marginalized people. Like the economic processes that they address, such political initiatives often transcend national borders.

In the pages that follow I analyze the practices of the Network, a coalition of women's organizations within the transnational antisweatshop movement[3] that acknowledges and even works within existing political and economic structures. This chapter critically examines the "self-limiting radicalism" that makes up the Network's strategic orientation (Cohen and Arato 1992). What do these practices tell us about how power and resistance operate within the contemporary "global system" (Sklair 1995)? Rather than evaluating the Network's practices in terms of a standardized notion of transformative potential, this chapter explores the conundrums that result from these practices and the political openings to which they give rise. This analysis, then, leads beyond narrow interpretations of transformative resistance toward a more nuanced approach to opposition that is critical, but also calls attention to the points of impact and influence of these women's practices.

In addition, this case calls for a more cautionary view regarding the emergence of an increasingly "global" civil society as embodying a strong liberatory potential. If it is true that civil society is increasingly being brought together on a global scale, then it is also true that, as Alvarez and her colleagues point out, this "global village" is neither happy nor homogenous (Alvarez et al. 1998b). Unequal access to power and resources are still prevalent, and there are still winners and losers, as groups compete heavily with one another. But who are these winners and losers, and when and under what conditions are transnational political strategies successful? What kinds of obstacles impinge upon these strategies? This chapter will use the case of the Network to shed light on these questions and to tease out the complexities of what M. P. Smith and Guarnizo term "transnationalism from below."[4] First, however, I will turn to a review of the ways in which Central America has been affected by the globalization of capitalism that will set the context for the discussion that follows.

Central America in an Age of Globalization

The past two decades have witnessed impressive shifts within the international economy. The globalization of capitalism, characterized by flexible accumulation strategies, dramatically increased mobility of capital, a shift from manufacturing production to that based on information processing, and the relocation of manufacturing jobs from First World nation-states to low-wage countries in the Third

World, has seen the emergence of the transnational corporation as a key player (Castells 1993; Sklair 1995; Sassen 1994). These changes have brought about the formation of a "global system" (Sklair 1995).

An international economy of sorts has existed for centuries, and since the years following World War II, foreign investment in multinational production has represented an important accumulation strategy for industrialized countries (particularly the United States). Nonetheless, the current moment has distinct characteristics. As Rouse (1995) puts it, "a dialectical relationship between the national and the multinational has been giving way to one between the national and the transnational" (353). Instead of large multinational corporations manufacturing at various national sites for self-contained markets, corporations are distributing a single production process among sites in different areas of the world and are using rapid telecommunications to coordinate simultaneous production across geographical locations (Rouse 1995, 367). Indeed, the rapid flow of capital, goods, people, and images across national boundaries, which communications and information technologies have made possible, is what has put the "trans" in "transnational" (Appadurai 1996).

The integration of Latin-American countries into the global economy has been accompanied by sweeping political transitions. The 1980s and early 1990s witnessed the demilitarization of many Latin-American states as military dictatorships gave way to electorally appointed neoliberal state regimes. Central America has seen particularly dramatic shifts in the political sphere with the end of civil wars in Nicaragua and El Salvador, the signing of the peace accords in Guatemala, and the opening of Honduras from a military dictatorship.

In accordance with their neoliberal orientations, Central-American state regimes have enacted legislation to attract foreign investment, and governments have cast their eyes on FTZs as a way to provide desperately needed jobs. The transnational apparel industry plays off this need for employment by selling its operations to the host country that offers the most benefits for the lowest costs (Tolentino 1996).

The apparel industry is one of the most globalized industries in existence (Bonacich and Waller 1994). To more easily access the burgeoning U.S. market and avoid import quotas, Asian-based transnational corporations have recently located production in Central America and the Caribbean. Making use of traditional systems of domination in a search for an ever cheaper, more docile workforce, transnational capital accumulation strategies specifically target young female labor markets. This reliance on a feminized, superexploited labor pool has prompted some to herald women workers as the "paradigmatic subjects" of the international division of labor (G. H. Spivak 1988).

Policies implemented within this era of globalization of capital have devastated organized labor. With their high degree of mobility, transnational corporations displace one group of workers only to integrate another more vulnerable sector, thereby pitting groups of workers against one another (Bonacich and Waller 1994). In many cases the feminization of labor has displaced a male, unionized workforce. On the other hand, trade unionism has entered a crisis because it has privileged class exploitation as the exclusive site of domination. Both the movement's failure to address the unique concerns of women workers and, indeed, the sexist practices of union organizers themselves have contributed to a delegitimization of the movement in the eyes of many in the new workforce.

Struggles based on other oppositional formations, not necessarily defined by class consciousness, such as feminist/women's and antiracist movements, have represented alternatives to "modern" modes of opposition. Like modern oppositional movements, such struggles occupy sites of contradictions generated by globalized processes. These contradictions "produce new possibilities precisely because they have led to a breakdown and a reformulation of the categories of nation, race, class, and gender, and in doing so have led to a need to reconceptualize the oppositional narratives of nationalism, Marxism, and feminism" (Lowe and Lloyd 1997, 21).

Organizers of maquila workers have been at the forefront of such initiatives by implementing new transnational forms of political organization, mobilization, and practice. These new modes of opposition recognize a "new" laboring subject, constituted by multiple, intersecting axes of domination. Creating and taking advantage of a globalized political space through localized grassroots initiatives, the collective practices of women maquila workers' movements have blown apart a simplistic notion of a global/local duality (M. P. Smith 1994). The words of Mary Tong, the director of the Support Committee for Maquiladora Workers, sum up the idea behind such initiatives: "Solidarity among workers should cross the border as easily as companies move production" (quoted in Lowe 1996, 167).

The Study

When the Network formed in September of 1996, I was in Nicaragua conducting ethnographic research with the Women Workers' and Unemployed Women's Movement, María Elena Cuadra (MEC).[5] Leaders of this group were key in spearheading the formation of the Network, and the participant observation I conducted with the MEC exposed me to the processes involved in the Network's formation and constitution. From 1996 to 1997, I attended three international meetings of the Network, which took place in Guatemala, Nicaragua, and Honduras. In addition, in June 1997 I traveled to San Pedro Sula, Honduras, to visit Network members and the communities in which they work.

As a guest of the Network, at each meeting I participated in the various activities that occurred in conjunction with the semi-annual meetings of the Network delegates. These included media events, training workshops, meetings with state agents and representatives from other organizations, as well as social activities such as meals and receptions. I conducted nine intensive, semistructured interviews with members of the Network. In addition, being housed with members and sharing meals and unscheduled time led to countless informal discussions with participants.

Based on my experiences with the Network and interviews with its participants, this research provides an in-depth picture of transnational politics. It contributes to an understanding of the ways in which social structures in an age of globalization shape the organized resistance of marginalized people and how these social actors respond to the new opportunities and limitations of the contemporary moment and shape the political terrain upon which oppositional struggles take place.

The Central American Network of Women in Solidarity with Women Workers in the Maquilas

The Network formed in 1996 after a meeting in Mexico organized by a group of women's organizations along the northern border. At this meeting both the Mexican and Central American groups decided to establish separate regional networks of women's organizations that work with issues pertaining to the maquilas. Funded by a Canadian nongovernmental organization (NGO), the first meeting of the Network was held in El Salvador with representation from autonomous women's groups from Nicaragua, El Salvador, and Guatemala. Subsequently, a group from Honduras and two other groups from Guatemala joined the coalition. Founders describe the Network's purpose:

> Given the situation of discrimination and super-exploitation in which women maquila workers live as a result of the process of globalization of the regional economy and given the lack of proper spaces and conditions that permit them to make demands and proposals and stake claims regarding their rights as women and as workers; we have come together in order to analyze, generate and contribute by means of this organization a space which could serve this purpose. (*Red Centroamericana de Mujeres en Solidaridad con las Trabajadoras de la Maquila* 1997, 1)

The Network meets every six months, and the role of host country for each meeting rotates. Meetings are attended by two or three appointed representatives from each organization belonging to the coalition. The events that occur in conjunction with the internal meeting are open to foreign visitors as well as maquila workers from the host country, members of the hosting organization, and other invited guests. The Network is completely dependent upon financial support from international NGOs. Most of its funding has come from Canadian and European NGOs and solidarity groups.

The general organizational term "network" is used to denote umbrellalike organizations that link diverse groups. Although every network is different, the general idea behind this organizational form is to allow diverse groups to organize around certain basic principles or issues. Thus, each organization within the Network is autonomous, and in the words of one participant, "The Network is not over and above (*encima de*) any one group." The loosely formed structure allows organizations with diverse histories, affiliations, perspectives, and priorities "to share and coordinate efforts in the search of alternative proposals in confronting the problem of the maquilas and to improve the conditions of women workers in the Central American region" (*Red Centroamericana de Mujeres en Solidaridad con las Trabajadoras de la Maquila* 1997, 1). Though the Network takes part in regional and international campaigns and activities, each organization must decide how best to implement these activities in their home countries. The idea is for each group to be able to address the specific issues facing the communities in which they work. For example, in Guatemala a large number of minors are employed in maquila factories. Not only are these children superexploited and exposed to extremely harsh work conditions, but they are too young to receive social security benefits in the form of medical coverage. The situation of these child workers is a major concern for the Guatemalan groups, while in Nicaragua and El Salvador child labor in maquila factories is not as predominant.

Organizations that make up the Network all work with communities where large groups of women are employed by maquila factories, and the principal organizers of all the groups have had substantial experience in popluar movements, particularly in trade union federations. The majority of the Network organizations formed as a direct result of gender-based conflicts within an organization of the Left. For example, the MEC formed as the result of contradictions and conflicts within a Sandinista trade union confederation (CST). Organizers, who formerly held leadership positions within the confederation's Women's Secretariat, either left or were ousted after a series of conflicts culminating in a dramatic coup in which the Executive Council refused to appoint the candidate elected by the women of the various federations as the next director of the Secretariat.

The Association of Women in Solidarity (AMES) split from the Syndical Federation of Food and Agroindustry (FESTRAS) in Guatemala after male leaders changed the federation's political orientation and strategy. The union cut off support to the Women's Committees that had formed to organize women in the maquilas. In addition, union leaders replaced the committees with a Women's Secretariat to which they appointed leaders, making all projects proposed by this Secretariat subject to approval by the male leadership. The Women's Committees had been nearly the only ones in Guatemala to successfully organize female maquila workers. After FESTRAS cut support to their efforts, basically casting off all organizing efforts in the maquilas, the leaders of the women's committees decided to form an autonomous organization.

Members of the Network see the formation of autonomous women's organizations as necessary in order to work for the particular concerns and needs of women maquila workers. Organizations' relations with feminist organizations and feminism have varied. Some organizations of the Network have embraced typically "feminist" approaches to issues such as domestic violence and reproductive health, and many groups openly identify as feminist; others remain suspicious of feminism, however. These women base their criticisms on the privileged class position of feminist organizers as well as what they perceive as a lack of consideration of class issues; feminist organizational practice in Central America has never been "of the masses," they say.

Most of the women hold extremely ambivalent and complex positions regarding unionism—at once highly critical of the traditional labor movement for its rigidity, corruption, and sexist practices, while acknowledging that in many cases "the first political organizing experience for [Central-American] women was in unions." Rosa María, an organizer from Guatemala, describes the culminating meeting that resulted in her and her *compañeras*' leaving the federation to form AMES: "They told us, 'Look, *compañeritas*, we're sorry, but we are going to restructure in this way. . . . And if you want to ask for authorization for your projects, fine. If not, you will have to leave.'" Like many of the Network's members, despite her vehement critique of unionism, Rosa María has mixed feelings:

> I still believe that syndicalism is the only mechanism that truly represents the workers. Now, that unions have not properly involved women is another matter . . . [*otros cinco pesos*]. . . . So, perhaps we are not against unions, as such. We are opposed to methods and attitudes, but we are not against the ideology of the unions. We have lived in the flesh the attitudes of the men and have a different expression.

A common experience among Network organizers within the union movement was exclusion from decision-making power. Manuela, from El Salvador, contends, "First they [union leaders] would tell us that yes, they wanted to talk [about gender issues], then they accused us of being *divisionistas*."

Network members criticize unions for leaving out women maquila workers from their agendas. They contend that it is only now that it is "fashionable" to work with this sector that the unions are turning to maquila workers. Still, Network members are highly critical of unions for continuing to apply the same methods in the maquilas as they had in traditional industrial settings in past decades and for failing to incorporate a "gender perspective" into their strategies for organizing this predominantly female sector.

Though some Network participants maintain active and friendly dealings with particular unions, in many cases relations with the labor movement are extremely tense, and even hostile. Some union leaders have accused the women of the Network of betraying syndicalism. Particularly in the cases in which the women's organizations' split from the labor movement was conflictive and hostile, some union leaders actively tried to subvert the efforts of the Network within the FTZs. For example, leaders of the CST have denounced the MEC or its strategies in public several times and have engaged in clandestine efforts to undermine its organizing initiatives.

In this manner the Network is an alternative to union representation, and is also a means to make visible "the social and labor reality of women." The organizations that make up the Network see the coalition as incorporating a "vision for addressing integral problems associated with the women of the maquilas and of developing processes of collective leadership." The organizations of the Network, then, are not just concerned with traditional labor issues. Network members work to empower women and improve their daily lives in all sectors of society. Their programs and strategies cut across the public/private divide by addressing women's social position at home, in the workplace and in society in general.

The organizations of the Network run programs for maquila workers on domestic violence and sexual abuse along with those connecting workplace violence on the shop floor with the larger issue of women's position in society. The groups of the Network also devote a great deal of effort to creating educational programs to teach women about their labor, human, and civil rights. Organizations administer revolving credit programs for maquila workers to use to improve their homes, and job training programs for workers and their daughters. One Honduran organization even established workshops for maquila workers to learn how to sew their own clothes. Ironically, though these workers labor all day at sewing, the piecemeal way in which labor is organized in the factories means that these women lack the skills for sewing an entire article of clothing from start to finish. Workers' low wages and the fact that many are the sole breadwinners in their large families makes sewing their own clothes an important economic strategy. In addition to such community-based programs, the organizations of the Network address women's role in grassroots politics and describe one raison d'être of the Network as being a means to make women visible within popular organizations. In the words of one organizer, "Now we are giving a face to our work. We have always been there, but now we want to receive recognition."

Organizing in the Information Age

The increased importance of the production, manipulation, and control of information has become a defining characteristic of the global system (Keck and Sikkink 1998a; Sassen 1994). Within the world economy, as competition is played out among transnational actors, information technologies make possible the extremely flexible, decentralized, and customized strategies of production coordinated among multiple locations (Bonacich and Waller 1994; Castells 1993). In the garment industry such extreme flexibility is reflected in "just-in-time production" strategies and the increasingly shortened fashion trends.

Control over information, however, is not only crucial for economic competitiveness. As grassroots politics has "gone global," social actors increasingly are engaging in "information politics" in an effort to achieve goals of social justice (Keck and Sikkink 1998a; M. P. Smith 1994). Wielding information as an instrument of power, social movement organizations can transmit knowledge or information through diffuse transnational channels (often using the media and telecommunications technology) to reach other international organizations and "foreign reference publics." Through these linkages international actors and institutions can then pressure state institutions or nationally located actors to bring about change (Brysk 1993). The practices involved in such politics include negotiation, lobbying, media campaigns, and electronically disseminated action alerts. New Social Movements and other nonstate actors depend on information to challenge institutions and influence change through persuasion and changing perceptions and values (Brysk 2000; Keck and Sikkink 1998a).

In the struggle to improve work conditions in the assembly factories of Central America, the important role of information is immediately apparent. There is little or no publicly accessible data regarding the characteristics of maquila workers, pay scales, benefits and production quotas. In addition, regulation of this industry by state or other institutions is almost nonexistent. Most maquila factory managements blatantly disregard state labor legislation. And regulating state agencies such as ministries of labor have been both unable and unwilling to enforce local laws. Thus, simply keeping track of what happens behind the closed doors of the maquila factories represents a crucial project for organizations interested in improving work conditions.

By definition, a "network" as an organizational form is characterized by the flow of information and services among members (Sikkink 1996). At their semiannual meetings members of the Network share reports on the latest changes and issues regarding the maquila industry in their country. They also circulate materials that they have developed for use in workshops and training sessions with workers. The host organization for each meeting coordinates the event by e-mail, fax, and telephone. Indeed, the establishment of communication technology (including telephones) was one of the coalition's first priorities. Members recognize the importance of communication within the Network, but also that communication by e-mail and fax matches the rapid mobility of capital within the Central-American region. Thus, members can warn and inform each other about factory conditions and relocations. Another goal is to create documentation centers in each of the organizations, that would hold databases and libraries of information regarding the activities of the transnational corporations, the labor conditions within maquila factories, and the occurrence of human rights violations.

The primary strategy of the Network has been to launch national, regional, and international campaigns to raise public awareness regarding the situation of maquila workers. The goal of one major campaign has been to pressure maquila factory owners to sign a "code of ethics" agreeing to uphold workers' human rights and comply with local labor laws (with particular reference to those laws that specifically apply to women). The lobbying and negotiation involved in this type of strategy have become the new tools of the trade for grassroots oppositional groups, marking changes in the political landscape of the Central American region. Negotiation and lobbying as political tactics require certain conditions—political spaces that allow dialogue and the participation of civil society.

The context in which organizations of the Network negotiate is different from union negotiations in "national" workplaces or those that would take place as a resolution to armed conflicts. In the latter situations, although negotiators from oppositional groups do not come to the table holding equal levels of power as their adversaries, they do hold an important trump card—the threat of a strike or violence. In the new transnational context, oppositional negotiators no longer hold this bargaining chip. Whereas in the heyday of unionism, force in numbers was the key to power at the negotiation table, in the new context of weak labor and high mobility of capital, information becomes the key commodity.

In order to engage in information politics, members of the Network devote a great deal of effort to monitoring conditions within the FTZs. State agencies like ministries of labor have proved to be extremely incompetent and ineffective in monitoring complaints of labor code violations, frequently turning a blind eye to violations within the FTZs in order to protect the interests of foreign investment and the only growing employment sector in most countries in the Central American region. As Keck and Sikkink (1998a, 16) point out, nonstate actors gain influence by serving as alternative sources of information, but to be credible the information produced must be reliable and well documented.

Needless to say, obtaining reliable information regarding shop floor conditions is not an easy task. Conditions from one factory to the next within the same FTZ can be very different. This is especially a problem in countries like Honduras, in which, at the time of this publication, there are 11 FTZs with more than 200 factories, employing approximately 100,000 workers (Bickham Mendez and Köpke 1998). To make matters worse, working conditions vary considerably from production line to production line, depending, among other factors, upon the supervisor for that line. Many workers themselves do not know if they receive payment for overtime hours or how such payment is calculated, and pay rates are determined by a complicated system of piece-rate wages sometimes combined with base pay scales which vary from factory to factory and frequently change.

Unlike union representatives, members of the Network do not have access to workers on the shop floor and must devise strategies for obtaining information from outside. For example, MEC organizers have created a network of promoters, maquila workers who represent the MEC within their factories. They meet once a month in the MEC's office to report on recent changes within their factories to impart such information as the latest brand names being processed in production lines. In addition, an MEC organizer visits the FTZ weekly and meets with workers at a spot outside the entrance to the zone. This organizer has a long history of experience as a union organizer and community activist. She and another MEC organizer reside in the same *barrios* as a great number of maquila workers. They also visit maquila workers at their homes and have family members who are employed in the FTZ.

Promoters collect pay stubs and brand tags from workers as well as social security statements, and copies are archived in the MEC's documentation center. In addition, they act as liaisons between movement organizers and workers who have suffered violations of their rights and wish to file complaints at a ministry of labor, referring workers with grievances to the MEC's office and putting them in contact with MEC organizers. The organization's documentation center also keeps a record of these cases and their results, as well as any information from the media regarding the activities of transnational corporations and state agents.

Negotiating National and Transnational Spaces

In their lobbying efforts and public awareness campaigns, the groups that make up the Network work to open and take advantage of different political spaces. Their strategic orientation regarding the maquilas is encapsulated in a campaign slogan: "Jobs, Yes . . . but with Dignity!" Thus, the Network does not call for the removal of the assembly plants, as this would leave women workers with no means of generating income. Acting as interlocutors for the women of the FTZs, Network organizers' commitment to improving women's daily lives makes them sensitive to testimonies like that of one Nicaraguan maquila worker: "I want my job and value it, because even though it tears me apart and exploits me, with my job I am able to feed my kids."

Such "radical reformism" or "self-limiting radicalism," as Cohen and Arato (1992) term it, is not particular to the Network. Scholars have noted it as being characteristic of New Social Movements (Alvarez et al. 1998a; Cohen and Arato 1992; Escobar and Alvarez 1995; Laclau and Mouffe 1985; Melucci 1994). This orientation acknowledges institutional structures and seeks to work within them for change. In the words of one Network organizer, "Our people are tired of these confrontational methods. We need to propose alternatives." So, unlike the oppositional movements of "before," the immediate goal here is not to seize the state or even to replace the capitalist system. The focus instead is to work "where the women are" to improve their daily lives given existing political and economic conditions. Network organizers themselves are very conscious of the limited range of their strategies. As one member put it, "We are asking for the minimum. We aren't even questioning the exploitation of workers. If the goal of the code of ethics were to dismantle the system of capitalism we would be fried."

In its implementation of the campaign, the Network's strategy has been for individual organizations to negotiate at the state and local levels. The Network organizes press conferences, and the local media spread the message of the campaign. The international character of the Network has not only drawn local media attention, but has added weight and legitimacy to members' negotiations with state agents and transnational capitalists.

It seems clear that the Network's strategic use of the media has contributed to increased public visibility of the issues facing maquila workers. Network members also report that shop-floor violence has decreased in some Central American countries. As part of the campaign "Jobs, Yes . . . but with dignity," Network members have met with state agents, factory owners, managers, and FTZ administrators to present their code and ask for support and have addressed governing bodies like the National Assembly of Nicaragua. In a landmark victory for the Network, Nicaragua's minister of labor, Wilfredo Navarro, was the first state agent to endorse the code of ethics, which he signed on February 1, 1998. Later, he adopted it as a ministerial resolution, which all factory owners in the Nicaraguan FTZ eventually signed, symbolizing their agreement to comply. In some cases factory owners have granted Network members access to certain factories and have entered into negotiations to allow the Network to monitor factory conditions.

Despite the Network's relative success in calling certain state agents and factory owners and administrators to the negotiating table, the political tools that the Network has chosen have also posed problems. For instance, the Network's negotiation techniques are borrowed from the business world and are designed to reach an agreement at any cost between relatively equal adversaries. It is questionable, then, that negotiation in and of itself can be an effective instrument for bringing about changes in social structures. The marginalized position of oppositional groups means they often come to the table making minimalist demands with little room for "cutting a deal." Similarly, mediation techniques require mediators to remain impartial. Some of the women of the Network have questioned if this is an appropriate tool for social justice.

Obstacles to Enacting Transnational Politics: Competition and Conflict in the Global System

The Network's strategies at the transnational level have been vaguer, and some groups have met with obstacles in implementing a transnational effort to bring about their objectives. While the Network's strategic orientation has enabled the coalition to open political spaces, at the same time its "self-limiting radicalism" has impinged upon options available to it and the effectiveness of its strategic practices. For example, the Network's strategy regarding the maquilas means that organizers must be extremely careful in their lobbying efforts not to pressure the factories to the point that they relocate production. This greatly limits the Network's ability to engage in the kinds of political maneuvering that have been successful for other transnational advocacy networks, such as international boycotts in the case of the Nestle corporation (Keck and Sikkink 1998a).

Other transnational networks have found the global media to be an important tool for implementing strategies of "information politics" (Keck and Sikkink 1998). For some groups of the Network the global media has been a useful mechanism for exerting pressure, while for others it has been a double-edged sword. For example, it was an international media campaign regarding the Kathy Lee line of garments that helped spark the development of the U.S. Apparel Industry Partnership's Workplace Code of Conduct and pressured the Honduran factory KIMI into allowing an independent monitoring team, which included members of the Network, to monitor conditions there. On the other hand, the experiences of other members of the Network demonstrate the difficulties and unpredictability involved in employing the global media.

In November 1997 the New York–based National Labor Committee (NLC), with the help of a solidarity organization in Nicaragua and the coordination of the Sandinista textile union, organized a visit of reporters from the television program *Hard Copy* to the country's only free trade zone. In a three-part series reporters used hidden cameras in entering the garment assembly factories (maquilas) of the FTZ to expose the working conditions. To add more shock value to the series, reporters exaggerated some claims, reporting that a barbed-wire fence surrounded the zone to keep the workers inside, and that minors as young as 13 were employed there.

A national uproar ensued when a local television affiliate picked up the segment and broadcast it in Nicaragua. Public opinion was split. Supporters of the maquilas, including neoliberal state agents, pointed to *Hard Copy*'s dealings with the NLC and described the report as a plot by U.S. unions whose jobs are threatened by offshore production. Meanwhile, the Sandinista labor movement called for the ouster of the foreign-owned factories. The headline of an editorial by former Sandinista Minister of the Interior Tomás Borge, in the oppositional newspaper *La Barricada,* read "*¡Que se vayan!*" (essentially, "They should leave!") (Borge 1997). Borge clearly articulated an extremist, "all or nothing" position: "The benefit received by the country is insignificant. Our national dignity is of greater value" (A4).

In response, more than 350 male and female workers marched on the Ministry of Labor calling for the factories to remain in operation. The Sandinista media portrayed this as workers being manipulated by the free trade zone corporation in order to protect their jobs, while supporters and neoliberal state agents cited the march as evidence that Nicaraguans supported the FTZ. Sandinista union and party leaders exchanged accusations of "national betrayal" with state elites, and each camp struggled to use the issue to demonstrate their representation of true "national" interests.

The Nicaraguan media also approached the leaders of the Nicaraguan members of the Network, the MEC, for their views. "We felt like a sandwich," said one MEC leader. Organizers chose to remain silent rather than have their views distorted in order to fit within the binary frame that the public debate had adopted. Thus, the more nuanced position of these women—that they wanted the factories to remain in the country but to respect the human and labor rights of workers—was effectively excluded from public discourse. All the workers who appeared in the *Hard Copy* segment were fired after the report aired in Nicaragua. "Are *they* going to give these people work?" an MEC organizer wondered of both state agents and the Sandinista labor movement. Network members have met with other barriers in enacting transnational strategies. For example, the Network plans to enter negotiations with international organizations and present its code of ethics to the Central American Parliament and the International Labor Organization (ILO) asking for political support from these institutions of "global governance" (Drainville 1998). However, members have found it difficult to gain access to them as well as to other transnational political spaces such as summits of Central American ministers of labor or Central American presidents. When the ILO held a conference in Nicaragua, only representatives of the labor movement and the media received official invitations. One representative from the MEC finally found a way to attend, but only after searching through her personal networks of old friends from the labor movement; they were able to secure an extra invitation for her. Similarly, in 1998 when the Department of Labor met in Washington, D.C., to discuss the sweatshop issue, human rights groups, trade unions (like UNITE) and student groups were there, but women's organizations were left out.

The Network has also sought to establish alliances with other regional and transnational networks in order to gain access to transnational political spaces, but has faced obstacles. For example, Inciativa Civil para la Integración Centroamericana (ICIC [The Civil Initiative for the Integration of Central America]), a network of Central American NGOs, was eager to meet with representatives of the Network. Members were disappointed, however, when ICIC's invitation to "join us" (no autonomous women's groups belonged to the initiative) indicated that the organization hoped that the Network would be a "women's branch" along with the "women's wings" of the other organizations in the initiative. They were not invited to join other members of the initiative at the 1997 summit of Central American presidents but instead were invited to participate in a "women's forum" to be held in Guatemala.

Another difficulty pertains to support for the Network's campaign on the part of solidarity organizations from the North. So far, all of the Network's funding has come from progressive NGOs from Canada and Europe. But the coalition has not yet determined how best to use the support of solidarity groups and individuals from the north. That is, the Network has issued no clear message regarding how international individuals and groups can best support its efforts. Thus, the international component of the Network's campaign has been based almost entirely on the dissemination information about work conditions and the code of ethics through transnational channels, using the Internet and linkages with groups from the North. The only thing that the organizations of the Network have clearly articulated is that they do not support consumer boycotts.

Again, this somewhat compromising position regarding the maquila factories greatly limits the amount of pressure that the Network is able to exert on factory owners, who can easily relocate production if the political arena becomes too heated. Coalition organizers acknowledge that the real power resides not in the factory subcontractors, but in the so-called "mother" (*matriz*) companies, transnational corporations like the Gap and J. C. Penney. The fear here, however, is that under boycott pressure, these companies will simply turn to other factories for their production needs—once again leaving the workers jobless. Indeed, this fear is not unfounded, as there have been several cases in Central America in which boycotted companies have withdrawn contracts from subcontractors, resulting in the shutdown of these factories.

Relations with Northern-based solidarity organizations pose other problems. Due to their greater access to material resources, such "global agents" have considerable influence over the shape that transnational corporative initiatives will take and who will be involved (Nelson 1997). The *Hard Copy* report reflects the continued orientation of many of the Northern NGOs that make up the solidarity movement toward the traditional organizational strategies of the labor movement. Network members have experienced other tensions with international NGOs that have exerted indirect and direct pressure for organizers to include unionist language and strategies in the campaign for the code of ethics. One Network member expressed her frustrations with individuals in such Northern groups who continue to be extremely invested in the ways of "before" and to espouse a limited vision of unions as the only truly appropriate organizational model for protecting workers' rights: "They have all these theories about the transformation of society, but . . . this is a process. It is step by step. It's not true that we are going to change the whole world—the whole economic system—from one day to the next."

Ironically, in many cases Network members have encountered more opportunities for political alliances within certain state institutions than within the transnational labor movement. Northern-based organizations such as the NLC have demonstrated a willingness to ally themselves with local trade union federations in working to establish independent monitoring teams within FTZ factories. Autonomous women's organizations, however, have been excluded from most of these transnational initiatives, reflecting a narrow vision of what constitutes a "labor organization." The tense relations between the unions and autonomous women's groups and the exclusion of women's organizations from independent monitoring groups have prompted the Network to pursue alliances with NGOs that have teamed up with corporations themselves to define standards to protect workers' rights and certify companies who meet these standards.

For example, the Council on Economic Priorities Accreditation Agency (CEPAA), a Northern-based NGO, accredits qualified organizations to conduct audits of factories and certifies companies and contractors who successfully pass the independent inspections. CEPAA has been vehemently criticized for excluding unions and other labor organizations and for its vertical decision making, based in the North (Clean Clothes Campaign 1998). The advisory board of the CEPAA consists not only of representatives of human rights organizations and NGOs but also of people from various corporations. Critics claim that CEPAA's (SA 8000) auditing system does not obligate companies to disclose the full names of their suppliers and subcontractors. Thus, a company could be certified while still subcontracting to uncertified suppliers.

Discussion

Though linkages among local groups across national borders continue to represent a highly significant and powerful form of oppositional mobilization, clearly there is much complexity involved in "transnationalism from below." Returning to the question posed at the beginning of this chapter, what do the practices of this transnational network tell us about how power and resistance operate within the "global" system? The Network's "alternative" strategies have at least been effective in calling state and local public attention to the situation of women maquila workers. As one Network member stated, "If there is something that has to be recognized, it is the space that we have come along opening up."

On the other hand, the Network's efforts to fully enter the transnational political arena have met with obstacles. Unlike human rights networks and other oppositional groups, such as the Ejercito Zapatista de Liberación Nacional (Zapatista National Liberation Army) of Chiapas, Mexico, the Network has had little success with influencing the global media and using international public opinion to pressure transnational corporations; instead, it has focused on localized negotiations and the use of local media. In addition, the Network has had difficulties engaging international supporters and NGOs within the campaign for "Jobs, Yes . . . but with Dignity." How can we explain participants' limited ability or willingness to access and operate at this transnational level?

In Keck and Sikkink's terms, the challenge that confronts the women of the Network is implementing effective "accountability politics" around the issues of women workers in maquila factories. Who should be the target actors of the Network's efforts to hold transnational corporations accountable for human and labor rights violations? In the current context of global capitalism, it becomes unclear whether the most effective lobbying strategy is to focus on state or global institutions or national or global civil societies. The Network's self-limiting radicalism, which has at least opened spaces at the state and local levels, impinges upon efforts to gain material leverage within national and transnational institutions.

Given that the overall goal of the organizations that make up the Network is to improve women's daily lives, the nature of the issues pertaining to female maquila workers—work-related issues involving both class and gender social structures—combined with conditions in the global economy and within a transnational political landscape do not lend themselves very well to the types of strategies that other transnational networks have found to be effective. For example, in the case of human rights violations in Argentina, human rights networks used information politics to target specific governments which in turn exerted pressure on the Argentinian state. Boycott strategies have also been effective for other networks (Keck and Sikkink 1998a). When political actors, however, adapt such practices to fit the complex issues facing women maquila workers, these strategies lose much of their material punch.

If Keck and Sikkink's assessment of transnational politics is correct, then the problem in engaging international public opinion to exert pressure becomes formulating a clear and direct "causal story" regarding who is responsible for the situation of maquila workers. Large companies like J. C. Penney can easily point to subcontractors who can just as easily blame individual supervisors for rights violations. Likewise, assigning blame to the state can be difficult, especially when protesters call for factories to remain in production. State actors can, and do, throw up their hands in the name of "competition in the global economy," claiming that they must make concessions in order to maintain the jobs generated by maquila factories.

Other actors have stepped forward to fill the void left by noninterventionist, neoliberal state regimes—NGOs, labor organizations, and others. However, salient contradictions have arisen within the various initiatives for establishing mechanisms for holding corporations accountable for labor and human rights violations. Gender blindness continues to be a problem within the transnational antisweatshop movement. Voluntary corporate codes of conduct, such as the SA 8000, also pose serious problems and have been accused by labor organizations of being "the fox guarding the henhouse." North/South tensions crosscut both transnational initiatives.

The tensions experienced by members of the Network call for an analysis of the power relations that occur within transnational organizing initiatives. In particular, a gender-blind analysis of the initiatives making up transnationalism from below provides an incomplete picture of power and resistance in the global system. The experiences of MEC organizers show that the transnational political terrain is highly gendered. Just as in the case of national politics, gendered structures of power and hegemonic definitions of the public/private split construct certain political spaces as male domains. We see this in the exclusion of autonomous women's groups from various political spaces—networks of NGOs, independent monitoring teams, institutions of global governance like the ILO, or transnational forums like international meetings of Central-American presidents.

In addition, the case of the Network points to the continued salience of power differentials even within the "new" era of globalization. The *Hard Copy* example reflects internal power dynamics within transnational political strategies, highlighting the importance of asking "Who controls information?" when viewing transnational political efforts. Who decides that an issue will receive "international" attention? It is important to recognize that all players do not have access to a transnational public sphere or to the global media. Because of power differentials within transnational political initiatives, local agents who manage to gain access to the global media can lose control of the information, which can lead to adverse results.

Consider, too, the union officials, who despite the crisis of labor movement, are willing to devote considerable efforts to destroying and undermining the work of the women of the Network. They stand in stark contrast to the state agents who, in some cases, have actually been supportive. All these examples lend risk nuances to the idea of transnationalism from below which reveal these processes as complex, multilayered, and rife with power differences.

Finally, this research calls attention to the importance of not dismissing the efforts of groups like the Network as being merely reformist. Instead of rating the Network's transformative potential according to some narrowly conceived definition of transformative potential, the case of the Network points to the need for an expanded analytical focus. A shift in focus to consider not only the Network's strategic orientation, but its democratic and feminist vision as exemplified in organizations' work at the grassroots level, allows for a deeper analysis of the implications of its practices. The feminist vision of the groups that constitute the Network reflect the idea that the personal is political, and the training and educational programs that these groups bring to the maquila workers bridge the public/private divide by making connections between what occurs on the shop floor and what occurs in the home and community. Thus, as in the case of women's gender politics in a variety of contexts, the Network's vision and work politicize the heretofore "private" or apolitical and challenges hegemonic definitions of the public/private split (See Dore 1997; Jaquette 1994; Jelin 1994; Radcliffe and Westwood 1993).

Turning attention to the processes that have led to the constitution of the Network also sheds light on significant implications of its practices. Members' development of a gender/feminist consciousness based on gender and class experiences led to their breaking with male-dominated popular movements to establish autonomous organizations. Thus, the formation of the Network has involved a process through which women have become more visible in grassroots politics and have articulated alternative conceptions of what constitutes political claims and who are legitimate political subjects. Such alternative conceptualizations indicate a shift in ways of "doing politics."

The women of the Network draw from a rich, cumulative oppositional history as political actors in order to negotiate the constantly fluctuating political landscapes of the global system. These social actors reconfigure and reinvent political practices in response to changes, shifts, and openings within national and transnational political arenas. An indepth study of these actors' practices calls for the recognition of a continuing and creative process generated from below. Political agents draw from a collective oppositional experience to formulate and remold strategic practices in order to fit particular conditions in the current transnational context. This is an ongoing process. Thus, there is reason to believe that the strategies used now by groups of the Network will not necessarily be those used in the future, as changes and transformations continue to occur within national and transnational political spheres. The minimalist demands that MEC organizers make now could very well be a necessary step that must be taken before larger demands can be articulated.

In assessing transnational politics, then, it is crucial not to overlook these aspects. Employing a gendered analysis that recognizes such microlevel processes, rather than adhering to a more traditional and outcome-oriented model of what constitutes social transformation, brings to the fore important complexities and provides a more complete picture of the inner workings of the so-called global village.

Notes

1. The terms *maquilas* and *maquiladoras* are used interchangably. They are synonyms.

2. Free trade zones are important components of the globalization of capital. Governments of developing countries often establish these zones to attract foreign investment and encourage transnational corporations to locate production within their borders. Import duties, customs fees, and taxes as well as local environmental and labor laws are often suspended for corporations willing to locate production within the borders of these zones. In addition, corporations are often given considerable breaks on the cost of utilities, and infrastructure is often improved in the areas surrounding these zones, thereby granting corporations access to airports and modern roads.

3. This chapter is based on ethnographic research that I conducted from 1994 and 1997 with support from a Fulbright Study Abroad Fellowship, a University of California (UC) Humanities Institute scholarship, a travel grant from the UC Pacific Rim Research Program, and a research grant from Sigma Xi. I thank Sarah England, Luis Guarnizo, Charles Hale, Rosemary Powers, and Roger Rouse for their helpful comments on earlier drafts. I presented versions of this chapter at the 1998 meetings of the American Sociological Association and the Latin American Studies Association.

4. One metaphor that has been used in relation to transnationalism has been to conceptualize it as emanating from "above" in the form of transnational capital, the global media, the increased power of international institutions of "global governance," and the nearly global dominance of neoliberal political doctrines; and from "below" in the form of the emergence of an increasingly "global" civil society brought on by transmigration, transnational social movements, and the explosion of local and transnational NGOs (See Smith and Guarnizo 1998).

5. Nonreferenced citations are from interviews with Network participants. All names of Network participants have been changed. Translations from the Spanish are my own.

9

Context, Strategy, Ground

Rural Women Organizing to Confront Local/Global Economic Issues

Betty L. Wells

THIS CHAPTER PRESENTS A CASE STUDY OF WOMEN WHO HAVE ORGANIZED IN response to, and in the context of, local/global economic processes through the Women, Food, and Agriculture Network (WFAN). This network of rural women committed to social change is based in Iowa and was founded in 1997. The resolve of founding members was rooted in their concern about systemic problems in agriculture and rural communities. The mission of WFAN—to link and amplify women's voices on issues of food systems, sustainable communities, and environmental integrity—conveys its breadth of focus and belief that women's voices are too rarely heard. I offer a grounded analysis of globalization by exploring WFAN's strategies for navigating the local/global divide. I explore the meaning of globalization and distinguish between globalization as the context in which organizing occurs and as the focus of organizing. WFAN's substantive concerns include the industrialization and corporate control of agriculture, trade liberalization, the consequences of biotechnology, and the effects of restructuring and structural adjustment policies on women. Members feel the effects of these global, system-level issues every day in myriad ways, whether being squeezed by vertical integration, working full time yet unable to afford health insurance, being disheartened by the poisoning of our waters and inhumane treatment of animals in large-scale confinements, or watching the demise of rural communities. WFAN challenges socioeconomic and conceptual frameworks of domination (see Warren 1991 and 1994, 184), notably conventional economic thinking about globalization and trade. I will suggest that strategies to navigate the local/global divide must be grounded; that is, they must be contextualized and firmly anchored in the places where we live and work.

Many advocates and opponents of globalization envision one global market. Advocates speak of it as both good and inevitable. Opponents—citizen movements and organizations such as WFAN—focus on the threat of global economic hegemony. They see the influence of the economic sector looming large without counterbalance from the state or civil society. These advocates propose alternatives to the one-world, one-economy, one-way globalization model and distinguish between globalization processes and globalizing ideologies and practices that consider only the market in structuring institutions (Currie 1998, 15). They advance beliefs, values, and practices that temper the market-centered model (table 9.1).

Whether understood as blurred identities and crumbling walls (e.g., Veseth 1998) or as reshaped political, economic, and cultural boundaries and widened political movements (e.g., Youngs 1999), globalization challenges conventional understandings of organizing. Globalization alters power relations and gives rise to new forms of resistance. For example, technology, while undoubtedly driving globalization, also extends intellectual reach and international understanding, enables us to cross international boundaries in larger numbers, virtually if not physically, and creates new networks of women/activists whose access to each other and to all sorts of information is unmediated by traditional institutions.

Following a brief overview of WFAN's origins, I will consider how WFAN confronts globalization-related issues within a globalizing context. Of particular focus are the conceptual, practical, and strategic challenges of negotiating what I call the local/global divide from the bases of gender and rurality/agriculture.

Table 9.1: Tenets of Market-Centered and Alternative Approaches to Globalization

MARKET-CENTERED	ALTERNATIVE
Economic sector is preeminent	Economic sector is tempered by state and civil sectors
Competition	Cooperation
Monolithic	Pluralistic
Winners and losers, individual benefit	Common good, mutual benefit
Market knows best, is ungovernable	Market requires human guidance
Direction of change is inevitable	Direction of change is volitional
Market is gender neutral	Market is gendered
Privatization, user pays	Access independent of means

Genesis of WFAN

The name, Women, Food, and Agriculture, originated in 1994 when Denise O'Brien of Iowa, current WFAN coordinator, and Kathy Lawrence of New York City formed a Women, Food, and Agriculture working group in preparation for the United Nation's Fourth World Women's Conference in Beijing to remedy the neglect of food and agricultural issues.[1] O'Brien subsequently represented U.S. agricultural women at the Rural Women's Workshop that preceded the 1996 World Food Summit and addressed a special session of the United Nations General Assembly in 1997 on behalf of the world's farmers. In spring 1997, a group of women, including O'Brien and myself convened in central Iowa and resolved to act on long-standing mutual concerns about rural and agricultural problems. In the words of one founder, "We decided to become the leaders for whom we had been waiting." This event marked the birth of the Women, Food, and Agriculture Network.

A significant formative event and precursor to the formal establishment of WFAN was a two-day workshop entitled "rural women, the economy and the environment," held in July 1997 at the Springbrook Conservation Education Center, Springbrook, Iowa. Twenty-five women from Iowa and Nebraska attended. Economic literacy training (ELT), employing methods of popular education, was central to the workshop. The group explored deep-seated attitudes toward money and reviewed key economic terminology. The workshop facilitator, international economist Pamela Sparr, guided the participants through an experiential exercise called Ah-Hah! (GATT-Fly 1993). This method contextualizes globalization by grounding it in participants' individual situations and making connections to the global economic and political system. Beginning with a specific local problem,[2] participants collectively drew a picture of the local/global system in which they live. This activity made visible interlocking economic and political forces affecting individuals and communities and made flows of capital and power concrete. It revealed how the local and global are connected "through parallel, contradictory, and sometimes converging relations of rule which position women in different and similar locations" (Mohanty 1997, 6).

The participants also engaged in the Trade Game and the Structural Adjustment Policy Game simulations. Through role-playing they vicariously experienced the effects of economic reform policies and the transition to a global economy, in particular how women are systematically disadvantaged by structural adjustment policies. Through the Trade Game they gained insight into the relationships between nations in the international economy, how large gaps in wealth among nations are created and maintained, and who benefits and who loses from trade—nationally, institutionally, organizationally, and personally.

WFAN's mission was established by consensus at a retreat in fall 1997. Founding members developed five goal statements (table 9.2). These goals have strategic implications. For example, goal 4—instigating change by cultivating networks that support communities of growers, consumers, workers, and others who strive for sustainability—signals recognition of the need to form coalitions and to cross geographic and conceptual divides such as rural/urban, local/global, and agricultural/nonagricultural. WFAN acknowledges past efforts but keeps its vision forward focused. WFAN challenges cultures of domination and institutionalized discrimination but always in the context of exploring alternatives.

Table 9.2: Mission and Goals of the Women, Food, and Agriculture Network (WFAN)

Mission:*	To link and amplify women's voices on issues of food systems, sustainable communities, and environmental integrity
Goals:**	To promote sustainable agricultural and community structures
	To insist on social and ecological justice for current and future human and nonhuman communities
	To provide opportunities for education on economics and environment that articulate a holistic view of agriculture, instill a sense of place, and draw forward useful experiences from the past
	To create networks that support communities of growers, consumers, workers, and others who strive for sustainability; increase effective access to and use of existing resources; engage participants in experiential learning; provide safe places for self-expression; and respect the spirituality of the land and people
	To advocate change by exploring alternatives and challenging the globalization of economies, cultures of domination and institutionalized discrimination, the disintegration of landscapes, and oppressive conceptual frameworks

* Established 10/28/97.

** Established 3/27/98.

WFAN has grown slowly but steadily. The network is centered in Iowa but includes members from more than 30 states and several countries. There are currently 100 active members with diverse backgrounds, ranging in age from 16 to 75. They include farmers, urban gardeners, environmental educators, community activists, academics, and others who care about a safe, healthy, and secure food supply. An additional 250 individuals receive the WFAN newsletter or subscribe to the listserv. A webpage is currently under construction [http://www.wfan.org.html].

Rethinking Organizational Strategies in a Globalizing Context

Any effort at coalition building or alliance formation must pay close attention to the specific situations of each group as defined by axes of gender, race, class, and sexuality. As Nancy Hartsock (1996, 256) makes clear, the feminisms of different groups emphasize political issues that are most salient in their particular social location. Theorists and strategists must focus on each group's specific situation because global processes are mediated through local practices, institutions, political structures, ideologies, and divisions of labor and prevailing cultural values (Sreberny 2000, 931). Our location shapes the look and feel of globalization.

Gender and rurality are WFAN's primary axes of concern. WFAN's strategies are contextual and grounded. Place provides the basis from which to negotiate the local/global divide. I next address some conceptual and strategic challenges of gender and rurality/agriculture as bases for organizing and the potential for members and allies in the rural/agricultural nexus.

Gender and Agriculture/Rurality as Bases for Organizing to Address Globalization

WFAN is organized by and for women, and most members are women. One founding member recalls the impetus for the group's establishment: "Our growing awareness of dissonance between public policy actions and our practical, locally grounded knowledge and experiences emerging from our unique social locations as women farmers, activists, professionals, and mothers became the motivating force for our organizing." WFAN's commitments to eradicating cultures of domination and to establishing social and ecological justice for current and future human and nonhuman communities are part of a progressive, feminist, activist agenda. Such goals are unlikely to garner support from a majority of rural and agricultural women. Feminist activists and theorists correctly note the limits of identity politics, that differences among women negate effective organizing based on gender alone. Nonetheless, identity politics and the construction of group identities remain an important political resource for social change (Hartsock 1996, 265). WFAN members are (mostly) women who share certain assumptions, interests, hopes, and worldviews.

WFAN is embedded in a rural context that further delimits and defines strategic possibilities. Mormont (1983, 562; 1990) observes that declining rural populations and diminished cultural strength bode poorly for the prospects of any rural group to mobilize a large cross-section of rural people. Rural culture is also notably patriarchal. Traditional stereotyping of gender roles is part of the agrarian social structure in the United States (Chafetz 1990), enforced through the family, religious groups, economic institutions, educational systems, and other regulatory institutions and promoted by relative isolation, and powerful sanctions (Wells and Tanner 1994). The status of rural and agricultural women in the United States continues to be marginal and secondary to men in many respects, and women continue to face discrimination and bias.

WFAN's mission, linking and amplifying women's voices, begs the question: Why are women silent? One reason is that culture, perhaps especially rural culture, silences. Censorship can be straightforward or subtle, as when women self-censor for fear of sacrificing relationships or conform to norms of courtesy. Language also silences, such as the abstract and elitist economic discourse surrounding the globalization debates.

Rethinking the Rural/Agricultural Nexus and Its Potential for Membership/Coalitions

How, then, might a group of mostly rural women even hope to make change? First, and significantly, rural women are less isolated than ever, and communications technologies foster new ties and strengthen existing ties. Second, allies are not limited to rural areas. Understanding rural as only agricultural, or agriculture and farming as only rural, limits potential for strategic alliance. Rural and agricultural are bound together, empirically and in peoples' minds, but neither farmers nor other agriculturists necessarily work or live in rural areas. Community gardens, farms, and farmers' markets thrive in urban areas, and many agricultural producers, processors, and researchers, as well food consumers, are urban dwellers. WFAN welcomes as members and allies urban and rural residents, whether farmer, gardener, consumer, environmentalist, or nonagricultural worker because agricultural, environmental, and food-related issues cross conventional spatial and conceptual boundaries. Third, WFAN engages members' collective energy and experience as activists, theorists, political strategists, and educators. A feminist and oppositional consciousness, a strategic division of thought and labor, communications technologies, and coalitions multiply the impact.

Strategic Positioning

Voice and experience are WFAN's raw materials, but theory provides the interpretive frame. Theory illuminates the concrete social relations through which we create our worlds and the way in which social structure shapes our daily lives (Hartsock 1996, 271). The task of theorists committed to social change is to construct, as a necessary adjunct to collective action and coalition building, theoretical bases for political solidarity. WFAN members theorize through practice and experience, but they also draw upon a more formal body of feminist theory. Theory reveals the shared structural features of different accounts of the world. Because the axes of domination are several, and different groups are privileged along some and disadvantaged along others, theory helps us recognize our experiences in the lives of others and reveals possible new coalitions and alliances. Feminist theoretical analysis is a tool for struggle against dominant groups and for the empowerment of the dominated (Hartsock 1996, 257).

In addressing the theoretical bases for coalition building, Hartsock (1996) emphasizes difference and heterogeneity, stressing multiple possibilities for understanding the world and multiple points of view. Correspondingly, WFAN works from multiple levels that reflect members' diverse levels of comfort, time, interest, and skill. WFAN strives to provide a nurturing space while engaging in politics and embraces practical strategies that relate to members' daily lives (e.g., microenterprise education), activist strategies (e.g., protest), and transnational strategies (e.g., organizing across national borders). The strategies presented next have practical, political, and transnational dimensions that help bridge the local/global divide.

Mentors, Role Models, and Mutual Support

Interpersonal communication, often veridical (face-to-face) and sometimes virtual, is the glue that holds WFAN together. Many WFAN economic strategies are also interpersonal, and the organization provides mentors, role models, and mutual support and recognition. Members hold few illusions about ultimate success. As one member clearly conveys,

> The kind of systemic change we need—be it related to issues of food security and sustainable agriculture, or education—is not really going to happen in my lifetime. That sounds pretty pessimistic. And sometimes I feel very discouraged. Don't we all? WFAN is such a positive experience for me, looking at one another and saying, "We can only change ourselves, and this is one way we can model that kind of behavior and one way of working together. We are not really about changing the entire planet but changing the 'world' in which each of us as individuals lives." And if this kind of behavior works in a small way, at the very places where we live, then I have hope that it can happen on a broader scale.

This resonates with Joanna Russ (cited by Judith Plant 1990, 21): Nobody can deal with all the issues—there isn't energy and time. But we can deal with *our* issues—the ones that affect us immediately—in a way that relates them to all the others. And I think that we had better because otherwise we're bound to fail. This willingness to take action, to be agents of change, ensures against failure.

Systematic strategy and practical experience are blended in a project in which WFAN connects aspiring female farmers with experienced women farmers and women landowners. Women, in sizable numbers, own significant amounts of land, especially land in the rental market (Effland, Rogers, and Grim 1993). This project strives to connect women landowners with landless women farmers or aspiring farmers. Through a pilot internship program, women farmers mentor novice farmers. Benefit is mutual, and those who desire to farm learn about farming practices from those who are farming. The farmers receive valuable labor from the inters. Support flows both ways, countering the isolation experienced by many women on the land and promoting the integenerational passing of knowledge (O'Brien 2001, 4).

Accessing Economic Language through Popular Education

Women find it difficult to question the general implications of economic policies in the dominant economic language, much less raise their gender implications. One way WFAN has helped members access economic language is through popular education on economics, such as that featured at the July 1997 workshop Rural Women, the Economy, and the Environment. Popular education continues to be a priority. In spring 2001, Denise O'Brien attended the Hemispheric Meeting on Popular Education and the Trade Agenda sponsored by the U.S.-based Economic Literacy Action Network and the North American Gender and Trade Network to further cross-national linkages and to identify trainers to conduct a new round of ELT in the Midwest.

Popular education on economics and social justice provides a gender analysis of the dynamic of globalization and enhances organizing and progressive movement building. It empowers women to name and oppose harmful political and economic processes and to develop a counterdiscourse (Marchand 1996). Experiential methods such as Ah-Hah! provide a framework for understanding the worldviews of the oppressed and help build participants' consciousness of alternative models and solutions. After the Ah-Hah! exercise, participants concluded that the next step was to "crack the nut" (founding member Katy Hansen used the nut as a symbol of current systems of domination) and to visualize a model with positive connections. This exercise in mapping and deconstructing the dominant economic paradigm and constructing an alternative one resonates with Noël Sturgeon's (1995, 35) assertion that social movements are critical and creative, oppositional and prefigurative.

Focusing on Food

Food is a both a material and symbolic focal point for WFAN's strategic efforts. Food establishes common ground, connecting producer-grower and consumer-eater, and rural and urban communities. Food issues highlight the irrationalities and inequities of the economic system and problems in the relation of capitalism to the natural world (Mormont 1983, 562, 571). Food grounds globalization. Food knits closer community ties by bringing people into a closer relationship with each other and the place where food is grown. Food production also highlights the continuing significance of rural knowledge. Food growing, processing, and preparation are a daily reality in the lives of many people, especially rural women, around the world.

WFAN supports a food system in which people have access to safe, healthy, and culturally appropriate food; farmers receive an adequate income; and farmworkers receive a living wage and labor under safe working conditions. WFAN asserts that food is a human right, concurrent with the statement produced by the Rural Women's Workshop prior to the World Food Summit in Rome:

> We cannot tolerate food insecurity. As women we believe that food is a fundamental human right which we are obliged to ensure; it must not be trivialized simply as a source of income, a commodity, a weapon or an object for genetic manipulation. Nutritionally sound and safe food is a necessity to life and production of food is a way of life. Food security implies access to sufficient, healthy and culturally appropriate food at all times and for all peoples of the earth. (Rural Women's Workshop 1996, 14)

Denise O'Brien helped write this statement and underscored this commitment at the 1997 USDA National Consultations on Food Security in Ames, Iowa. O'Brien, who represented WFAN and was the only woman on the eight-person panel. International Priorities, Actions, and Initiatives, insisted that the concept of food as a fundamental human right be included in the panel's report.

WFAN supports an extended network of local, small-scale food enterprises. Members include Community Supported Agriculture producers and members of food-focused organizations (e.g., the Iowa Network for Community Agriculture and the National Organic Consumers Association). In addition, several WFAN members serve on the Iowa Local Food Policy Task Force, a statewide body commissioned by Iowa's secretary of agriculture. WFAN has also hosted regional workshops on food-related microenterprise developments (Hutchison and Nelson 1999, 7). Participants from the workshops shared their experiences at the National Town Meeting in Detroit (Wirth and Hutchison 1999, 7), and ideas generated at these workshops are continuing to produce results nearly four years later.

Inequities in food distribution also foster potential alliances with low-income communities, both rural and urban. In November 2000, WFAN members Virginia Moser and Stacey Brown represented WFAN at the World Poor People's Summit to End Poverty. The summit was sponsored by the Poor People's Economic Human Rights Campaign and the International Campaign for Economic Justice, hosted by the Kensington Welfare Rights Union—a conference designed by, and for, poor people. Brown (2000b, 5) reports:

> Poverty in urban and rural areas manifests itself differently. We [WFAN] work with farmers who are losing their land because they can no longer make a living growing food, and we work with farmers who grow food for alternative markets. The poor people we met in New York City struggle daily to get food to their plates . . . [and] don't have a choice about what they eat and where it comes from. We produce organically, and poor people can't afford to pay for food. Their issues may seem totally different from ours, but the result is the same. We are all poor. . . . A cycle keeps people in poverty. Farmers cannot get a fair price for their food and many people cannot afford to pay that fair price. (5)

Locally, WFAN connects with low-income families and communities through healthy-food voucher programs. Member Linda Nash, a farmer and Community Supported Agriculture grower, on principle refuses to sell her organic produce at prices that she and others in her rural area cannot afford. Consequently, she chooses not to market to affluent urban markets in Chicago, Milwaukee, or Madison, but rather in a radius no farther than 15 miles from her farm in northeast Iowa.

WFAN takes a critical stance toward the practices and the economics of industrial agriculture. WFAN is one of 33 endorsers of the Farmers' Declaration on Genetic Engineering in Agriculture. Among the 10 demands of the endorsers is the following:

> Demand that the corporations and institutions that have intervened in the genetic integrity of life bear the burden of proof that their actions will not harm human health, the environment or damage the social and economic health of rural communities. These corporations must bear the cost of an independent review guided by the precautionary principle and conducted prior to the introduction any new intervention.

WFAN's spring 2000 meeting featured Martha Crouch, plant scientist and noted activist and critic of biotechnology. Crouch helped WFAN members to understand some of the science of biotechnology and to deconstruct the globalizing discourse as it pertains to the search for the "perfect food," golden rice being her case example (Crouch 2000).

In February 2001, WFAN members Virginia Moser and Stacey Brown attended A Natural Call to Action Conference in Chicago, sponsored by the Genetic Engineering Action Network. Moser and Brown gained knowledge of local/global efforts to resist the proliferation of genetically engineered crops into domestic food supplies. Moser and Brown will share this knowledge and materials at WFAN's summer meeting. This meeting will also feature local members who are engaged in various ways in genetic engineering issues, whether as scientists, farmers, or activists.

By these and other actions, food links WFAN to others in our rural communities and others worldwide. Monoculture agriculture is not news to the rural Midwest. In the name of profit, soybean and corn monocultures and megascale livestock confinement operations have replaced diversified farming systems. Transnational parallels are abundant and staggering in their implications. As monocultures have replaced traditional polycultures, dependence on food and seed imported from international markets has increased, limiting food choices and food security. Food has become a transnational commodity and is the weapon deployed by multinational corporations to enforce what Shiva (2000, 17) calls food totalitarianism. Food totalitarianism is the result of control of entire food chains by a few multinational corporations and the destruction of alternative "diverse, safe foods produced ecologically."

Cross-border Networking and Organizing

WFAN opposes globalization and transnational trade agreements (e.g., NAFTA) by supporting cross-border organizing of women workers and activists and by working in coalition with labor, farmer, church, environmental, and indigenous people's organizations. The borders crossed may be between countries, or within countries, such as rural and urban women in the United States. While groups from different countries or regions may have different tactical or strategic positions on trade, honest and open dialogue can foster mutual understanding and synergy. At the international level, cross-border organizing can reveal similarities in downward economic pressures in diverse localities and link diverse local practices (Grewal and Kaplan 1994, 19).

In October 2000, Stacey Brown represented WFAN at the Second South-North Gathering of Peoples of America Building Alternatives to Neoliberalism in Chiapas, Mexico. Brown (2000a, 4) observed strategic differences among the U.S. participants. The coordinators, from the Center of Economic Justice and the Globalization of Alternatives North and South, were internationally oriented and highlighted the protests against the World Trade Organization in Seattle and the International Monetary Fund in Washington, D.C. In contrast, delegates from grassroots organizations, many of whom were people of color, preferred to focus on issues such as ending criminal prosecution of women under welfare reform, unmasking the institutional racism behind police brutality, and building local food systems. Brown says that she, along with these groups, wanted to

> build our analysis against neoliberalism through the true experiences of our communities and to connect those experiences with the strategies and experiences of the groups from other countries . . . to talk about more than the protests and more than what was happening on an international level: we needed to look at the history of organizing in the U.S. against race, class, and gender oppression and the direct effects of neoliberal policies in our communities. (4)

Brown's observation brings to mind Sassen's (1993, 65) caution that social movements, like transnational capital, can privilege the global at the expense of local place-bound activities in households, work sites, and communities. As Brown further observed, they can also privilege the urban at the expense of the rural. This dynamic is persistent, but a grounded analysis that connects rural to rural, as well as local to global and rural to urban, can challenge these questionable dualities.

Place: The Ground from Which to Navigate the Local/Global Divide

Navigating the local/global divide requires multistage, multi-issue, multilevel, and coalitional strategies. Separating spheres of action into the local and the global, and into hierarchical rankings of local, regional, national, and international, is still common practice, but these abstractions may be of limited utility. Elsbeth Probyn (1990, 186) finds, "The idea that politics is inscribed on this abstraction we call the local . . . [is] both ludicrous and problematic." The local exists only as a fragmented set of possibilities, a momentary politics of time and place. An unspecified local, says Probyn, becomes the site for an unnamed politics.

Place, rather than "the local," is WFAN's ground. The importance of place permeates all five of WFAN's goals. To founding member Danielle Wirth (1996), place sets the parameters for ethical deliberations. Wirth's place in central Iowa was once the heart of the tallgrass prairie bioregion with soil composed of rich, dark organic matter over two feet deep. The prairie that provided the soil's wealth has been replaced by a monocultural regime of corn and soybean agriculture that has polluted water resources and destroyed biological diversity and natural habitat. To Wirth, agriculture is *the* environmental issue in Iowa.

Place is also contested space. Probyn uses locale to designate a place that is a setting for a particular gendered event, for struggles between being positioned by patriarchal practices and everyday pleasures. The ideal articulation of place and event is never reached. Contradictions and disjuncture are ever present: the place of home and the gendered event of family, or the place of body and the gendered event of reproduction. The family reproduces the conditions of a fundamentally unjust society in which women invest because of the pull of place. This pull is especially strong in rural areas and, together with powerful silencing mechanisms, may explain the reluctance of many rural women to embrace feminism. Feminist theory must locate itself in terms of both victimhood/complicity and agency.

Place is the logical starting point for strategy formulation. Extending Sturgeon's (1997) conception of environment, place is the site of an embodied activism, an arena for collective political action and the formation of alliances from which to deploy a strategic politics. This conception of place can render the local into something workable, somewhere to be worked upon, and to be worked more deeply in—and against (Probyn 1990, 186). A focus on place need not exclude a focus on macro-economic forces such as global capitalism. Once our feet are firmly on the ground, we can then reach beyond, to transcend space to a transnational feminism.

Conclusion

WFAN aspires to make change and challenge local/ global restructuring despite the daunting sweep of globalization and patriarchal rural culture. By starting in a place, a rural place, by privileging the rural in rural/urban relations and the female in female/male relations, and by illuminating and acting against the conditions that silence women, WFAN begins to uncouple the event of patriarchy from its site. The knowledge of place is powerful and provides the possibility of reclaiming our ground and rearranging globalizing practices.

Rethinking levels of analysis and abstraction and reconfiguring conventional analysis and thinking informs strategies to navigate the local/global divide. WFAN strives to work from multiple stages that reflect members' diverse levels of comfort, time, interest, and skill. WFAN strives to provide a safe place for women, to give voice to women, and to engage in politics. WAFN embraces practical economic strategies (providing food-related microenterprise education), activist economic strategies (advocacy, protest), and transnational economic strategies (cross-border organizing).

WFAN's strategies are thus necessarily stitched into a particular time and place. WFAN's perspective on social justice is global, but members' feet are on their home ground. Although rooted in place, WFAN also transverses space because members and allies face challenges that cross rural/urban, agricultural/nonagricultural, local/global, natural/social, and public/private divides, and lines of race, ethnicity, class, age, sexual orientation, and culture. Despite a primarily rural and agricultural focus, addressing local/global economic issues requires transversing such divides and coming up with multifaceted, multi-issue, multilevel, and multiparty (coalitional) strategies. WFAN privileges women over men, place over global/local abstractions, practice over theory, and rural over urban, but also constructs change strategies that transverse locales, identities/positions, and conventional dichotomies/constructs through experiences and strategies that invite inclusive and forward movement.

Notes

1. Shortly thereafter Kathy Lawrence began working with Just Foods as executive director, building food systems in New York City; she is now executive director of the National Campaign for Sustainable Agriculture, and a member of WFAN.

2. Three problems were offered as starters: deer eating Nan Bonfils's corn; the high price of rice in Sierra Leone, suggested by workshop participant Margaret Kroma; and the impact of the IPSCO Steel in Muscatine, Iowa, an example offered by founding member Mary Steinmaus. We started with the deer problem, which was compounded by the location of the farm next to a state park. The rice and steel examples were added as the exercise proceeded.

10

Linking Local Efforts with Global Struggle

Trinidad's National Union of Domestic Employees

Marina Karides

> The local and the global are indeed connected through parallel, contradictory, and sometimes converging relations of rule which position women in different and similar locations as workers.
>
> —Chandra Talpade Mohanty,
> "Women Workers and Capitalist Scripts" (1998)

THE COLLECTIVE INTERNATIONAL POLITICAL ACTIVITY OF WOMEN'S GROUPS HAS immediate implications for state policymaking in Third World or postcolonial contexts. Nations that participate in international forums and agree upon documents such as the Nairobi Forward Looking Strategies for the Advancement of Women (1985) and the Beijing Platform for Action (1995) are held accountable to these agreements by the international community and local women's groups. As a participant in these international agreements and forums, the National Union of Domestic Employees (NUDE) of Trinidad and Tobago has held its government responsible nationally and internationally for the rights of domestic workers. Trinidadian domestic workers, the majority of whom are single parents, earn an average of 56 cents an hour, even though minimum wage legislation requires employers to pay workers at least $1 an hour. Yet these women workers, unlike other workers, are not provided a state forum in which to make known their exploitative wages and other grievances. Employers of domestic workers, therefore, can escape state regulations and employment policies.

Since its beginning in the mid-1970s NUDE has struggled to have domestic workers recognized under the nation's Industrial Relations Act. Enacted in 1972, this act provides an Industrial Court in which unions and workers can present their grievances against unfair employment practices and hold employers accountable to state employment policies. To address domestic workers' explicit exclusion from having their cases heard in Industrial Court, NUDE has engaged in international activism that it links with local action. Through its representation at international women's conferences and participation in the international campaign Wages for Housework, NUDE has made its case known in various parts of the world. The union has contributed to developing international agreements regarding women and has used its international activity to campaign for the rights of Trinidad's domestic workers. This chapter focuses on three ways that NUDE links the local with the global: through involving itself with international activism; holding state officials accountable to international agreements, and publicizing their international activity locally.

To examine NUDE's strategies I analyzed 63 newspaper articles and editorials, 10 public speeches, and 6 letters to government officials, all published, presented, and written between 1990 and 1998. In addition, I conducted interviews with six NUDE members, including two officials of the union, and attended three union meetings. I use the information gleaned from these sources to delineate and describe each of the three methods NUDE uses in its campaign for the recognition of domestic workers under the Industrial Relations Act. I consider how this grassroots women's group uses the global arena to empower its local struggles.

In the next section, I consider the economic and political constraints of Third World states in relation to women's political activism. This is followed by a summary of Trinidad and Tobago's political and economic context. I then review each of NUDE's three organizing tactics and conclude by considering members' assessment of the effect of the union's international activity on the status of Trinidad's domestic workers.

International Activism and the Constraints of the Postcolonial State

The state has been the catalyst and site of women's political action as well as a focal point for feminist analyses. Setting the parameters of national gender ideology, states can contribute significantly to the oppression or liberation of women. Though a significant amount of research on women and the state in wealthy nations has been conducted in the last 20 years, little research has focused on women and Third World states (Afshar 1996; Alexander and Mohanty 1997a). Western-biased feminist and political theories do not account for the postcolonial circumstances that activists in the Third World must necessarily face and address (Mohanty 1997). Third World women's rights activism must confront both the national and international political economic systems that affect the daily lives of women.

The dependent economic position of Third World or postcolonial states in the global economy shapes the political activism of women's groups in these nations.

According to dependent development theorists, Third World states are trapped between the needs of local and foreign capital (Evans 1979; So 1990). Postcolonial nations such as Trinidad and Tobago depend on advanced capitalist nations for economic survival (Evans 1979; Fernandez-Kelly 1985; Safa 1987; Ward 1990). Lacking large amounts of capital, Third World nations must maintain conditions such as low taxes, minimal regulation, political stability, and a low-wage labor force to attract foreign investment (Evans 1979; So 1990). At the same time, the local elite influence political and economic policies. The local elite's strength lies in their votes and their political organizations; they can oust one political regime and install another when they are dissatisfied with state policies that compromise their profits for those of foreign capital's (Evans 1979). Therefore, to sustain economic development and political viability, Third World nations must mediate between the needs of local and foreign capital.

Though Evans's (1979) analysis of Third World countries provides a way of understanding the constraints of the Third World, it neglects to consider how women's groups, unions, and other grassroots organizations can shape state policies in these nations. Women and other marginalized groups have effectively organized to challenge exploitative or oppressive state policies (Fainstein 1987). Though these groups suffer from their nation's economic and political subordination in the global political economy, the constrained position of Third World states also may provide local grassroots groups an avenue into state policymaking.

Along with economic globalization has come a number of internationally coordinated campaigns, meetings, and agreements that address a host of social issues, such as human rights, labor exploitation, women's rights, and environmental concerns (Hirasawa 2000). Transnational networks of activists play an increasingly important role in international and regional politics. Many scholars and practitioners argue that this global activism represents the positive side of globalization and has had progressive effects on international and national policies regarding women, human rights, and the environment (Keck and Sikkink 1999). More critically, others suggest that international agreements such as those regarding human rights are least successful in Third World countries and are used to codify human rights violation as a Third World phenomena (Reich and Sacks 2000). Generally, research in this area indicates that globalization, broadly conceived, has mixed results in improving the livelihood of the poor and the oppressed—increasing both economic exploitation and political opportunity (McCorquodale and Fairbrother 1999; Moghadam 1998).

Organizations such as NUDE have used international campaigns and agreements to pressure their government to address the concerns of their constituency. Third World participation in international agreements and forums has helped to establish these nations as modern and credible in the eyes of Western political and economic leaders. Dependent on foreign capital, Third World states have an economic interest in presenting themselves as modernized. For instance, research demonstrates that the larger the foreign investment in a nation, the greater the likelihood that the nation had participated in international environmental agreements.

In addition to participating in global forums, many nations incorporate values and organizational structures associated with Western capitalist countries to demonstrate their economic and political preparedness for capitalist development. The modernization approach, dominating policies of economic development since their inception in the late 1950s, assured poor and undeveloped nations that with modern values and structures they would soon advance to the same level of development as wealthy core nations (So 1990).

In the last several decades, the participation of women in the labor force has become a marker for modern social and economic structures. By appearing to advance the position of women, a nation can present itself as not tethered to traditional values. In other words, women's participation in the labor force implies that a nation has a modern society with a forward-moving value system rather than being attached to "backward" cultural values. The participation of women in the labor force also is attractive to multinational capitalists who view poor Third World women as a cheap source of labor (Safa 1995). Though the rhetoric of a free market economy is one of increasing egalitarianism throughout the world, gender and development scholars have established that women and Third World workers in general are increasingly exploited in a globalizing economy (Moghadam 1998; Ward 1990).

Yet international and local organizations truly committed to social justice can use the rhetoric of egalitarianism associated with globalization to fight against the exploitation of workers. Women's groups can expose their nation's gender-biased practices in an international arena. Globalization and the blossoming of an international activist community provide another option for grassroots women's organizing efforts. While postcolonial states often function as instruments of global ruling class interests in neglecting the needs of the mass population, the organizing efforts of NUDE demonstrate that the underrepresented masses can use the globalizing world economy to get their issues addressed. By linking their local struggle with international activism, NUDE has shaped state policies regarding women and domestic work. In the next section I provide a brief background of Trinidad's economy and the status of women workers to provide a frame for NUDE's campaign.

Political and Economic Context

Trinidad's labor market is shaped by the nation's oil-reliant economy (World Bank 1995). Trinidad's energy sector earns up to 70 percent of the nation's foreign revenue, but it employs less than 3 percent of the population. Even during its most successful economic period of the 1970s, when oil prices shot up dramatically, unemployment remained above 10 percent (Hintzen 1985; Pantin 1993; World Bank 1995).

In addition to already limited job opportunities, Trinidadian women also must deal with discrimination in the formal labor market. Women are restricted from high-wage positions and relegated to low-wage formal jobs (Clarke 1993; Coppin and Olsen 1992; Women's Affairs Division 1995). For instance, Trinidad continues to employ a Night Work Ordinance that bans women from the highest paying jobs in the petroleum industry (Clarke 1992). Gender discrimination in Trinidad's labor market is also evidenced by wage differences—women earn half as much as men in the formal labor force (Women's Affairs Division 1995). In addition, although women typically attain higher educational levels than men do, they receive lower economic returns on education than do men in the same ethnic group (Coppin and Olsen 1992). Faced with limited job opportunities and discrimination in the formal labor market, women have historically turned to domestic service, street vending, or other types of informal (undocumented and unregulated) work to earn income (Clarke 1992).

In the late 1980s, a dramatic drop in the international price of petroleum almost halted the nation's economy. A lender to the IMF until 1984, Trinidad and Tobago turned to the institution for economic assistance in 1988. Forced to meet IMF's structural adjustment policies, Trinidad had to retrench state employment and cut the social programs it had used to alleviate employment problems (EIU 1998; World Bank 1995).

Changes in global economic conditions deeply influence national politics, particularly in countries with an oil-based economy like Trinidad. The People's National Movement (PNM), controlling the nation parliamentary government since it became a republic in 1962, benefited politically from the upswing of the petroleum industry in the 1970s but eventually took the heat for the downturn in the economy in the late 1980s. In the 1986 national elections the PNM for the first time lost control of the government. The political party that gained power was the National Alliance of Reconstruction (NAR), often referred to as a coalition party.

The politics of Trinidad and Tobago are dictated by the tensions between the republic's racial and ethnic groups. Descendants from Africa and India each make up 40 percent of the population, and Chinese, Syrian/Lebanese, and whites make up the remaining 10 percent. The PNM, identified as representing the interests of the African-Trinidadian population, and the United National Congress (UNC), which is considered to represent the East Indian population, have battled for control over the parliamentary government in recent decades. The UNC was reelected in 2000, defeating the PNM by a small margin, and dominates parliament. While the UNC's reign for the last five years is associated with economic growth resulting from the expansion in natural gas– and petroleum-related industries, it is also tied to the persistent poverty, increasing income inequality, and high levels of unemployment that characterize the nation.

Currently 18 percent of women are unemployed, and 28 percent of employed women are actually self-employed—most of them in the informal sector (CSO 1999). To address the economic hardship of unemployment, underemployment, and discrimination in the formal labor market, women engage in informal work such as domestic service, which is labor intensive and requires minimum capital. Domestic employees as well as other informal workers suffer low earnings, lack formal employment benefits, and are not covered by the national insurance program.

Trinidad's state actors address the high levels of unemployment by promoting microenterprise development and self-employment as the premier solution to poverty eradication, employment creation, and economic growth (Ministry of Trade 1997). Yet domestic workers, who *have* independently found means of earning income, continue to face some of the most exploitative conditions in the labor market and remain unrecognized as workers under the Industrial Relations Act.

The Industrial Relations Act explicitly states "that domestics are not to be considered workers for the purpose of protection and representation." Instead the relationship of domestic workers to their employers continues to be governed by the Master and Servants Act, put in place in the early 1800s by the British colonial government to regulate the relationship between domestic workers and their employers after the abolition of slavery (Brereton 1981; Reddock 1994).

Since domestic workers are governed by the Master and Servants Act, they are denied guarantees granted to other workers. A full-time workweek, which is stipulated as 40 hours for most employees, is 44 hours for domestics. Another example of the impact of colonial legacy on domestic workers is their exemption from severance benefits, which requires employers to provide full-time employees with a retirement package such as a pension plan. Rather, the Master and Servants Act dictates that retiring domestic workers receive only one month's pay—which in most instances is not forthcoming (Le Blanc 1998).

Domestic workers are also excluded from the nation's social security program. Trinidad's National Insurance System (NIS) functions similarly to the United States' Social Security system, with workers and employers each contributing to the nation's social security fund. In Trinidad, the NIS provides employees with monthly social security payments upon retirement, compensates workers for permanent or temporary injury, and also pays for leave in case of sickness or pregnancy. Though it is mandatory for employers to register all their workers under the NIS, if employers of domestic workers choose not to, they experience no sanctions. In addition, domestic workers, as self-employed persons usually with more than one employer, do not even have the option of making both the employer and the employee payments to the NIS, leaving them with little in retirement savings.

NUDE Starts Up

The first steps toward the formation of a domestic workers' union were taken in 1974. A group of domestic workers approached Clotil Walcott, then an active and well-known activist of the Shipbuilders and Ship Workers Allied Union (SSAU), for support in gaining some kind of protection from exploitative labor conditions (Walcott 1998). As domestic work, street vending, and other forms of informal work are how most low-income women earn a living in Trinidad, these women organized themselves within their respective communities. Beginning organizing efforts were mostly carried out by word of mouth through the sharing of information and domestic work experiences with friends and neighbors. Walcott, well known for her activism against gender discrimination in the labor force and within the trade union movement, was the obvious candidate to help these women form a union. She is recognized as a national leader for women workers' rights, and has received national, regional, and international awards for her advocacy of domestic worker rights.

Initially, domestic workers were accepted as a branch under the SSAU. Soon after, however, Walcott left the larger union because, like many unions, it was not addressing the concerns of women workers. Walcott then helped establish NUDE as an independent entity (Clarke 1992). In 1982 NUDE was registered under the Trade Union Ordinance and became officially recognized by the central government (Le Blanc 1998). Ten years later, NUDE officially expanded its membership from domestic workers "to include in the union all workers who may be desirous of joining the union NUDE for effective representation." NUDE organizers explained that they were interested in providing representation for informal workers, who engage in undocumented and unregulated labor and lacked representation because they were unable to gain employment in the formal labor force.

NUDE is one of many organizations across the globe addressing the challenges of organizing an informal labor force. Globally, more and more workers are finding informal means of employment (Cross 1998; Portes, Castells, and Benton 1989; Rakowski 1994; Ward 1990), and in many Third World regions more workers are found in the informal rather than the formal employment sector. Unlike most formal workers who labor together in one location, informal workers are particularly difficult to organize because they are often isolated from one another and have more than one employer. Domestic workers' grassroots organizing tactics can inform future efforts toward organizing an individualized and contingent labor force. NUDE has begun to address "the challenge for collective organizing in a context where traditional union methods (male workers) are inadequate as strategies for empowerment" (Mohanty 1997, 6). NUDE's organizing strategies of addressing local concerns with international involvement contributes to the international organization of informal workers.

NUDE's Experience: Women, Class, and International Activism

Divisiveness along class lines has been difficult for women's activist organizations (Naples 1999) and persists even at the international level. NUDE members explain that their international ties are with women's groups from other nations that tend to represent a similar class of workers, mostly poor and working-class women. Locally, NUDE members feel that as representatives of domestic workers their efforts are not widely supported by other Trinidadian women's groups because the needs and struggles of these mostly upper- or middle-class women's groups are not informed by the concerns of poor and working-class local women.

NUDE criticizes many of Trinidad's women's groups for not using their participation in international conventions and agreements to advance the position of low-income women in Trinidad. They explain that women in these other organizations are highly regarded internationally but are unknown locally and inaccessible to most Trinidadian women.

Class differences separate groups in ways that transcend a simple lack of mutual support, however. The more affluent groups, though struggling for justice in their own cases, actively perpetrate injustice toward the domestic workers through their dependency on cheap domestic help. In effect, they are part of the problem that NUDE is trying to solve. Le Blanc of NUDE says, "Remember, all these people are upper class, they are employers of domestics, so what you're fighting for is you're fighting for benefits that they have to put out to domestics."

In one startling example, NUDE was excluded from a regional conference, Vital Voices, held in Port of Spain, Trinidad, which was focused on the implementation of the Beijing Platform of Action (*Briggs* 1999; *Newsday* 1999). Though the organizers of the conference said that budgetary constraints made them unable to accommodate more women's groups, NUDE members blamed their exclusion on the fact that any gains they made would be losses for the more afflluent groups. Most of those women participating in the conference would have domestic workers, they noted.

The international activist strategies of NUDE may provide a way for overcoming local class barriers that hinder the union's struggle. Class divisions among women's activist efforts is particularly disempowering for poor and working-class women, who lack the social and economic power of their wealthier counterparts. The organizing efforts of domestic workers and working-class or poor women have been given scant attention (Naples 1998a). Yet NUDE's response to class divisiveness has encouraged the international women's movement to incororate the needs of all women workers, domestic and otherwise, in its struggles for gender equity. NUDE's slogan bespeaks incontrovertible logic: "House work is work, so therefore workers who do this work are workers." NUDE has campaigned locally and globally for almost 20 years to change the status of domestic workers in Trinidad and Tobago. Unable to challenge unfair employment practices in the Industrial Court, NUDE must find alternative tactics. And so the group engages in international political discourse by attending conferences and engaging in campaigns such as Wages for Housework. It then publicizes its international activity as well as the local conditions of domestic workers in the nation's widely read newspapers and at national and regional conferences. The point of this publicity effort, organizers say, is to show Trinidadian citizens the "cosmopolitan nature of NUDE's cause" and gain support for their campaign. NUDE follows these efforts by communicating through letters, public media, and in public or government forums to state officials that it is the state's local and international responsibility to include domestic employees under the Industrial Relations Act, holding employers accountable to international agreements and women workers.

Wages for Housework

Wages for Housework is focused on the recognition of women's unwaged household work as productive labor and contributive to the gross national product (GNP). It is a campaign that seeks to make known the gendered organization of household labor, women's disproportionate share of this work, and the need for women to be compensated for this labor. A network of women in both poor and rich countries, Wages for Housework also demands that wages for housework come first of all from military spending.

NUDE became a member of the international campaign when the union's leader, Walcott, attended her first international women's conference in Mexico in 1975 and met Selma James, the founder of Wages for Housework (Walcott 1998). Realizing the similarities between their campaigns, the two organized an impromptu workshop to consider how they could build upon the affinities of their struggles. Participants in the workshop concluded that the low wages and exploitative labor conditions of domestic workers directly result from the fact that women's household labor is unpaid (Walcott 1998). These two groups reached an understanding, now commonplace within feminist scholarship, that the devaluation of women's labor and labor activities associated with women is based on the assumption that women's work is a natural extension of their reproductive roles. In other words, it is not "real work"; real work is what men do.

Instead of returning to Trinidad after the conference, Walcott accepted an invitation to travel with James to England to further develop their campaign, after which Walcott returned to Trinidad to initiate the Trinidadian branch of Wages for Housework. The union then used the international campaign to politicize domestic workers' rights as part of a global agenda for the remuneration of women's work. After that, the union routinely put local concerns into a global context. NUDE locally organized internationally coordinated events such as conferences, protests, and annual marches on International Women's Day. It also participated in International Time Off for Women, an annual event in which women across the globe picket and protest for the recognition of their major contribution to the economy. In addition, NUDE organized workshops to inform the public of the international campaign and its own involvement.

The many years of struggle by women activists involved in Wages for Housework reached its apex at the Beijing conference in 1995 when the remuneration of women's work was accepted as part of the Platform for Action, an agenda for women's empowerment that builds upon the Nairobi Forward Looking Strategies of 1985. Included in the platform and agreed upon by all governments participating is the commitment to "the recognition of the economic value of women's work in the home, in domestic food production and marketing, and in voluntary activities not traditionally remunerated" (United Nations 1995). Six thousand government representatives from 189 countries and 4,000 representatives of women's nongovernmental organizations all agreed to make efforts to acknowledge women's economic contribution and adhere to the many agreements made through changes in national policies of their respective countries.

Since the conference, Trinidad and Tobago is one of only 15 nations that have made the recognition of women's unpaid work a state policy. In 1995 the nation's parliament passed the Unremunerated Work Bill, giving official recognition to women's traditional household labor as work. Beginning with the country's 2000 census, women's as well as men's unremunerated work will be incorporated into the national accounting system. Though it was NUDE's international and local efforts toward recognition of women's unwaged work that prompted the state's passage of the Unremunerated Wage Bill, domestic workers remain unrecognized under the Industrial Relations Act; unpaid domestic work is officially work, but paid domestic workers are not officially workers. It is this contradiction that NUDE publicizes in the national media and uses in its dealings with state officials.

Keeping the Public Informed

NUDE actively uses the print media in its struggle for domestic workers' rights. Articles and editorials regarding the union's efforts appear in each of the nation's three daily newspapers, the *Trinidadian Guardian, Newsday,* and *Daily Express.* With 97 percent of its adult population literate, Trinidad has one of the highest literacy rates among Caribbean nations (UNDP 1997). From interviews I conducted with newspaper vendors and my social interactions with Trinidadians, I learned that these three daily newspapers have a wide circulation and are read and discussed by wealthy, middle-class, and low-income or poor members of the population.

Reviewing the articles and editorials in these newspapers, as well as locally presented addresses by NUDE, the central themes that emerge regarding domestic workers are the contradiction in state policy, government's accountability to international agreements, and NUDE's participation in international activity. Taken together, these themes demonstrate NUDE's commitment to informing the Trinidadian public about the connection between conditions faced by local workers and the global economy.

NUDE members convey that the circumstances facing Trinidadian women are not unique. In an editorial published on Emancipation Day, a national holiday recognizing the liberation of African Trinidadians from slavery, Walcott writes,

> In 1980 the United Nations and the ILO published statistics showing that women do two-thirds of the world's work for five percent of the income and own only one percent of the assets, showing that women world wide are at the bottom of an international hierarchy of work and wealth and on the front line of poverty.
>
> This figure means that poverty, racism and war can not be abolished without abolishing the slave status of women, and, in particular, the slave status of the majority of Black and other women of color who are the poorest of the poor.
>
> We have to get rid of the colonial mentality existing in our society and to abolish the Master and Servants Act, called the "Slave Act" which says domestic servants are not workers. How can we celebrate Emancipation Day and at the same time glorify waged slavery and dismiss housework? (Walcott 1993)

Using the nation's heightened awareness of slavery during the holiday, Walcott ties in the global status of women of color with the local issue of domestic workers. This editorial draws together women's international status, the role of colonialism and postcolonialism, and the current status of Trinidadian domestic workers. Actively using the print media as a campaign tool, NUDE explains the contradiction between the international agreements the government participates in and the exclusion of domestic employees from the Industrial Relations Act. This helps to inform the general public and domestic workers of the union's activities. In addition, publicizing their participation in the international arena and the government's responsibility to international agreements strengthens their case. An article written just after NUDE's participation in the Beijing conference explains,

> Clotil Walcott took her cause to Beijing in September, to the Fourth World Conference on Women. She came back recently, triumphant because governments at the conference agreed to measure and value unwaged work. Walcott's reaction to this agreement was that now the Trinidad and Tobago Government would have to amend the Industrial Relations Act to recognize domestic servants as workers. (Mills 1995)

Publicizing the numerous events it has coordinated on its own and with international organizations, NUDE has swayed public opinion in its perception of domestic work and domestic workers.

NUDE uses the public forum to declare that changing the status of domestic workers under Trinidadian law is part of its government's international responsibility. A speech given by Ida LeBlanc at a regional meeting on sustainable development held in Trinidad and published in the *Guardian*, states:

> The refusal to recognize domestics as workers, works against the achievement of the Unremunerated Work Act and the Convention of the Elimination of all Forms of Discrimination which affects women's overall economic status, with wider implications for women's relative lack of social power. (NUDE 1998)

NUDE's attack on the government for not implementing the Platform for Action is apparent. And the newspaper headline, "NUDE Calls for Equal Treatment for Low Income Workers . . . Calls on Govt to Honour Commitment to Beijing Platform," illustrates that the media are well informed of NUDE's mission.

In addition, NUDE publicizes its exclusion as a union from bargaining rights on the behalf of domestics. Union leaders claim this is a violation of the United Nations Convention on the Elimination of All Forms of Discrimination against Women. Le Blanc explains, "Discrimination against women trade unionists violates the principle of equality of rights and respect for human dignity. It is also an obstacle to the participation of women on equal terms with men" (Webb 1999).

NUDE's rhetoric in the local media focuses on notifying the public of its international efforts as well as the international agreements to which the nation is accountable. By publicizing the contradiction between the employment status of domestic workers and the government's international responsibility, the union garners support for its campaign. Throughout its existence NUDE has been able to increase its membership. It has also gained the attention of Diana Mahabir-Wyatt, a feminist senator who has pursued the union's campaign in parliament.

Holding Government Responsible

In discussing how her international participation relates to her interaction with the central government, Walcott says in an interview:

> Anytime I go to a conference and I come back, I take my report and I send it to the prime minister, so he knows what is doing in each country. . . . I let him know what took place. So they really know the kind of fight I was fighting, you understand?

As an organization, NUDE does not skip a beat keeping governmental leaders attuned to the latest international agreements and how they relate to the status of domestic workers. Direct correspondence with government officials informing them of their international responsibility is one of NUDE's most powerful tactics. Exploiting the state's desire to be perceived as a modern nation, NUDE maintains that the nation's global status relies on upholding international agreements. A letter sent to the prime minister by the union two weeks after members attended the conference in Beijing states:

> As you probably know the Platform for Action (PFA) agreed on by governments at the Fourth World Conference On Women held in Beijing, China sets out economic, political and social priorities which will affect women and our national communities well into the 21st century . . . In implementing this Platform for Action therefore, the government of Trinidad & Tobago will now need to amend the Industrial Relations Act, to recognize domestic servants as workers under that Act.

The Platform for Action, which NUDE helped formulate, provides the organization with international support for its campaign of almost 20 years. NUDE not only brings the Platform for Action to the attention of the prime minister but also articulates how the platform applies to the particular situation of domestic workers in Trinidad and Tobago. In another letter, also directed to the prime minister NUDE officials wrote:

> Since 1975, when the women of Iceland took a "Day Off" and thereby caused the entire economy of Iceland to grind to a halt, there are no longer

> doubts about the importance of women's contribution or about the potential economic and therefore social power of women. It is criminal for this economic contribution to continue to be hidden and for women to continue to suffer the greatest poverty and overwork—according to the International Labor Office, double the workload of men—which are the penalty of the invisibility of their work.

NUDE uses statistics gathered by international organizations as well as events in other parts of the world to locate the oppression of Trinidadian women within an international context.

When the minister of labor was questioned on the status of domestic workers under the Industrial Relations Act during parliamentary proceeding, he told members that "no decision has been taken to change this situation." In a collective letter responding to this statement, NUDE said:

> It is the view of our Union that the Honourable Minister's reply simply did not answer the question with the completeness and precision that was necessary. . . . Our members' exercise of their rights, and their enjoyment of the constitutional guarantee of the equality before the law is severely infringed upon by the Industrial Relation Act. We are not satisfied that our members' loss of such a fundamental and hard-won right—the right to be recognized in law as workers—is based on principles that are just, fair, and proper . . . If it is the view of the Honourable Minister and/or the Government of Trinidad and Tobago that the relevant section of the Industrial Relations Act should not be amended so to include domestic employees as "workers," then would the Hounourable Minister inform our Union of the basis for such a view?

In another letter written to Elton Prescot, Chairman of the Standing Tripartite Commttee on Labour Matters, the union uses international agreements to apply pressure on the state to change the status of domestic workers so that minimum wage ordinances are enforceable. The letter states:

> Therefore it would be strange for a roadblock to be raised in the case of domestic workers and low income workers in ensuring effective enforcement of the Minimum Wages Act. Therefore you must honor this country's commitment to ILO convention 111 by enacting or amending legislation that supports a policy of non-discrimination.

Clearly, NUDE is persistent in stating the similarities between its local campaign and the agenda of the international community. The fact that domestic workers continue to be governed by the Master and Servants Act is inconsistent with the modern image that Trinidad and Tobago tries to project. The attendance by NUDE members at international events at which they "represent the grassroots women of Trinidad and Tobago . . . forcefully putting their case to the international community" demands that the Trinidadian government be accountable in the international arena.

Conclusion: Real or Surface Change in State Policy?

Currently NUDE is evaluating the impact of its participation international conferences and campaigns, and the use of international agreements and statistics for improving the status of domestic workers in Trinidad and Tobago. The organization as a whole generally is split between two perspectives. Some members argue that international involvement, while requiring much time and energy, has helped to achieve changes in state policies regarding women and domestic work. Others feel that state policy has not been impacted by the union's international efforts. Although the government of Trinidad and Tobago participate in international agreements regarding the status of women, this has not led to any real change in the position of low-income women in Trinidad and Tobago.

In one union meeting, a member argued that most of the agreements incorporated into the Platform for Action have not been legislated in Trinidad and Tobago nor in many other nations. Members, unsure of the effects of the union's international participation, suggested that these international agreements on women's status might actually deter the improvement of Third World women's living conditions. They argue that agreements made on paper allow a nation to *appear* as if they are addressing the concerns of women without really taking action. As one member said, "It looks nice on paper because of the conference, the paper they have for the Caribbean, and you see about Trinidad, everybody seeing that, they say, 'Well, boy, you pay domestic workers.'"

A nation such as Trinidad and Tobago can look advanced and modern in the global arena by formally agreeing to international conventions regarding women's status while actual living conditions of women deteriorate. Yet many NUDE members feel that their international activism has been instrumental in making small but important changes in government legislation regarding women and domestic workers and feel that their international involvement adds weight to the case they are making

Clearly NUDE's local and international activism has affected international and state policies. NUDE's persistent campaigning and involvement with the Wages for Housework campaign contributed to the government of Trinidad and Tobago becoming an international leader in accounting unremunerated work in national statistics. The passage of the Unremunerated Work Bill reinforces NUDE's case for changing the status of domestic workers under the Industrial Relations Act. In addition, NUDE's international campaigning may also have contributed to the inclusion of domestic workers under the National Insurance System and Minimum Wages Act. The problem remains, however, that although employers of domestic workers should ascribe to these laws, there is no arena to address domestic workers' grievances against delinquent employers. Presently, a change in the status of domestic workers is being debated in parliament, and for the first time parliament is giving serious consideration to providing domestic workers full rights and recognition as workers and, therefore, access to the Industrial Court. Many members feel that the possible change in legislation is a product of politicians' concern with negative evaluation by their international counterparts. Whether or not domestic workers get recognized as workers under the Industrial Relations Act, it is clear that the status of domestic workers has come up for parliamentary debate only because of NUDE's activism. Publicizing its case to the international community and using international clout in the local context is arguably one of NUDE's most important campaign tools.

The fact that domestic workers continue to be governed by the Master and Servants Act and are excluded from the Industrial Relations Act challenges the government's posture as a modernized country. As the most developed country in the Caribbean, the Republic of Trinidad and Tobago is especially conscious of presenting itself as a sophisticated and modern society (Ministry of Trade 1997). By exposing nationally and internationally the remnants of colonial legislation in state policy, NUDE challenges the nation's international image.

NUDE's linkage of international and local activism offers grassroots women's groups a model for organizing beyond the national arena. In addition, the union offers some ideas on how to organize an informal labor force. The union's long persistence alone serves as an exemplar for women activists.

Note

I gratefully acknowledge the participation of NUDE members in the completion of this manuscript and thank the organization for willfully providing me with information. Parties interested in contacting or contributing to NUDE can write to the National Union of Domestic Employees, Mount Pleasant Road, Arima, Trinidad, or call (868) 667-5247. I thank Joya Misra and Ivy Kennelly for comments on early drafts. I am especially indebted to the editors for their detailed review of this chapter.

11

Women Activists in Mali

The Global Discourse on Human Rights

Susanna D. Wing

MALIAN WOMEN HAVE ALWAYS BEEN ACTIVE POLITICALLY. WOMEN'S ASSOCIATIONS (*musotonw*) in Bamana villages regularly sent representatives to village meetings (Jorio 1997, 42).[1] After the electoral code reforms of 1951, rural women throughout the French Soudan voted in greater numbers than did men as a result of electoral laws that favored women. Throughout the 1950s, women were active in local and international women's organizations. Following independence in 1960, women's organizations were officially linked to the ruling party, Union Soudanaise-Reassemblement Démocratique Africain (US-RDA) and later Union Démocratique du Peuple Malien (UDPM), although Rosa de Jorio (1997), in her comprehensive study of women's formal associations in Mali, argues that they were only partially subordinated to the parties in power and retained a certain amount of autonomy.

At the 1991 National Conference that marked the country's transition to democracy, only 52 women were among the total 1,034 registered participants (CTSP 1991).[2] Although these few women managed to achieve the protection of equal rights for women and children in the constitution, women's rights remained peripheral to the main debates discussed at the conference. Despite these indicators, the participation and influence of women in Malian politics has increased dramatically over the last decade. Since 1991, Mali has pursued political liberalization, and the proportion of female representatives in the National Assembly rose from 2 percent in 1992 to 12 percent in 1997, after just one round of legislative elections (Tamboura 1997, 4, 10). During the same period the number of female ministers in the president's 22 member cabinet rose from two to six (Traoré, 1997, 3). Since its debut in 1994, the annual Éspace d'interpellation démocratique has provided a forum for women to demand respect for the constitution and the protections it affords women and children. By 1998, women's rights were on the agenda of the *concertations régionales* for Projet d'Appui à la Réforme de la Justice and were discussed in each of Mali's eight regions.

In this chapter, I shall argue that the Malian government has created a space within which female citizens can discuss their rights. The resulting dialogue on women's rights is linked to the participation of Malian women in a global discourse in which women leaders bridge the gap between the international community and local women. In the process, individual women become adept at participating in politics at the international, national, and local levels. The discourse on women's rights varies in content at each of these levels of political life. Global arguments for women's equality and the protection of their universal human rights, derived in part from the Forth World Conference held in Beijing, China, must be adapted to local conditions relative to the role of women in politics, the economy, and the family. To grasp the overall picture of human rights in Mali, understanding the interaction between women from urban and rural communities is critical. In an effort to close the perceived gap between these diverse communities, rights are directly linked to the democratization process and nation building rather than to a more "distant" global struggle for women's rights.

Following a brief discussion of women's interests and the relationship between globalization and women's rights, I shall analyze the strategies that women have developed in order to strengthen their role in Mali's nascent democracy. Based on interviews conducted in the regions of Koulikoro, Sikasso, Mopti, and Ségou in 1994 and 1997–98, I discuss the role played by women's associations in the process and, in particular, the role of such organizations as Association des juristes Maliennes (AJM), an association of female lawyers, Groupe Féminin Droit de Suffrage (GFDS), a group for women's voting rights, and Observatoire des Droits de la Femme et de l'Enfant (ODEF), a watch group for the protection of the rights of women and children. Each of these associations has projects that are funded by international donors. Such organizations, thriving on the promotion of civic rights and growing awareness of these rights, illustrate the extent to which globalization has influenced the dialogue within Mali on democracy and human rights. I conclude with an analysis of the critical role that associations and women play in nation building.

Women constitute more than 50 percent of the Malian population, and their diversity complicates the very idea of "women's interests" that is fundamental to the discussion in this chapter. I shall present the activities of several associations that are very different from one another and address the broad gap between rural and urban women, elite and non-elite women. In addition to gender, shared identities such as ethnicity and class cross the urban and rural divide. Similarly, the role played by extended families in Malian society establishes a link between urban and rural areas.

Women's organizing is important because one of the reasons many women are prevented from exercising their rights is that they do not know of the existence of such rights. This is complicated by low female literacy and a lack of awareness of legal issues.[3] These barriers to dialogue must be overcome for women to participate effectively in constitutional dialogues. The examples provided in this chapter explain the ways that women's associations in Mali are addressing this issue.

Globalization and Women's Rights

Globalization has broadened the dialogue on women's rights throughout the world. International networks created during the United Nations Decade on Women (1975–85) and in the wake of the United Nations' Fourth World Conference on Women in Beijing (September 4–15, 1995) helped put women's rights as human rights on the international agenda (L. West 1997, xiv). Toward the end of the UN Decade for Women in July 1985, a program titled Forward Looking Strategies for the Advancement of Women (FLS) was adopted by delegates from 157 governments meeting in Nairobi. By 1995, 131 countries had ratified the UN Convention on the Elimination of All Forms of Discrimination against Women (CEDAW) (Peterson and Runyan 1999, 218). Discussion of CEDAW arises in interviews with leaders of women's associations in Mali's capital, Bamako, as well as in development program reports from donor organizations.[4] These examples illustrate the extent to which the global discourse on women's rights has permeated the discourse at the urban level and within international donors. However, it is important to understand how this international discourse relates to lives of women in rural areas.

Bilateral and multilateral donors have increasingly made development assistance conditional on political and economic liberalization. The United States Agency for International Development (USAID) has established strategic objectives for its development initiatives that include democratic governance. Donors such as USAID, the French Ministry of Cooperation, Germany's Frederik Ebert Foundation, and the Centre Canadien d'étude et de Coopération Internationale (CECI) are particularly active in programs that promote public awareness of issues such as excision, commonly known as female genital mutilation, and civic education. Despite the reliance of women on international funding, the success of this dialogue on rights, paradoxically, depends on the ability of women leaders in Mali to present themselves as separate from the international human rights movement. Instead, they must be viewed as women whose ideals are specifically Malian and part of the new Malian democratic initiative. This separate identity allows leaders of the movement to become insiders and gain acceptance into local communities. As one woman who had not attended the Beijing conference explained, women returning from China quickly learned that mentioning Beijing often led to negative remarks labeling a woman as "Westernized" and "feminist" and thus not connected to Malian realities.[5]

In May 1993, the government mandated the creation of the Commissariat de la

Promotion des Femmes (CPF), an official government body that would advise the prime minister's office on issues concerning women. The CPF did not become operational until 1994, and critics believed that it disregarded concerns from *la base*, focusing instead on the upcoming conference in Beijing (Jorio 1977, 203–204). By supporting institutional contacts or participation in international women's conferences, the CPF often offended women who were occupied with local issues (204). The divide between the elite women leaders who would participate in Beijing and those who were concerned with issues that were directly relevant to Malians hobbled the Malian women's movement in 1994. Furthermore, the position of the CPF created disaffection of *la base* from the activities of the government under President Alpha Oumar Konaré regime. The extent of this division was evident at a legal clinic sponsored by the AJM in Kayes, located in Mali's westernmost region. A participant noted that with respect to the Beijing conference, "*nous n'avons rien compris.*" ["We didn't understand anything"]. Mme Douré Bamou Diarra, a representative of the AJM, responded,

> Beijing had the reverse effect. It is a platform during which the difficulties confronted by women were raised. However, certain subjects evoked do not relate to our realities. Our battle is a question of economic means. We must give women the means to blossom while freeing them of weighty tasks, and teaching them how to read and write. (quoted in Karabenta 1996, 4)

Despite the concerted effort made in Beijing to be inclusive of problems women face in the developing world, many Malians felt that the conference had little to do with what they faced on a day-to-day basis. Thus, women eager to participate in international women's conferences were forced to balance their international experience with local Malian issues. Mme Diarra was partaking in a project to promote the rights of women, yet she distanced herself and her organization from Beijing. The participation of these women in a global movement, though central to their understanding of women's rights, places them in a precarious position in which they must establish a strong connection to local women or risk being ineffectual. In order for the human rights discourse to be effectual in Mali, it must emphasize issues raised within particular communities at the local level. Both the AJM and ODEF helped this process with the success of their mobile legal clinics, going into villages where efforts to preserve what is viewed as "traditional" and Malian are most evident. If the dialogue on women's rights is to be effective, clearly it must take place at this level.

The effort to balance global interaction with local participation is evident in organizations such as Association pour le Progrès et la Défense des Droits des Femmes Maliennes, the Groupe Féminin Droit de Suffrage (GFDS), and ODEF, whose members include internationally prominent leaders. The president of the Association pour le pregréss, Mme Fatimata Siré Diakité, was awarded the Chevalier d'honneur from the French government in 1998; Maitre M'Bam Diarra N'Douré, who is president of the GFDS, was the sole female member of the transitional government, Comite' de transition pour le Salut du Peuple, and is currently the coordinator of a judicial assistance program operated by the United Nations Center for Human Rights in Burundi. Finally, Maitre Diarra Fatoumata Dembélé, vice president of GFDS, president of ODEF, and vice president of the Fédération des Juristes Africaines (Federation of African Women Lawyers), is very visible within the international community in Mali. Despite the international status of these leaders, the women's associations operate numerous grassroots-oriented projects throughout the country. The Association pour le progrès has a very extensive membership base in each of the eight regions in Mali. Mme Diakité is perhaps one of the most criticized figures in the women's movement. She is labeled as "Westernized" because of her close ties with France, and as one of the leaders who, after participating in the NGO Forum on Women in Huairou outside of Beijing, had priorities that were not "Malian." Yet, she has successfully promoted a network of women throughout the country who preach women's rights and lead the debate against excision.

Globalization has brought increased communication between these women leaders and donor organizations. Many donors encourage development projects from women's associations or require a certain number of women to benefit from a project. Donors have made efforts to ensure that women are placed in decision-making roles in projects, after becoming aware that many such projects were controlled by men who initially used women to gain access to the funds. The increase in women's associations has helped improve the odds of a successful project. Where women's associations are vibrant, they are useful in ensuring that those intended to benefit from projects actually do. Thus, decisions made at the national level are implemented with consultation at the local level.

The reaction to the Beijing conference and the criticism of the Malian women who attended, often with government support, resulted in the current situation in which women are more involved in projects at the local level. The women who participated in the conference were forced, upon their return to Mali, to address the issues of human rights as raised from within their communities. The CPF, in conjunction with the Coordination des associations et ONG Féminines au Mali (CAFO), and other like-minded groups established a Policy Plan for 1996 to 2000 that makes reference to Beijing, as well as CEDAW and the African Platform for Action. Education, health, women's rights, economic development, women's participation in public life, and the environment were prioritized in the Plan. Budget allocations for 1996 to 2000 specify that 11 billion fcfa were to be spent over four years: 42 percent on economic development, 32 percent on education, 15.8 percent on institutional "reinforcement," 5 percent on health, 2.7 percent on environment, 1.6 percent on rights, and .9 percent on public life (Commissariat de la Promotions des Femmes, n.d., n.p.). With 75 percent of the budget allocated for economic development and education, the CPF and NGOs were responding to a growing concern that economic roles of women must be increased and that promoting education would help to address this problem. Economics and education are also the issues most easily linked to development of the Malian nation as a whole. When previously excluded women enter the political process, all Malians will benefit.

Women, Politics, and Associations in Mali

> The village chief held meetings in his home. In the same room, his wife sat behind a curtain. After hearing his visitor's case and before making any decisions, the chief announced that he had to think about his stance on the matter presented to him. His guest would then leave and the chief would be free to discuss the issue with his wife. Only after deliberating with her would he make his final decision.

This story, part of the oral tradition in Mali, is told frequently by Malians who advocate a more significant role for women in contemporary politics. In this particular instance, it was told by a participant in a GFDS seminar on women's civil and political rights, held in the town of Sikasso. Women, she argued, have always been integral to the politics of their communities. Whereas they were once consulted only behind closed doors, today women must not be afraid to lift the curtain and participate openly and publicly in political campaigns and events. Other women chimed in, saying that Malian women are taught that if they choose to speak out they will be considered arrogant and disrespectful. Thus, in public, they have learned to let others speak for them.[6]

Women's long-standing importance in community decision-making was clearly balanced against the deeply rooted cultural impediments to their own political participation. In the continuing process of democratization, these women from rural communities find themselves in an environment that encourages their participation as Malian citizens. Yet, how are they to balance these disparate ideas, remain true to their own culture, and still participate fully in the vigorous political changes taking place?

Let us begin with a brief historical account of women's political participation in Mali. In her work on women's formal associations in Mali, Jorio (1997) provides a familiar description of the role of women in politics. Her analysis of the colonial period prior to independence and the period of socialist rule (1960–68) emphasizes the role of women as mothers. Their primary obligation was to nurture the citizens and dedicate themselves to the creation of a domestic environment that promoted good health, proper education, and morals within the family. It was by these means that women were expected to contribute to national construction (132). They were also given tasks within the party, including "diffusion of information, party cards, and folkloric performances" (154). Such tasks were considered to be within the realm of acceptable female activity.

Since the US-RDA (1960–68) and throughout the Comité Militaire de Libération Nationale, CMLN (1968–79) and the UDPM (1979–91) periods, women have been represented as receptacles of traditional African values. Women are "gardiennes averties des lois et règlements garantissants la stabilité des foyers, la perennité de nos valeurs morales et culturelles" ["Keepers of the laws and rules that guarantee the stability of the household, the continuity of our moral and cultural values"] (Kante 1987, 2, quoted in de Jorio 1997, 260).

When women are perceived as "receptacles of African values," protecting them from the influences of "modern" life becomes critical; as mothers pass traditions on to their children, they would help to preserve African cultures. Women's political activism presented an obvious challenge to this role.

However, during a GFDS seminar on political and civic rights of women, discussion included negative views about women who begin to prepare dinner, particularly during Ramadan, while at work in the office. Certainly women do this to speed up the preparation at home because at sundown, husbands and families who have fasted all day are ready to have their meals served. This is an illustration of the ubiquitous double workday of women, and yet rather than challenging the gender roles that lead to this situation, women criticize their counterparts for appearing "lazy" at the office. That women are expected to perform in a certain manner at work, but also must have dinner ready for their families when they get home, was never raised as a topic at issue during the seminar. In this case, the traditional role of women remains unchallenged. Indeed, such a challenge would likely have raised derision among the participants as being a feminist idea that was not part of their Malian reality.

Women's associations' role in ceremonial activities is both familiar and widespread. Frequently called upon to participate in naming ceremonies and similar family events, women's associations helped to provide not only the necessary numbers of women at such events, but were also able to assist in meeting the expenses (de Jorio 1997). The Union Nationale des Femmes du Mali (UNFM) national women's association was created in December 1974 to unite women at the national level. The nation's first lady, Mariam Traoré, was the president of UNFM. Ghana, Mali, and Nigeria are three of the many countries where the wives of political leaders have been chosen to lead either the national association for women or the women's wings of ruling political parties. Thus, these groups instead of being effective voices against authoritarian regimes, were often co-opted by the regimes themselves. With the fall of Moussa Traoré and his party in 1991, the association his wife led was dissolved. In 1994, many women in power were still considered suspect by leaders of women's associations as a result of this history of co-optation. The female head of the CPF was described by numerous women interviewed as a "sellout," and women representatives to the National Assembly were not widely supported by women's associations because members felt that these representatives did not fight for the interests of women.[7]

As the political arena opened up following the transition, women's associations spread quickly. An umbrella organization for women's associations, Coordination des associations et ONG Féminines au Mali, was created in order to serve as a liason between the CPF and women's associations across the country (Jorio 1997, 205). The umbrella organization included 50 member organizations in 1994 (Jorio 1997, 205), and after just four years, by 1998, that number had more than tripled, reaching 191. In Mopti, the umbrella group was instrumental in the election of Bintou Sanankoua to the National Assembly in 1997, having organized its members to support her candidacy. Regardless of their party affiliations, members came together to support Mme Sanankoua.[8]

I turn now to a few examples of the work being done today by women's associations, particularly in the area of women's rights and civic participation.

Women's Rights and Civic Participation

Elite urban women have used their international networks to their advantage at the regional and local levels. Throughout the country they have created local branches of national organizations and have used these organizations to help promote political campaigns and development projects. The ties among women throughout the country have contributed to an ever-broadening awareness of women's rights. The women's movement in Mali depends on these links between rural and urban, educated and uneducated women because misunderstandings and conflict between nonliterate and literate women have been commonplace in Mali. The conflict between women of different economic, social, and cultural backgrounds was exacerbated by the role that UNFM and other earlier centralized women's organizations played in perpetuating state interests rather than women's interests. This divide is evident today in the skepticism of some women with respect to Beijing.

Women frequently belong to numerous associations, each with its own purpose. In Mopti, most women interviewed were members of three to four associations. Several women were members of the Collectif des Femmes au Malil (COFEM), a politically focused collective of women. Other organizations listed were often professional associations or credit associations that provided funds to women on a rotating basis.[9] Credit associations have long been a part of Malian life. Of interest here is the explosion in the numbers of existing associations and the numerous groups to which any one individual belongs. The flourishing of associations, I argue, is a result of the events of 1991 that led to democratic elections in 1992. The environment in which rights and political participation are discussed freely is a result of Konaré's emphasis on dialogue as a mode of governing, as well as the role played by international donors encouraging transparency and democratic governance.

Growing Awareness of Women's Rights

Analysis of three women's associations, all of them active with respect to women's rights, may serve to illustrate the growing national dialogue. Reports from legal clinics of the AJM and ODEF provide a glimpse of how women are using these NGOs to access their rights. The AJM sponsored a mobile legal clinic that provided local women an opportunity to discuss issues directly affecting their lives. Lawyers from the AJM traveled to communities outside of Bamako and contributed to debates on citizen rights taking place in remote areas, thus creating one of the more successful arenas for discussing human rights. The AJM also spearheaded a radio show, *La Voix des Femmes*, broadcast on Radio Guintan nearly every day for a month. ODEF provided cliniques juridiques as well as debates concerning topics either selected by women within the target community or by ODEF members. Topics included the rights of women in marriage and parental obligations to the family. In one Bamako neighborhood, the women of the area requested a discussion of the sensitive matter of inheritance rights (ODEF 1997, n.p.). Such neighborhood meetings often included 50 to 100 people.

In addition, the seminars provided by GFDS in Mopti and Sikasso illustrate another forum used to raise awareness of women's rights in these regions. The seminars included representatives of women's associations throughout the region. For three days, participants learned the technicalities of presenting themselves as candidates as well as the intricacies of the Malian electoral system. In one instance, women from Yanfolila described how their local women's association had created a play in which they discussed the importance of women's voting and being politically active. They presented this skit at numerous locations in the area. While these examples cover only a brief period (1996–98), they give a sense of the issues that were of the most immediate concern to the participants.

With respect to the activities of both the AJM and ODEF, the primary issues discussed by participating women revolved around divorce. In many cases women are unaware of their rights in a marriage and their ability to end a marriage. In Ségou, 55 participants attended a clinic sponsored by the AJM in 1997 to discuss marriage law. During a clinic in Kayes, many questions revolved around divorce, monogamy, inheritance, and responsibilities within a marriage. In certain instances, women were assisted in assuring that their complaints were brought to court to be tried. Participants wondered, for instance, "what is the position of a married woman with respect to the monogamy settlement when the husband wants to re-marry?" Or with respect to inheritance and marriage, one participant asked, "In the case of the husband's death, how can the widow or widows be protected from abuse by their brothers-in-law (expulsion from the house)? Is it legal to divide the inheritance between married women and those who are divorced?" (ODEF 1996, 7). The AJM encouraged women to have civil weddings so that their rights are protected. A religious marriage, which is commonly practiced throughout the country without a civil procedure, does not legally bind the spouses in the eyes of secular law. While many Malians respect the obligations of religious marriages, others use the lack of a civil union to their advantage and leave their spouses without resources. A civil wedding at least provides the partners with legal recourse. As a result of this discussion, a participant asked, "Comment faire coordiner coutume et lois? Vous dites qu'on ne doit pas tenir compte de la croyance réligieuse pour accepter les mariages" ["How do we coordinate custom and law? You say that when we accept marriages, we must not take our religious beliefs into account"] (Karabenta 1996, 4).[10] Her concern was that with an emphasis on the importance of civil marriages, Malians would become less tolerant of religious differences and the dominent role that religion held over civil law.

In 1998, the AJM had planned a public awareness project concerning excision. In many of these forums, women often request that men be included in discussions concerning women's rights. In one extreme case, the AJM representatives arrived in Kasila, a village 45 kilometers from Bamako. The women who met them said they should go to greet the village chief. Upon arrival in the chief's compound, they found that all the men from the village had gathered together and wanted to know what the visitors planned to discuss with the women of the village. The anatomically explicit discussion concerning excision took place in front of the men, with a griot, a member of a certain caste (*jeliw*), asking questions for the participants. The topics being discussed are often viewed as not suitable for mixed audiences. The use of a griot to relay questions permits the asking of questions that may not be considered appropriate for discussion by other village men. Ironically, the representatives from the AJM were not able to speak to the women of the village that day because of the interest of the men in discussion on the topic. However, the chief encouraged the women to return and discuss the same information with the women, as previously planned.[11] This example is important in that it illustrates aspects of Malian culture that impact the discussion of rights. In this instance, men, who are so often excluded from public awareness campaigns, were involved in this campaign to stop excision. And it is hoped that the women of Kasila were able to participate in the campaign as well.

Each of these clinics was held in a small town, outside of the capital, and regularly included 50 participants, and in some instances, more than 100. The clinic in Markala included 128 participants.[12] It is in these forums that traditions are often discussed and questioned. Women are curious about how constitutional law protects them and how this relates to traditional practice. For example, in Bamako, the need to revise the practice of dowry was raised in an ODEF clinic (ODEF 1995, n.p.). This newly created discursive space thus allows for deliberation over the importance of the various types of law that function in Mali—secular, religious, and traditional.

In addition to legal clinics, AJM also created a support unit for the exercise of civic rights by citizens, which began in December 1995. Funding for these projects comes from such sources as USAID, CECI Canada, and Coopération Belge, and the discussion supports the education of Malian citizens. It is increasingly evident that there is a dependence between the international arena and the national, regional, and local discussions that center on the constitution, its protections of Malian citizens, especially women, and that this dependence blurs the divide that exists between "authentic" and "Western influenced."

The first GFDS seminar on women's civic and political rights took place in Sevaré, with participants from all over the Mopti region. The second was in Sikasso and once again included a wide array of selected participants who were representatives of women's associations. It was hoped that these women would form the foundation needed to create networks of women in more remote areas that would encourage women's active political participation. Follow-up on the results of the seminar in Sevaré revealed that several participants gave lack of money as the reason so little networking had taken place since the seminar. However, women in Bandiagara, in Dogon country, were very successful in using a federation of women's associations to continue dialogue on rights at the village level across this very rural area.

Nation Building and the Discourse on Human Rights

As Malian women discuss voting in rural areas and encourage both political participation and dialogue on civic rights, they contribute to the transition toward a more democratic nation. The AJM distributed posters and fliers that used female characters to promote peaceful participation in elections as well as an awareness among men and women of the role for both sexes in the electoral process. President Konaré has stated, "Democracy has given us social dialogue as a method of government. . . . The more people participate, the more importance they attach to the work of building our nation. With participation and transparency we have managed to limit ethnic tensions that tear at so many African countries" (French 1996, A3). Critical to this quote is the notion of a link between dialogue and nation building. While Konaré emphasized the role of dialogue in reducing ethnic tension, I wish to consider the importance of women in this process. The networks described earlier in this chapter are instrumental in extending the dialogue on rights into rural areas. As a consequence, the growing role of women in politics and development has reflected a positive image upon the majority party Alliance pour la Démocratie au Mali, internationally and locally. In this way, the government benefits from encouraging women's participation in the increasingly decentralized dialogue on rights.

In this chapter, I have considered the ways in which women are promoting a discourse on rights. This discourse, I argue, is directly linked to nation building and constitutionalism. Central to the constitutional project must be participation on the part of the citizenry and knowledge of constitutionally protected rights at all levels of society. Hence, constitutional literacy plays a critical role in democratization. By leading the drive to promote discussion concerning laws that affect their lives, women empower all citizens to learn about their rights and to use them. Women contribute immensely to the development of constitutionalism in Mali by helping to create an open discourse on rights within the state.

Conclusions

Some scholars have argued that resistance to the Beijing Platform stemmed from "conservative male-dominated religious institutions, states, and movements" (L. West 1999, 187). Yet, such criticism negates the validity of arguments made by women who did not attend the Beijing conference and complain of a gap between the discussions in Beijing and their own realities. In the sense that these realities are based on the status quo, they represent conservative views. While examples throughout this chapter illustrate the connections between the global discourse on rights and local initiatives, it is important to recognize the ways in which the discourse was adapted to Mali. Specifically, Beijing was rarely referred to directly by women leaders promoting women's rights, neither by those who had attended the conference nor by those who had not; instead, reference was frequently made to Mali's new democracy and the role of dialogue within it. Helping to build a more democratic nation and women's role in this nation-building effort became central to discussions on rights.

No movement can be successful without a strong foundation with a basis in local values. Just such a foundation is being created today in Mali through women's associations and their networks across the country. Certainly resentment existed between Malian women who were compensated to attend the Beijing conference and those who were rebuffed by the CPF when they sought funds to promote their own small-scale projects. The CPF and the Konaré regime were forced to balance demands on meager resources and pay more attention to issues critical to *la base*. True dialogue within *concertations régionales* was part of the solution.

The gender-sensitive development index, created by the United Nations Development Program provides a measure for quality of life, including life expectancy, educational attainment and income, as adjusted for gender disparities (Seager 1997, 104). Mali is one of the 10 countries in the world with the widest gap between men and women; more than 45 percent of Malian families are polygamous (Seager 1997, 16, 19). Today, thanks to legal reforms, Malian women can marry and sign a pact of monogamy with their husbands. While problems still exist, this marks a significant change from the recent past in which a woman had little choice in the man she would marry, let alone who else he might choose to marry in the future. Though it is certainly true that entry into the political sphere is limited at first, it is important to recognize the strides that have been made and consider whether men have as much control as is suggested. Do they have the ability to "allow" women to act in certain ways, or will women continue to unite and choose how to challenge male authority and when to do so? In Mali, marriage law, inheritance rights, and excision are key issues now being discussed across the country. Slowly, changes are taking place with respect to excision and dowry. With reference to education, criticisms have been made concerning male-biased classrooms and the need to provide environments that are conducive to learning for both males and females (Soumaré 1995). Such changes have an effect on the control that men will be able to exercise over women.

During the Sikasso seminar women were asked whether their husbands influenced their vote in elections. The overwhelming majority of participants stated that they voted for the candidate of their choice, not necessarily one their husbands preferred. One woman acknowledged pressure from her husband and was encouraged by other women to insist on her right to vote as she wished. If that was not possible, they suggested, she could simply remain nonconfrontational and vote behind the curtain for whomever she wanted to support. Her choice would always be secret. If asked for whom she had voted, the other women encouraged deception if she felt threatened by her husband. This example illustrates the ways that women currently come together to support one another, recognizing the conflicts that other women may face within their marriages. By offering support to their co-participant, they encouraged her at least to follow her own path, even if she did not wish to confront her husband openly.

In Mali, as Barbara Callaway (1991) argues in the case of Kano, Nigeria, men are not likely to give up their positions of power to women, so while they support women's education and political activism, religious and traditional law concerning inheritance are rarely challenged. Traditional law and religious law today provide a similar backdrop to the discussion that cultural norms and morals provided in the late-nineteenth and early-twentieth-century struggle for universal suffrage in the United States, as well as the long debate over the ill-fated Equal Rights Amendment. In each case, there exists a fear of altering the roles traditionally ascribed to men and women. As Malians deliberate their understandings of traditions and cultural preservation in their new nation, the rights of individuals versus those of ethnic groups are central to the debate. A leader of the struggle for women's rights expressed clearly the conflicts that they face. She noted, "I am in favor of culture, but never culture that oppresses women."[13]

Notes

I wish to thank Aminata Maiga Touré and Fatoumata Dembélé Diarra for their guidance while I was in Mali conducting research for this chapter. In addition, Richard L. Sklar, Carole Pateman, and Edmond J. Keller must be thanked for their comments on previous drafts. I am also indebted to all the women in Mali who spent countless hours sharing stories and insights about Malian politics.

1. See the autobiography of Soudan Aoua Kéita (1975), *Femme d'Afrique,* for analysis of politics and colonialism.

2. These numbers are useful in that they show the gender disparity. However, they are not an accurate account of the nearly 2,000 participants in the conference. Even with an increase in numbers, the gender ratio would be unlikely to have changed.

3. When resources are scarce, boys are given preference and attend school. Girls, if lucky enough to go to school, are often removed for marriage at an early age, or withheld because they are perceived as a risk (it is often feared that they will return pregnant, frequently the result of rape).

4. Interviews with CADEF and ODEF. See UNICEF and RDM 1998.

5. Interview, Hippodrome, Bamako, February 1998.

6. GFDS seminar, Sikasso, April 1998.

7. Interviews conducted in Bamako, August 1994.

8. Interview March 11, 1998, at the Coordination de la Promotion des Femmes.

9. Ibid.

10. Unfortunately, unlike other AJM reports, this one does not include responses given to participants.

11. Interview with Mme Bouaré Bintou Samaké, AJM, March 18, 1998.

12. See above Ségou reports, 11–13.

13. Interview, November 12, 1997, Badalabougou.

IV
Activism in and against the Transnational State

12

The Limits of Microcredit

Transnational Feminism and USAID Activities in the United States and Morocco

Winifred Poster and Zakia Salime

As one of the most active and dominant nongovernmental organizations (NGOs) for women's causes, the United States Agency for International Development (USAID) has been instrumental in establishing transnational alliances among women in the last decade. It has done this by sponsoring global conferences, by linking international organizations like the United Nations to grassroots organizations, and by funding local associations that provide services to women. However, such activities are also highly contested, with questions raised about whose interests are actually represented. Many feminist scholars have begun to reassess USAID, critically examining its efforts in various regions of the world.

In order to observe more directly the *transnational* influences on these dynamics, however, we compare USAID-sponsored organizations in *two* contexts—the United States and Morocco. Activists in these locations organize around the common theme of microcredit, yet the type of women involved and the strategies they propose vary considerably. We start in the United States with the USAID head office in Washington, D.C., where its global microcredit policy is formulated, and Chicago, where USAID hosted its annual International Women's Business Conference in 1999, convening entrepreneurs and political leaders from around the world for discussions of microcredit. Subsequently, we turn to Fez, Morocco, and the Moroccan Association for Solidarity without Borders, a USAID-funded grassroots women's organization administering microcredit to poor women. Although slightly different in their organizational forms, both of these settings represent locations where microcredit discourse is constructed and implemented. We contrast them to reveal how—within the larger context of USAID—activism surrounding microcredit transforms across the North and South.

Through participant observation, document analysis, and in-depth interviews of these organizational contexts, we address two issues. First, we contrast the First World *discourses* of microcredit as a global strategy for women's empowerment, with the Third World *application* and *experience* of these policies. In particular, we chart the contradictions in policies that aim to put women at the center of development programs, but have unintended consequences in shifting the responsibility of household income support from men to women, and household labor from women to their daughters. Similarly, policies aimed at invoking "solidarity" among women (by disbursing loans to groups rather than individuals) have counterproductive effects in creating tensions as well as cooperation among women. Second, we discuss the international political relations that obstruct the process of organizing among women's microcredit groups locally and transnationally. We reveal a complicated transnational web of funding, which involves not only the international agencies and the state, but varying forms of big and small local women's organizations. The resulting hierarchy among the NGOs hampers the possibility of linkages of women's microcredit associations—either within the same region or across national borders. Thus, rather than being the savior of poor women around the world, these microcredit programs and the highly tense relations they create among NGOs, the state, and international donors can be antithetical to women's empowerment and transnational feminist movements.

Globalization and the Context of Women and Microcredit

At the heart of the microcredit trend is the process of globalization. In particular, dynamics of economic restructuring, development discourse, and NGOs have been crucial in shaping the discourses of microcredit for women—especially in the South. To start with, restructuring of the global economy has severely restricted labor market opportunities for Third World women. This has been especially accelerated by the "structural adjustment programs" of international financial institutions such as the World Bank and the International Monetary Fund (IMF). Their programs for allocating loans to poor countries and the attached debt repayment policies have devastated local economies, particularly by requiring governments to devalue their currencies and suspend basic social services like health care and education. Women are hit the hardest by such measures: They face an intensified burden from taking on second jobs, a reduction in food and clothing as the limited household resources typically go to men, and an increase in violence (Ault and Sandberg 1997). Furthermore, these programs hurt women in terms of access to formal-sector jobs. In Morocco, for instance, women were deliberately blocked from many occupations during the 1980s when structural adjustment was at a peak: "Public administrations favored male candidacy and rejected the female ones under the pretext that during economic crises it is more appropriate to offer jobs to men and not to women" (Daoud 1993). This unequal access to jobs by gender was sustained during the 1990s as well; the rate of women's employment decreased from 17 to 16 percent between 1995 and 1998, while the rate for men increased from 52 to 53 percent (Secretary of State 1999).

Partly in response to this phenomenon, there has been another major trend within global economic restructuring affecting women in the South—the rise of the *informal* economy. Informal work is defined as unprotected labor (Ward 1990), which means that it is neither "on the books" of employers nor recognized or regulated by the state (Collins and Gimenez 1990). It usually includes activities such as domestic services, commerce and trading, small-scale home production of handicrafts or food to sell on the market, or subcontracting of illicit products within homes or semicovert enterprises. Although once thought to be a passing phenomenon, the informal economy has been thriving, particularly since the 1980s (Benería 2000; Portes, Castells, and Benton 1989). Moreover, with shrinking opportunities in formal-sector markets, informal work has become especially important for women as they look for sources of income. Because informal work straddles the formal economy and household, it often "provides the intermediate link" between public and private spheres and the most accessible form of paid work for women (Ward 1990). Thus, in many regions of the world—especially Africa—women represent the large majority of informal workers, as well as the majority of informal economy contributors to national gross domestic products (GDPs) (Benería 2001).

Not surprisingly, there is a great deal of gender stratification in informal work. Women typically participate in the informal economy to subsidize their earnings and maintain the class position of their families, whereas men do so as a profit-seeking endeavor and often as a means of occupational mobility. In turn, while men's informal work is characterized by high pay, opportunity, and power, women's work is more often poorly paid, isolating, and routine. Many also argue that women's work in the informal economy is central in maintaining the global capitalist system: It provides services that sustain households, augments wages for families on the brink of poverty, and allows capitalists to bypass expensive and politically threatening labor relations that exist in the formal economy.

While economic restructuring has reshaped the patterns of women's labor market activities, dynamics of "development" have reshaped the orientations that international agencies have taken regarding aid to poor women. Promotion of self-employment has increasingly become the dominant model of assistance to women in the Third World. This has come largely in response to the "successes" of the Grameen Bank in Bangladesh. Started in 1976, this bank began by giving small loans to men and shifted to women in 1983 (Kabeer 1999). It experienced such high rates of return (90 percent) on such large volumes ($500 million in 1995) that it no longer requires sponsorship from governments or international agencies

(McMichael 2000). This model is being replicated around the world now, and women are being targeted in larger and larger proportions.

The broader source of this shift lies in paradigms of foreign aid in the North. Some argue that strategies for alleviating poverty have transformed over the last century from "development," which favored nation-states as the agents, to "globalization," which favors international markets, financial institutions, and corporations as agents (McMichael 2000). This has accompanied a change in focus from "development as charity" to "development as business," in which private lending associations are favored over public service agencies to assist the poor. Microcredit has an important role in this context:

> [T]he development community is riding the microcredit band-wagon given that it is consistent with the dominant paradigm of self-help, decentralization, and stimulating "social capital" at the local level to promote community-based entrepreneurship, and given that structural adjustment programs have forced the poor into self-employment. (McMichael 2000, 295–96)

Feminist critics point out that these forms of aid rely upon a neoliberal economic agenda of development through individual women rather than through structural changes in the economy (Kabeer 1999; Prugl 1996). Along these lines, we argue that the discourses of microcredit in USAID also divert attention (intentionally or unintentionally) from the disastrous effects of IMF and World Bank austerity measures, and deflect the potential for more transformative programs of women's economic advancement outside of the informal economy.

Finally, a third dynamic of globalization that has affected the role of microcredit for women is the growth of NGOs. These organizations—which export microcredit programs from the First World and implement them in Third World countries—have increased exponentially over the last decade. Indeed, at least half of the women's NGOs in Morocco were founded after 1985 (Ministry of Employment and Social Affairs 1995). This trend has been prompted by privatization, the massive withdrawal of many Southern governments from the public sector, and the resulting increase in need for community-based services by the poor. The dynamics of NGOs become important, however, in terms of their capacity to negotiate between international sponsors and local grassroots women. Moreover, recently there has been lively debate among scholars as to whether NGOs hinder or promote women's empowerment and international solidarity (Tinker 1999a). Some characterize the debate in terms of two views (Basu 2000a): one in which transnational women's organizations are eclipsing and co-opting local associations through their linkages with the state (Alvarez 1999), and another in which NGOs are helping local associations thrive by creating viable global feminist networks (Moghadam 2000).

We would like to contribute to this debate by revealing a case where both trends seem to be emerging. First, we find consistencies with the "cooptation" thesis, but also argue that the picture is more complicated than previously portrayed. Rather than simply an issue of NGOs co-opting local movements, the case of USAID in the United States and Morocco demonstrates the existence of many other mediating factors: namely the state and its interests in privileging some NGOs over others, the hierarchical relations among NGOs, and the precarious interests of the international agencies, which shift frequently. Moreover, dynamics of NGOs are also related to the class politics of the NGO leaders themselves, and their conflicting interests in seeking state and international support, in meeting the needs of their clients, and also in enforcing their middle-class development agendas on working-class women (Alexander and Mohanty 1997; Staudt 1990). Thus, it is the relationship of all these factors that creates tensions for leaders of grassroots NGOs.

Second, we also find some evidence of local benefits to transnational networking. However, we find that the opportunities for this are highly constricted by the relations among the above actors. Local grassroots associations in Morocco are permitted to engage in such activities only when powerful NGOs and the state provide an occasion to do so. In fact, even *regional* networking among microcredit associations is impeded by hierarchies among the NGOs. Thus, we need to ask how it is possible to find opportunities for *international* feminist linkages in the context of transnational organizational webs.

We did field work in two locations using participant observation, interview, and document analysis methods. From the United States, we examined USAID's official policy through reports, policy statements, and congressional addresses produced by its head office in Washington, D.C., and we participated in an international microcredit conference held in 1999 in Chicago, Illinois: "Lessons without Borders: Women Mean Business." From Morocco, we conducted a case study of a USAID-sponsored NGO, the Moroccan Solidarity without Borders Association. This research was conducted in December 2000, through interviews with organization leaders, agents who administer the loans, and women who receive the loans. We also observed two of seven microcredit centers where women come to pay their loans, visited with clients in their homes, and analyzed NGO and Moroccan government documents.

Our study begins by looking at USAID in the United States context with an analysis of its head office policy and its Chicago conference. In this section, we highlight the principal elements of USAID microcredit philosophy and the way it reflects the interests of the North. We also reveal how this philosophy is adopted and articulated by world microcredit leaders as they gather for the conference. From there, we move to Morocco and explore the dynamics of USAID microcredit programs in the South. We examine the complicated network of local and international actors shaping the operations of a grassroots microcredit NGO. Then we trace the series of events that shifts the relation between USAID and the NGO, and creates different tensions for NGO leaders and clients. We conclude by emphasizing the disjuncture between the formation of microcredit policy in the North and its implementation in the South, and the obstacles this process poses for transnational feminist activism through NGOs.

A View of USAID in the First World

USAID is one of many international funding organizations from the United States that supports women's development activities worldwide. What makes this one unique, however, is that it is sponsored by the U.S. government. USAID began its formal commitment to women's issues in 1973, when the Foreign Assistance Act was amended to include the incorporation of women into national economies as part of the foreign aid policy (Lycette 1999). Shortly after, USAID set up an Office of Women in Development (WID), which was crucial in eliminating many of the egregious male biases in USAID policy that had existed to that point. For example, the agency began collecting data on women as well as men, and including women in programs that had previously been reserved for men. In addition, the WID office developed specific programs to enhance the role of women in the development process, such as those on family planning and educational enhancement.

The Philosophy of Microcredit

Microcredit, or a small-business loan, is the primary *economic* component of the WID agenda. In this paradigm, access to credit for running one's own business is seen as the best strategy for promoting labor market opportunity for women. The ideological rationale for such an agenda is rooted in a neoliberal framework in which empowerment is achieved through individual means. It is a bottom-up approach to development, in which women are responsible for raising their own economic status by means of small amounts of cash. In such a framework, there is little consideration for structural barriers to that process or any collective responsibility by the state, NGOs, social service organizations, or others. Moreover, it is a policy that focuses narrowly on women, sometimes without regard for the larger context of their families, social networks, or communities.

Thus, the practical aim of the program has been to raise the participation of women in self-employment to that of men. WID stipulates: "Country strategies, projects and programs should be designed so that . . . the percentage of women who receive benefits would be in approximate proportion to their traditional participation in the activity or their proportion of the population—whichever is greater"

(Lycette 1999, 2). In other words, gender parity is the officially stated priority for women's economic empowerment. What is interesting about the microcredit program, however, is that WID shifted from a view that "microcredit is good for women" to a view that "women are good for microcredit." Not only did WID start to target women as recipients for the program, but it decided to make these programs *predominantly female*. In a report to the U.S. Congress, WID directors stated,

> USAID's Microenterprise Development programs . . . bring a special focus on women. Overall, USAID supports loans and business services for a clientele of microentrepreneurs that is more than 50 percent female. In many cases, women constitute up to 90 percent of entrepreneurs receiving services of loans for business development. In recent years, this has translated into approximately $150 million a year focused on women business owners. USAID has maintained this focus on women as entrepreneurs for over a decade and will continue to do so in future programming. (USAID 1999, 20)

The question becomes, then, If the larger USAID mission is for *proportional representation* of women to that of the larger population or the economic activity, why are microcredit programs weighted to favor women? With much candidness, the director of USAID notes, "In microenterprise, there was no particular compelling rationale, at least in the 1970s and early 1980s, for a focus on improving the lot of women entrepreneurs. [Yet] . . . when women were included in microenterprise projects (initially, inadvertently), we saw very strong performance: high repayment rates, good project success" (Lycette, 1999, 2–3). Thus, the motivation for this focus on women has less to do with any philosophical commitment to "women and development" than with practical issues of loan repayment and program success.

Indeed, the relation of USAID to its own funding source, the U.S. government, is an important factor in how WID orients its policy. Because of its quest for external legitimacy, USAID seeks to prove its "success"—both in terms of global representation of its programs and financial security of the loans. One of the immediate effects of the WID policy agenda is a passion for numbers. USAID leaders aim to illustrate that microcredit has reached the largest number of women possible around the world. Their documents on women's participation in microcredit read like stock market reports: "During 1996, USAID microenterprise programs in 54 countries supported more than 300 institutions. More than 1 million clients were reached . . . with the average loan size about $300—more than two-thirds of the clients were women" (USAID n.d.-c). Indeed, quantitative measures are used exclusively as indicators of women's empowerment. In its report to Congress, WID lists its measures of program success as the number of clients receiving small business loans, gross educational enrollments by sex, increases in annual achievement test scores by third-graders, the percentage of women voters who vote in elections, and similar measures (USAID 1999). WID is particularly proud of the program in Morocco, where success is measured in terms of "the number of business licenses granted to women." Under this framework of getting as many women as possible involved in microcredit, the success of the program is defined in purely quantitative terms—rather than in the *quality* of women's lives. Neglect of the latter issue leads to many unintended consequences for how the programs affect women's daily lives. Problems are also evident in the way USAID regulates the terms and conditions of funding for microcredit programs in NGOs.

The Terms and Conditions of Microcredit Programs

One of the most significant effects of the WID discourse for NGOs in Third World countries is the issue of gender within the funding requirements. USAID has recently included the number of women participating in the program as a condition for support: "The extent to which field Missions are addressing gender issues in their programming can now be a factor in how much funding they receive for future programming" (Lycette, 1999, 4). With such a condition, NGOs are effectively discouraged from including men in their programs. While such a plan sounds as if it would help women, it can have the opposite effect on their household dynamics, as we will illustrate below.

Another consequence of the WID discourse is that *informal* sector programs are favored over those in the *formal* sector, even though the conditions of the informal work are insecure and there are often serious risks to women's safety (Boris and Prügl 1996; Collins and Gimenez 1990). However, development programs tend to favor this type of work for microcredit, since informal-sector jobs are already widely available to women, and are much easier to promote than formal-sector jobs. A USAID policy statement asserts, "Special programs of non-formal education and vocational training must be provided to help these women develop skills for employment in the formal sector and increased income earning opportunities in the informal sector" (USAID 1982). Formal-sector jobs are included in the general plan, but only in terms of "non-formal education and vocational training"—in other words, premarket skill enhancement rather than market-based material support. Thus, it is only in the informal sector that USAID provides financial resources in the form of microcredit loans. The problematic aspect of this approach is that USAID enhances women's opportunities in highly erratic and unprotected sectors of the economy, rather than through job creation in the more secure and unionized sector of the formal economy.

A third condition of funding that emerges from this agenda is a particular arrangement for disbursing microcredit loans to women entrepreneurs called the "solidarity group." Rather than providing loans to individual women, USAID requires that loans be allocated to small groups. A regional report explains the rationale for this:

> Microenterprise development is an economic strategy well-suited to local urban communities. Lending to groups rather than individuals creates group solidarity, which, in turn, harnesses peer pressure and peer support. It also represents an opportunity for empowerment of local communities through education and training, not just access to capital. (USAID n.d.-a)

Under the rhetoric of "solidarity," these programs promise that group lending will promote cohesion and "support" among poor women; microcredit will be conducive to and complementary to other development programs, like education and training; and finally, giving microcredit to groups of women will enhance the community as a whole. Indeed, there is a taken-for-granted and unreflective tone to discourses such as these that fails to consider the incongruities of such policies with the lived experiences of women receiving the loans. In fact, few of these promises are fulfilled in the case of the Moroccan women in our study, as we will show below; solidarity groups create as much tension as they do cohesion; microcredit creates so much work for women that it overshadows the possibility of participating in other development programs; moreover, microcredit ultimately traps low-income families in their socioeconomic position rather than enabling mobility.

Finally, it is important to note that, couched within these grand pronouncements of support for poor women in Third World countries, there are also subtle hints of tension in USAID policy when it comes to the local NGOs that represent such women. This is particularly true of USAID's orientation toward grassroots organizations, which is sometimes articulated in distrustful terms:

> Typically, organizations selected to undertake income-generating activities for women have had little technical expertise and yet have been selected because they are organizations exclusively of women. The objectives of these programs tend to be welfare-oriented and ill-defined; their activities often fail to provide women with real opportunities for generating income over the long term. AID should support the upgrading and development of implementing institutions based on their technical capability or potential expertise. AID will support the funding of women-specific organizations only to the extent that they meet with this criterion. (USAID 1982, 11)

Indeed, USAID—like many other First World funding agencies—has a tendency to differentiate NGOs according to what they consider "responsible" versus "irresponsible" local associations when it comes to managing money and instituting microcredit programs. The implicit bias in these categorizations is that "technical expertise" is often valued over being "women specific." Moreover, the former qualities are more often found in the wealthier, state-supported NGOs than in the poorer, autonomous ones. Indeed, "responsibility" is determined not so much in terms of representing the interests of grassroots women but in terms of financial and bureaucratic viability. Such categorizations are harmful because they contribute to the hierarchies among local NGOs, which is a central issue in our analysis here.

Organizing for Microcredit in Chicago

In the summer of 1999 , USAID hosted the Second Annual International Women's Business Conference in Chicago. The conference is connected to a particular initiative of USAID called "Lessons without Borders," established in 1994 through a collaboration of USAID Administrator Brian Atwood and former vice president Al Gore. The purpose was to promote an exchange between policy planners and community activists across national borders, to share development strategies, and find mutual solutions to a variety of problems, like those of health care and education. The program's interest in microcredit led to the establishment of an annual conference with the theme "Women Mean Business: A Global Exchange."

What this event shows with respect to our study is how WID discourses were articulated and reproduced on a global scale. Indeed, the neoliberal formula for women's empowerment was appropriated by policymakers and local businesswomen alike. In addition, many of the USAID policies were legitimated with new discourses not necessarily present in the organization's formal documents. Finally, even the most economically marginalized women at the conference reproduced this agenda as well, illustrating the power of the discourse as it travels the globe.

The Participants

The participants of the meeting reflected the global elite of microcredit campaigns. Several hundred politicians, businesspeople, and activists (mostly female) from 30 countries attended. The conference also included a number of high-profile speakers, including Queen Rania of Jordan, USAID Ambassador Harriet C. Babbitt, Illinois Senator Richard Durbin, and—via videotaped message—former first lady Hillary Rodham Clinton. The majority of the other speakers were microcredit planners: bank representatives, representatives of consulting companies, government officials, and leaders of nonprofit service organizations or NGOs. In addition, there were a few microcredit recipients—the "exemplary" ones—who had received loans and achieved great success with them. Conspicuously absent from speaking roles in these meetings were the intended beneficiaries of USAID microcredit. According to its stated goals for the microcredit program, Lessons without Borders' first aim is to "assist the efforts of the poor, especially women" (USAID n.d.-b). However, few of these people were represented as speakers in the 25 sessions at this event. Rather, members of USAID-sponsored NGOs, flown in from around the world (and who constituted roughly two-thirds of the conference participants) were meant to observe the "experts" rather than talk with them. This disjuncture led to a number of tensions and contradictions in articulating women's policy strategies.

Discourses of the Global Elite

Speakers at the large-scale events of the conference—the keynote and plenary sessions—invoked the individual-based, neoliberal paradigm regarding the sources and solutions of women's economic disadvantage. Several presenters emphasized how the central problem for women is restricted access to capital. For example, Hillary Clinton spoke of women being turned away from banks, and Ambassador Babbitt emphasized that women worldwide are left out of economic decision-making processes. Maria Otero of Accion International remarked that less than 10 percent of self-employment credit loans are given to women and that, therefore, what is needed is to "value women's contributions in business, expand women's economic opportunities, and bring an urgency to women's business worldwide." Thus, the prevailing ideology of women's subordination involves blocked opportunities to credit.

In turn, if barriers to capital are the problem, then small-business loans are the solution. Even when some speakers expressed the need for a variety of strategies to empower women, they still pointed to microcredit as the central vehicle. Queen Rania stated, in her keynote address,

> There are many ways to increase women's economic opportunities. . . . A key component is expanding access to credit. Microfinance has proven to be an experience worth being shared and further developed throughout the world. Numerous communities are beginning to benefit from outcomes, and we should look into ways to expand its effects as a tool for socio-economic development. (Rania 1999)

Indeed, the general tone of the conference reflected this unquestioning support for microcredit and its potential.

The discourses by these world leaders also reflected a new legitimation of the gender focus of microcredit programs, which involved a particular characterization of women's innate abilities in managing business matters. Many speakers similarly commented on women's strengths in juggling multiple demands—and still achieving amazing feats. Ambassador Babbitt cited women's talent in "multitasking" as their biggest competitive advantage as entrepreneurs. Likewise, one of the most popular speeches came from the representative of Shorebank Advisory Services, who used an image from Bangladesh to capture this theme. She described a poster of Laxmi, a goddess with many hands, each tending to a different task simultaneously: one caring for children, one cooking dinner, one carrying water, one caring for her husband, and yet another running a street vending business. This Laxmi image was then invoked by speaker after speaker in the subsequent presentations, as a model of how capable women are in handling microcredit.

What is especially notable about this discourse, however, is the way it used in conjunction with "poor, Third World women" and the context of development. Indeed, the valorization of poor women's skills in "single-handedly" solving their own problems (as well as those of their families) reinforces the notion that development is best treated from the bottom up, and that woman should be starting point (UNIFEM 2000). When phrased in these terms, poor women are constructed as superbeings who are inherently capable of overcoming the entire weight of development single-handedly—that is, pending their microcredit disbursement. In such a scenario, why should anyone ask men, the state, unions, or international bodies to interfere? But as flattering as it may seem to praise women's multiple skills, this ideology has problematic implications in justifying development schemes that place much of the responsibility on women. Ultimately, this rhetoric of the self-empowering Third World woman provides a rationale—where before there was little—for the women-centered policies of USAID.

Voices from Below: Reproducing the Discourses

Even though there were few opportunities to hear from the microcredit recipients themselves at this event, the voices we did hear from the Third World tended to reflect these same themes. The small-business and NGO leaders from industrializing countries reproduced the uncritical discourses regarding microcredit and its role in development. From Bolivia, a microcredit director said that "loan giving would break the cycle of dependency among the poor," and that women merely need to "seize opportunities" and "take risks" to enhance their economic power. A leader of an entrepreneur association in Ghana pointed out tensions of infrastructure and international debt in her country, but ultimately advocated strategies of building "networks for partnerships" and "sharing of information on the availability of goods and technology" rather than any material or structural changes in policy.

The discourses of nonwhite speakers from the United States also reinforced the self-empowering themes of poor women. An African-American entrepreneur described the astounding hurdles she overcame to build a successful business in the food industry—Michele Foods. She began as a divorced, welfare-dependent, single mother of three girls, who wanted to start a business. After selling all of her possessions for startup capital, she moved into her mother's house, where she manufactured products in the basement. After surviving years of hard physical work—and a brain tumor—she finally achieved a nationally recognized business. She attributes this success to the multigenerational contributions of the women in her family, once again legitimizing the notion that poor women are expected to build their own support networks when enduring severe hardships.

The purpose of this discussion is not to place blame on these women microcredit leaders, because many of them have devoted their lives to increasing opportunities for underprivileged women—some at much personal cost. For example, a woman from Latin America described how she was stigmatized by colleagues and society for just proposing the idea of loans for the poor. Similarly, although many of the proposed solutions for women's economic problems tended to be at the individual rather than structural level, they are still important in breaking the isolation for women entrepreneurs. This was articulated well by a South African construction contractor who said she had never met another female business owner in her country, much less from other regions of the world.

Instead, the aim of the discussion is to examine how the subtle and not-so-subtle dynamics of a conference such as this coalesce to reinforce the WID agenda of microcredit. One key factor is the lack of representation by microcredit recipients at the WID conference. Another is the lack of critical perspectives toward microcredit. There were few forums in the conference to express alternative views to this prevailing ideology, nor any events to discuss the philosophy or implementation of microcredit programs. There were sessions, however, on business strategy, technology, and human capacities, but no sessions on how to run a microcredit program or what some of the obstacles might be. Thus, this conference illustrates how USAID policy is being formed and supported at the First World level, and how even Third World microcredit leaders are adopting this dominant discourse leading to its exportation around the world.

A View of USAID in the Third World

We illustrate some of the difficulties of transporting these policies overseas and implementing them at the grassroots level through the case of the Moroccan Association for Solidarity without Borders (AMSSF), a USAID-funded, grassroots microcredit organization in Morocco. We argue that the obstacles faced by AMSSF are rooted in the ideology of microcredit, and in the transnational bureaucratic web in which it must operate. We also argue that the resulting tensions are experienced differently by AMSSF leaders and AMSSF clients: Organizational leaders feel strain as they attempt to maintain and expand their grassroots service organization within a hierarchy of NGO, state, and foreign actors; members feel strain as they negotiate the demands of microenterprise activities, with those of the NGO programs, their families and households.

AMSSF started its activity in 1989 as a sociocultural NGO in the city of Fez. Originally, it provided training programs in sewing and embroidery, but this metamorphosed into a microcredit program in 1993 when some members wanted to set up an individual microenterprise. In order to respond to the community, AMSSF leaders sought USAID funding. With this support, AMSSF increased its membership from two clients to about 600 over the period of 1993 to 1997, and eventually to about 2,000 between 1997 and the present (the relevance of these periods will become clear below).

The major activity for which AMSSF clients seek microcredit is informal trade, which is the case in many other regions of the world as well (Blumberg 2001). Many of the clients are poor immigrants from rural regions around Morocco, who end up geographically isolated in the suburbs of Fez where job opportunities are particularly scarce. Therefore, many travel at least once a week to the Spanish border in northern Morocco (fig. 12.1) to buy European wholesale goods (especially clothing, home furniture, and auto parts) that are cheaper than those made in Morocco because there are no taxes. The rest of the week, microentrepreneurs commute to various regions of Morocco, primarily to the rural areas near Fez, where they sell their goods to retailers at open markets.

These women receive loans ranging from 200 DH ($20) to 1,500 DH ($150) to support such activities. There are many conditions and requirements for these loans. Payments must be submitted on a weekly basis, and no matter the amount of the loan, the total reimbursement is due within a period of four months. If loans are paid off in this time period, the client is eligible for another loan of a higher amount. The maximum loan, however, for any individual at any point in their membership with the organization is 1,500 DH. (The loan amounts and requirements change when AMSSF switches its sponsor organization, so that its current policies are slightly different). Another important condition (which does not change) is that loans are provided only to groups of five—not to individual microentrepreneurs. Thus, there is one loan per group, and one payment per group. If one member of the group is not ready to repay the loan on time, the other members must pay for her/him.

At present, the organizational structure of AMSSF includes a central administrative office and seven service centers around the country, at which 22 agents directly manage the loans. These agents often make individual trips to each member's home. Aside from microcredit programs, AMSSF also offers development programs in literacy, health, and rights.

The Context: A Transnational Web of Aid

AMSSF grew as an organization through a complex web of transnational and local actors. Although it started as an autonomous grassroots organization providing microcredit for poor entrepreneurs, it was able to maintain itself and expand its activities only through international support. There are several international and national actors in the story of AMSSF (see fig. 12.2). The first is USAID. In the early 1990s, USAID sought to provide development assistance in Morocco but did not want to deal directly with the public. Rather, its interest was in working through mediating organizations, which it considered more experienced and trustworthy. Therefore, it turned to the second group involved in this scenario—the big NGOs. USAID provided funds to one big NGO—Catholic Relief Services (CRS), a U.S.-based world wide organization operating with offices in Morocco among other nations (Salahdine 1992). CRS, in turn, created and allocated funds to another NGO—the Moroccan Association for Solidarity and Development (AMSED). AMSED is another big NGO, but one that has more familiarity with grassroots organizations better than CRS because of its local origins in Morocco.

However, because AMSED does not have direct contact with clients, it in turn delegated this responsibility to yet another organization. This was AMSSF, a member of the third group in the NGO web—the small NGOs. AMSSF is considered such partly because of its size, but more for its grassroots orientation. AMSSF

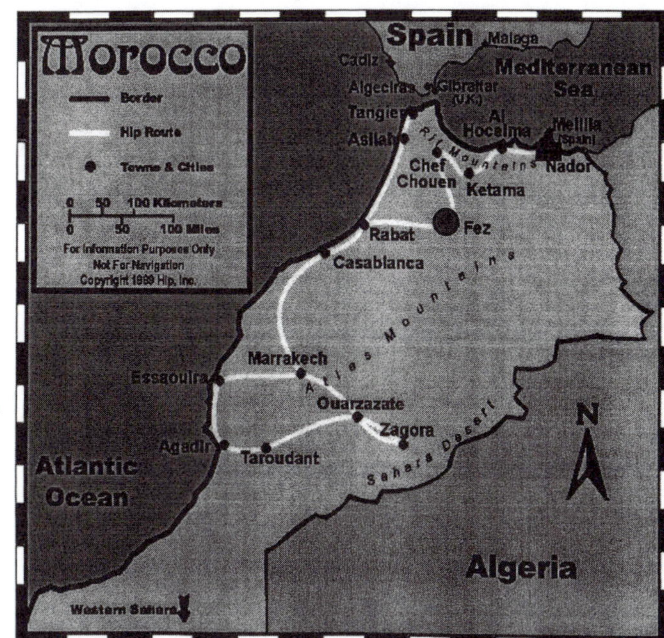

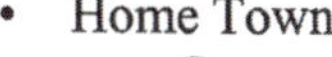

FIGURE 12.1: *Informal Trading Routes of Moroccan Women.*

was responsible for setting up and managing the microcredit programs, with the financial support and oversight of ASMED. Put together, the transnational chain of funding went as follows: Microcredit funds were transferred from USAID to CRS, then to AMSED, which would make decisions about procedures and the use of money, and finally to AMSSF for implementation. Thus, even though USAID does not have direct influence on AMSSF in this scheme, USAID is active as the source of both funds and policies.

There are additional actors in this scheme that make the chain more even more complicated. One is another big NGO called "Zakoura." This NGO has been in Morocco for quite a while, but started its Fez operations in 1996. It is an important player in this scene, because it is the only other major microcredit association in Fez and has a much larger membership than AMSSF. This is in part because it has a larger funding base through local private-sector sponsorship alongside international aid. Finally, the last actor in the web—but not by any means the least influential—is the state. The Moroccan government, specifically the arm of the Ministry of Industry, plays a large part in casting the relations among the various NGOs by enhancing the legitimacy of some over others.

Complicated as it is, this bureaucratic web benefits many of the groups in-

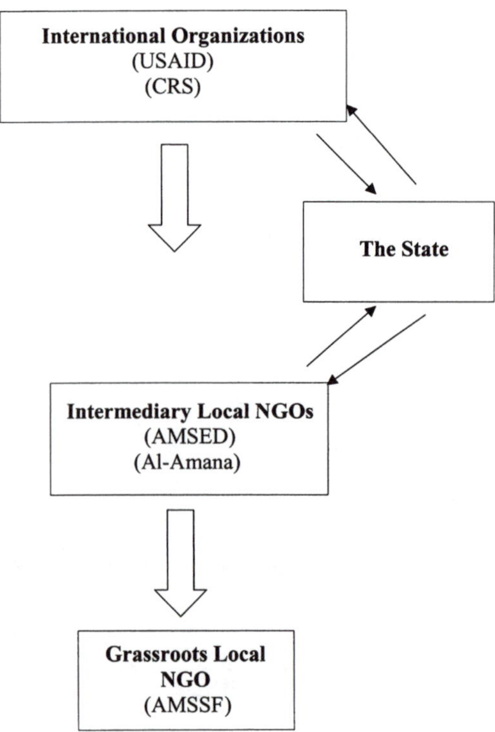

FIGURE 12.2: *Links among Actors in the Transnational Organizational Web.*

volved. First, it benefits transnational organizations like USAID because it is able to work through organizations that are locally based but still highly controllable. (Indeed, some foreign associations create their own NGOs with Moroccan names in order to mask their outsider identity). Second, the state benefits because it gains the attention and funding of international organizations. Third, the big NGOs benefit by gaining favors from the state (such as training, housing and infrastructure, and indirect access to government funds) as well as international assistance and visibility from groups like USAID and the United Nations. For the small NGOs, however, the benefits are not so straightforward. Although they gain access to funding unavailable otherwise, they also experience strains from the complicated hierarchical relationship of the other actors. However, this situation impacts AMSSF leaders and their female clients in different ways.

Tensions for AMSSF Leaders Seeking Aid

AMSSF leaders quickly learned that mediating relations in the NGO web was not easy. They also learned that this web is dynamic, changing, and requires frequent adaptations. Thus, the tensions for AMSSF leaders can be characterized by two stages.

The Early Stage: Braving the Lengthy and Hierarchical NGO-IGO Chain

The first stage was based upon the USAID-CRS-AMSED-AMSSF chain, which the members of AMSSF describe as "painful" and "frustrating." They recount the experience of seeking money through this maze as hierarchical, hegemonic, rigid, and slow. AMSED, they explain, "had no contact with the grassroots and their own needs." On the whole, AMSED procedures did not take into account the concrete problems faced by the organization or the real needs of microentrepreneurs. This underlying tension generated many practical strains for AMSSF leaders.

One major problem was maintaining the financial base of the organization. Most troublesome were the procedures for funding subventions from AMSED. Rather than providing funds on a regular basis (i.e., annually, as other NGOs did), or even on a rolling basis according to the needs of the clients, AMSED would renew funding to AMSSF *only when all of the clients had repaid their loans.* The intention was to ensure AMSED's financial security. However, the erratic nature of these procedures created many problems for AMSSF directors. They had to negotiate the conditions of attribution of new loans and urge AMSED to provide them almost daily. Complicating this dynamic was the dependence of AMSED on CRS subventions, and in turn, the dependence of CRS on USAID funding. This meant a highly constricted flow of funding.

A second major problem for AMSSF leaders was a lack of autonomy in managing the loans for their clients. AMSED did not allow the local directors to have independence in terms of the procedures for the loans or the reimbursements. Rather, AMSED had to comply with the rules about repayment as described. The consequences for clients were grave, with AMSSF unable to maintain continuous loans to its clients—even the most responsible ones. Directors frequently had to cut off funds and suspend their activities until new funds were provided by AMSED. This policy became, in effect, a sanction for the most successful clients of AMSSF. The president of AMSSF stated that her organization was trapped between the demands of the seekers of microcredit, the urgency of their financial needs, and the constraints imposed by AMSED.

The third major problem was blocked access to microcredit management and training. Because AMSED focused its support in monetary terms only, AMSSF was left struggling for informational resources. This problem was exacerbated by the fact that AMSED became an obstacle between AMSSF and other transnational women's organizations. Being the bigger and more legitimate NGO, AMSED had firsthand access to training programs, networks, and conferences hosted by international groups, and it reserved the spaces for its own staff. Consequently, AMSSF became increasingly marginalized from the international networks, and suffered from lack of exposure to management knowledge and training necessary for its microcredit program.

On the whole, then, AMSSF leaders objected in this early stage to the underlying philosophy of AMSED policies. This philosophy, asserted the president of AMSSF, "stems from the idea that people cannot be trusted and are not responsible. The local actors are not considered ready to deal with the questions of money management, and the grassroots population are not considered mature enough to use the loans in an effective manner." Changing the procedures became a source of conflict between AMSSF and AMSED, as the proposals for organizational change by AMSSF leaders were rejected. As we will show next, such conflicts lead to the severance of the financial relationship between USAID and AMSSF, but not an end to their interactions within the microcredit scene in Morocco.

The Later Stage: Intensified Competition for Clients

In the late 1990s, three crucial events transformed the bureaucratic web: a change in AMSSF's outlook toward its sponsors, a change in USAID's approach toward microcredit NGOs in Morocco, and a change in Moroccan state laws regarding microcredit NGOs. Though the culmination of these events had some liberating effects for AMSSF, it ultimately meant new forms of subordination as the NGO political constellation shifted into a new hegemonic pattern.

The first disruption in the original NGO relationship occurred when AMSSF leaders sought new funding sources. They turned to the United Nations Development Program, which they believed had some advantages over USAID-AMSED support. The biggest improvement was in the financial securities—with the UN program, subventions are *directly* transferred to AMSSF rather than through mediating NGOs. In addition, funds are transferred on a predictable yearly basis, rather than sporadically when client loans are paid. Loan amounts were also increased, so that AMSSF leaders could raise the range of disbursements to 500 DH ($50) to 4,000 DH ($400). On top of this, AMSSF experienced much more autonomy in running its programs. Leaders were allowed to participate in framing the terms of the contract with their sponsorship organization and were given greater independence in managing their client loans.

Another important benefit to the new arrangement was in improving links to other transnational women's organizations. The UN program reserved money for training and participation in conferences, which allowed AMSSF directors access to information and networking at the transnational level. Thus, almost immediately after the partnership with this funding source, AMSSF was able to participate in two international conferences—one in Bolivia and one in Lebanon—through a microcredit training program called Microstart. The knowledge gleaned from these training sessions was fundamental in equipping AMSSF staff with management skills for running the organization, and also in repositioning its political relationship to the bigger NGOs. Members of AMSSF expressed the impact in these terms: "Before the workshops we did not know what was going on around the world, especially in terms of procedures, problems, and solutions. But as soon as we came back, we decided to impart to AMSED our own conception about microcredit, and to fight against the existing assumptions about our capacities and clients." By gaining a comparative view of the different agencies and funding programs, AMSSF leaders took a crucial step in promoting a new self-image and gained a clearer picture of the bureaucratic web they were operating in and of their own power to negotiate new relationships among the different funding agencies. Indeed, a concrete indicator of the success of this new partnership is demonstrated in AMSSF's leap in membership—it was able to go from 600 to 2,000 clients. Still, the unfortunate fact is that many new tensions arose in this period.

The second event that happened around this time was a change in USAID's approach to microcredit programs in Morocco. Specifically, the policy changed from supporting small local NGOs through bigger ones to a policy of creating *its own NGO*, which would be under USAID's direct control would be provided with direct funds. This resulted in 1997 in the creation of Al Amana. This is a very large NGO—at 30,000 members—set up in Fez as a first step in broadening its scope to the entire Moroccan region. Having such an expansive organization meant that

Program in 1998. In the process, this has meant an entirely new set of characteristics attributed to women and men: women are said to be responsible, serious, and trustworthy (particularly with regard to handling business matters in microcredit programs), whereas men are said to be careless and unreliable. Moreover, women—and in particular those from poor families—are identified as the main providers of their family's survival and well-being.

The Moroccan state is also implicated in this policy shift. It too has demonstrated a remarkable change in its attitude toward women and microcredit. Historically, the state has defined women as peripheral to development and subordinate, politically and financially, to men in the family. These notions are legalized in the Moroccan "Codes of the Mudawwanah," which are religious-based laws dating back to 1957 (right after the country's independence in 1956): Code 1 states that the husband is the head of the family and for this reason (Code 36), the wife has to show respect and obedience. Code 115 stipulates that the husband is responsible for the financial security of his wife, regardless of her assets (Moulay R'chid 1991). What is remarkable is how these legal proscriptions have endured despite their contradictions with women's roles in the larger society. For instance, women's actual participation in the economy is considerably large at 35 percent (especially compared with other Arab countries). Moreover, the Moroccan constitution (which is a separate from the Codes of Mudawwanah) presents a much more egalitarian notion of male-female relations within the family. Nonetheless, the conception of women that has dominated state discourse is that of homemakers who are dependent on men for their material needs and who are unimportant for societal progress.

In the last decade, though, there has been a profound transformation in the gender discourse of the state. Faced with an increasing need for international funding, the state has realigned its discourse to reflect that of international agencies. The culmination of this discourse is that poor women are now conceived of as the *agents* of development. The ideology is also reflected in the discourse and policies at the local level, with leaders of AMSSF reporting that women clients are more reliable than men at paying back loans. The point, then, is that there is a transnational dynamic that reinforces the "women as most suitable microentrepreneur" philosophy among all these actors.

At face value, the policy of favoring women sounds like a reasonable one. However, the women of AMSSF report that this agenda has a multitude of negative consequences. The most important of these is a shift in the burden of household maintenance to women, and away from men. Microcredit may have increased women's ability to earn an income, but it has also increased their financial responsibilities with regard to their families. Many are taking on the burden of being the sole earner in the household. Because of this burden, as well as the intensity of the payment schedule for the loans, women have to work even harder in their economic activities. This can be seen in the grueling schedule some of these women keep. In a typical trading day, a microcredit woman has the following routine: she catches a bus between 1 and 3 A.M.; sleeps on the bus; arrives at the northern trading towns between 6 and 7 A.M.; purchases goods all day long; and takes a bus back home at 10 P.M. The other days of the week, she leaves at 5 A.M. to travel to local rural markets, sells goods during the day, and returns late in the evening.

In contrast, men's participation in this process is limited—sometimes only dropping women off at the bus stop. Moreover, during Salime's visits to these women's homes, men were observed to be mostly sleeping, often until late morning. Although this may not be representative of all men's behavior, husbands' contributions to the households observed in this study appear to be minimal. This is because working-class men have limited employment options, forcing them to resort to marginal work (such as seasonal or part-time jobs) or unemployment (which is 14.4 percent for men in Morocco). AMSSF's policies concerning men do not help to alleviate this situation: Not only is there a woman-focused admittance policy, but also a "one member per family" policy. This means that women members cannot enlist their husbands in the program, preventing the possibility of a family business endeavor. Indeed, rather than allowing the participation of multiple household members, the program mandates that it is women alone who must run the microcredit business for the family.

The effects of this gender imbalance are evident in national level. The proportion of women as heads of household has increased dramatically over the last few decades—52 percent of poor households are now headed by women (Secretary of State 1999), compared to 20 percent in the early 1990s and 10 percent in the 1970s (Ministry of Employment and Social Affairs 1995). This trend is also associated with increased social problems as evidenced by the fact that the illiteracy rate among those who head households is almost twice as high among women (92 percent) than men (53 percent) (Ministry of Employment and Social Affairs 1995). Nonetheless, women who head households are slightly more likely to ensure the education of their children: the percentage of children from female-headed households who are in high school is 79 percent, versus 71 percent from male-headed households (Ministry of Economic Provision and Planning 1998).

This points to a second consequence of women-focused policies: an increased burden on daughters. Microentrepreneur women are often so concerned about repaying their loans that they involve the entire family in their trading activities, even though this practice is officially proscribed. Girls in particular bear a tremendous responsibility in this situation, taking part in labor both inside and outside of the household. In many cases, daughters are often in charge of *all* the housework and must substitute for their mothers in trading when they become sick or are absent from work. During all three research visits to women's homes for this study, young girls were observed to be busy doing housework or else involved in their mothers' businesses. Many women testified that without their daughters' help, they would not be able to make it. And though most of the women interviewed in this study insisted that their daughters go to school, one of them expressed how difficult it is for daughters to manage school duties with other chores. "My daughter cannot do any homework during the day. She has to take care of everything because I am not here, and when I come back I am very tired. She will do her homework during the night when everybody is almost ready to go to bed." Thus, young girls in these situations could be said to suffer from a "triple burden" of work, household, and school duties in comparison to their mothers' "double burden."

A third consequence of women-focused policies is a diversion of working women away from other development activities. The intense pressure of the loan requirements leads women to focus all their energy and time on microcredit activities, to the exclusion of other programs and workshops. For instance, although most women are illiterate, they have no time to benefit from the literacy programs organized by AMSSF's sister organization. Ironically, AMSSF's literacy program is composed mostly of housewives and young girls, and has tremendous difficulties in attracting its own microentrepreneurs. Moreover, working women have no time for additional programs, such as health workshops, job training sessions, and political rights seminars. In this way, the broader goals of women's empowerment are eclipsed by the demands of microcredit.

One might say, then, that these policies have gone too far in favoring women. Though they provide extensive opportunities for women in the economy, it has come at the expense of discouraging men's participation, destabilizing intrahousehold relations, and obstructing women's development in areas such as literacy and health care. (In Bangladesh, there are even more serious consequences; Grameen Bank microcredit programs are said to be associated with increased male violence against women [UNIFEM 2000; S. C. White 2000]). In our case of AMSSF, these programs play a major role in shifting family income responsibility from men to women, and household labor responsibility from women to their educated daughters. In turn, rather than enhancing women's independence from the family structure, the microcredit programs reinforce the dependency of the family on women and on the informal economy.

"Solidarity Groups" as the Basis for Loans

Aside from these gender-based requirements, a second feature of the microcredit programs causes tensions for women. These are the "solidarity" requirements. Quite contrary to their name, these groups result in more tension among participants than they do cohesion. Despite any philosophical motivation that NGOs have regarding collective strategies for development, the practical motivation for this policy is to use the women themselves as policing agents. The idea is that participants monitor one another and thereby independently guarantee loan repayment without the organization getting involved. Although there are many sources of conflict within the groups, the most salient is derived from the nonpayment or delay in payment by one or more members of the group.

Indeed, during Salime observations at an AMSSF microcredit center, many leaders of the solidarity groups reported tremendous difficulties with one or two members of their groups. They said that managing the conflicts took a lot of time and energy, involving long negotiations with the member who refused to pay. As one woman put it, "Violence does not give any result. You should talk and convince." Indeed, some women stated that they had lost close friends because of this money issue. The AMSSF's attitude toward this issue does not help the situation, as it has a policy of not getting involved in intragroup tensions, and furthermore, provides no training in conflict resolution. It is completely up to the group to solve its own problems.

Exclusion of Men from Women's Solidarity Groups

Yet another source of strain for women is the policy concerning the gender composition of the solidarity groups. Because 20 percent of AMSSF's clients are men, the issue arises as to the placement of men and women in various groups. Tensions develop when the solutions of organizers conflict with those of the members. For example, although the international sponsors make no regulations regarding the gender specificity of the solidarity groups, AMSSF directors decided to segregate the groups by gender. Among the main reasons for such a decision were stereotyped assumptions about people of rural and poor backgrounds. Managers of the program assumed that female clients practice seclusion and therefore desire social distance from nonfamilial men. Accordingly, having men in the solidarity groups would be problematic because of the need for frequent contact and home visits between the members to organize payments.

However, many women stated that they would *prefer* to have men in their groups. One reason is that they receive visits from male microcredit agents. As part of the routine of loan oversight, AMSSF agents make personal calls to client homes. Even though these agents are typically male, they visit all clients regardless of their gender. Thus, female clients wished for male members in their groups so these men could interact with the male agents. Another reason is to assist in communicating with outsiders. The leader of one group explained, "Men are helpful to women. They can take care of your needs, especially the questions related to outside." Another woman added, "Men are more serious and more comprehensive and are ready to help. You won't have problems with men. They respect your commitment." Moreover, many microentrepreneurs asserted that their husbands would not contest the presence of a man in the group, since husbands were more interested in women's contribution to the family budget than in their wives' relationships with men in their microcredit activities. In certain ways, then, women perceive favorable aspects to men's involvement in their groups.

A critical perspective is needed regarding discourses of the clients, though, just as with those of the leaders. For instance, positive accounts of male members by women clients are counterbalanced by more problematic accounts by AMSSF leaders. In an earlier phase, the leaders did make an attempt to integrate the solidarity groups by gender and found that a power relationship developed between male and female members. Men were domineering and ordered the women around, or else refused to reimburse the loans and consequently left women with the burden of the debt. This suggests there is another side to the behavior of male members. A second problematic aspect to the discourses of female clients is how they perpetuate certain notions of gender segregation. Just as the women seek to disprove assumptions about female modesty by the AMSSF leaders, they simultaneously support a dichotomy of public/private spheres. This is apparent in their rationales for men's participation in the solidarity groups: Men are supposedly needed for "external" contacts and management of microcredit activities, while women are needed for "internal" family management and support. While this is an obvious contradiction to women's actual practices (e.g., they spend most of their time in the public sphere doing trading), they seek to present an image in which the public sphere is masculine and the private sphere is feminine. Why they perpetuate this ideology is unclear. What is clear, though, is discourses of gender segregation come from both leaders and members. Furthermore, their notions are very different and sometimes conflicting.

Many of these tensions reflect a class division between leaders and members. Like most NGOs around the world, AMSSF is headed primarily by educated, middle-class organizers (Alvarez 1999). That this generates tensions between leaders and members has been shown in studies of women's NGOs around the world (Ford-Smith 1997; Kannabiran and Kannabiran 1997; Wekker 1997). Such tensions manifest themselves in many forms—not only in terms of income level and residence (urban versus rural), but also in terms of education, language (Western versus local), and strategies (research and data collection versus service and activism). In the case of AMSSF, some of these factors become integral to relations between leaders and clients. In fact, they may be present as well in the interview process for this study. Salime's impression is that part of the motivation for female clients to represent male colleagues favorably was to enhance their own status as liberated women in the eyes of the researcher herself who is a middle-class Moroccan woman.

The fact remains, nonetheless, that AMSSF leaders are enforcing a program that the clients find unhelpful in their daily lives. Even if the leaders had in the past a sensitivity to client concerns by instituting mixed sex groups, this sensitivity did not endure. Furthermore, however benign leaders' motives may be in respecting clients' customs regarding interpersonal relationships, these motives reflect their own stereotypes rather than the clients' actual needs (or at least their own interpretations of them). The result is that leaders end up implementing a single-sex policy for solidarity groups without exploring alternative strategies which may suit client needs better. Indeed, one such strategy may be to empower women *within* mixed-sex groups, so they could better handle misbehavior by men.

Increasing Debt and Dependence on NGOs

The last, but by no means least important, type of tension women experience is increased debt and dependence upon the microcredit organizations. This is a result of the broader organizational context of state and international funding regulations, and especially the inter-NGO competition. In particular, the demand for increasing numbers of clients influences NGOs to keep women in their programs rather than alleviating their poverty or assisting them in upward mobility. There are two important ways in which this influence happens.

First, the drive for clients keeps women dependent upon the lending organization. In theory, the leaders of AMSSF should encourage a cycle of clientele moving through the organization because of the limited range of the loans that they can offer—some women starting out at low range loans, some advancing to greater loan amounts as they pay off the previous ones, and others leaving the organization as they reach the maximum loan amount. (Indeed, the other organizations like Al Amana offer much higher loans, in the range of 1,500 to 10,000 DH [$150to 1,000] compared to AMSSF's current range of 500 to 4,000 DH [$50 to 400].) However, because of the intense competition between the organizations for clients, leaders do not encourage their own members to leave. As the director of the microcredit centers said, "Our aim is to keep the clients in our program; otherwise we are just preparing them to go to other programs or to the bank." Thus, rather than reflecting the larger goal of integrating women into development by increasing their revenue and enhancing their capacity of entrepreneurship, the transnational web generates (however unintentionally) a system that keeps women for prolonged periods in the same range of loan.

Second, the drive for clients also increases women's indebtedness to multiple NGOs. As described earlier, the competition among microcredit programs encourages women to acquire loans from more than one NGO at a time. Indeed, many solidarity groups were in debt to several programs at once, which increased the strains within the groups. Thus, quite opposite to the ideal of helping women smoothly manage their investments and expenses, the NGOs are perpetuating a dynamic of financial insecurity for these women. Furthermore, coordination among the different NGOs to make sure clients are not multiplying their loans is not on the agenda. Indeed, their main concern is that women stay in their programs and pay back their loans, regardless of their other activities.

Women are not without agency in these situations, however. Some show a particular finesse in taking advantage of the inter-NGO competition, and playing one organization off another. In one of Salime's observation sessions at an AMSSF credit center, a woman described how she had just left Al Amana. She had abandoned her solidarity group there because one of the group members failed to pay her share of the loan. Rather than remaining trapped by the rules of Al Amana however, the woman sought out a new loan from AMSSF to continue her microenterprise activities. Thus, women are not victims of this system, but take action to navigate within and even resist it.

Conclusion

The undeniable fact is that over the last decade in particular, microcredit NGOs have provided new economic opportunities for many women that may not have been possible otherwise (UNIFEM 2000). They have incorporated millions of people into the workforce worldwide, especially in economies where there are few other job opportunities for either men or women. In the case of Morocco, they have also motivated (knowingly or unknowingly) a long-term continuation of income generation for women, through the household transmission of microcredit skills from mothers to daughters. Indeed, these microcredit programs have prepared many daughters for entering the world of microenterprise in general, if not for the specific jobs initiated by their mothers. Furthermore, recent findings from other regions of the world confirm many advantages to these programs: women's solidarity groups have fewer conflicts than men's, women microentrepreneurs tend to pay back loans more frequently than men (Blumberg 1995), and women entrepreneurs contribute more of their income to the household than male entrepreneurs (Espinal and Grasmuck 1997). Thus, despite all the tensions described above, there are many benefits of microcredit to be highlighted.

Indeed, this analysis is not aimed at denying the positive outcomes of microcredit programs, or even rejecting the idea of microcredit for women. Rather, our critique is aimed at questioning the assumptions that lie behind the use of microcredit as a means of incorporating women in development, and the ways in which microcredit programs are currently administered at the international, state, local, and organizational levels. We argue that there are crucial limitations in the ideological frameworks of microcredit that originate in First World settings like USAID, which are then transported and rearticulated globally through NGOs, and finally reinforced through state governments and local associations. In particular, the problem is in defining, on one hand, microcredit as the *primary* strategy for empowering women economically, and on the other hand, women as the *primary* or *exclusive* members for microcredit programs. Underlying both these themes is the assumption that development is largely the responsibility of women. There were many costs to this approach in AMSSF, including magnifying women's burden as providers for the family, discouraging male responsibility in household maintenance, and increasing the household workload for other family members, especially daughters. For this reason, we argue that there is a pressing need to expand the framework of economic empowerment campaigns to focus on *gender* rather than just women or men. In the words of development scholar Sara White (2000),

> [T]reating gender as solely a women's issue seriously underestimates the scale of the battle to achieve a more just society. This has major implications for the GAD [gender and development] approach, in relation to the issue of "empowerment.". . . It is very clear that if women's empowerment is to be sustained, it must be complemented by a change for men. (210)

This means that rather than excluding men from microcredit, these programs should attempt to enlist more equitable participation of men in *both* income-producing and family household activities.

Our study also has implications for discussions about NGOs and their relation to transnational feminist politics. We argue, to begin with, that there is a need to expand our theoretical understanding of NGOs and the context in which they operate. In the case of Morocco, there is a complicated transnational web of funding that involves a diverse set of actors, each of which is also internally diversified. The category "international agencies," for instance, is not monolithic but quite varied in terms of its policies and orientations toward NGOs (Alvarez 1999). On one hand, USAID funding (through AMSED) was crucial to AMSSF's organizational growth but also created tensions for members with its loan regulations; while the UN Development Program, on the other hand, had advantages in terms of its disbursement processes and training support, but generated new strains in terms of requirements on numbers and types of clients. Another point is that there are varying kinds of NGOs: some that are more powerful through the legitimacy of the state or private industries, and others that are more independent and strongly tied to local populations but also more politically fragile. Indeed, it is the relationship among the NGOs (through manipulations by the state and international agencies) that creates some of the greatest tensions for AMSSF leaders, in the form of competition for clients. In turn, these inter-NGO dynamics enhance the dependence of women on the organizations, and direct women away from other development programs that might free them from the severe problems of illiteracy and the informal economy.

Furthermore, there are important intraorganizational dynamics as well. The disjuncture between the class and regional backgrounds of the member and the leaders generates unique types of strains. Although much of the policy that leaders enforce in the organization originates from the international funding sources, some of it is also negotiated by the leaders themselves, and often reflects their own privileged biases. In this sense, the case of AMSSF certainly speaks to the need for a greater voice and more participation by the women clients in the policymaking process of the programs that guide their lives.

Finally, transnational web of funding works in many ways to impede the process of grassroots activism and the political articulation of the interests of the entrepreneur women. One way this is evident is in obstructing collective organizing among the NGOs themselves. Recently, there has actually been a proposition among the microcredit NGOs in Morocco to form a "federation" to represent client base. However, rather than having a democratic partnership among the organizations, Al Amana insisted on leading this federation. This caused both AMSSF and Zakoura to reject the plan, because they saw it as maintaining the hierarchy between the big and small associations. Thus, the hierarchy among NGOs hinders the potential for alliances that might create a basis of strength from which to contest the state or international agencies. In addition, the transnational web of funding also impedes international alliances among NGOs. As was shown in the case of AMSSF, the state and even some big NGOs are very powerful in restricting the access of grassroots groups to transnational feminist organizing.

However, it is also important to point out the glimmer of light in this story. Although many scholars argue that the process of "NGOization" has the effect of demobilizing feminist activism (Lang 1997), our case does not necessarily provide such a discouraging account. It is true that AMSSF became subject to pressures of both international organizations and the state, and was forced to make concessions in its agenda and its organizational structure in order to accommodate those demands. However, at the same time, it was also able to negotiate within the bureaucratic web to a certain degree. It was able to realign itself and take advantage of the various funding options (just as the women clients did), making use of the programs that would allow them the greatest flexibility in asserting their own interests and best represent (as far as their social position permitted) the "true" needs of their clients. In addition, it was able to use the international organizations to gain access to transnational feminist organizing, which would have been difficult otherwise.

Fortunately, there are growing examples of this kind of creative strategizing by local women's groups. A group of rural women in Brazil maintained their autonomy within the transnational funding network by relying on their own funds as much as possible, providing training sessions to members on interpersonal empowerment techniques during meetings with international donors, inviting these donors to their organization for a firsthand view of the women's activities, and appropriating and refashioning the transnational discourses of gender to their localized needs (Thayer 2001). These cases suggest that there is potential for grassroots organizations to use NGO linkages to create a global feminist alliance.

Note

Direct correspondence to Winifred R. Poster, assistant professor, Department of Sociology, University of Illinois at Urbana–Champaign, 326 Lincoln Hall, 702 S. Wright St., Urbana, IL 61801, poster@uiuc.edu. We are grateful to the participants of the study for their generous offerings of time and knowledge, and to Nancy Naples and Manisha Desai for their excellent comments. The opinions expressed herein are those of the authors alone.

13

"No Discrimination Whatsoever"
Women's Transnational Activism and the Evolution of EU Sex Equality Policy

Rachel A. Cichowski

Women as legal experts and policy activists have played a central role in the evolution of supranational social policy in Europe. The purpose of this chapter is to examine the mechanisms that affect women's involvement in European integration and international policy processes more generally. This analysis draws upon research from integration scholars, public policy experts, and feminist theory, and introduces a policy dynamic that explains activism and participation in terms of policy designs and issue constructions. In particular, I examine the evolution of sex equality policy in the European Union (EU)[1] through a case study of the Equal Pay Principle (Article 141).[2] I focus on the role of women activists in creating and shaping the scope of this European policy sector. This analysis adopts an interdisciplinary approach to examine how sex equality became an integral part of what was intended to be an international economic agreement. The research demonstrates the significant effect that national and transnational women's activism can have on international policy outcomes. A systematic study of this dynamic remains absent from our current understanding of global politics.

Are global policy decisions and international cooperation inherently removed from direct citizen participation and pressure? Or do supranational policy processes provide activists with increased political power both in national arenas and at the international level? This suggests an interesting puzzle for scholars and activists examining the changing role of women activists in both global and national policy processes. The evolution of sex equality policy in the European Union presents a particularly interesting test case for this puzzle. The dominant theoretical understandings of European integration (intergovernmentalism) explain policy decisions in terms of national government bargaining and attribute no independent strength to citizen pressure in this international process (e.g., Garrett 1992; Moravcsik 1993 and 1998).[3] But a growing body of feminist scholarship has begun to reveal the integral role of women's activism both nationally and at the European level in constructing an entire EU policy sector independent of national government control (Hoskyns 1996; Pillinger 1992; Sohrab 1996). Unfortunately, these studies have yet to gain theoretical and practical prominence as evidence of the increasing role of citizen activism in the process of European integration. This failure is not surprising, as the field of international politics has long been criticized for its lack of feminist analysis (Enloe 1989; Hoskyns 1996).

This chapter contributes to feminist scholarship that highlights the effects of globalization and international politics on women's activism (e.g., Grewal and Kaplan 1994; Yuval-Davis 1999). In particular, it builds on recent scholarship that questions the dominant understanding of supranational politics in Europe by providing evidence that transnational society and national activists have functioned as key independent forces in the expansion of European policy sectors (e.g., Cichowski 1998 and 2001; Sandholtz and Stone Sweet 1998). Furthermore, this analysis adopts a feminist perspective and builds on the frameworks provided by policy scholars to better understand how policy processes in the European Union have empowered women (e.g., Hoskyns 1996; Pillinger 1992; Schneider and Ingram 1990 and 1997; Smith and Ingram 1993).

Figure 13.1 provides the general framework that will guide this analysis. This framework draws from Schneider and Ingram's (1997) policy design model and also explicitly adopts a feminist perspective of EU policy processes (Hoskyns 1996; Pillinger 1992). The causal circle comprises three main variables: issue construction, policy design, and societal construction. Issue construction pertains to the factors affecting how EU policy issues are framed. These factors include economic knowledge and discourse, social construction of target population, political institutions, and political power. These issue constructions generate specific policy designs

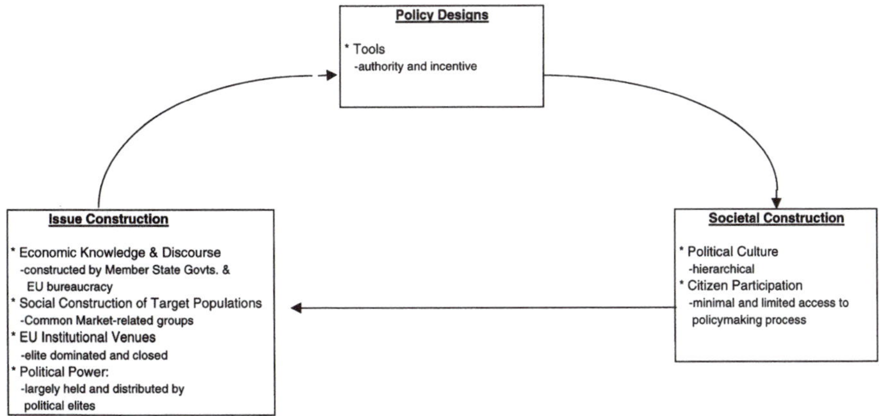

FIGURE 13.1: *Intended Policy Construction in the EU.*

and in particular a set of tools that comes to characterize the policy. The policy designs then shape societal construction, in particular the political culture and citizen participation norms developed in the EU. Finally, this dynamic reflects the consequences that this societal construction has on future issue construction in EU policymaking.

The causal nature of this framework is particularly helpful for my analysis as it allows us to understand the effects that Article 141 and women's activism had on future European policymaking. This dynamic also allows us to examine how a law can have consequences different from those intended by its creators and how women can exploit international opportunity structures to change national policy. Figure 13.1 provides an overview of the intended evolution of Article 141 and can be seen as a general conceptualization of how EU policymaking was intended to evolve. This analysis will focus on this overall process, but will do so in terms of how Article 141 allowed for a deviation from this model.

My analysis will be organized in three parts. Part I provides the foundations of this historical analysis: the origins of Article 141 and how this treaty provision provided the opportunity for activism. The remaining two sections examine how this fair competition provision was transformed into social justice policy, governing not only equal wage, but also issues such as maternity leave and discrimination in employment. Part II focuses on the policy dynamic that characterized Article 141, particularly the interaction of issue construction, policy design, and subsequent societal construction. By studying the policy designs of Article 141, we are able to understand how an economic policy governing international cooperation was exploited for social justice purposes. Finally, Part III focuses on how the transformation of Article 141 led to the expansive development of EU sex equality legislation and highlights the role of activist women in this development. Also, I will provide a feminist critique of the limitations embodied in this type of sex equality policy.

I. Historical Roots of EU Sex Equality Policy: Transforming Article 141

Article 141 provided that member states ensure and maintain the principle that women and men receive equal pay for equal work.[4] Member states were required to implement the principle by the end of the first stage of the European Economic Community (or Common Market), December 31, 1962.[5] It was the French delegation that originally demanded that an equal pay provision be included in the 1957 Treaty of Rome. France was the only country to possess equal pay laws at the time, and French employers saw this as a potential barrier to fair and equal competition among member states. The role of activist women can be traced back to this initial policy stage of getting the issue on the agenda, for the existence of this French law was a repercussion of political activism by Frenchwomen in the 1940s (Hoskyns

1996). However, the intention of EU architects was not based in a concern for equality between the sexes.

Scholars observe that member state agreement to the equal pay provision was founded in an attempt to "placate the French," rather than in a serious commitment to provide for equal pay in national markets (Warner 1984, 143). In fact, implementation of such a measure at the time would have resulted in considerable costs and restructuring of the labor market. In the six member states, women constituted almost 30 percent of the waged workforce. And legal provision for equal pay varied widely: Four countries had some provision, but Belgium and the Netherlands lacked any legislation. Dutch pay disparities were in the order of 40 percent, with many sectors of the economy relying on low-paid female labor. Treaty debates were characterized by Dutch resistance to the idea of equal pay (D. Collins 1975).

These varying national positions also reflected an overarching conception of the relationship between social protection and the functioning of the Common Market. In particular, two opposing logics undergirded treaty negotiations in 1957. The French believed a "harmonization" of social costs was necessary in order to provide a fair playing field for businesses across the member states once barriers to the free movement of goods and persons were removed. Rightfully so, French businesses were concerned that mandated national social legislation, such as equal pay and longer paid holidays, would increase the costs of production in France and thus, put French industry at a comparative disadvantage. On the other hand, German negotiators were skeptical of the need to equalize social costs by way of treaty provisions. They believed that harmonization of social costs would be an inevitable consequence once the Common Market was established. The position taken by Germany stemmed from a more general commitment to low levels of government interference in the area of wages and prices (Ellis 1998, chap. 2).

These opposing traditions resulted in the treaty's minimal social provisions. The French delegation persuaded the other member states to accept a very specific provision on equal pay (Article 141) and a similarly narrow provision regarding paid holidays (Article 141a). These negotiations remained strictly focused on fair competition, with the original placement of the principle in the portion of the treaty dealing with competition distortion. However, both provisions were ultimately shifted (though the text unchanged) to social provisions as an attempt to develop at least some harmonization of social costs within the treaty (Mosley 1990). Stated generally, Article 141 was inserted into the treaty for economic reasons, but was placed in the position of having social consequences. Its inclusion laid down a precise legal obligation for member states, yet at the same time it also embodied a general social ideal or instrument (at least indirectly) to harmonize social policy. The policy consequences of this treaty provision were not foreseen.

Until the late 1960s, the member states saw Article 141 as a distant set of ideals.

Not one national government had undertaken domestic policy changes to enshrine this equal pay principle. However, Article 141 was far from dead, as it was soon to regain life as a result of two types of activism, both taking place in Belgium and both led by women. Along with its importance for developing European sex equality norms, these cases of activism are particularly significant as they paved the way for subsequent inclusion of women activists in the European policymaking process, a process largely dominated by men at the time and largely closed to direct citizen input (Hoskyns 1996).

The first case occurred in the spring of 1966 when women workers at the Herstal arms factory called a strike because of the inequality of pay between men and women. The preceding Fall, one of the main Belgian labor unions had held a seminar in Brussels on the problems of women in the workforce, and Article 141 had been a topic of discussion. A group of women who participated in the Brussels seminar returned to the Herstal factory and set up a committee to address women workers' concerns. This exchange of ideas and communication of needs provided the foundation for a well-organized strike by more than 3,000 people (see Hoskyns 1996). Article 141 gave ordinary citizens the ability to change the policies that affected them the most, their basic earnings.

Article 141 also fostered another type of activism through litigation. Elaine Vogel-Polsky, a young Belgian lawyer who specialized in social and labor law, saw Article 141 as a stepping-stone to expanding women's labor rights. It was largely through the jurisprudence of the European Court of Justice that the social right embodied in Article 141 was brought to life. Through a series of test cases in the late 1960s, Vogel-Polsky and other lawyers were able to work with the European Court of Justice to expand the scope of the article and to provide real situations in which Article 141 was applicable.[6] Almost 20 years after the adoption of this principle, the court ruled on the "direct effect" of Article 141 and in doing so endowed community citizens with individual rights enforceable under EU law. The significance of this ruling far surpassed that of expanding sex equality rights, as it in effect helped further transform an international treaty into a supranational constitution (see Cichowski 2001; Stone Sweet and Caporaso 1998). Yet from the sex equality policy perspective, it also represented a powerful step.

The court's action initiated an expansion in the scope of Article 141 that became the driving force behind EU sex equality legislation in the 1970s and 1980s (e.g., Cichowski 2001). These cases "opened the way for women within the [European] Commission's own bureaucracy to push for stronger policy" (Hoskyns 1996, 74). Furthermore, these landmark judicial decisions have formed the basis of a continuous line of jurisprudence, driven primarily by national legal activists, that has in effect developed and institutionalized women's policy at the European level (see Cichowski 2001). Article 141 opened the door to such an opportunity.

II. Policy Design and Its Consequences

Against this policy history, we look to the specific policy design of Article 141 to help understand how this distant treaty provision evolved into the basis of the EU sex equality policy. In particular, I focus on the three main variables in this policy dynamic: issue construction, policy design, and societal construction. Referring back to figure 13.1, we are able to see how the issue construction of Article 141 was typical of EU policymaking and led to a certain set of policy designs. However, when examining the policy tools more closely we are able to see the unintended consequences these designs had on EU societal construction. Furthermore, by examining these unintended consequences, we are able to see how Article 141 changed participatory norms in the EU, in particular, by providing the opportunity structure for women activists, and how this subsequently changed the direction of EU policymaking.

Issue Construction

The European policymaking process is an unprecedented form of supranational policy development. It is characterized by "the policymaking attributes of a modern state, across an increasingly wide range of policy sectors" (Richardson 1996, 3) yet it is a governance structure that is above the state. The successful development of this policy process can be understood as strategic action on the part of EU economic experts and national government elites to construct this process in terms of economic knowledge and discourse.[7] Without this construction, the reality that national sovereignty is slowly (or rapidly, depending on the policy sector) being usurped would be unacceptable to national governments and their citizens. Furthermore, this economic construction is characterized by patriarchal decision-making structures that have all but excluded women's issues from the original scope of EU policy (Hoskyns 1996; Pillinger 1992).

Bureaucrats in the European Commission and national governments as represented in the Council of Ministers dominate the EU policy process. Further, the policy officials in both of these institutions are not directly elected by the people, but instead are career civil servants or appointed national government ministers. This process has also developed within largely "male-dominated" institutions in which ultimately national elites have "stuck fast to unchanging patriarchal relations" (Hoskyns 1996, 10; Pillinger 1992, 168). Not surprisingly this process is criticized for its democracy deficit as the only directly elected institution of the EU, the European Parliament, remains relatively powerless in comparison (Dinan 1994). The power of expert knowledge in EU policy development is illuminated by the increasingly "excessive policy-making role" that commission bureaucrats have played in the development of European integration (Christiansen 1996, 80; Richardson 1996, 3).

This dominance of economic knowledge and discourse has reinforced EU institutional strength by securing political power within EU institutions and national government elites. The intended logic of EU policymaking implicitly retained political power above the reach of direct citizen control. By drafting Article 141 in terms of Common Market goals (which prioritizes stronger implementation standards), the treaty privileged EU institutions and national governments. The commission is granted the ability to commence enforcement proceedings if a national government fails to implement the principle into national law. In exchange, however, the narrow reach of this law gives national governments the power to interpret the principle in a manner they see as congruent with their own national policy priorities. The construction of Article 141 left little room for citizen political empowerment (or so the drafters thought). Again, it is the underlying motivations behind the equal pay principle that eventually alters these power distributions.

Who was the supposed target population of Article 141? Similar to Schneider and Ingram's (1997) observations of American public policy, the EU policy process is characterized by social constructions that "extol the virtues" of certain target populations, which inevitably focus policy debates and determine policy designs (102). Their typology of target populations is instructive in understanding why Article 141 was constructed as a fair competition policy and not a sex equality principle. By understanding the political risks involved with benefiting "contender" populations, we can see why the French framed this policy in terms of equal competitive practices, even though the population that really stood to benefit was not the business community. In examining Article 141, we also can see how the implicit meaning in this policy ended up benefiting a target group different from the one intended by treaty negotiators.

Article 141 can be interpreted as benefiting two different target populations; an "advantaged" group and a "contender" group. The advantaged population is the business community, and the contender population consists of women activists. The social construction of these two target populations differs, and in particular they possess varying degrees of political power. Ultimately, they present policymakers with different risks and opportunities. Advantaged groups are "powerful and positively constructed," while contender populations are often "powerful but negatively constructed as undeserving" (Schneider and Ingram 1997, 102). Again, in terms of the goals of the treaty, European integration was seen as a uniting of economic markets and not cultures or value systems. The business community is the population most positively linked to economic cooperation and thus policies benefiting this "advantaged" population presented little political risk to member state governments.

The real beneficiaries of Article 141 were not initially evident from the wording of the treaty provision. It was the ability of women legal activists to find this benefit and use it that created a shift in the explicit target population of this policy. It is interesting to see how the dual nature of this policy actually created a situation in which an emergent contender population usurped a policy from an advantaged target population. Treaty drafters favored the politically optimum situation. They framed the equal pay principle in terms of a beneficial policy to an advantaged group. This policy reinforced a strong representation of national economic interests on the European policy agenda. Furthermore, its rules were highly universalistic as Article 141 created a general principle that would be applied to all businesses throughout the EU. Following the dictates of a policy design model, we would expect beneficial policies that target advantaged groups to be constructed in a more universalistic pattern (Schneider and Ingram 1997).

Impact of Policy Design on Societal Construction

The previous section focused on the role that expert knowledge and economic discourse and social constructions played in the development of Article 141. We saw how these factors created a particular issue construction that was intended to reinforce EU institutional and national government political power, while discouraging citizen participation in the policy process. In particular, it perpetuated a male-dominated policy process that allowed little space for women's issues or inputs. In this section, I will discuss the policy designs that resulted from this issue construction and then examine how this has produced a particular societal construction.

Article 141 presents an interesting case of the potential unintended consequences of policy designs and in particular the role of policy tools in this process. As emphasized above, national variation was provided for in the implementation of Article 141. Policy tools played a significant role in how varied this implementation process ended up becoming. By examining the policy tools utilized in Article 141,

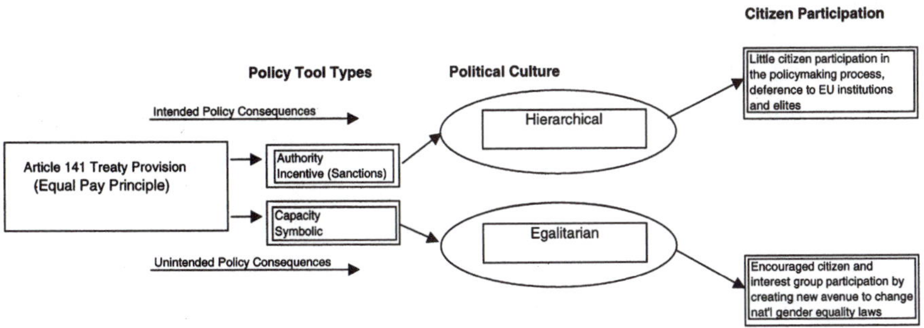

FIGURE 13.2: *Policy Consequences of Article 141.*

we are able to illustrate how in fact policy designs can embody a set of intended policy tools and end up with a very different outcome depending on how the policy is interpreted and by whom. I will first detail the intended tool types and their intended societal effects and then contrast them with the implicit tool types of Article 141 and the unintended policy consequences that followed. Figure 13.2 gives an overall picture of these intended and unintended consequences.

Intended Policy Consequences

The drafters of Article 141 constructed this provision in accordance with other Common Market–related policies. In doing so, they laid down what was intended to be a straightforward statement that prohibited unequal pay for equal work. From this intention we can see that this policy design used "authority tools." As described by Schneider and Ingram (1990), authority tools are "statements backed by the legitimate authority of government that grant permission, prohibit, or require action under designated circumstances" (514). Authority tools are most often found in governmental structures that emphasize hierarchical relationships. Implicit in these tools are the assumption that both agents and targets will comply with the "leader-follower" relationship involved in this policy design. This is particularly significant in the case of EU policy, as policymaking is intentionally a national government decision, yet integration ultimately depends on citizen compliance with these new European laws.

Article 141 also used incentive tools as it laid down strict sanctions for noncompliance. Employees wronged by failure to apply to this principle must have the right of recourse through judicial processes to pursue their claims. Similarly, national governments that failed to implement this principle into national law faced enforcement litigation. As a policy design model predicts, we would expect authority and incentive tools to lead to a particular type of political culture and citizen participation.

The prevalence of authority and incentive tools in EU policy has led to a distinctively deferential political culture. Article 141 was intended to promote a similar culture. It was designed to remain at the elite level for implementation and encourage citizen adherence to this hierarchy of decisions. The policy tools prevented or minimized citizen participation by not creating the space for citizen input. Not only does this affect the implementation of this single provision, but it has the repercussion of setting a norm for EU policymaking. Returning to figure 13.1, we can reemphasize that it is from this hierarchical societal construction that new issue constructions are created and thus we can see how the European Union has been able to perpetuate its norm of deference. In the case of Article 141, the dynamic did not unfold as intended by its creators.

Unintended Policy Consequences

The drafters of this provision did not expect the societal construction created by Article 141. Hoskyns (1996) gives an historical account of this outcome:

> At no time are the interests of women considered even obliquely or the issues of social justice raised. The distance from the reality of work or any real struggle seems complete. However, the potential for a stronger implementation of equal pay was embedded in the history of the article and, paradoxically, in the history of the EC itself. It took activist women to realise these possibilities—and switch the debate from one of economic rationality to a demand for rights. (57)

This unintended policy outcome revealed that the provision possessed a very different second set of policy tools that applied to a very different target population. While drafters thought they were designing an economic policy with a strict authoritative statement, they in fact were creating a capacity building policy for women. Capacity tools can be used to change agency practices and to promote the use of innovative programs (Schneider and Ingram 1990, 518). This is exactly the effect Article 141 had. It provided women throughout Europe with a new legal basis to demand change in national policies that enshrined sex inequalities. This is evidenced from the court cases discussed earlier (see also Cichowski 2001). Article 141 also embodied symbolic tools that aided in creating this social justice policy outcome. The ambiguity of the text gave citizens the ability to convince governments that it embodied values of justice and equality far beyond the actual concerns stated in the policy.

The resulting political culture and citizen participation was then also considerably different than expected. The capacity and symbolic tools created a political culture that promoted egalitarian values, albeit within a larger deferential structure. The progressive interpretations of this policy by individuals and the court fostered the development of equality on a social and individual basis, not just in terms of economic value. Article 141 also opened the door to opportunities for citizen participation in EU policymaking. It created the space, both psychological and physical, for a discussion of European values on sex equality. Women activists, as lawyers, lobbyist and policymakers, were given a legal basis to participate in the evolution of this policy. Even when a national government adopted a conservative interpretation of Article 141, women were able to overturn these national laws in favor of a more expansive reading of the policy intention.[8] The court, activated by women activists, brought about significant and expansive reform in national equality policies concerning pensions and employment rights.[9] This increased participation had direct consequences for the future of sex equality policy in the European Union (Cichowski 2001; Ellis 1998; Kenney 1992 and 1996; Prechal and Burrows 1990; Stone Sweet and Caporaso 1998). The next section addresses this final loop in the circle.

III. Activism and the Development of Equality Legislation

This section explores the subsequent development of EU equality legislation, and the role of activists in this evolution. Article 141 created the legal basis for this expansion, but it took the work of women activists, as academics, lawyers, labor activists, and European Commission policymakers to realize this opportunity. While these have been great successes for women throughout Europe, they also presented limitations. I will end this section by suggesting the inherent constraints of this type of equality policy.

EU Equality Legislation

Three pieces of EU legislation were passed between 1975 and 1979, which clarified the goals set out in Article 141. They were the Equal Pay Directive, the Equal Treatment of Work Directive, and the Equal Treatment in Social Security Directive.[10] These policies were heavily influenced by a comprehensive study carried out in 1968 on the status of women's employment in the member states. The author was a French sociologist and activist, Evelyne Sullerot, who had pioneered academic studies on women's work in Europe. However, the policy debates surrounding the Equal Pay Directive remained similar to the original discussions of Article 141 as it remained primarily conceptualized as an employment issue. Yet within these negotiations, there was a continual pressure, from women activists in the commission and national legal network, to expand the scope of this EU policy area. This pressure and the effect it had on the two Equal Treatment directives is depicted in the following account of the policy debate:

> During the course of the equal pay negotiations there were constant reminders from Sullerot, the commission, and in the end even the European Court of Justice that this was not a sufficient policy to tackle women's inequality. It needed to be expanded. The next two directives, while remaining within the employment field, were much broader and raised issues such as child care and dependency, which crossed the public/private divide and were therefore more controversial (Hoskyns 1996, 93)

Due to both the decision-making procedures at this time and the sacred nature of these policy decisions, these directives were all adopted under unanimity voting.[11]

In order to reach consensus among all member states, the resulting legislation failed to address and clarify the sometimes sensitive issues of discrimination and general equality. However, this lack of clarity created an opportunity for legal activists to invoke EU rules against their own national governments. The directive states that "no discrimination whatsoever on grounds of sex" will be allowed under EU law. Scholars have observed that this general "whatsoever" expression has given ample opportunity to both litigants and the court to expand the directive's scope. This includes one court decision that found protection against dismissal for transsexuals within the scope of EU equality law.[12] Furthermore, the directive failed to clearly provide a definition for the concept at the heart of the legislation, namely, how is indirect discrimination embodied in general equality? This ambiguity would later be at the center of a series of cases brought by legal activists before the court.[13]

Together Article 141 and these three directives provided the basis for European sex equality law. The Council of Ministers subsequently added only two directives to this policy area in the 1980s,[14] both of which are largely symbolic. Furthermore, the passage of the Single European Act in 1986 did little to alter equality policy as laid out in the treaty and secondary legislation (Hoskyns 1996). National governments, in particular those of Germany and the United Kingdom, continued to exhibit a reluctance in developing this EU policy area. Germany from the earliest discussions regarding Article 141 argued that social costs, in particular wages and prices, should be subject to minimal government interference (Ellis 1998). Germany was reluctant to implement the EU Equal Treatment measures, and was criticized in a commission study for adopting too narrow a view of equality.[15] However, this narrow implementation has subsequently been corrected by litigation fueled by a German legal network for women.[16] The United Kingdom's reluctance differs in that it stems not so much from a belief in minimal government interference but more explicitly minimal EU interference in its national social protection law. Yet the outcome has been the same. The United Kingdom's attempts to constrain the reach of EU social policy have been trumped by rulings of the European Court of Justice that have been driven primarily by the work of legal activists in the British Equal Opportunities Commission (see Alter and Vargas 2000).

Innovations in EU equality legislation and treaty provisions have experienced a roller-coaster ride in the 1990s. The early part of the decade demonstrates an overall reluctance on the behalf of national governments, the United Kingdom in particular, to expand or clarify equality policy. While the Agreement of Social Policy provided explicit equality rights, it was relegated to an annex of the Treaty on European Union (1992) in order to accommodate the British government's insistence on its opt-out position on further social protection. Furthermore, some have interpreted the national government's addition of a specific Protocol in the Treaty on European Union to reverse an expansive and costly ruling by the European

Court of Justice regarding pensionable age under Article 141, as a way of restricting both the court's activism and the scope of Article 141.[17] This time period also witnessed the passage of the Pregnancy Directive (92/85) which pertained to the safety and health of pregnant workers. While the directive provided minimal protection at the EU level as a result of UK insistence, women activists throughout Europe have pushed for greater pregnancy protection under EU law through litigation. The result has been an extensive case law on pregnancy and maternity rights that has enabled the European Court of Justice to expand this directive beyond it minimalist protections (see Cichowski 2001).

The end of the decade brought a distinct shift in treaty-based advances in EU sex equality policy. Scholars have suggested that this shift may have been influenced by transnational activism inspired by the 1995 Conference at Beijing's strategy of empowerment (Rossilli 1997). With the passage of the Amsterdam Treaty in 1997, all member state governments agreed to the formal inclusion of fundamental social rights into the treaty. The Agreement on Social Policy has now been absorbed into the treaty after the conclusion of the United Kingdom's opt-out position. Article 118 (now Article 137) includes "equality between men and women with regard to labour market opportunities and treatment at work" in a list of activities that member states promise to complement and support. A second enabling provision is Article 6a (now Article 13), which reads:

> Without prejudice to other provisions of this Treaty and within the limits of the powers conferred by it upon the Community, the Council, acting unanimously on a proposal from the Commission and after consulting the European Parliament, may take appropriate action to combat discrimination based on sex, racial or ethnic origin, religion or belief, disability, age or sexual orientation.

Article 141 has also undergone changes that adopt earlier positions taken by the court, such as the concept of equal pay for work of equal value. Furthermore, Article 141 now includes a paragraph that encourages positive action by providing that

> with a view to ensuring full equality in practice between men and women in working life, the principle of equal treatment shall not prevent any Member State from maintaining or adopting measures providing for specific advantages in order for the under-represented sex to pursue a vocational activity or to prevent or compensate for disadvantages in professional careers.

This inclusion and expansion of formal sex equality rules in the treaty bodes well for future legislative innovations in this policy sector. In particular, Treaty Articles 136–145 are now governed by the codecision procedure in which qualified majority voting is utilized except in proposals regarding social security.

Inherent Limitations

Though clearly the development of at least minimal equality policy at the EU level has benefited many women, this equality may be limited. I will end this analysis by discussing possible limitations of EU equality policy. Feminist scholarship has begun to recognize the serious shortcomings of policy based purely on equality and of policies that fail to acknowledge the diversities embodied in the category of "women" (Lovenduski 1997; Pillinger 1992; Sohrab 1996). This feminist critique is not intended to diminish the accomplishments that women have so far attained in constructing a space for women's issues at the European level, but instead to emphasize the continued need to broaden the scope of this policy area.

EU policy on women has largely developed in terms of equality laws. The positive benefits of this policy are clear, as overt discrimination in employment opportunities, social security benefits, and wage were minimized (see Elman 1996; Sohrab 1996). Mazey (1988, 82) describes EU equality policy as having "doggedly chipped away at the vast edifice of sexist practices and policies" yet concludes that the policy fails to go beyond "formal" equality. This is the inherent problem with sex equality laws and why they alone cannot remedy the social inequalities and injustices facing women. Traditionally, sex equality laws were conceptualized in terms of justice as defined by social contract theory. It is seen as equality before the law (Meehan and Sevenhuijsen 1990). Feminist theorists have revealed the problematic nature of this derivation of equality (e.g., Pateman 1988). Equality through such a framework requires women to demand their rights in terms of the prevailing patriarchal discourse. They are forced to stress the similarities between women and men. Ultimately, this does little to change the underlying structures that caused the subordination of women in the first place. Furthermore, it perpetuates the unrealistic perceptions of women's position in the labor market by continuing to ignore women's unpaid labor in child rearing.

Sohrab (1996) explains this as a conflict arising from the "sameness-difference model." This conflict is at the center of EU sex equality policies. She characterizes this policy area as extending the "same treatment to women when they are the same as men (women as paid workers) and different treatment when they are different from men (women as dependents and carers)" (Sohrab 1996, 53). This is exemplified by EU legislation, such as Directives 76/207/EEC and 79/7/EEC, in which women are extended the same opportunities as men in employment and benefits, yet are given special benefits or compensation (e.g., lower pension age and limitations on night work) for their social roles as caregivers. This approach fails to even question the basic assumptions that perpetuate a system in which women are the assumed caregivers.

The limitations are made clear in a European Court of Justice ruling that involved the clarification of Directive 76/207/EEC. In the *Hofmann* case,[18] a German man claimed that a German law was incompatible with the protection allowed for maternity leave by the European law. The German law offered a daily allowance to women who remained at home with the child until it was six months of age. Mr. Hofmann, whose partner returned to work after her eight-week maternity leave, remained home with the child until it was six months of age, but he did not receive the daily allowance. The court did not concur that the directive extended these special rights to men and ruled that the directive "is not designed to settle questions concerned with the organisation of the family, or to alter the division of responsibility between parents" (paragraph 24).

Clearly, this ruling illustrates the limitations of this directive and even reveals its detrimental effects on attempts to change social roles associated with child rearing. Feminist scholarship has emphasized the need to share child rearing between men and women in order to truly change the subordination of women (Chodorow 1978). However, EU sex equality policies do little to change the underlying structure of an economic system in which women are dependents and placed in subordination to men. Policies reflect societal norms, and as long as women persist as the main caregivers in the family and community, government policy will continue to perpetuate this relationship.

Another main limitation of EU sex equality policy is the assumed category of "women" it is benefiting. Generally, EU women's policy has constructed women as a unified and homogenous category. Furthermore, until recently, EU policy clearly viewed this category as "white women in paid employment" (Hoskyns 1996, 9). This totalizing construction hides the real diversity of women across the European Union. Women working at home, women who are black or of an ethnic minority, and migrant women are all absent from the scope of this policy sector. Feminist scholars emphasize the problems with such general conceptualizations of women and argue for the importance of pluralist approaches—which emphasize the importance of a women's personal experience, race, and class—in examining women's subordination to men (e.g., Alexander and Mohanty 1997a; P. H. Collins 1990; J. W. Scott 1992; D. Smith 1990; Spelman 1988). The feminist movement in Europe became aware of this diversity of interests through the activism of lesbian women in Britain and also the activism of black and ethnic minority women in Britain and the Netherlands who criticized the "hegemony of the white women in the feminist movement" and demanded that their histories and experiences be heard (Hoskyns 1996, 8).

The tension between similarities and diversity presents a challenge to EU policymakers. The patriarchal structure presents a unifying reality, yet women's experience, sexuality, ethnicity, culture, and access to resources present considerably different levels of domination by this structure. Furthermore, diversity is particularly acute in the European Union as its 15 member states embody considerably different socioeconomic levels and varying cultural norms and values. From the role of women as political leaders to family policy spending there is a clear demarcation in Europe between the Nordic countries (Sweden, Finland, Denmark) and the southern countries (Italy, Greece and Portugal,) on the status of women in politics and the development of policies that reflect the interests and concerns of women (see Gardiner and Leijenaar 1997; McBride Stetson and Mazur 1995).

Conclusions

Women's transnational activism enabled by Article 141 led to the expansive development of sex equality policy in the European Union. By studying this process in terms of a dynamic model, we are able to understand how activists were able to develop these supranational policy outcomes. This analysis has examined the creation, implementation, and evolution of Article 141. This analysis revealed the significant impact that policy designs have on women's participation in EU policymaking. I found that although the issue construction of Article 141 was economic, the dual nature of its text led to a set of both intended and unintended policy outcomes. The drafters intended to produce a competition policy that targeted business and perpetuated a norm of elite domination and patriarchal control over the policy process. Instead, Article 141 served as a social justice provision that empowered women and enabled the expansive development of European sex equality policy.

This empowerment must also be understood in terms of its limitations. This study has illustrated how the ambiguous and flexible nature of EU policymaking created an unintentionally hospitable environment for women's activism (as legal experts and policy activists) and the expansion of EU competence on women's issues. Simultaneously, this analysis has also offered a clear argument for why sex equality policies are at the most only the foundation for policies that can actually abate the inequalities confronted by women throughout Europe. Policies that fail to embrace the diversity of culture, race, and experience of women will do little to alter the patriarchal structures perpetuating their subordination. Though the women of Europe should be pleased with their clear success of getting their interests on the agenda, they must continue to use the opportunities afforded them through the European Union to broaden the scope of women's policies. Transnational exchange of information among women's legal networks, equality units, and women's organizations will be increasingly important with the enlargement of the EU to include central and eastern European countries. In particular, the status of women in these accession countries stands to benefit greatly from these links, as their current lack of an established network of women's interests will inhibit successful implementation and adherence to EU sex equality policies.[19]

The study also suggests general conclusions regarding the linkages between global politics and women's transnational activism. This relationship has only begun to be studied by feminist theorists and policy experts, and a systematic study clearly remains absent from the international relations literature (Bretherton and Sperling 1996; Hoskyns 1986 and 1996).[20] The analysis revealed the following general relationship: International policy can create psychological or physical space that enables national women activists to engage in transnational discussions on common issues. In the spring of 1966, a Belgium labor union discussed the implications of Article 141 for women workers. Following the event, women organized, and the result was a 3,000-person strike protesting wage inequalities between men and women (Hoskyns 1996). Furthermore, as we saw from this study, in the early 1970s, national activist labor lawyers such as Vogel-Polsky shifted their national litigation strategies to include the European Court of Justice.

This creation of space in turn provides the setting for more permanent inclusion in international policy processes. Today, more than 40 years after treaty negotiations on Article 141, women activists have increasingly become involved in EU politics in Brussels through their work within research centers (e.g., the Centre for Research on European Women), umbrella organizations (e.g., the European Women's Lobby), commission-sponsored networks (the National Legal Experts Group on Equal Treatment), and consultancy firms (Engender). It is through this series of interactions that women are able to more fully participate in the international governance process and create policies that recognize their diverse interests. Awareness and utilization of this dynamic relationship will be essential for the continued empowerment of women worldwide.

Notes

1. The term *European Union* (EU) refers to the present governance structure in Western Europe that includes 15 national governments. These governments are called member states.

2. Prior to 1998, Article 141 was numbered as Article 119. Article 119 of the 1957 Treaty of Rome provided that member states ensure and maintain the principle that women and men receive equal pay for equal work. An amended version of this provision is now Article 141 under the 1998 Treaty of Amsterdam. For consistency, this analysis will refer to the treaty provision by its new numbering (Article 141).

3. *European integration* in this chapter refers to the process by which the European Union (referred to as the European Community before being renamed in 1992) has developed and continues to evolve as a policymaking arena. It refers to the processes by which an

international agreement between independent European nation-states has developed into an institutionalized supranational governance structure that grants rights to individuals. See Dinan 1994 for an in-depth discussion of this historical process.

4. Full Text of Article 141 from the Treaty of Rome:

> Each Member State shall during the first stage ensure and subsequently maintain the application of the principle that men and women should receive equal pay for equal work.
>
> For the purpose of the Article 'pay' means the ordinary basic or minimum wage or salary and any other consideration, whether in cash or in kind, which the worker receives, directly or indirectly, in respect of his employment from his employer.
>
> Equal Pay without discrimination based on sex means:
>
> a) that pay for the same work at piece rates shall be calculated on the basis of the same unit of measurement; b) that pay for work at time rates shall be the same for the same job.

5. At the time, there were six member states: Belgium, France, Germany, Italy, Luxembourg, and the Netherlands.

6. Case 80/70 *Defrenne I* and Case 43/75 *Defrenne II* are examples of this litigation. See Cichowski (2001) for a discussion of this case law.

7. The use of the general concept "economic knowledge and discourse" in this chapter refers to the articulation of "expert knowledge" by those individuals of the technical profession who use economic rationality and the scientific method to define problems and develop the most cost-effective solution. This is influenced by definitions of "scientific knowledge" in Schneider and Ingram 1997. It also refers to the general framing of policy debates in terms of cause and effect relationships as related to the Common Market. This concept of "knowledge and discourse" is also similar (both in definition and framing power) to the knowledge contributed by "epistemic communities" to international policy coordination (Haas 1992).

8. For example, see Case 286/85 *McDermott and Cotter v. Minister for Social Welfare* ECR 1987, 1453.

9. For example, see Case 43/75 *Defrenne II* ECR 1976: 455; Case 14/83 *Von Colson* ECR 1984: 1891; Case 177/88 *Dekker* ECR 1990: 3941; Case 152/84 *Marshall I* ECR 1986: 723, Case 32/93 *Webb* ECR 1994: 3567.

10. Council Directive 75/117/EEC, Council Directive 76/207/EEC, and Council Directive 79/7/EEC.

11. Unanimity voting requires that all member states agree to pass the legislation.

12. Case C-13/94 *P v. S and Cornwall County Council* ECR 1996, 2143.

13. *Bilka-Kaufhaus GMbH v. Karin Weber von Hartz* Case 170/84 ECR 1986: 1607.

14. Council Directive 86/378 and Council Directive 86/613.

15. COM (80) 832 final February 11, 1981.

16. Case 14/83 *Von Colson* ECR 1984: 1891, and *Hofmann* 184/83 ECR 1984: 3047. See also Tesoka 1999.

17. *Barber v. Guardian Royal Exchange Assurance Group* Case 262/88 ECR 1990: 1889.

18. *Hofmann v. Barmer Ersatzkasse*, Case 184/83 ECR 1984: 3047.

19. See Rai, Pilkington, and Phizacklea 1992 and Lovenduski 1997 for a discussion of the absence of grassroots feminist activism in the former state socialist systems.

20. Recent international relations scholarship has begun to examine the role of transnational activism in international policymaking in the issue areas of the environment and human rights (e.g., Brysk 1993;1996; Haas 1992).

14

Redefining Security

Okinawa Women's Resistance to U.S. Militarism

Yoko Fukumura and Martha Matsuoka

ON THE EVE OF THE GATHERING OF THE HEADS OF STATE FROM THE UNITED STATES, France, Italy, Canada, the United Kingdom, Japan, Germany, and Russia (the "G8"[1]) in Okinawa in July 2000, a group of Okinawan women hosted an international meeting of women to strategize about women's responses to globalization and militarization. The International Women's Summit to Redefine Security was held in Naha and drew women from Okinawa, Japan, South Korea, the Philippines, the United States, and Puerto Rico. Following their summit, the women issued a statement:

> The purpose of this meeting was to challenge the principle of 'national security' on which the economic policies of the G8 are based. These economic policies can never achieve genuine security. Rather, they generate gross insecurity for most peoples of the world and devastate the natural environment. These economic policies are inextricably linked to increasing militarization throughout the world. Militaries reap enormous profits for multinational corporations and stockholders through the development, production and sale of weapons of destruction. Moreover, militaries maintain control of local populations and repress those who oppose the fundamental principles on which the world economic system is based. (East Asia–U.S. Women's Network Against Militarism 2000)

The statement sent two messages. First, national security interests do little for women in East Asia and the United States. Instead, principles of "national security" provide the rationale for an increased global militarization that privileges profit over people. In doing so, the global militarized economy breeds deep insecurity by increasing the economic and environmental vulnerability of local communities, particularly that of women and children. Second, women resisting the presence of U.S.

militarism in their respective communities were organizing across national borders to put forth alternative frameworks for global security and sustainability. Challenging the traditional paradigms of "security," the women instead assert a framework of security based on the following four key tenets (Reardon 1998):

- The environment in which we live must be able to sustain human and natural life;
- People's basic survival needs for food, clothing, shelter, health care, and education must be met;
- People's fundamental human dignity and respect for cultural identities must be honored; and
- People and the natural environment must be protected from avoidable harm.

With these principles in mind, women from Asia and the U.S. gathered in Okinawa to raise awareness and visibility of the local Okinawan women's resistance to the U.S. military and the negative impacts of globalization and militarization. Not only is the framework relevant to the struggle of East Asian women against the U.S. military, it also illuminates examples of women struggling worldwide to survive increasing economic and environmental insecurity in a global context in which neoliberal economic policies push for the privatization of state assets, lower barriers to trade, and elimination of restrictions of transnational movement of capital. For Asian women in particular, examples include the Cordillera People's Alliance struggle to stop the takeover of their indigenous land by multinational corporations and national Philippine development strategies; young Laotian girls of the Laotian Organizing Project leading their refugee community in Richmond, California, in a grassroots movement to make government and the corporate oil refineries accountable to the community; the international campaigns of activist organizations such as Gabriela to stop the degradation and sexual exploitation of Asian women; and the formation of Sweatshop Watch, an organization formed to monitor corporate practices and stop the exploitation of women's labor.

In the case of Okinawa, this framework of alternative security emerges from a dynamic of material conditions facing women across East Asia who live with the ongoing presence of the U.S. military. The emergence of women's resistance to militarism must be seen in context of the relationship between the U.S. military presence and globalization in East Asia. In a revealing speech delivered at University of California, Los Angeles, in October 1998, then Secretary of Defense William Cohen remarked, "U.S. troops would be the most professional and most ready military in the world in order to protect the emerging and stabilizing capital markets around the globe." His remarks, in the wake of the Asian financial crisis, explicitly tie the presence of the U.S. military to the future of globalizing economies and to the support and protection of national governments in the struggle to develop markets. Though his rhetoric made direct the link between the U.S. military and globalizing economies, John Feffer (2000) argues that the relationship between the military and globalization in East Asia is much more complex than Cohen implies and that policies of globalization and U.S. militarism "do not always mix well in East Asia." Feffer notes:

> Certain military imperatives, such as a regional missile defense system, have driven wedges between countries that neoliberals want to unite through free trade. Moreover, certain economic trends, such as the deregulation of financial markets, have weakened some of the very countries that U.S. troops and battleships are pledged to protect. Herein lies the central problem for U.S. policy toward East Asia: the tension between core military and economic objectives. U.S. military strategy in the region depends on the maintenance of the Cold War, with North Korea, China, or a set of new "threats" substituting for the Soviet Union. U.S. economic strategy, although initially forged in the crucible of the Cold War, is increasingly dependent on breaking down ideological divisions in the region. (22)

The combination of neoliberal economic policy and Cold War military strategies, or "gunboat globalization," Feffer argues, must be replaced by a multilateral policy framework that assumes the cooperation between and within countries in East Asia. Certainly, governmental actors are key in this transformation of policy, but Feffer also acknowledges the role of civic actors and activism that challenge military budgets, labor conditions, and employment security:

> A true multilaterialism—independent of the United States, economically equitable, and accountable to the citizens of the region—cannot be solely created by government officials. As transnational movements in East Asia are discovering, true multilaterialism must be built from the ground up. (22)

An examination of Okinawan women and their resistance to U.S. militarism suggests that such a strategy to address globalization and militarization may be possible in Asia. Using the case study of Okinawa Women Act against Military Violence (OWAAMV), a nongovernmental, grassroots organization, this chapter examines the cultural, historical, political and economic context of antimilitarism in Okinawa. Drawing on the ideology and strategies used by OWAAMV women, we argue that their activism suggests alternative paths of security and development in the face of globalization and militarization.[2]

The Context for Antimilitarism

The physical and economic context of the U.S. military in Okinawa is a result of the political relationship between Okinawa and Japan and the legacy of World War II. Once known as the kingdom of Ryukyu, Okinawa was annexed and renamed in 1879 by imperial Japan, becoming the first foreign country to be so absorbed. Colonial systems of government and education were imposed on Okinawa in which "centuries-old national systems of government, justice, education, honours, etc. were destroyed and replaced with double-decker colonial societies where the Japanese military, administrators, educators, professionals, and businessmen dominated disenfranchised natives" (Taira 1997, 143). Land reforms between 1899 and 1903 abolished communal land tenure and introduced a system of private property and inheritance. Lebra (1966) argues that this single act "ushered in a series of changes which altered the whole fabric of village life," most notably the exclusion of peasant families from land bases. The economic dislocation of these households forced many families to sell their daughters to brokers to work as prostitutes, particularly in Tsuji, the island's licensed "entertainment district" (Mercier 1996, 51; Okinawa Women Act against Military Violence 1996).[3] With these reforms, official policy focused directly on the eradication of Okinawan culture and the transformation of Okinawans into Japanese nationals (Lebra 1966, 18). Japanese educational systems were institutionalized, forcing the introduction of standardized Japanese language and the subordination of all things Okinawan.

During World War II, Okinawa was the site of the only land battle between the United States and Japan. An intense battle destroyed the built and natural environment, particularly in the central and southern portions of mainland Okinawa (Ota 1999).[4] During the four months of heavy fighting, more than 200,000 people were killed; approximately 122,000 of these were Okinawan civilians, nearly one-quarter of the Okinawan population (Tamamori and James 1999, 10). Entire families were also destroyed due to the mass suicides committed by many Okinawans in fearful response to the Japanese imperial propaganda that warned Okinawans against the "barbarians" of the West (Keyso 2000, viii; Ota 1999, 16;).[5] Many Okinawans believe that the Battle of Okinawa was strategically directed toward Okinawa by Emperor Hirohito to spare lives and destruction on mainland Japan and to leverage better surrender terms from the Allies. Okinawans also believe that the central government in Tokyo sacrificed them again in 1952 when Japan retained "residual sovereignty" over Okinawa but the U.S. military, through its occupation, exercised de facto sovereignty (Johnson 1999, 24).

For Okinawan women, physical monuments recognize this tragic chapter of their history. The Shiraume no To memorial, for example, marks the site where 74 students from the Okinawa Second Girl's High School and their 11 teachers committed suicide when it became apparent that the Battle for Okinawa would end in defeat for Japan (Robinson 1969, 46). Himeyuri no To marks the site where 143 students and 15 teachers of the Okinawa First Girl's High School, who served as nurses to the Japanese army, died. Robinson notes, "During mop-up operations they apparently hid or were working in [the] cave. Details of what happened are not clear but apparently they were called to come out, refused, and were killed" (46). While there are different accounts of the fate of these women and girls, Rabson (1999) writes that the legendary Himeyuri Student Corps were conscripted into service as nurses to the Japanese military, but "such sacrifices only swelled the numbers of victims in a tragically misguided cause. Japanese soldiers ordered mass suicides of Okinawan civilians to stretch dwindling food supplies, and forced others out of overcrowded caves and tunnels into heavy enemy fire." In addition, Okinawan women were subject to the Japanese military's policy of providing "comfort women," sexual slaves, to the approximately 100,000 soldiers deployed throughout the Okinawan islands. Approximately 500 Okinawan women and an estimated 1,000 abducted Korean women were sent to the 130 military brothels established in houses, public buildings, barracks, storehouses and even caves to service the Japanese military (Okinawa Women Act Against Military Violence 1996).

Though the U.S. occupation of Japan ended in 1952, Okinawa remained under direct control of the U.S. military until 1972. During this time Okinawan people carried passports to travel to the Japanese mainland, used U.S. dollars, and drove on the right side of the street as in the United States. Even following reversion to Japan in 1972, the dominance of the U.S. military remains in Okinawa at the invitation of the Japanese government. Between 1945 and 1972, U.S. forces designed and built 56 military installations in Japan; 39 are still located on the main island of Okinawa and the surrounding islands of Okinawa Prefecture (fig. 14.1). Though Okinawa makes up only .6 percent of the Japanese territory, roughly 75 percent of all U.S. military installations in Japan are located there. They occupy approximately 20 percent of the developable land on the main island of Okinawa, limiting the development of local economic infrastructure in a region that has above-average unemployment (6.0 percent compared to 3.4 percent in the rest of Japan in 1997) and below average per capita income (70 percent of other Japanese in 1998) (Bandow 1998; Okinawa Prefectural Government 1998). Coastlines, airspace, and prime agricultural land still remain in control of the U.S. military (McCormack 1998, 2).

Moon (1997) and Takazato (1996) refer to these U.S. military facilities as sites of oppression and violence that represent a history of military violence against women. Historic research by George Kerr ([1958] 1975) documents that the first act of U.S. military violence against Okinawan women occurred in 1854 with the arrival of Admiral Perry and the rape of a 50-year-old Okinawan woman by one of his crew members. After the incident, Perry demanded a trial not of the rapist but for the local Okinawan men who chased the crew member and caused him to fall to his death. The Okinawan men were tried; one was sentenced to banishment from the island for life; the others were banished for eight years. According to historical recounts, Perry demonstrated his "keen sensitivity" by presenting to the rape victim a "handsome present" consisting of a few yards of cotton cloth (G. Kerr [1958] 1975, 331; Mercier 1996, 51; Okinawa Women Act against Military Violence 1996).

Military violence, particularly rapes and assaults against women, continue 150 years after Perry's arrival. More than 200 cases of rape and assaults against women have been formally reported and documented since 1945. Of these recorded crimes, no charges were filed in 15 percent of the cases, more than 60 percent resulted in only incident reports to Okinawa and U.S. military authorities, and only 20 percent of the cases ended in arrest or prosecution (Okinawa Women Act against Military Violence 1997).[6] According to the Status of Forces Agreement (SOFA), suspect service members are not automatically transferred to local authorities. Instead, Japanese law enforcement agencies must, as stated in Article 17, section 5, of SOFA, "file complaints with the prosecutors' office based on clear suspicion." Johnson (1999) notes that SOFA therefore gives the United States the right to refuse Japanese requests to hand over suspects when they are affiliated with the military (117–18).[7]

The U.S. presence also brings a threat and legacy of military toxics that has harmed not only the health of women and children, but the natural environment as well.[8] Little is known about the extent of military contamination on military bases

FIGURE 14.1: *U.S. Military Facilities on Okinawa.*

in Okinawa because there has been minimal site research conducted. However, analyses of environmental conditions at similar military posts in the U.S. suggest that high levels of contamination exist in and around the facilities in Okinawa. For example, contaminants such as oil products, petroleum paint, paint thinner, lubricating oil, lead, PCBs, asbestos and contamination from underground storage tanks are commonly found on air bases. In addition, artillery firing exercise waste such as empty shells and unexploded ammunition and missiles exist in areas used for live firing ranges and in areas that were heavily damaged during war.

Though a comprehensive environmental assessment has not been conducted by the Okinawa prefectural government, the Japanese national government, the U.S. military, or the U.S. government, a range of military toxics exist. A 1998 study by the prefectural government reports that babies born to women living near Kadena Air Base showed significantly lower birthweights than those born in any other part of Japan, attributable to severe noise generated by the base (Kirk et al. 1999, 1). A 1984 study shows that cleaning agents from Kadena Air Base regularly leak into public drainage systems. These cleaning agents as well as Agent Orange defoliant were used frequently during the Vietnam War and launched by aircraft from Okinawa; both contaminants have been found in local waterways. In 1996, 120 tons of substances including mercury and PCB were discovered at the former Onna Communications Site on the west coast of central Okinawa. In February 1997, bullets containing depleted uranium were found on the island of Torishima and in its surrounding waters. A 1998 study shows that wastewater containing oil from Camp Kinser is routinely dumped into Okinawan public sewer systems. In addition, ongoing military drills such as the urban guerrilla training conducted at Camp Hansen produce red soil erosion, destroying marine life such as the edible sea grass *mozuku*.

Though the United States and Japan have agreed to begin transferring military facilities and base lands back to Japanese civilian administration, local government officials and nongovernmental organizations (NGOs) in Okinawa are concerned about the public health and natural environmental impacts of military toxics, and the fact they have only limited access to information on environmental issues related to the bases. Local efforts to address U.S. military toxics are confined by the regulatory and legal frameworks that pertain to the U.S. military presence in Japan, SOFA, the international treaty between the United States and Japan signed following the end of World War II.[9] Title 4 of SOFA states:

> The United States is not obliged, when it returns facilities and areas to Japan, on the expiration of this Agreement or at an earlier date, to restore the facilities and areas to the conditions in which they were at the time they became available to the United States Armed Forces, or to compensate Japan in lieu of such investigation.[10]

Taira (1997) argues that this political situation reflects Okinawa's "dual oppression" by Japan and the United States set in place by the occupation of the United States from 1945 to 1972 (165–66). Decision making about the bases remain in the political spheres of Tokyo and Washington, D.C., and within the parameters of international legal instruments such as SOFA and the U.S.-Japan Security Treaty. These legal frameworks create a structure in which Okinawan voices—whether locally elected or at the grassroots—are negligible influences in national and international discussions. In the absence of Okinawan political influence, local and national development processes prioritize the interests of Japan as a state and its national role in the global economy and in regional security and trade (McCormack 1998, 2).

Women's Resistance to the Military

When the world's media flocked to Okinawa in the summer of 2000 to cover the G8 Summit, Okinawans staged a prefecture-wide protest to raise awareness of the negative effects of the U.S. military in Okinawa. Nearly 30,000 Okinawan people linked arms in protest to form a human peace chain around Kadena Air Base, the largest U.S. Air Force base in the Pacific, timed for the arrival of President Clinton. Just days before, a young schoolgirl had been assaulted by a drunken U.S. Marine while she slept in her home; the same week, another U.S. serviceman committed a hit-and-run in which an Okinawan man was struck while crossing a street.

These Okinawan acts of resistance against the U.S. military were not new, however. In 1955, the first prefecture-wide demonstration against the United States occurred in response to the "Yumiko-chan incident," in which a six-year-old girl was raped and murdered by a U.S. military officer. A similar protest erupted in 1970 when a drunken serviceman killed an Okinawan woman in a hit-and-run accident. One week later, a second hit-and-run accident injured an Okinawan man in Koza, the district outside Kadena Air Base. According to reports, military police fired shots to intimidate the crowd that gathered, setting off what is known as the Koza rebellion, where thousands of Okinawans rose up and burned American cars and buildings in and around Kadena Air Base (Hosaka 1999). In the 1980s, Okinawa women, supported by women from the Japanese mainland, organized a hunger strike to protest the construction of an urban guerrilla training camp in the village of Onna. The citizen movement against the training facility viewed the U.S. military as threatening a sacred site as well as the environment. The training site would violate Mount Onna as a place of spiritual worship, be a potential threat to the safety of nearby residents, and cause the erosion of iron-rich red soil, which in turn would destroy the ecosystem of the coral reefs surrounding Okinawa.

In 1995, about 85,000 people came together in Naha, the capital of Okinawa, in the largest public demonstration and rally in postwar Okinawa, to protest the brutal rape of a 12-year-old schoolgirl by three U.S. servicemen. The rape, and specifically the girl's decision to report the rape to local authorities and make public the crime committed against her, catalyzed a resurgence of antimilitary activism in Okinawa. Carolyn Francis (1999) writes,

> Parents, teachers, and students, many of whom up until now remained silent on the troubling issue of the mammoth U.S. military presence, rose up as one, raising their voices to declare, 'No More!' in the largest, most broad based and longest lasting citizen protest in postwar Okinawan history. Their response sent unexpected tremors reverberating not only throughout Japan, but also throughout the U.S., ultimately shaking the very foundations of the U.S.-Japanese defense relationship spelled out in the U.S.-Japan Security Treaty and the more detailed U.S.-Japan Status of Forces Agreement. (189)

That nearly 1 in 10 people within the entire prefecture turned out for the demonstration signified a clear revival of the antimilitarism movement, which focused for the first time on the U.S. military presence as an act of violence against women and children. Fueling the movement were protests of the legal procedures that privilege the U.S. military. Following the rape, the accused were not turned over to the Japanese authorities for 25 days. The men eventually stood trial in Okinawa, were found guilty, and are now serving sentences of between six and one-half and seven years in Japan. Over the course of the trial and sentencing, the protests continued. Finally, on September 8, 1996, a year after the rape, the people of Okinawa went to the polls to vote on the first prefecture-wide citizen referendum in Japan's history. The nonbinding but highly symbolic referendum, asked, "Do you support the continued presence of U.S. military in Okinawa?" Sixty percent of voters cast ballots; 90 percent voted "no," raising a loud voice against the presence of the U.S. military in Okinawa (Johnson 1999, 12).

The visibility of the issues of women and children in the reemergence of antimilitarism was due to the active leadership role of Okinawan women, and in particular Okinawa Women Act Against Militarism (OWAAMV). Since its formation, campaigns and activities have reflected a perspective on militarism that recognizes women's rights as human rights and the military as an affront to human security.[11] Keiko Itokazu, co-chair of OWAAMV and an elected member to the Okinawa Prefectural Assembly, says:

> Our campaigning is not anti-U.S., but against military forces. The Japanese forcibly involved women in Okinawa in that wheel of destruction. During

> the war, not just women from Okinawa and the mainland but all over the region, Taiwan and Korea, were all called in to serve the requirements of the military. The military always forces women into this unproductive process of destruction; that is what their existence and logic is all about. Only with that sort of logic, war logic, could the destruction of our natural environment and the denial of women's human rights be possible. (Itokazu 1996, 11)

In a report to the International Conference on Violence against Women in War and Armed Conflict Situations OWAAMV argued that (1) even in times of "peace," the long-term military presence results in violence against women; (2) military facilities represent sites of violence, illustrated by deployment of U.S. military forces from Okinawa to engage in conflict in Korea, Vietnam, and the Persian Gulf; (3) training facilities used by military personnel expose residents and civilians to physical and psychological domination and risk to safety; (4) the extent of violence against women is related to the attitudes of the host government, reflecting the status of women, human rights, and the legal system that is in place to protect the status of women in society; (5) violence against women and the violation of their human rights is related to the economic relationships between the country deploying the military presence and the country receiving the military presence; and (6) the military is a male-dominated structure that maintains constant war-making readiness, domination, and violence (Takazato 1997a).

Japanese feminist scholar Yayori Matsui (1998) further notes that OWAAMV's activism is drawn from a framework of alternative security.

> Okinawan women challenge the very concept of security by asking whose security it is if women and children are raped and harassed by military men and put under fear and threat. They forcefully call for people's and women's security, not security of the state. They claim that violence against women cannot be prevented without confronting and doing away with U.S. military dominance and without achieving demilitarization in the Asia-Pacific region. They emphasize that the army itself is a mechanism of violence. They also broadened the concept of violence against women from war and armed conflict situations to cover the situations of long-term military presence, because women near military bases are constantly victimized by sexual violence, even if there is no war or armed conflict. (61)

Ueunten (1997) suggests that OWAAMV has been able to frame antimilitarism in a way that goes beyond nationalism, one which moves toward a broader sense of community reflecting the historical evolution of the Okinawan diaspora. The political and economic history of Okinawa, the international relationships between the United States and Japan, and the colonial legacy of both nations in Okinawa serve as a complex backdrop for any local antibase struggle. Traditional explanations using colonial theory to describe Okinawa's history and future have limited the historical and potential agency of Okinawans to define their own history and future. Ueunten argues, however, that the activism of OWAAMV challenges these explanations by putting forward a type of activism which recognizes and emerges from the implications of Okinawan history, culture, and political and economic conditions under Japanese and U.S. rule.

Institutionalizing a Movement

Though less than six years in existence, OWAAMV draws on their own history and experience of organizing and brings these struggles into a cohesive resistance against the U.S. military within a framework of redefined security. The founding of OWAAMV reflects an important convergence of earlier organizing with the almost simultaneous events of the fourth UN Women's NGO Conference held in Huairou, China, and the rape of the 12-year-old schoolgirl by three U.S. servicemen in the late summer of 1995. The timing of the rape and the level of organization of the women's delegation to Beijing were critical in forming OWAAMV and spurring the resurgence of activism against the U.S. military in Okinawa.

Ten years earlier, a broad base of women's organizations coalesced to establish the annual Unai [sisterhood] Festival, a public gathering of women including labor activists, artists, feminists, alternative natural childbirth groups, peace and human rights activists, a group for mothers' and children's issues, recycling groups, international cooperation groups, a women managers' society, and a consumers' cooperative (Mercier 1996, 54). While not all groups involved with the Unai Festival are involved directly in the antimilitary activism, they have become organized through the festival to create an alternative women-based community in Okinawa where one did not previously exist. Akibayashi (1998) notes that the organizing of the initial *Unai* Festival itself emerged from exposure by Okinawan women to the 1975 UN Conference in Mexico City, which initiated the Decade of Women, and the World Conference in Nairobi in 1985: "The *Unai* Festival was born to articulate the experiences of Okinawan women who participated in the NGO Forum in Nairobi where three women of (OWA) [Okinawa Women Act against Military Violence] held a workshop on the prostitution problems in Okinawa" (Akibayashi 1998).

It was out of this coalition that Okinawan women organized with women from mainland Japan to stop the construction of an urban guerilla training camp in Onna Village in the late 1980s. In one case, the women sat in the middle of the road to stop trucks from delivering supplies to the base. On October 9, 1989, the daily newspaper *Ryukyu Shimpo* reported on the women's hunger strike:

> For 30 hours, Suzuyo Takazato, newly elected Naha City councilmember, accompanied by Yoko Marosawa, women's history researcher, and Chiyo Saito, a member of the editorial women's magazine *Agora*, went on a hunger strike to support the opposition movement in Onna against the construction of the training facility. The hunger strike took place the day after the Okinawa Women's Unai Festival. Some women from the Japan's Women Conference who came from the mainland to attend the conference in Okinawa were so moved by the Onna-son struggle that they continued the hunger strike after Ms. Takazato and the other two women had finished.

In addition to direct actions, women activists began providing counseling and social services to prostitutes and women working in military base towns. In 1994 the group began organizing its participation for the Beijing Conference to focus on issues of militarism and its impact on women, children, and the environment. Instead of joining a delegation of women from mainland Japan, women organizers decided to organize their own Okinawan-based group, forming a delegation of 71 women from throughout the prefecture. Preparation included English teaching programs, informal discussion groups, and a pre-Beijing meeting sponsored by the women's division of the prefectural government (Akibayashi 1998, 23). Workshops on the topic of militarism and women focused on themes of peace, the environment, traditional customs that discriminate against women, labor issues, the aging society, and an Okinawa women's network (Akibayashi 1998, 23).[12] Over the year of preparation, the delegates organized media coverage and ultimately invited reporters to become part of the delegation. As a result, the activities of the delegation were the topic of heavy media coverage, and the activities of the women while in Beijing were the subject of daily reports in the Okinawan newspapers.

When the delegation returned from Beijing in early September, they quickly learned that the young rape victim had made public the crime committed against her by the U.S. servicemen. Francis (1999) writes,

> All of the Okinawan participants attending the Beijing conference felt buoyed up by the support and solidarity of women from throughout the world, as they realized how many others faced problems similar to theirs. . . . Their elation was short-lived however, for they were met at the airport in Okinawa by colleagues who informed them of the rape, the news of which had been made public two days earlier. . . . The women who had been in Beijing went into action immediately, calling a press conference for

> the following date, September 11, to issue a statement. . . . The same group organized a "Rally of Okinawa women, children and islanders against military violence," held 12 days later on September 23. This rally provided an opportunity for ordinary Okinawans to express their thoughts and feelings concerning the rape, since the program included a 'One-minute Speech' open-microphone hour. Long lines of women waited their turn at floor mikes to pour out their anger, sorrow, and sense of helplessness. (190)

In the aftermath of the rape, OWAAMV became the first grassroots women's group in Okinawa focused specifically on the impact of militarization on women and children.

Strategies for Action

OWAAMV has grown to approximately 200 members. Co-chairs are elected annually, and a 10-woman steering committee leads the group. The steering committee meets once a month and on an as-needed basis; the general membership meets every six months. OWAAMV supports itself through donations, honoraria, and membership dues of 2,000 yen per year (approximately $20). All decisions are made through consensus of the members. Co-chair Suzuyo Takazato (1999) notes that "in Okinawan culture, consensus is the only way. Though we as women quarrel and disagree on certain issues, we come together and move onward together."

Activities of OWAAMV reflect five key strategies: direct action and protest, education and awareness, building networks and alliances, electing women to public office, and youth development and leadership.

Direct Action and Protest

The emergence of OWAAMV and its continuing activities illustrate the central role of direct action and protest in women's organizing throughout Okinawa and the world. The experiences of direct action and protest provided the base for the formation of OWAAMV following the 1995 rape. Since then, the organization has undertaken other forms of direct action such as a 12-day women's sit-in protest and signature campaign in November 1998 to raise Okinawan awareness of military violence against women. On the fifth day of the sit-in, a 25-member delegation traveled to Tokyo to deliver an appeal with 55,000 signatures to the Japanese prime minister, the Foreign Ministry, and the U.S. Embassy to protest the rape and the U.S. military presence in Okinawa (Francis 1999, 192). Additional examples of direct action include organizing demonstrations such as the human chain formed around Kadena Air Base in 1999 and during the G8 Summit in July 2000.

Education and Awareness

A core area of OWAAMV work focuses on raising awareness of the effects of the U.S. military in Okinawa. Members have compiled a detailed chronology of acts of violence committed by U.S. military members against Okinawans and documented the presence and impact of military toxics. With this research, they make presentations to women's organizations, peace and environmental groups, labor unions, churches, and student organizations within Okinawa and in mainland Japan in order to expand their membership and build their campaigns.

In mid-1998 OWAAMV began a campaign along with U.S.-based environmental organizations to protect the endangered *dugong*, a species of manatee found off the western coast of Okinawa. The Okinawan women see the survival and preservation of the *dugong* as necessarily tied to the prevention of the construction of a proposed military heliport that would destroy the habitat of the *dugong* and as a way to preserve the delicate marine ecosystem of the coral reef. In addition, OWAAMV is involved in campaigns focused on the cleanup of toxic contamination at military installations. These campaigns include demands for access to information, adequate funding to conduct public health and toxics assessments, and the staff and money to clean up military sites when they close and to get pollution-prevention measures started at operating sites.

OWAAMV leaders recognize the necessity of building international pressure to push the Japanese government to take action on environmental cleanup of the military bases in Okinawa. In collaboration with another NGO, the Okinawa Environmental Network, a representative from OWAAMV attended the International Grassroots Summit on Military Base Cleanup held in Washington, D.C., in October 1999. Together with activists from 10 countries in which the United States has military bases, a Host Country Bill of Rights was created to demand a set of guidelines to address the harm of toxics created by U.S. military activities in host countries (International Grassroots Summit on Military Base Cleanup 1999). These organized trips to participate in and speak at international events have been a large part of OWAAMV's work. Visits to and from international conferences are widely covered in the local Okinawan media, reflecting OWAAMV's commitment to building a cadre of media reporters, many of whom are women, to report on their struggles. In their visits to the United States in 1996 and 1998, delegates included columnists from the Okinawan press who provided daily reports from the delegation.

Following the 1995 rape, OWAAMV organized a four-city (San Francisco Bay Area, Boston, Honolulu, and Washington, D.C.) women's peace caravan through the United States and met with elected officials and community organizations to raise awareness of the effects of the U.S. military on women and the environment in Okinawa. A similar peace caravan was organized in 1998, stopping in Los Angeles, San Diego, and Washington, D.C. Both caravans included teachers, local government representatives, youths, and community organizers.[13] In addition to community forums and radio programs, the delegates met with U.S. government officials such as Congressman Ronald Dellums of California (then head of the Armed Services Committee of the U.S. House of Representatives), California State Senator Hilda Solis, U.S. Senators Barbara Boxer and Dianne Feinstein of California, and staffs from the U.S. Department of Justice, Department of Defense, and State Department. In October 1998, the group helped organize and participated in a congressional briefing sponsored by Congress members John Conyers, Barbara Lee, and Cynthia McKinney.

Issues of concern during the caravans and the congressional hearings were articulated in four key areas: (1) U.S. military violence against women, including domestic abuse, rape, and prostitution; (2) environmental damage, including the need for cleanup of U.S. bases in Okinawa and the public health effects of toxics; (3) Amerasian children; and (4) Status of Forces Agreements and Treaties that determine the scope and scale of U.S. military presence in Okinawa. During its 1998 trip, the group presented the following specific demands at the Congressional briefing (Okinawa Women Act against Military Violence 1998):

- We call for a full investigation of all past U.S. military crimes against women in Okinawa
- We call for the reduction and realignment, not the mere moving around of U.S. military bases within Okinawa; moreover, we call for the removal of U.S. military forces, especially the Marine force, from Okinawa
- We call for a halt of the plan to build a new offshore heliport base in Okinawa that will cause environmental destruction
- We call for full disclosure of all past military base toxic contamination in Okinawa, for the establishment of a toxic cleanup plan and for the clarification of responsibility for cleanup; to achieve these goals we call for the revision of the Status of Forces Agreement
- We call for the guarantee of the human rights of women and children and the necessary passage and enactment by each of the countries involved to realize that guarantee.

Other international educational strategies include organizing a delegation of women and youths to participate in the Hague Appeal for Peace talks in May 1999. A key objective was to demand action by the international courts to address issues of military violence against women in the Pacific. With the announcement that the G8 Summit would be held in Okinawa in July 2000, the group developed a set of activities and actions designed to develop alternative analyses and critiques of the global economic and military system. Recognizing the media opportunities provided by the G8 Summit, the group also agreed to organize an International Women's Summit as a way to focus media attention on militarization and its negative effects on women, children, and the environment in Okinawa. OWAAMV developed a series of local educational workshops to raise issues such as globalization and alternative security paradigms. At the invitation of the group, feminist scholar Betty Reardon led a workshop to discuss women's rights as human rights and to outline her framework of security, which is based on elements of human needs rather than national needs.

Building Women's Networks and Alliances

The work of OWAAMV and the networks it has developed locally, regionally, and internationally have contributed to the learning and transformative process of women's skills and leadership. The formation of these networks constitutes what Keck and Sikkink (1999) call *transnational advocacy networks* that link actors in civil societies, states, and international organizations. By forming a broad set of networks, OWAAMV is able to "multiply the opportunities for dialogue and exchange." Through these networks against militarism, it has created a broad set of political alliances as well as support, information, and potential resources.

In the months following the formation of OWAAMV, members made connections with women's and antimilitarist organizations in mainland Japan. Akibayashi (1998) notes that OWAAMV and its network building work rests on the idea that women's rights are human rights and that there is a damand for the dignity of all women and children whose rights have been denigrated in a patriarchal society (37). The groups activism is rooted in this ideology but at times has met with resistance within Okinawa. For example, OWAAMV works closely with citizen groups in Henoko to block construction of a proposed military heliport. The community position on the proposed base in Henoko is still divided, in large part because Tokyo is exerting increasing pressure to accept the proposal. OWAAMV recognizes that the relocation of Futenma Air Station to another site in Okinawa fails to address issues of human rights and overall security for Okinawa, and members work with Henoko women to organize the community to protest against the proposal and for the ultimate removal of all U.S. military bases. Similarly, though some activists in Okinawa argued that the relocation of a live artillery range from Okinawa to Yufuin, a small town in Kyushu (just north of Okinawa prefecture), was a way to alleviate the military impact in Okinawa, OWAAMV took a hard stance against militarism, vowing that it would oppose military activity anywhere to protect human rights. Today, though the live artillery range did locate in Yufuin, OWAAMV continues to work with citizens groups there to oppose the range exercises. In a statement developed in 1998, OWAAMV states:

> We seek the removal of U.S. military forces, especially the U.S. Marines from Okinawa. But we do not want those forces to be merely transferred to another location. Instead we seek the transformation of our society that is permeated with weapons and violation, into a community built on mutual trust and partnership. To this end, we seek to enlarge our network with women throughout the world to break the silence and join together to create a society that respects the human rights of all persons.

This framework also extends to a global context. Takazato (1997b) notes:

> We know that when military personnel return home to the U.S., their training in violence returns with them; thus, the targets of violence now become their American wives and girlfriends. For these reasons, I believe we must work together to achieve not only an Okinawa free of military bases and military forces. We must also transcend national barriers and create a peaceful global society that is free of military violence.

OWAAMV's use of international networks reflects its intent to develop relationships and strategies with other women's organizations in the region and internationally that will strengthen their local work and build a broad antimilitary movement. In 1997, OWAAMV joined with women's groups from South Korea, the Philippines, Japan, and the United States to form an international women's network, the East Asia–U.S. Women's Network against Militarism. The purpose of the network is to build stronger relationships and campaigns against the presence of U.S. military troops and bases in the network member countries. At the initial network meeting in Okinawa, 40 women focused on (1) violence committed by U.S. military personnel against civilians, especially women and children, and its effects on the victims; (2) the plight of Amerasian children abandoned by their military fathers—many of these children are subsequently socially marginalized and forced into a system of prostitution around U.S. bases; (3) the threat that military toxics pose to the public and to the environment; and (4) the status of various official agreements and treaties governing U.S. bases and military personnel. In the past five years, the network has met twice—in Washington, D.C. (1998) and in Okinawa (2000)—and now has more than 90 members. The next gathering is planned for Seoul, Korea, in 2002.

Participation in the network has resulted in information sharing and collective strategy development, both of which have boosted OWAAMV's efforts. For example, women gained access to information about the legal framework and historical evolution of SOFAs that define the roles and responsibilities of the United States in host countries. Comparing the SOFAs of Japan, Korea, and the Philippines with the SOFA between Germany and the United States, members of OWAAMV lobbied their government officials to take up the revision of SOFA as a way to address the harm done by the U.S. military to women, children, and the environment.

Electing Women to Office

A primary strategy of OWAAMV is to organize women to run as candidates for political office. Suzuyo Takazato, co-chair of OWAAMV, is an elected member of the Naha City Council. Keiko Itokazu, the other co-chair, earned a living as a tour guide in Okinawa before being elected to the Prefectural Assembly. From 1993 through 1998, Mitsuko Tomon, OWAAMV member, served as vice governor of Okinawa; in June 2000, she was elected as the first woman Diet (national government) member from Okinawa. The founding of OWAAMV in 1995 has enabled women to use the organization as a political base to become elected to city councils, town assemblies, and prefectural government. Such a strategy, Takazato (1999) argues, results in Okinawa having the highest number of women in elected office of all Japan's prefectures.

Youth Leadership

Even before the formal founding of OWAAMV women activists supported the development of young Okinawan leaders in the women's movement against militarism. Mayumi Tengan, a young mother who participated in the Beijing delegation along with three other young Okinawan women, notes,

> It was good for me to be in Peking. It gave me the opportunity to network with other women from around the world and to find out what sorts of issues they have to deal with in their home societies. . . . When we got back to the island [Okinawa] the four of us decided to form a group called Young Voice. It is a support group of sorts made up of young women between the ages of twenty and thirty. What we hope to do through this group is increase awareness among young people in contemporary Okinawan society about political, military, and social issues affecting us. (Kelso 2000, 122)

In 1997, OWAAMV helped launch another youth project, Deactivate Our Violent Establishments (DOVE) as part of the initial meeting of the East Asia–U.S. Women's Network meeting held in Okinawa. The purpose of DOVE is to provide a forum for young Okinawan men and women to learn about and discuss the presence and negative impact of the U.S. military on local Okinawan culture, politics, and economy. The formation of DOVE recognized the need to provide historical, cultural, and political context for those who did not directly experience World War II or the movements of the 1960s and 1970s such as the U.S. occupation and the reversion of Okinawa to Japan. In addition, most of the students were in high school when the 1995 rape occurred and had no earlier direct exposure to military crimes or to the social protests that followed. Responding to the need of youths to critically understand militarism, DOVE sponsors lectures and training sessions that impress upon them the connections among their own Okinawan identity, the U.S. bases, and violence against women, children, and the environment.

Approximately 100 local college and high school students have participated in DOVE discussions and organizing efforts. Key to the establishment and ongoing work of DOVE is the involvement of an OWAAMV member who is a university lecturer and English teacher. She has incorporated critical Okinawan history and cultural identity into her English courses. Since the Japanese education curriculum does not include Okinawan history (even in Okinawa), the strategy of integrating critical Okinawan history into English curricula enables Okinawan or Japanese students to learn the history of struggle under U.S. military occupation. This knowledge can help to motivate them to participate in the continuing debates on the U.S. military presence in Okinawa. Many of these Okinawan students are energized when they recognize the Okinawan history of protest as their own.[14] Yuka Iha, a founding member of DOVE, states,

> Some high school and college students like to become friends with GIs to speak English and learn about American culture. I have had many girlfriends who had GI boyfriends and I have heard many terrible things from them. I became interested in trying to understand what the U.S. military really is. (Quoted in Francis 1999, 190)

Through DOVE and the international networks they are involved with, OWAAMV plans to develop a technical training and educational exchange program for youth leaders to work with nongovernmental organizations in the United States, Philippines, Japan, and Korea. The purpose of this training program will be to enable youths to obtain skills such as advocacy, translation, training, environmental assessment, and so on to address issues of violence against women and base cleanup and base reuse in Okinawa.

Paths to Genuine Security

Through its activism, OWAAMV continues to point to the U.S. military's role in creating conditions of insecurity for women, children, and the environment. At the same time, the group recognizes that the military base lands held by the United States must be returned to local government control if alternative paths of development are to be achieved. The broad membership and support base of OWAAMV reflects its ability to organize across lines of class, nation, and the division between urban and rural. It also illustrates the resonance of militarism as a critical issue for women, and it positions antimilitary activism in a broader context of redefining national security. These themes of antimilitarism and security resonate with the ecological feminist framework developed by Seager (1993) and Kirk (1997). The framework identifies economic and political institutions as "perpetrators of ecologically unsound investment." Both argue that within this framework, it is possible to make global connections across lines of difference—race, class, and nation—to build alliances. Specifically, Kirk argues that an ecological feminism

> must oppose the structural/social economic adjustment policies of northern governments, as well as militarism and the culture of violence it generates and requires. This means opening up a public debate that challenges and opposes the values and practices of this economic system—its hazardous production processes as well as its consumerist ideology—rather, framing progress in terms of sustainability, connectiveness and true security. (361)

For Okinawan women, the opportunity to demonstrate these forms of alternative security is fast approaching. In late 1998, the Special Action Committee on Okinawa (SACO) report outlined a Base Return Action Program announcing the return of nine U.S. military posts in Okinawa to the Japanese government by the year 2001; 14 by 2010; and 17 by 2015. On an island with little developable land, the closure of these military sites, including the immediate return of Futenma Air Station (1,200 acres), presents an opportunity to develop Okinawa's local economy. Plans emerging from the prefectural government have included such concepts as the "Multimedia Island," a plan to develop a multimedia industry in Okinawa. The concept argues that such a plan will "create jobs for 24,500 people or one percent of the entire labor population in the nation, which is expected to reach 2.45 million by 2010, in the area of information and communications." Other highlights of the reuse concept include the development of a resort in the northern part of the island, the establishment of a new urban development at Futenma Air Station, and the expansion of the Naha military port (Okinawa Prefectural Government 1998).

The alternative security framework put in practice by OWAAMV triggers a critique of such development approaches. It is unclear, for example, whether a "Multimedia Island" concept will address the key issues of meeting people's basic needs, ensuring that the environment will sustain human and natural life, honoring people's human dignity and respect of cultural identities, and ensuring that people and the environment be protected from avoidable harm. Beyond a critique of existing development proposals, OWAAMV must now face the challenges of how to create everyday examples and models of this alternative security framework. Based on the experiences of military base closure, conversion, and reuse in the United States and the Philippines, the challenge of creating development that will serve the local community is a daunting one. Three key considerations are (1) the cleanup of military toxics; (2) the need for a overall reuse plan that addresses the needs of local people, particularly women and children; and (3) a well-organized and powerful political force to ensure that cleanup and reuse processes are fully funded and implemented.

In the eight years between 1988 and 1995, the U.S. Department of Defense closed 12 domestic military sites in the San Francisco Bay Area and transferred the land and facilities to local and other nonmilitary governmental bodies. The process of converting formar military lands into civilian uses requires the cleanup of environmental toxics, the development of a reuse and redevelopment plan, and implementation of the plan. To date, at least $1.6 billion have been spent on environmental cleanup alone at the sites (*Los Angeles Times* 2000). Hunters Point Naval Shipyard, in San Francisco, has been closed for more than 25 years and not fully reused because of the presence of military toxics. The problem of cleanup is partially technological as scientists and engineers work to find ways in which to clean up the toxics. But the problem is also highly political. In 2000, the United States plans to spend $1.72 billion on the cleanup of its domestic bases; all overseas bases will share $165 million (International Grassroots Summit on Military Base Cleanup 1999). Okinawans have little access to the decision makers in Washington who allocate military base cleanup funding. While OWAAMV has documented the impact of military toxics and begun to develop relationships with U.S.-based activists on issues of military toxics and cleanup, it is clear that more capacity must be developed in Okinawa to engage in activism specifically focused on issues of military toxics and cleanup.

Second, as former military land becomes available for local reuse, OWAAMV is poised to play a powerful leadership role in determine the scope and framework of local development plans. Toward this end, it is able to draw on earlier successful experiences. OWAAMV have helped develop community-serving projects including a Prefectural Women's Building that provides programs, services, and resources to and about women in Okinawa. Other efforts include a domestic violence and rape hotline and counseling center. Plans are under way to develop a women's shelter modeled after such successful shelters as the Asian Women's Shelter in San Francisco and My Sisters Place in South Korea. While not to the scale necessary to generate economic activity equal to an operating military base, the models established by the women represent possible approaches to develop other community-based projects and the locally controlled institutions that will further these projects. They are tangible, physical and relevant examples of development that reflect principles of alternative security and provide real critiques of development processes that have little to do with local resources.

Using these examples as prototypes, OWAAMV may be able to promote its agenda for alternative security and development. The task itself is daunting especially in the face of powerful political and economic interests that privilege U.S. and Japanese corporate and government interests over the interests of the people. Yet as McCormack (1998) argues, the current development road consisting of military bases, public works, and tourism is unsustainable in the long term.

> Okinawa now faces a choice between being incorporated in the nation-state–centered regional and global order as a hyper-peripheral hyper-dependent backwater to be despoiled by the "slash-and-burn" of rampant development (*ran-kaihatsu*) or, alternatively, becoming a base for the creation of a 21st century's new, decentralized, sustainable and naturally balanced order. The latter could only be accomplished by a prodigious concerted effort, almost certainly of an international character. (7)

Third, the struggle of military base cleanup and reuse requires broad political support that spans Okinawa, Japan, and the United States. There are important lessons to be learned from earlier base conversion efforts. In the Philippines, women organized to develop a reuse plan for Subic that recognized the need for reuse activities that addressed the needs of women and children. Government officials, however, opted for a plan that emphasized the need to attract foreign investment, promoting development such as free trade zones, hotels, casinos, and large-scale resorts. Similar lessons from base reuse at the Alameda Naval Shipyard in California suggests that community-based plans require a strong organized constituency to build the political power necessary to get community plans adopted in formal reuse processes (Matsuoka 1999). Having reviewed the citizen-initiated reuse plan developed for the Subic base in the Philippines and met with activists involved in the Alameda base closure, OWAAMV is aware of what it will take to organize and develop the political will to support a citizen-based plan. Currently the organization's organizing strategies focus on mobilizing women around issues of women's rights as human rights, not of base conversion and reuse issues. Shifting focus to a base conversion agenda even with women's issues as a central focus will require a revisiting of organizing strategies. How OWAAMV chooses to develop its future organizing strategies remains an important question.

Conclusion

This chapter has attempted to outline the dimensions of Okinawan women's activism against militarization. It illustrates how women in Okinawa have built an organization as well as the leadership, networks, and power to influence the debates on military presence in Okinawa. Through this resistance and political activism, Okinawan women have developed a proactive stance toward political self-determination, democracy, and overall security for women and children. Their struggle is not only an act of resistance against the U.S. military and the complicit government of Japan, but also a struggle to build a community-based vision of security in the face of increasing globalization. The movement has helped frame proactive development alternatives to the military industrial complex that exists in Okinawa and the Pacific region. Moreover, their resistance exemplifies what Feffer (2001) suggests may be a strategy of bottom-up multilaterialism. Thus, some of the seeds of an alternative development path have been planted. But much remains to be done.

The possibility of reusing closed military sites presents an immediate opportunity and daunting test of OWAAMV's intention and ability to shape future local development in Okinawa. While women have put in place a framework and examples of community-based projects to meet the needs of women, children, and the environment, the scope and scale of these projects remains relatively small in relation to the ongoing presence and dominance of the U.S. military. Yet these examples embody and emerge from a women's activism that has laid a path of resistance that has at its core an alternative vision of peace and security.

Notes

This chapter represents the collective work and struggle of Okinawa Women Act against Military Violence, the East Asia–U.S. Women's Network against Militarism, and the Okinawa Peace Network. The authors appreciate the contributions of Suzuyo Takazato, Margo Okazawa-Rey, and Carolyn Bowen Francis. Jacqueline Leavitt at UCLA provided guidance, support, and necessary resources. Thanks are due especially to Gwyn Kirk, who helped frame arguments and had limitless patience, commitment, and insights to give to this chapter.

1. The G8 and its annual summit were established in 1975 for the major industrial democracies (which now include Russia) to discuss key economic and political issues facing their nations and the international community as a whole. Discussion items for the 2000 G8 Summit included debt relief for developing countries, information technology, and globalization; the role and scope of the U.S. military was not specifically discussed in formal G8 discussions.

2. The terms *militarization* and *militarism* are used throughout the chapter as defined by

Kirk and Okazawa-Rey: "a system and worldview based on the objectification of 'others' as enemies, a culture that celebrates war and killing. This worldview operates through specific military institutions and actions."

3. OWAAMV and Mercier also note that following the land reforms of the Meiji era, a 1914 census revealed that more than 1,000 women lived and worked in a district established in the mid-1600s to serve the Satsuma officials, Chinese envoys, and local officials.

4. Ota notes that the Battle of Okinawa was the first battle on Okinawan soil since the Mongolian invasion in the thirteenth century.

5. It is difficult to know how many of the 122,000 Okinawan civilians who died during the Battle of Okinawa were killed in crossfire, killed by Japanese soldiers, or committed suicide. Wartime history is a particularly controversial issue and continues to be debated within Japan, particularly within the Ministry of Education (Monbusho), the agency responsible for approving all textbooks in Japan. Taira (1999) notes that in 1982 the Ministry of Education deleted from a draft of a high school history textbook the following sentence: "About 800 civilians of Okinawa prefecture were murdered by the Japanese troops on grounds that they hindered the fighting." Okinawans strongly protested, and the local government urged the Monbusho to reinstate the sentence to emphasize the truth of the civilian killings by the Japanese army. Several lawsuits were filed against the Monbusho; one suit was appealed and reached the Japanese Supreme Court who ruled with the Monbusho and against reinstatement of the original textbook statement. Recently, there has been increased activism in Korea as well as the Philippines to demand that the Monbusho include a more adequate and correct version of Japan's role in wartime history in those countries as well.

6. OWAAMV notes that these figures do not reflect the numbers of rapes and assaults that are never reported to public authorities because of shame, humiliation, or fear. They also note that following the report of the rape of the 12-year-old girl in 1995 and the establishment of a rape hotline and crisis center, the number of reported rapes and assaults against Okinawan women by U.S. military servicemen has increased.

7. Johnson also notes that the SOFA with Korea requires American suspects to be handed over to local authorities only if they have been convicted by a U.S. military court.

8. The term *military toxics* is used here to refer to contaminating materials used by the military during war and military operations that cause threats to human health and the environment.

9. U.S. military bases and troops in foreign countries are governed by security treaties signed between the United States and host countries. Status of Forces Agreements (SOFAs) are the policy framework that lay out specific guidelines set forth by security treaties. Though the specifics of responsible parties may differ by SOFA in individual countries, the SOFA outlines scope and responsibility for issues such as environmental cleanup of military bases, criminal acts by U.S. servicemen, and other issues which might arise between the two countries. See also Kirk and Bowen Francis 2000.

10. Similar Status of Forces Agreements were signed between the United States and the

nations of Germany, the Philippines, and South Korea outlining the role and responsibilities of the United States in these host countries. Considerable discrepancy exists among these SOFAs; the one with Germany, for example, gave that country more rights over environmental cleanup than did those with Asian countries. For a detailed comparative analysis of these SOFAs and their effects on women, see Kirk and Bowen Francis 2000.

11. For more work on feminist concepts of international and human security, see Reardon 1998 and Matsui 1998.

12. Titles of the 11 workshops were (1) Women and the Environment; (2) Uji Dyeing; (3) The Military: Structural Violence and Women; (4) The "Comfort Women" Issue in Okinawa; (5) Action for Abolition of Nuclear Weapons; (6) Enforced Relocation to the "Malaria" Area in Wartime; (7) Women and Peace; (8) Traditional Cultural Practices and Discrimination against Women; (9) Aging Society and Social Welfare; (10) Women and Work/Labor; and (11) The Unai (Sisters) Network.

13. The 1996 delegation was made up of 13 members; the 1998 delegation, 12 members.

14. Yoko Fukumura, a member of OWAAMV and the co-author of this chapter, continues to be active in DOVE.

V
Conclusion

15

The Challenges and Possibilities of Transnational Feminist Praxis

Nancy A. Naples

THE COMPLEX PROCESSES OF GLOBALIZATION AND RESISTANCE HIGHLIGHTED IN this book demonstrate the contradictory array of possibilities for our collective future. This *politics of possibilities* has two faces. One vision of this future foregrounds the oppressive consequences of global capitalism and military conflicts that constrain the achievement of economic justice and peace throughout the world. The other reflects the possibilities for resisting imperialism and for achieving equality and justice for people around the globe.[1] The case studies in this collection highlight this latter vision and focus attention on the challenges and possibilities of a transnational feminist praxis. The former vision is crystalized in the September 11, 2001 terrorist attacks and the subsequent bombing of Afghanistan. The events of September 11 have jolted people in the United States and around the world to contemplate possibilities of continued attacks from the global network of terrorists as well as to prepare for a global war against terrorism. These events give urgency to the call for a transnational feminist praxis informed by a rich understanding of grassroots feminist analyses of peace building and organizing across differences and across national borders.

Transnational feminist praxis foregrounds women's agency in the context of oppressive conditions that shape their lives. Although the primary justification for the U.S. retaliatory bombing of Afghanistan is to destroy al Qaeda, concern has been expressed about women's oppression under Taliban rule. For example, in an address to the nation on November 17, 2001, U.S. first lady Laura Bush highlighted women's loss of freedom in Taliban-controlled Afghanistan. However, missing from the dominant media and government discourse on women in Afghanistan is an acknowledgment of their role as political actors and political analysts. No mention is made, for example, of the Revolutionary Association of Women of Afghanistan (RAWA) that was established in 1977 to fight for human rights, adequate health care, education, and economic justice, and for democratic and secular rule in Afghanistan.

The case studies in our book highlight the role of women in helping to shape a future free of the oppressive features of globalization. The authors profile the challenges of resistance to the oppressive economic and political regimes as well as the possibilities for solidarity across class, culture, and national borders. In this concluding chapter I focus on the contradictory politics of location and neoliberalism as they constrain women's effectiveness as international political actors. I also outline how postliberalism can open up the possibilities for transnational feminist praxis.

Globalization and the Politics of Location

The dominant discourse on *economic globalization* stresses the speed of communications and financial transactions that seem to render local economic activities and face-to-face transactions obsolete. However, as Saskia Sassen (1996) argues, "many of the resources necessary for global economic activities are not hypermobile and are, indeed, deeply embedded in place." In fact, she explains, "global processes are structured by local constraints, including the composition of the workforce, work cultures, and prevailing political cultures and processes" (631). Sassen, along with feminist geographers and Third-World feminist analysts, emphasizes the importance of place and locale in exploring the dynamics of globalization as well as articulating strategies of resistance. In fact, as Vandana Shiva (1997) notes, *localization* can provide "the countervailing citizens' agenda for protecting the environment and people's survival and people's livelihood" (43). In this section, I explore the "politics of location" in transnational feminist praxis and highlight some of the significant lessons derived from the case studies in the collection.[2]

Localization involves "subjecting the logic of globalization to the test of sustainability, democracy and justice" and "reclaiming the state to protect people's interest" (Shiva 1997, 43).[3] Local resistance strategies developed in response to oppressive forms of globalization may not necessarily offer effective counterhegemonic alternatives (see Kaplan 2002; Mackie 2001; Santos 2001; Sklar 1999; Tabb 2001).[4] Many scholars have written about the limits of locality-based struggles. For example, David Harvey (1999, 351) notes in his discussion of the environmental movement that "particularistic militances—fighting an incinerator here, a toxic waste dump there, a World Bank dam project somewhere else, and commercial logging in yet another place" do not provide the grounds from which to challenge the global processes that generate environmental degradation. He argues that a transnational movement must move beyond "narrow solidarities and particular affinities shaped in particular places . . . and adopt a politics of abstraction capable of reaching out across space, across the multiple environmental and social conditions." In a related vein, Leslie Sklar points out that "[t]he knowledge that workers, citizens, churches, and other concerned groups all around the world are monitoring their activities clearly encourages some TNCs [transnational corporations] to act more responsibly than they otherwise might be doing" (299).[5]

Contributors to *Women's Activism and Globalization* recognize the limits of local struggles that fail to challenge the extralocal processes that shape them. Yet the authors also view the local as a site of *politicization* where activists collectively develop analyses of the complex economic, political, and social processes that contour locally experienced problems (see Naples 1998b). Authors depict locality and place as sites in which women generate the collective vision of an economically, politically, and socially just world. The *local* is also the site where activists work toward building the just world they envision by creating "more inclusive organizations and approaches that may help them confront capital more effectively in the future" (Dickinson and Schaeffer 2001, 220). For example, Betty Wells (in this volume) emphasizes the very "local" ways a small group of women built a network of activists, farmers, and consumers opposed to oppressive modes of capitalist production. As they worked together to organize Women, Food, and Agiculture Network (WFAN), they developed a vision that went beyond an exclusively economic one. Their political analysis also includes a political and social critique of the dominant processes of globalization. Their broad analysis provides a vehicle to link the issues of a variety of constituencies. For example, they define food security as a basic human right and see it as tied directly to sustainable agriculture and environmental health and safety, thus bringing together the interests of small farmers, consumers, and environmentalists.

These local sites are also highly contested places where members redefine their identities and strategies in the context of ever-changing community dynamics and international relations. Winifred Poster and Zakia Salime (in this volume) describe the process by which AMSSF (the Moroccan Association for Solidarity without Borders), was transformed from a small grassroots group that provided microcredit for poor entrepreneurs to a part of a hierarchical network of organizations that refocused the relationships between the leaders and clients in AMSSF. This ever-changing complex funding arrangement including relying on the Moroccan Association for Solidarity and Development (AMSED) to access financial assistance from Catholic Relief Services working in Morrocco who in turn received funding from USAID. As a consequence, they lost the autonomy to manage their clients' loans. In addition to the externally imposed tensions they encountered, leaders and clients also experienced internal tensions based on their class differences. Despite these multiple tensions, Poster and Zakia remain optimistic about the potential for grassroots groups like AMSSF to use nongovernmental organization (NGO) linkages to create transnational feminist alliances.

Optimism about the significance of women's local activism in the context of economic globalization is reflected in Jennifer Bickham Mendez's analysis of the

Central American Network of Women in Solidarity with Maquila Workers. The Network has raised the consciousness of local and state officials about the problems faced by women maquila workers. Network members have also experienced a deepening in their gender consciousness that led them to create autonomous women's groups and challenge male-dominated social movement organizations. As a consequence, women have gained greater visibility in local politics and legitimacy as political actors.

To further complicate our notion of the "local," it is important to point out that many of these sites for building alliances and political strategies may not be coterminous. Drawing inspiration from Benedict Anderson's (1983) notion of "imagined community," feminist scholars stress the myriad of ways that women who may never meet can draw strength from each other and organize across differences (see Mackie 2001; Mohanty 1991b). Solidarity across "often conflictual locations and and histories" derives from "the political links we choose to make among and between struggles" (Mohanty 1991b, 5). The Internet has facilitated the process of organizing across specific locales and further illustrates how the global lands in place. What may appear distant and remote is brought into view through a technology that also helps promote the very conditions against which people struggle. Yet how women activists use this technology must also be understood contextually as Ellen Kole (2001) demonstrates in her analysis of WomenAction in Africa. WomenAction was developed to facilitate the participation of nongovernmental organizations in evaluating the implementation of the Platform for Action developed during the United Nations Conference on Women Beijing in 1995.[6] Not surprisingly, Kole found that women's groups in Africa use the Internet in a manner that differs from the way women in the western world access and use the Internet. As importantly, diverse groups of African women use the Internet in ways that differ from each other.

As evident through the work of a number of authors in this collection, women have been able to create cross-class, cross-race, and cross-national coalitions that are enriched by the diversity of resources, political skill, and experiences. Sharon Navarro (in this volume) details how activists in La Mujer Obrera in El Paso work across the Mexican–United States border to achieve seven basic goals including access to stable employment, housing, education, nutrition, healthcare, peace, and political liberty. Clare Weber's chapter (in this volume) on the cross-national organizing between Nicaragua and organizations based in the United States demonstrates that knowledge and other resources can transfer from South to North as well as North to South when participating organizations remain self-conscious and actively work against power imbalances. In other cases, most clearly illustrated in Alexandra Hrycak's study (in this volume), cross-class, cross-cultural, and cross-national alliances further reinforce inequalities across and within national contexts.

Neoliberalism and the Politics of Accountability

Many of the cases reported in *Women's Activism and Globalization* emphasize the continued significance of the liberal claims for economic, social, and political rights. Many feminist scholars are concerned about the limits of the modernist, liberal framework for achieving political, social, and economic justice. The rhetoric of *liberalism* argues for a division between the so-called civic and political spheres, and between economics and politics (see Bayes, Hawkesworth and Kelly 2001, 3). University of Delhi law professor Upendra Baxi insightfully points out that "the neoliberal frame, even when cloaked in 'people-friendly' global governance, is about creating . . . 'market-friendly NGOs' that can cooperate with, and be co-opted by, but do not oppose CSOs [civil society organizations], states, and international organizations that support a neoliberal agenda" (quoted in Runyan 1999, 211).[7]

A key dimension of *neoliberalism* is the framing of social, political and economic issues in terms of "human rights." After years of organizing, feminists have achieved recognition for "women's rights as human rights." However, as Inderpal Grewal (1999) warns, by globalizing women's human rights discourse, the "notion of essential gender finds new impetus" (507).[8] As further evidence of the limits of neoliberal discourse, the recognition of poverty as a human rights issue has had much less success on the international political stage. The neoliberal human rights frame has been criticized most harshly by activists and scholars interested in native Indian and indigenous peoples' struggles for political sovereignty and for territorial rights. As Alexander and Mohanty (1997, xxxiv–xxxv) explain, "there is no language or conceptual framework to imagine territorial sovereignty as a feminist demand—or to theorize decolonization as a fundamental aspect of feminist struggle" (xxxiv–xxxv). However, a group rights claim as developed through the struggles of American Indians raises another issue of "who belongs or does not belong to the group and redefinitions and representations of traditions that define the group" (341; also see Grewal 1999; Howard 1992).[9]

Yet the discourse on human rights can be an effective tool for achieving progressive goals. Drawing on the Universal Declaration of Human Rights, United Nations Secretary General Kofi Annan invited corporations to follow the Global Compact, a voluntary effort to enlist transnational corporations in efforts to improve the human rights of people around the world (Tabb 2001). Organizations such as NUDE have used international human rights agreements like the Universal Declaration of Human Rights to pressure their government to address the concerns of their constituency (see Karides in this volume). As Rachel Cichowski demonstrates (in this volume), women activists in Europe have successfully advocated for the Equal Pay Principal to be adopted by the European Union and have, in turn, drawn on this principal to press for similar policies in member states that had yet to pass such legislation. Susanna Wing (in this volume) documents how the women in the Sahelian State of Mali have used the international discourse on women's rights to increase women's activism on behalf of their constitutional rights and their political representation. Wing notes that after Mali began to pursue political liberalization in 1991, women succeeded in increasing their representation in the legislative seats from 2 percent to 13 percent in one electoral season.

Mary Meyer and Elisabeth Prügl (1999) stress that the significance of international documents is not that governments will quickly adopt them but that national and local groups can use such documents to hold their governments accountable. In effect, the groups can use these "universal standards" in different local contexts to further their own aims (also see Hoskyns 1999). Yet, it also remains to be seen how, and under what conditions, certain international statutes can be enforced at the level of the nation-state. For example, Meyer raises this question in the context of the terms of the Convention on Violence against Women established by the Inter-American Commission of Women, which also is known by its Spanish acronym, CIM (Comision Interamericana de Mujeres). As an autonomous commission of the Organization of American States (OAS), it cannot participate actively in the politics of enforcement.

The human rights frame was generated in the context of violence perpetrated by oppressive military and political regimes. More recently the frame has been used to highlight injustices in western countries like the United States. For example, the Permanent People's Tribunal held a special session in Spain on 1989 and determined that "the US government was denying the People of Puerto Rico their most fundamental human right: the right to self-determination" (Committee for Human Rights in Puerto Rico 2000, 143). When Amnesty International turned its attention to human rights violations in the United States and identified abuses in prisons and jails as well as in the treatment of asylum seekers and other immigrants, they generated a great stir among U.S. officials (Maran 2000, 49). The organization's campaign, Rights for ALL, added the United States to a list of countries that includes such well-known violators as Turkey, China, Sudan, Indonesia, and Colombia.

Amnesty International's report emphasized the problems that female prisoners face such as sexual abuse by male guards and being placed in leg irons or shackles, both of which, according to the report, are common practices. Radhika Coomaraswamy of Sri Lanka, special rapporteur on violence against women, charged that the United States "is criminalizing a large segment of its population, a segment overwhelmingly composed of poor persons of color and increasingly female" (61). When Coomaraswamy requested permission to visit three prisons in Michigan, the governor of the state refused her request. This response illustrates the extent to which the human rights frame has been used to maintain a hierarchical distinction between the "Western world" and non-Western nation-states. Viewing policies and practices in Western nation-states that increase economic, social, and political inequalities in the Western world through the human rights frame reveals the colonialist, ethnocentric, and racist assumptions underlying neoliberal policy.

NGOs and International Politics

In response to global economic restructuring and international trade agreements as well as neoliberal policies, women are organizing through a variety of networks, transnational organizations, as well as through traditional vehicles like the International Ladies Garment Workers Union. In addition, they have put global restructuring on the agenda of national women organizations and are organizing across borders (Runyan 1996, 246). For example, Jennifer Bickham Mendez's chapter in this volume examines the efforts of the Network for Maquila Workers Rights in Central America. This network challenges the effects of global economic restructuring and neoliberal politics and policies in their effort to improve the situation of women maquila workers. Women workers in the network document their working conditions and gather detailed information about how fast they work, what they produce, for which TNCs, and their relationships with supervisors and others in managerial position. This information is used for local unionizing efforts and is communicated through network NGOs to enable groups in the North to undertake public consciousness-raising.

Marina Karides's chapter in this volume analyzes transnational activism and unionizing efforts of another major sector of the informal economy, namely domestic workers. She shows how Trinidad's National Union of Domestic Employees (NUDE) has worked for the rights of domestic workers, who are primarily women, by using the global rhetoric and international agreements signed by Trinidad to make the government accountable at home. When the government declined to address the grievances raised by NUDE, its activists wrote letters to various government ministers reminding them of their international commitment and undertook a public consciousness-raising campaign about the relationship between local and global injustices. Thus, through a form of public shaming they were able to make some changes, though to date they have not been successful in achieving all of their demands.

Many of the recent analyses on the role of NGOs and transnational networks highlight the limits as well as the possibilities of these organizations and advocacy networks for progressive social change (see Keck and Sikkink 1998a). Sonia Alvarez (1999) raises a major concern in her discussion of what she calls "the Latin American feminist NGO boom" (181). She notes three troublesome trends:

> First, states and inter-governmental organizations (IGOs) increasingly have turned to feminist NGOs as *gender experts* rather than as citizens' groups advocating on behalf of women's rights. Second, neoliberal States and IGOs often view NGOs *as surrogates for civil society*, assuming they serve as "intermediatirs" to larger social constituencies. And third, *States increasingly subcontract feminist NGOs* to advise on or execute government women's programs. (181, emphasis in the original)

NGO is a deceptively short acronym applying to a wide array of groups with more or less access to resources, to political influence, and to diverse membership. However, as a consequence of the processes Alvarez identifies, many feminist NGOs are transformed from advocates to professionals serving the needs of neoliberal states. Since the early 1980s, the contradictions inherent in the process of professionalization and institutionalization of feminist practice have become a focus of numerous scholarly accounts and a major concern among feminist activists.[10] For example, in the case of the battered women's movement, the development and expansion of battered women's shelters and rape crisis centers stand as a testament to the success of feminist political activism of the 1970s. On the one hand, battered women's shelters and rape crisis centers are now a site for organized public advocacy, community education, and crisis intervention on behalf of battered women as well as a place where incest survivors, rape victims and children, the elderly, and other abuse survivors find political allies and supportive services. On the other hand, the institutionalization of the activism against violence against women in shelter-based services and rape crisis centers has raised concerns for the continued vibrancy of the feminist antiviolence movement.[11] In this regard, Clare Weber (in this volume) demonstrates the value of transnational feminist networks for rendering visible the limits of local and national organizing against violence against women. Nicaraguan women activists who met with U.S. antiviolence activists discussed their different organizing strategies and what they saw as the limits of the U.S. approach for ending violence against women.

As Weber and other authors in this book emphasize, to understand how local activists connect their organizing with transnational feminist movements, one must explore the institutional and network links among various actors at different sites. In the field of international relations, the term "civil society" is used to reference an extensive network of social interactions and institutions that mediate between individuals and the state (Warkentin 2001, 1). Global civil society is defined as a network that provides various "channels of opportunity for political involvement" (19; also see Wapner 1995). Networks associated with the so-called global civil society have more or less autonomy from local, national, and international institutions of the state.

In a special issue on gender and globalization of *Signs*, the coeditors note the frequency by which scholars of globalization distinguish between so-called spheres of civil society, state, and multinational corporations (Basu, Grewal, Kaplan, and Malkki 2001; also see Laclau 1994). Feminist analysts challenge the division of social, political, and economic life into these separate spheres. The role of the military in supporting multinational corporations provides the most powerful illustration of the intersection of civil society, the state and economic institutions (see Enloe 1983a, 1983b, 1990, 2000). Yoko Fukumura and Martha Matsuoka (in this volume) detail women's resistance to U.S. militarism in Okinawa and explain the complex role the U.S. military plays in supporting global trade, destroying the local environment, and placing residents of the Pacific region in jeopardy. The NGO, Okinawa Women Act against Military Violence (OWAAMV), has been effective in its struggle against the U.S. military present in Okinawa but OWAAMV activists are concerned that once the military sites become available for local development, another battle over control of the development process will ensure.

Nongovernmental organizations are one of the main mechanisms for participation in the so-called global civil society. Exclusive attention to NGOs renders invisible the multitudinous informal ways women organize on behalf of themselves and their communities (see Naples 1998a, 1998c). Furthermore, as political scientists Ann Marie Clark, Elisabeth Friedman, and Kathryn Hochstetler (1998, 2) point out, the fact that the number of NGOs with shared transnational goals has increased does not necessarily mean that a global civil society has been achieved. To begin with, these organizations are often founded and led by middle class, professional women, and have had little success incorporating poor women. For example, Meredith Weiss (1999), in her discussion of the role of NGOs in Singapore, describes the narrow class background of the Association of Women for Action and Research (AWARE), which she calls "the only avowedly feminist group in Singapore" (71). She reports that AWARE, founded in 1985 by 50 members grew to approximately seven hundred members by the late 1990s. Though the most active leadership comes from educated, middle-class women, the organization remains committed to working across class and other differences. Weiss reports that the leadership of AWARE appear "quite open to input from rank-and-file members; however, since such input is seldom forthcoming, this accessibility is rarely tested" (74).

Further complicating the politics of NGOs in the context of globalization are the relationships between Western and Northern NGOs and those in other parts of the globe. For example, constructions of feminism promoted by Western-based international feminist organizations and funding agencies often conflict with national women's movements in many locales, as Alexandra Hrycak details in her chapter in this volume. Differences in power and resources are also constructed in terms of a "North/South divide." However, in their analysis of NGO participation in United

Nations World Conferences, Clark, Friedman, and Hochstetler (1998) conclude that the divide between the North and the South may not be the primary source of contestation. They explain that "this divide partially overlaps more persistent divisions between the new generation of small grassroots organizations focused on local action and more professional, often larger and older, organizations with long-standing activists at the UN" (29). Rather than viewing these divisions as an expression of inequality among feminists in the North and those in the South, it is important to acknowledge the ways in which class and status differences frequently characterize relationships between women's groups within nation-states (see, e.g., Jad 1995). Anthropologist Deborah Mindry (2001) demonstrates this in her analysis of women's organizations in South Africa. She characterizes the role of the western imperialist and racist "politics of virtue . . . which constitutes some women as benevolent providers and others as worthy or deserving recipients of development and empowerment" (1189). Other scholars have also noted the significant alliances formed across the so-called First and Third Worlds by right wing religious groups and demoninations (see Kaplan, Alarcón, and Moallem 1999).

The Significance of the United Nations for Transnational Feminist Praxis

Many of the authors in this collection, along with others writing on transnational feminist organizing, also stress the significance of international conferences, especially UN-sponsored events for expanding women's participation in the global political arena.[12] As Dianne Otto (1996) points out in her review of the changing relationship between NGOs and the UN, NGOs have had a somewhat antagonistic relationship with the UN and have only recently begun to fund openings for direct participation in UN conferences and other events. However, through parallel conferences and effective lobbying, NGOs have influenced official proceedings and gained more effective roles in UN deliberations. However, Otto wonders whether the UN, with its "state-centric world view," can "rise to the challenge of reorienting its focus to be inclusive of peoples as well as states" (128). Currently, representatives from NGOs who are consultants to UN organizations like UNESCO (the United Nations Educational, Scientific and Cultural Organization) or UNICEF (the United Nations Children's Fund) may attend their meetings as observers and make proposals with permission from the presiding officer. However, these recommendations are merely advisory and may not be acted on by the specific UN groups.

Despite the limitations of the UN structure, women's groups have used UN conferences to build a transnational women's movement and bring their local concerns to the international political stage (see Seidman 2000). Eve Sandberg (1998) persuasively argues that the three United Nations world conferences on women

(Mexico, 1975; Nairobi, 1985; Beijing, 1995) served as a catalyst for Zambian women's domestic organizing, legitimated their activism, and provided resources and strategies for successful mobilization though these benefits accrue more to elite women than to less privileged Zambian women. Feminist scholars also note that a focus on preparation for UN conferences often has the effect of diverting attention from the issues of most direct concern to local activists (see Alvarez 1999).[13] In their discussion of the Alliance for Arab Women (AAW), Nawal Ammar and Leila Lababidy (1999, 15)—mother and daughter who are founding members of AAW—acknowledge the significance of the UN conferences for Egyptian women's domestic organizing but also point out that

> [s]ince the UN Third Conference on Women in Nairobi in 1985, some nongovernmental organizations concerned with women's issues in Egypt have changed their focus from welfare work to development of empowerment skills. Reasons for such changes are numerous, but most salient has been the priority of international funding sources. (15)

Elisabeth Friedman (1999, 357) concludes her analysis of the impact of UN conferences on the women's movement in Venezuela by stressing that "the stage of the national movement, its sources of funding, and the politics of particular national administrations all interact with conference preparation, with quite different outcomes at different junctures."

Manisha Desai addresses the contradictions of the United Nations for "transnational feminist solidarities" in her chapter in this volume (also see Wing in this volume). Her description of the four phases of UN policies on women demonstrate the effectiveness of transnational organizing for the incorporation of women into the design and implementation of UN programs. Despite inadequate funding for the implementation of UN programs designed to improve women's lives in different parts of the world and the failure to gain support from nations like the Unites States for the Convention on the Elimination of All Forms of Discrimination against Women (CEDAW), Desai argues that the establishment of programs like the International Research and Training Institute for the Advancement of Women and the United Nations Development Fund For Women, and the adoption of CEDAW by the UN, demonstrate the power of women's international organizing as well as help promote the expansion of transnational solidarities among women. The UN Conferences on Women provide further opportunities for women activists from around the world to share their experiences, learn from each other, and develop strategies to counter the intensification of religious fundamentalism, militarization, poverty and sexual abuse, and to expand women's political participation. Women's influence on the transnational political stage is further demonstrated by their leadership and broad-based participation in world conferences on the environment, human rights, population, social development.

Postliberalism and the Politics of Feminist Praxis

In contrast to the liberal approach that is predominant in international organizing, Dianne Otto (1996) argues that a "postliberal perspective, which decenters states and stresses the importance of local participation in the international community, is allied with a postmodern understanding of power . . . [as] conceptualized as dispersed throughout the global polity rather than . . . centralized in the state and the economy" (134). In shifting from a liberal to a postliberal frame, feminist scholars explore the possibilities for a transnational feminist politics that will work against global inequalities of region, gender, race, class, and sexuality and toward what Ernesto Laclau and Chantal Mouffe (1985) term "radical and plural democracy" within movement organizations and coalitions. The postliberal approach to women's movement politics recognizes that the feminist struggle is not based on "a definable empirical group with a common essence and identity—that is, women—but rather as a struggle against the multiple forms in which the category 'women' is constructed in subordination" (Mouffe 1993, 88l; also see Basu 1995; Grewal and Kaplan 1994).

The essays in *Women's Activism and Globalization* provide further evidence of the diversity of women's movements around the world as well as within different nation-states (see Basu 1995; Dickinson and Schaeffer 2001; Gluck et al. 1998). Like the authors in *The Challenge of Local Feminisms* (Basu 1995), we are interested in rendering visible "what actually existing women's movements have achieved and failed to achieve, of the challenges yet to be confronted together and separately" (4). In this collection, we define "women's movements" very broadly. Referring to women's movements in the plural as recommended by Gluck and colleagues (1998) reflects a deepening awareness of how the multitude forms of women's activism throughout the world all work to challenge patriarchal hierarchies. We also include forms of collective struggle that may not have achieved the level of a "movement." For example, Betty Wells's chapter in this volume analyzes the work of rural women who have been traditionally left out of women's movements. These women engage in local activism, offer insightful indigenous knowledge about daily survival strategies, and participate in national and transnational organizing.

Revisioning women's movements to include the diversity of women's political analyses and strategies also requires us to rethink the labels used to categorize feminisms more generally. Third World and postcolonial feminists have effectively criticized the imposition of the Western feminist worldview in women in different parts of the world (e.g., Hubbard and Solomon 1995). In the introduction to her edited collection, Basu (1995) discusses the widespread resistance to feminism, but she points out that many Third World critics "go on to identify indigenous alternatives to Western-style feminism" (18–19). Rather than pose indigenous and Western feminism as mutually distinctive alternatives, recent analyses demonstrate the interdependence of women's movements and feminist analysis in different parts of the world. As Gay Seidman (2000) illustrates in her case study of gendered politics in South Africa, "the international flow of ideas and resources has become a basic element in local debates involving gender equity" (123).

Victoria Bernal (1999) turns to the Tanzania Gender Network Programme (TGNP), a feminist group based in Dar es Salaam, to explore the relationship between the local and the global. She finds that the organization voices its concerns in language common to women's organizations worldwide, emphasizing that "Tanzanian NGOs such as TGNP speak an international language of democracy, human rights, and development" (1). When communicating in their national language, Kiswahili, the Tanzanian feminists sometimes simply adopt the English terms (as in the cases of "gender mainstreaming" and "patriarchy"), leading, Bernal writes, "to what some have called 'Kiswahenglish" (1). However, Bernal concludes, "Neither the view of local organizations as somehow operating independent of their global context, nor the view of such organizations as mere puppets of external forces will allow us to explore the potentials and pitfalls in the globalized terrain of contemporary post-colonial political activism" (1).[14]

In the context of increased mobility and displacement, distinctions between home/abroad, insider/outsider, and Third World/First World, have become difficult to maintain. In her contribution to *Women's Activism and Globalization*, Bandana Purkayastha compares and contrasts her community activism during the latter part of twentieth century as an Indian-born woman in the United States with her mother's activism during the earlier part of the century in a rural Indian village. She argues that community activism facilitates the transmission of resistance strategies to counter the negative effects of global economic restructuring in local contexts.

Many of the lessons we have learned through more nationally defined feminist politics will continue to serve us as we expand the horizons of feminist organizing. These lessons include how to respond to problems that arise in organizing across class, race, ethnicity, sexualities, space, and religious and political perspectives; how to sustain feminist activist engagement over time; how to build and mobilize effective coalitions; how to create democratic structures at all levels of organization; and how to negotiate the politics of language, funding, representation, and social movement framing.

Along with the politics of naming, the politics of location, the politics of accountability, and the challenges of fighting against the scattered hegemonies of capitalism and patriarchy (see Naples in this volume), research on transnational feminist praxis reveals a number of contradictions that require careful consideration before we pass judgment on the limits or possibilities of different political strategies, organizational forms, or social movement frames. This collection of case studies deepens our understanding of the complexities, challenges, and possibilities of grounded struggles against oppressive forms of globalization associated with antidemocratic international politics and capitalist expansion.

Notes

1. I would like to acknowledge Manisha Desai for her insightful comments on this chapter and for contributing the frame, "politics of possibilities." Her reflections on the events of September 11 form the basis for this opening discussion of the contradictory possibilities of globalization.

2. In her book *Questions of Travel*, Caren Kaplan (2000, 160) interrogates Rich's (1986) notion of "the politics of location" feminism. She observes that "[t]he local appears as the primary site of resistance to globalization through the construction of temporalized narratives of identity (new histories, rediscovered genealogies, imagined geographies, etc.), yet that very site prepares the ground for appropriation, nativism, and exclusion."

3. Resistance can take many forms. As economist William Tabb (2001) points out, "Resistance can have a strong element of moral witness (speaking truth to power), of rebellion (I'm mad and I won't take it any more), of reformist goals (our mutual ideals are violated, let us live up to our agreed-upon principles as in the adoption of the Universal Declaration of Human Rights), and of revolutionary transformation (the institutions of structured inequality and destructiveness are necessary to preserve their power; the system must be overthrown and a fundamentally different one put in its place)" (197).

4. Boaventura de Sousa Santos (2001) views "counter-hegemonic globalization" as "focused on the struggle against social exclusion, a struggle which in its broadest terms encompasses not only excluded populations but also nature" (20)

5. As sociologist Leslie Sklair (1999) notes, "[g]lobal production chains can be disrupted by strategically planned stoppages, but this generally acts more as an irritation than as a real weapon of labor against capital" (298). Sklar (1999) identifies several examples of anticonsumerist social movements that have the potential to pose such challenges. He describes the Seikatsu Club in Japan, which is "based on the idea of consumer self-sufficiency through cooperatives" (303) and Goss's suggestions for reclaiming the mall "for the people" by, among other strategies: "1. expose commodity fetishism, and force advertisers and retailers to become more honest;" and "2. resist the economic and spatial logic of malls by helping community groups struggle against redevelopment" (304–305).

6. Beijing 5+ was held at the United Nations in New York City five years after the Beijing Conference.

7. Transnational feminists are not blind to the limits of neoliberal framing For example, during the Vienna NGO Forum in 1994, Runyan (1999) reports, a coalition of groups—the Network Women in Development Europe based in Brussels, Alternative Women in Development, National Action Committee on the Status of Women in Toronto, and Canadian Research Institute for the Advancement of Women—produced a report entitled "'Wealth of Nations—Poverty of Women' countering the optimistic rhetoric associated with globalization found in the ECE [Economic Commission for Europe] region draft platform" (215).

8. Grewal (1999) notes that the effort "to keep various kinds of difference alive in the womens' [*sic*] human rights arena is a difficult one, made even more difficult by the asymmetries of power within states, nations, and groups that both construct and fracture contemporary global conditions" (507; also see Charlesworth 1994).

9. In their study of *Activists Beyond Borders*, Margaret Keck and Kathryn Sikkink (1998a) also point out the limits of the rights frame for stemming violence and other abuses in Guatemala during the 1970s and 1980s and in Colombia in the 1990s.

10. Myra Marx Ferree and Patricia Martin (1995) define "institutionalization" as "the development of regular and routinized relationships with other organizations" (6).

11. With the institutionalization of shelters, shelter work was frequently depoliticized and redirected toward an increasingly social service orientation. See Ferraro 1983; Loseke 1992; Matthews 1994; P. Morgan 1981; and Sullivan 1982.

12. According to Nawal and Labibady (1999), the most notable UN conferences for transnational feminist organizing include those held in Copenhagen in 1980, Nairobi in 1985, Cairo in August 1994, Copenhagen in March 1995, Beijing in August 1995, and Istanbul in August 1996 (154–155). Also see Pietilä and Vickers 1994.

13. Gayatri Spivak (1996) offers one of the most devastating critiques of the Beijing conference "as an example of 'Women' as 'global theater, stated to show participation between the North and the South, the latter constituted by Northern discursive mechanisms—a Platform for Action and certain power lines between the UN, the donor consortium, governments, and elite Non-Governmental Organizations." Spivak argues that "what is left out" of this performance piece "is the poorest women of the South as self-conscious critical agents, who might be able to speak through those very nongovernmental organizations of the South that are not favoured by these objective-constitution policies" (2).

14. Una Narayan (1996) effectively argues, "Many Third-World feminist issues are hardly "foreign imports" or "Westernized agendas" imposed by feminists onto contexts where "culturally authentic" nonfeminist women would entirely fail to see what the feminist fuss was about." (12). Also see Seidman (2000).

Bibliography

Abdullah, Hussaina. 1995. "Wifeism and Activism: The Nigerian Women's Movement." Pp. 209–25 in *Women's Movements in Global Perspective*, ed. Amrita Basu. Boulder, CO: Westview.

Abraham, Margaret. 2000. *Speaking the Unspeakable: Marital Violence among South Asian Immigrants in the United States.* New Brunswick, NJ: Rutgers University Press.

Abubikirova, N. I., T. A. Klimenkova, E. V. Kotchina, M. A. Regentova, and T. G. Troinova. 1998. *Directory of Women's Nongovernmental Organizations in Russia and the NIS.* Moscow: Aslan.

Acker, Joan. 1990. "Hierarchies, Jobs, Bodies: A Theory of Gendered Organizations." *Gender and Society* 4:139–58.

Afshar, Hale, and Carline Dennis. 1992. *Women and Adjustment Policies in the Third World.* New York: St. Martin's.

Afshar, Helen. 1996. *Women and Politics in the Third World.* London: Routledge.

Agarwal, Bina. 1997. "The Gender and Environment Debate: Lessons from India." Pp. 68–74 in *The Women, Gender, and Development Reader*, ed. Nalini Visvanathan, Lynn Dagan, Laurie Nisonoff, and Nan Wiegersma. London: Zed.

Agnew, John A., John Mercer, and David Sopher, eds. 1984. *The City in Cultural Context*. Boston: Allen & Unwin.

Aguilar, Ana Leticcia, Blanca Estela Dole, Morena Herrera, Sofia Montenegro, Lorena Camacho, and Lorena Flores. 1997. *Movimiento de mujeres en Centroamerica.* Managua, Nicaragua: Programa Regional La Corriente.

Akibayashi, Kozue. 1998. "Okinawa Women Act against Military Violence: A Preliminary Study on a Feminist Challenge to Militarism." Master's thesis. Columbia University Teachers College.

Akiner, Shirin. 1997. "Between Tradition and Modernity: The Dilemma Facing Contemporary Central Asian Women." Pp. 261–304 in *Post-Soviet Women: From the Baltic to Central Asia*, ed. Mary Buckley. New York: Cambridge University Press.

Alexander, M. Jacqui, and Chandra Talpade Mohanty, eds. 1997a. *Feminist Genealogies, Colonial Legacies, Democratic Futures.* New York: Routledge.

______. 1997b. "Introduction: Genealogies, Legacies, Movements." Pp. xiii–xlii in *Feminist Genealogies, Colonial Legacies, Democratic Futures*, ed. M. Jacqui Alexander and Chandra Talpade Mohanty. London: Routledge.

Alter, Karen, and Vargas, Jeanette. 2000. "Explaining Variation in the Use of European Litigation Strategies: European Community Law and British Gender Equality Policy." *Comparative Political Studies* 33:452–82.

Alvarez, Sonia E. 1990. *Engendering Democracy in Brazil: Women's Movements in Transition Politics*. Princeton, NJ: Princeton University Press.

______. 1998. "Latin American Feminisms 'Go Global': Trends of the 1990s and Challenges for the New Millennium." Pp. 293–324 in *Cultures of Politics, Politics of Cultures: Re-Visioning Latin American Social Movements*, ed. Sonia E. Alvarez, Evelina Dagnino, and Arturo Escobar. Boulder, CO: Westview.

______. 1999. "Advocating Feminism: The Latin American Feminist NGO 'Boom.'" *International Feminist Journal of Politics* 1(2):181–209.

______. 2000 "Translating the Global: Effects of Transnational Organizing on Local Feminist Discourses and Practices in Latin America." *Meridians* 1(1):29–67.

Alvarez, Sonia E., Evelina Dagnino and Arturo Escobar, eds. 1998a. *Culture of Politics, Politics of Cultures: Re-Visioning Latin American Social Movements*. Boulder, CO: Westview.

______. 1998b. "Introduction: The Cultural and the Political in Latin American Social Movements." Pp. 1–29 in *Culture of Politics Politics of Cultures: Re-visioning Latin American Social Movements*, ed. Sonia E. Alvarez, Evelina Dagnino, and Arturo Escobar. Boulder, CO: Westview Press.

Ammar, Nawal H. Ammar, and Leila S. Lababidy. 1999. "Women's Grassroots Movements and Democratization in Egypt." Pp. 150–70 in *Democratization and Women's Grassroots Movements*, ed. Jill M. Bystydzienski and Joti Sekhon. Bloomington, IN: Indiana University Press.

Ancheta, Angelo. 1998. *Race, Rights and the Experience of Asian Americans*. New Brunswick, NJ: Rutgers University Press.

Anonymous. 1998. Personal interview, November 4.

Anonymous. 1999. Personal interview, March 17.

Aoua Kéita. 1975. *Femme d'Afrique: la vie d'Aova Kéita racontée par elle même*. (Paris: Presence Africaines).

Appadurai, Arjun. 1990. "Disjuncture and Difference in the Global Cultural Economy." *Public Culture* 2(2):1–23.

______. 1996. *Modernity at Large: Cultural Dimensions of Globalization*. Minneapolis: University of Minnesota Press.

ArcEcology. 1998. "The Report on Equal Employment Investigation by the Military Base Related Employee Task Force of Okinawa Prefecture."

Arnold, Cindy. 1999a. Personal interview, January 9.

______. 1999b. Personal interview, June 21.

Arrieta, Refugio. 1998. Personal interview, November 5.

Atkinson, Dorothy, Alexander Dallin, and Gail Labidus, eds. 1977. *Women in Russia*. Stanford, CA: Stanford University Press.

Ault, Amber, and Eve Sandberg. 1997. "Our Policies, Their Consequences: Zambian Women's Lives under 'Structural Adjustment.'" Pp. 493–96 in *Feminist Frontiers IV*, ed. Laurel Richardson, Verta Taylor, and Nancy Whittier. New York: McGraw-Hill.

Baca Zinn, Maxine, and Bonnie Thornton Dill, eds. 1994. *Women of Color in U.S. Society*. Philadelphia: Temple University Press.

Baden, Sally. 1997. "Recession and Structural Adjustment's Impact on Women's Work in Selected Developing Regions." In *Promoting Gender Equality at Work: Turning Vision into Reality*, ed. Eugenia Date-Bah London: Zed/ILO.

Bald, Suresht. 1995. "Coping with Marginality: South Asian Women Migrants in Britain." Pp. 269–301 in *Feminism, Postmodernism, Development*, ed. M. Marchand and J. Parpart. London: Routledge.

Bamyeah, Mohammed A. 2000. *The Ends of Globalization*. Minneapolis: University of Minnesota Press.

Bandow, Doug. 1998. "Okinawa: Liberating Washington's East Asian Military Colony." *Policy Analysis* (Cato Institute), September 1.

Banerjee, Nirmala. 1988. "Working women in colonial Bengal: Modernization and Marginalization." Pp. 269–301 in *Recasting Women: Essays in Indian Colonial History*, ed. Kumkum Sangari and Sudesh Vaid. New Delhi: Kali for Women.

Barnet, Richard, La Barricada, and John Cavanagh. 1994. *Global Dreams*. New York: Simon & Schuster.

Barth, Fredrik. 1969. *Ethnic Groups and Boundaries*. Boston: Littlefield & Brown.

Basch, Linda, Nina Glick Schiller, and Cristina Szanton Blanc. 1994. *Nations Unbound: Transnational Projects, Postcolonial Predicaments and Deterritorialized Nation-States*. Langhorne, PA: Gordon & Breach.

Basu, Amrita, ed. 1995. *Women's Movements in Global Perspective*. Boulder, CO: Westview.

______. 2000a. "Globalization of the Local/Localization of the Global: Mapping Transnational Women's Movements." *Meridians* 1(1):68–84.

______. 2000b. "MillerComm Lecture. Mapping Transnational Women's Movements: Globalizing the Local, Localizing the Global." Presented at the UIUC Area Centers joint symposium "Gender and Globalization," University of Illinois, Urbana-Champaign.

Basu, Amrita, Inderpal Grewal, Caren Kaplan, and Liisa Malkki. 2001. Editorial: Special Issue on Globalization and Gender. *Signs: Journal of Women in Culture and Society* 26(4):943–48.

Beck, Ulrich. 2000. *What is Globalization?* Cambridge, UK: Polity Press.

Benería, Lourdes. 1996. "The Foreign Debt Crises and the Social Costs of Adjustment in Latin America." Pp. 11–27 in *Emergences: Women's Struggles for Livelihood in Latin America*, ed. John Friedman, Rebecca Abers, and Lilian Autler. Los Angeles: UCLA Latin American Center Publications.

______. 2000. "Changing Employment Structures and Economic Insecurity: A Global Gender Perspective." Presented at the Women and Gender in Global Perspectives Symposium, "Risks and Rights in the 21st Century," University of Illinois, Urbana-Champaign.

______. 2001. "Shifting the Risk: New Employment Patterns, Informalization, and Women's Work." *International Journal of Politics, Culture, and Society* 15(1):27–53.

Benería, Lourdes, and Shelley Feldman. 1992. *Unequal Burdens: Economic Crises, Persistent Poverty, and Women's Work*. Boulder, CO: Westview.

Benería, Lourdes and Gita Sen. 1982. "Class and Gender Inequalities and Women's Role in Economic Development," *Feminist Studies* 1(spring):157–76

______. 1997. "Accumulation, Reproduction, and Women's Role in Economic Development: Boserup Revisited." Pp. 42–50 in *The Women, Gender, and Development Reader*, ed. N. Visvanathan, L. Dagan, L. Nisonoff, and N. Wiegersma. London: Zed.

Berkovitch, Nitza, and Karen Bradley. 1999. "The Globalization of Women's Status: Consensus/Dissensus in the World Policy." *Sociological Perspectives* 42(3):481–98.

Bernal, Victoria. 1999. "Gender Activism and the Globalization of Civil Society in Tanzania." Unpublished manuscript, University of California, Irvine.

Bickham Mendez, Jennifer, and Ronald Köpke. 1998. *Mujeres y Maquila*. San Salvador: Fundación Böll.

Blank, Rebecca M. 1997. *It Takes a Nation: A New Agenda for Fighting Poverty*. Princeton, NJ: Princeton University Press.

Bleyer, Peter. 1992. "Coalitions of Social Movements as Agencies for Social Change." Pp. 102–17 in *Organizing Dissent*, ed. William Carroll. Toronto: Garamond.

Blumberg, Rae Lesser. 1995. "Gender, Microenterprise, Performance, and Power: Case Studies from the Dominican Republic, Ecuador, Guatemala, and Swaziland." Pp. 194–226 in *Women in the Latin American Development Process*, ed. C. E. Bose and E. Acosta-Belen. Philadelphia: Temple University Press.

______. 2001. "'We Are Family': Gender, Microenterprise, Family Work, and Well-Being in Ecuador and the Dominican Republic, with Comparative Data from Guatemala, Swaziland, and Guinea-Bissau." *History of the Family: An International Quarterly* 6:271–99.

Bonacich, Edna, and David V. Waller. 1994. "Mapping a Global Industry: Apparel Production in the Pacific Rim Triangle." Pp. 21–41 in *Global Production: The Apparel Industry in the Pacific Rim*, ed. Edna Bonacich, Lucie Cheng, Norma Chinchilla, Nora Hamilton, and Paul Ong. Philadelphia: Temple University Press.

Bookman, Ann, and Morgan Sandra, eds. 1988. *Women and the Politics of Empowerment*. Philadelphia: Temple University Press.

Booth, Karen M. 1998. "National Mother, Global Whore, and Transnational Femocrats: The Politics of AIDS and the Construction of Women at the World Health Organization." *Feminist Studies* 24(1):115–39.

Borge, Tomás. 1997. "¡Qué se vayan!" *La Barricada* November 21, p. A4.

Boris, Eileen, and Elisabeth Prügl, eds. 1996. *Homeworkers in Global Perspective: Invisible No More*. New York: Routledge.

Borthwick, Meredith. 1984. *The Changing Role of Women in Bengal, 1849–1905*. Princeton, NJ: Princeton University Press.

Bose, Christine E., and Edna Acosta-Belén, eds. 1995. *Women in the Latin American Development Process*. Philadelphia: Temple University Press.

Boserup, Ester. 1970. *Woman's Role in Economic Development*. New York: St. Martin's.

Boulding, Elise. 1988. *Building a Global Civic Culture: Education for an Interdependent World.* New York: Teachers College Press.

Bowen Francis, Carolyn. 1999. "Women and Military Violence." Pp. 189–203 in *Okinawa: Cold War Island*, ed. Chalmers Johnson. Cardiff, CA: Japan Pacific Resource Institute.

______. 1998. "Women's Struggles against U.S. Bases in Okinawa: Focusing International Attention on the Rape of a Young Girl." *Women's Asia 21 Voices from Japan*. Vol. 2. Tokyo Japan: Asia Japan Women's Resource Center.

Braidotti, Rosi, Elise Charkiewicz, Sabine Hausler, and Sadkia Wieringa. 1997. "Women, the Environment, and Sustainable Development." Pp. 54–61 in *The Women, Gender, and Development Reader*, ed. Nalini Visvanathan, Lynn Duggan, Laura Nisonoff, and Nancy Wiegersma. London: Zed.

Brecher, Jeremy, John Brown Childs, and Jill Cutler, eds. 1993. *Global Visions*. Boston: South End Press.

Brecher, Jeremy, and Tim Costello. 1994. *Global Village or Global Pillage: Economic Reconstruction from the Bottom Up*. Boston: South End.

Brecher Jeremy, Tim Costello, and Brendan Smith. 2000. *Globalization from Below: The Power of Solidarity*. Boston: South End.

Brereton, Bridget. 1981. *A History of Modern Trinidad 1783–1962*. Kingston, Jamaica: Heinemann.

Bretherton, Charlotte, and Liz Sperling. 1996. "Women's Networks and the European Union: Towards an Inclusive Approach?" *Journal of Common Market Studies* 34:487–508.

Briggs, Joanne. 1999. "Domestic Workers Left Out of Conference." *Trinidad Guardian* October 1.

Brown, Stacey, 2000a. "Second South-North Gathering of Peoples of America." *Women, Food, and Agriculture Newsletter* 3, December, p. 4.

______. 2000b. "The World Poor People's Summit to End Poverty." *Women, Food, and Agriculture Newsletter* 3, December, p. 5.

Browning, Genia. 1987. *Women and Politics in the USSR: Consciousness Raising and Soviet Women's Groups*. New York: St. Martin's.

Brysk, Allison. 1993. "From Above and Below: Social Movements, the International System, and Human Rights in Argentina." *Comparative Political Studies* 26:259–85.

______. 1996. "Turning Weakness into Strength: The Internationalization of Indian Rights." *Latin American Perspectives* 23:38–57.

______. 2000. *From Tribal Village to Global Village: Indian Rights and International Relations in Latin America*. Stanford, CA: Stanford University Press.

Buckley, Mary. 1997. *Post-Soviet Women: From the Baltic to Central Asia*. New York: Cambridge University Press.

______, ed. 1989. *Perestroika and Soviet Women*. Cambridge: Cambridge University Press.

Buell, Frederick. 1998. "Nationalist Postnationalism: Globalist Discourse in Contemporary American Culture." *American Quarterly* 50(3):548–91.

Bulbeck, Chilla. 1998. *Re-Orienting Western Feminisms: Women's Diversity in a Postcolonial World.* Cambridge: Cambridge University Press.

Bunch, Charlotte, and Niamh Reilly. 1994. *Demanding Accountability: The Global Campaign and Vienna Tribunal For Women's Rights.* New York: UNDP.

Burns, Bradford. 1987. *At War in Nicaragua: The Reagan Doctrine and the Politics of Nostalgia.* New York: Harper & Row.

Butegwa, Florence 1998. "Globalization and Its Impact on Economic and Social Rights in Africa." Paper prepared for AAS and HURIDOCS.

Buvinic, Mayra, Catherine Gwin, and Lisa M. Bates. 1996. *Investing in Women: Progress and Prospects for the World Bank.* Washington, DC: Overseas Development Council in Cooperation with the International Center for Research on Women.

Bystydzienski, Jill M., ed. 1992. *Women Transforming Politics: Worldwide Strategies for Empowerment.* Bloomington: Indiana University Press.

Bystydzienski, Jill M., and Joti Sekhon, eds. 1999. *Democratization and Women's Grassroots Movements.* Bloomington: Indiana University Press.

CAFO (Coordination des Associations et ONG Féminines du Mali). 1998. "Liste des Associations Membres de la CAFO."

Callaway, Barbara J. 1991. "The Role of Women in Kano City Politics. " Pp. 145–59 in *Hausa Women in the Twentieth Century*, ed. Catherine Coles and Beverly Mack. Madison: University of Wisconsin Press.

Campbell, Bruce, Maria Teresa Gutierrez Haces, Andrew Jackson, Mehrene Larudee. 1999. *Pulling Apart: The Deterioration of Employment and Income in North America under Free Trade.* Ottawa, Ontario: Canadian Center for Policy Alternatives.

Cancian, Francesca M. 1996. "Participatory Research and Alternative Strategies for Activist Sociology." Pp. 187–205 in *Feminism and Social Change: Bridging Theory and Practice*, ed. Heidi Gottfried. Urbana: University of Illinois Press.

CAPRI. 1997. *Directorio ONG de Nicaragua 1996-1997.* Managua: Centro de Apoyo a Programas y Proyectos.

Carrington, Roslyn. 1998. "Overworked and Underpaid." *Trinidad Guardian,* October 25.

Castells, Manuel. 1993. "The Informational Economy and the New International Division of Labor." Pp. 15–43 in *The New Global Economy in the Information Age*, ed. Martin Carnoy, Manuel Castells, Stephen S. Cohen, and Fernando Henrique Carodoso. University Park: Pennsylvania State University Press.

______. 1997. *The Power of Identity.* Malden, MA: Blackwell.

CEHAT. 1995. *FIVE Years of CEHAT 1991–1995.* Mumbai: CEHAT.

CEI (Centro de Estudios Internacionales). 1997. "Taller 'Estrategias de Negociación en Procesos de Cabildeo.'" Managua, Nicaragua: CEI.

Central Statistical Offices. 1999. Labor Force Survey, Trinidad & Tobago.

Chafetz, Janet Saltzman. 1990. *Gender Equity: An Integrated Theory of Stability and Change.* Newbury Park, CA: Sage.

Chanana, Karuna. 1994. "Social Change or Social Reform: Women, Education, and Family in Pre-Independence India." In *Women, Education, and Family Structure in India,* ed. Carol Mukhopadhyay and Susan Seymour. Boulder, CO: Westview.

Charlesworth, Hilary. 1994. "What Are 'Women's International Human Rights'?" Pp. 58–84 in *Human Rights of Women: National and International Perspectives.* Philadelphia: University of Pennsylvania Press.

Charlick, Robert B., and Susanna D. Wing. 1998. "The Political Economy of Educational Policy Reform in Mali: A Stakeholder Analysis." Washington, DC: USAID/Management Systems International.

Charlton, Sue Ellen M., Jana Everett, Kathleen Staudt, eds. 1989. *Women, the State, and Development.* Albany: State University of New York Press.

Chaudhury-Sethi, Rita. 1994. "Smells Like Racism: A Plan for Mobilizing against Anti-Asian Bias." Pp. 235–53 in *The state of Asian America: Activism and Resistance in the 1990s,* ed. K. Aguilar San Juan. Boston: South End.

Chilsen, Liz, and Sheldon Rampton. 1988. *Friends in Deed: The Story of U.S.-Nicaragua Sister Cities.* Madison: Wisconsin Coordinating Council on Nicaragua.

Chinchilla, Norma Stoltz. 1995. "Revolutionary Popular Feminism in Nicaragua: Ideologies, Political Transitions, and the Struggle for Autonomy." Pp. 242–70 in *Women in the Latin American Development Process,* ed. Christine E. Bose and Edna Acosta-Belén. Philadelphia: Temple University Press.

Chodorow, Nancy. 1978. *The Reproduction of Mothering.* Berkeley: University of California Press.

Chow, Esther. 1994. "Asian American Women at Work." Pp. 203–228 in *Women of Color in U.S. Society,* ed. Maxine Baca Zinn and Bonnie Thornton Dill. Philadelphia: Temple University Press.

Chaudhury-Sethi, Rita. 1994. "Smells Like Racism: A Plan for Mobilizing Against Anti-Asian Bias." Pp. 235–52 in *The State of Asian America: Activism and Resistance in the 1990s.* ed. K. Aguilar San-Juan. Boston: South End Press.

Christiansen, Thomas. 1996. "A Maturing Bureaucracy?: The Role of the Commission in the Policy Process." Pp. 77–95 in *European Union: Power and Policy-Making,* ed. Jeremy Richardson. London: Routledge.

Cichowski, Rachel. 1998. "Integrating the Environment: The European Court and the Construction of Supranational Policy." *Journal of European Public Policy* 5(3):387–405.

______. 2001. "Judicial Rulemaking and the Institutionalization of EU Sex Equality Policy." Pp. 113–36 in *The Institutionalization of Europe,* ed. Alec Stone Sweet, Wayne Sandholtz, and N. Gligstein. Oxford: Oxford University Press.

Clark, Ann Marie, Elisabeth J. Friedman, and Kathryn Hochstetler. 1998. "The Sovereign Limits of Global Civil Society: A Comparison of NGO Participation in UN World

Conferences on the Environment, Human Rights, and Women." *World Politics* 51(1):1–35.

Clarke, Roberta. 1993. *Women in Trade Unions in Trinidad and Tobago*. Geneva: International Labor Office.

Clean Clothes Campaign. 1998. "Comments on SA 8000/Guidance." Unpublished memo.

Clements, Barbara. 1979. "Work among Women." Pp. 149–77 in *Bolshevik Feminist: The Life of Aleksandra Kollontai*. Bloomington: University of Indiana Press.

______. 1992. "The Utopianism of the Zhenotdel." *Slavic Review* 51(3):485–96.

______. 1994. *Daughters of Revolution: A History of Women in the U.S.S.R.* Arlington Heights, Illinois: Harlan Davidson.

Clough, Michael, 1996. "Shaping American Foreign Relations: The Critical Role of the Southeast." Report of a new American global dialogue (Stanley Foundation).

Cohen, Jean L., and Andrew Arato. 1992. *Civil Society and Political Theory*. Cambridge: MIT Press.

Collins, Doreen. 1975. *The European Communities: The Social Policy of the First Phase.* Vol. 2, *The European Economic Community 1958–1972.* London: Martin Robertson.

Collins, Jane L., and Martha Gimenez, eds. 1990. *Work without Wages: Comparative Studies of Domestic Labor and Self-Employment.* Albany: State University of New York Press.

Collins, Patricia Hill. 1990. *Black Feminist Thought: Knowledge, Consciousness, and the Politics of Enlightenment.* Boston: Unwin Hyman.

______. 1991. *Black Feminist Thought: Knowledge, Consciousness, and the Politics of Empowerment.* New York: Routledge.

Commisariat à la Promotion des Femmes Maître d'Oeuvre du Plan d'Action. n.d. "Plan d'action pour la promotion des femmes 1996–2000" Bamako: République Démocratique du Mali, Commissariat à la Promotion des Femmes.

Committee for Human Rights in Puerto Rico. 2000. "International Tribunal on Violation of Human Rights in Puerto Rico." *Social Justice* 27(4):143–51.

Coppin, Addington, and Reed Olsen. 1992. "Earnings and Ethnicity in Trinidad and Tobago." *Journal of Development Studies* 34:116–34.

Council for Mutual Economic Assistance. 1985. *Women in Socialist Society.* Moscow: Council for Mutual Economic Assistance.

Coyle, Laurie, Gail Hershatter and Emily Honig, "Women at Farah: An Unfinished Story." Pp. 117–43 in *Mexican Women in the United States*, ed. Magdalena Mora and Adelaida del Castillo. (Los Angeles: Chicano Studies Research Center, University of California, 1980).

Cross, John C. 1998. *Informal Politics: Street Vendors and the State in Mexico City.* Stanford, CA: Stanford University Press.

Crouch, Martha L. 2001. "From Golden Rice to Terminator Technology: Why Agricultural Biotechnology Will Not Feed the World or Save the Environment." Pp. 22–29 in *Re-*

designing Life? The Worldwide Challenge to Genetic Engineering, ed. Brian Tokar. London: Zed Books.

CTSP (Comité de Transition pour le Salut du Peuple). 1991. "Rapport de la Commission de Verification des Mandats," July 31.

Currie, Jan. 1998. "Globalization as an Analytical Concept and Local Policy Response." Pp. 15–20 in *Universities and Globalization,* ed. Jan Currie and Janet Newson. Thousand Oaks, CA: Sage.

Dallin, Alexander, and Gail Lapidus, eds. 1995. *The Soviet System: From Crisis to Collapse.* Boulder, CO: Westview.

Daly, Mary. 1978. *Gyn-ecology: The Metaethics of Radical Feminism.* Boston: Beacon.

Daoud, Zakya. 1993. *Feminism and Politics in Maghreb: 1930–1992 (Feminisme et Politique au Maghreb: 1930–1992).* Paris: Maisonneuve et Larose.

Date-Bah, Eugenia. 1995. "Women in the Global Labor Market: Empowerment and Enabling Environment for Progress." Pp. 43–49 in *Women and the United Nations,* ed. Filomina Chioma Steady and Remie Toure. Rochester, VT: Schenkman.

Dawson, Jane. 1996. *Eco-Nationalism: Anti-Nuclear Activism and National Identity in Russia, Lithuania, and Ukraine.* Durham, NC: Duke University Press.

Deb, Chitra. 1984. *Antahpurer Atmakatha.* Calcutta: Anando.

Desai, Manisha. 1995. "If Peasants Build Dams, What Will the State Have Left to Do? Practices of New Social Movements in India." *Research in Social Movements, Conflict, and Change* 19:203–18.

Deutch, K. W. 1966. *Nationalism and Social Communications: An Inquiry into the Foundations of Nationality.* Cambridge: MIT Press.

______. 1996. From Vienna to Beijing: The International Women's Human Rights Movement." *New Political Science* 35 (spring):107–19.

"Development Co-Operation Report." 1996. Republic of Trinidad and Tobago.

Dickenson, Torry D., and Robert K. Schaeffer. 2001. *Fast Forward: Work, Gender, and Protest in a Changing World.* Lanham, MD: Rowman & Littlefield.

Dinan, Desmond. 1994. *Ever Closer Union?: An Introduction to the European Community.* Boulder, CO: Lynne Rienner.

Dore, Elizabeth, ed. 1997. *Gender Politics in Latin America: Debates in Theory and Practice.* New York: Monthly Review Press.

Dragadze, Tamara. 1997. "The Women's Peace Train in Georgia." Pp. 250–60 in *Post-Soviet Women: From the Baltic to Central Asia,* ed. Mary Buckley. New York: Cambridge University Press.

Drainville, Andre. 1998. "The Fetishism of Global Civil Society: Global Governance, Transnational Urbanism and Sustainable Capitalism in the World Economy." Pp. 35–63 in *Transnationalism from Below,* ed. Michael Peter Smith and Luis Eduardo Guarnizo. New Brunswick, NJ: Transaction.

Dudwick, Nora. 1997. "Out of the Kitchen into the Crossfire: Women in Independent Armenia." Pp. 235–49 in *Post-Soviet Women: From the Baltic to Central Asia*, ed. Mary Buckley. New York: Cambridge University Press.

East Asia–U.S. Women's Network against Militarism. 2000. "Final Statement." Presented at International Women's Summit to Redefine Security, Naha, Okinawa, Japan, June 22–25.

East Asia–U.S. Women's Network against U.S. Militarism. 1999. "Project Summary."

Economist Intelligence Unit. 1997–1998. *Country Profile: Trinidad and Tobago, Surinam, Netherlands, Antilles, Aruba.* London: Economist Intelligence Unit.

Effland, Anne B., Denise Rogers, and Valerie Grim. 1993. Women As Agricultural Landowners: What Do We Know about Them? *Agricultural History* 67(2):235–36.

Einhorn, Barbara. 1993. *Cinderella Goes to Market: Citizenship, Gender, and Women's Movements in East Central Europe*. New York: Verso.

El Paso Greater Chamber of Commerce. 1997. "The El Paso Labor Market: A Training Gap Analysis, Final Report," December.

El Puente CDC/La Mujer Obrera. 1999. *Building Employment and Economic Development Bridges in South Central El Paso for Displaced Workers, Strategic Plan.* El Paso, TX: La Mujer Obrera.

Ellis, Evelyn. 1998. *European Community Sex Equality Law*. 2nd ed. Oxford: Oxford University Press.

Elman, Amy, ed. 1996. *Sexual Politics and the European Union: The New Feminist Challenge.* Oxford: Berghahn.

Elson, Diane, and R. Pearson. 1981. "Nimble Fingers Make Cheap Workers: An Analysis of Women's Employment in Third World Export Manufacturing." *Feminist Review* 7:

Enloe, Cynthia. 1983a. *Does Khaki Become You?: The Militarisation of Women's Lives*. Boston: South End.

______. 1983b. "Women Textile Workers in the Militarization of SE Asia." Pp. 407–25 in *Women, Men, and The International Division of Labor*, ed. June Nash and Maria Patricia Fernandez-Kelly. Albany: State University of New York Press.

______. 1989. *Bananas, Beaches, and Bases: Making Feminist Sense of International Politics.* London: Pandora.

______. 1990. *Bananas, Beaches, and Bases: Making Feminist Sense of International Politics.* Berkeley: University of California Press.

______. 2000. *Maneuvers: The International Politics of Women's Lives*. Berkeley: University of California Press.

Eschle, Catherine. 1999. "Review Essay. Building Global Visions: Democracy and Solidarity in the Globalisation of Feminism." *International Feminist Journal of Politics* 1920:327–31.

______. 2001. *Global Democracy, Social Movements, and Feminisms.* Boulder, CO: Westview.

Escobar, Arturo. 1995. *Encountering Development: The Making and Unmaking of the Third World.* Princeton, NJ: Princeton University Press.

Escobar, Arturo, and Sonia E. Alvarez, eds. 1992. *The Making of Social Movements in Latin America.* Boulder, CO: Westview.

Espinal, Rosario, and Sherri Grasmuck. 1997. "Gender, Households and Informal Entrepreneurship in the Dominican Republic." *Journal of Comparative Family Studies* 28(1):103–28.

Espiritu, Yen. 1992. *Asian American Panethnicity: Bridging Institutions and Identities.* Philadelphia: Temple University Press.

______. 1997. *Asian American Women and Men: Labor, Laws, Love.* Thousand Oaks, CA: Sage.

Evans, Peter. 1979. *Dependent Development.* Princeton, NJ: Princeton University Press.

"Extensive Pollution Stalls Base Conversions." 2000. *Los Angeles Times,* May 1.

Faber, Daniel, ed. 1998. *The Struggle for Ecological Democracy: Environmental Justice Movements in the U.S.* New York: Guilford.

Fainstein, Susan S. 1987. "Local Mobilization and Economic Discontent," Pp. 323–42 in *The Capitalist City: Global Restructuring and Community Politics,* ed. Joe R. Feagin and Michael P. Smith. New York: Basil Blackwell.

Falk, Richard. 1999. *Predatory Globalization: A Critique.* London: Blackwell.

Farnsworth, Beatrice. 1980. "The Zhenotdel during the NEP." Pp. 284–308 in *Aleksandra Kollontai: Socialism, Feminism, and the Bolshevik Revolution.* Stanford, CA: Stanford University Press.

Feffer, John. 2000. "Gunboat Globalization: The Intersection of Economics and Security in East Asia." Special issue on Globalization, Militarism, and Armed Conflict. Okazawa-Rey and Kirk, co-editors. *Social Justice* 27(4):45–62.

Fernandez-Kelly, Maria Patricia, 1983. *For We Are Sold, I and My People: Women and Industry in Mexico's Frontier.* Albany: State University of New York Press.

Fernandez-Kelly, Maria Patricia, 1990. "Power Surrendered, Power Restored: The Politics of Work and Family among Hispanic Garment Workers in California and Florida." Pp. 130–49 in *Women, Politics and Change,* ed. Louise Tilly and Patricia Gurin. New York: Russell Sage.

Fernandez-Kelly, Maria Patricia, and Anna M. Garcia. 1985. "The Making of an Underground Economy: Hispanic Women, Home Work, and the Advanced Capitalist State." *Urban Anthropology* 14:59–90.

Ferraro, Kathleen. 1983. "Negotiating Trouble in a Battered Women's Shelter." *Urban Life* 12(3):287–306.

Ferree, Myra Marx, and Beth B. Hess. 1994. *Controversy and Coalition: The New Feminist Movement across Three Decades of Change,* rev. ed. New York: Twayne.

Ferree, Myra Marx, and Patricia Yancey Martin, eds. 1995. *Feminist Organizations: Harvest of the New Women's Movement.* Philadelphia: Temple University Press, 1995.

Fisher, Julie. 1993. *The Road from Rio: Sustainable Development and the Nongovernmental Movement in the Third World.* Westport, CT: Praeger.

Fitzgerald, David. 2000. *Negotiating Extra-Territorial Citizenship: Mexican Migration and the Transnational Politics of Community.* San Diego: Center for Comparative Immigration Studies at the University of California, San Diego.

Flores, Maria Antonia. 1998. Personal interview, October 13.

Fong, Timothy. 1998. *The Contemporary Asian American Experience: Beyond the Model Minority.* Upper Saddle River, NJ: Prentice Hall.

Fontana, Marzia, Susan Joekes, and Rachel Masika. 1998. "Global Trade Expansion and Liberalisation: Gender Issues and Impact." Brighton, U.K.: Institute of Development Studies, University of Sussex.

Forbes, Geraldine. 1996. *Women in Modern India.* Cambridge: Cambridge University Press.

Ford-Smith, Honor. 1997. "Ring Ding in a Tight Corner: Sistren, Collective Democracy, and the Organization of Cultural Production." Pp. 213–58 in *Feminist Genealogies, Colonial Legacies, Democratic Futures,* ed. M. Jacqui Alexander and Chandra Talpade Mohanty. New York: Routledge.

French, Howard W. 1996. "In One Poor African Nation, Democracy Thrives." *New York Times,* October 16, A3.

Friedberg Elisabeth J. 1999. "The Effects of 'Transnationalism Reversed' in Venezuela: Assessing the Impact of UN Global Conferences on the Women's Movement." *International Feminist Journal of Politics* 1(3):357–81.

Fuentes, Annette and Barbara Ehrenreich. 1983. *Women in the Global Factory.* INC Pamphlet No. 2. Boston: South End Press.

Gabriel, Christina, and Laura Macdonald. 1994. "NAFTA, Women, and Organizing in Canada and Mexico: Forging a Feminist Internationality." *Millennium: Journal of International Studies* 23(3):535–62.

Gamson, Joshua. 1996. "The Organizational Shaping of Collective Identity: The Case of Gay and Lesbian Film Festivals." *Sociological Forum* 11:231–62.

Gamson, William. 1990. *Strategy of Social Protest.* Belmont, CA: Wadsworth.

______. 1992. "The Social Psychology of Collective Action." Pp. 53–76 in *Frontiers in Social Movement Theory,* eds. Aldon Morris and Carol McClurg Mueller. New Haven, CT: Temple University Press.

Garcia, Mario T. 1981. *Desert Immigrants.* New Haven, CT: Yale University Press.

Gardiner, Frances, and Monique Leijenaar. 1997. "The Timid and the Bold: Analysis of the 'Woman-Friendly State' in Ireland and the Netherlands." Pp. 60–87 in *Sex Equality Policy in Western Europe,* ed. Frances Gardiner. London: Routledge.

Garrett, Geoffrey. 1992. "International Cooperation and Institutional Choice: The European Community's Internal Market." *International Organization* 46:533–60.

GATT-Fly. 1993. *AH-HAH! A New Approach to Popular Education.* Toronto, Ontario: Between the Lines.

Geertz, Clifford. 1973. *The Interpretation of Cultures.* New York: Basic Books.

________. 1976. "Art as a Cultural System." *Modern Language Notes* 91:1473–199.

GFDS (Groupe Féminin Droit de Suffrage). 1998. Sikasso seminar transcript, April 3.

Giddens, Anthony. 1990 *Consequences of Modernity.* Stanford, CA: Stanford University Press.

Gilkes, Cheryl. 1988. "Building in Many Places: Multiple Commitments and Ideologies in Black Women's Community Work." Pp. 53–76 in *Women and the Politics of Empowerment,* ed. Ann Bookman and Sandra Morgan. Philadelphia: Temple University Press.

______. 1994. "'If It Wasn't for Women': African American Women, Community Work, and Social Change." Pp. 229–48 in *Women of Color in U.S. Society,* ed. Maxine Baca Zinn and Bonnie Thornton Dill. Philadelphia: Temple University Press.

Gilot, Louie. 1999. "Displaced Workers Want City to Help Find Jobs Quickly." *El Paso Times,* August 31.

Glenn, Evelyn. 2000. "Citizenship and Inequality: Historical and Global Perspectives." *Social Problems* 47:1–20.

Glenn, Guillermo. 1999. Personal interview, January 27.

Gluck, Sherna Berger, with Maylei Blackwell, Sharon Cotrell, and Karen Harper. 1998. "Whose Feminism, Whose History? Reflections on Excavating the History of (the) U.S. Women's Movement(s)." Pp. 31–56 in *Community Activism and Feminist Politics: Organizing across Race, Class, and Gender,* ed. Nancy A. Naples. New York: Routledge.

Goldberg, Gertrude Schaffner, and Eleanor Kremen, eds. 1990. *The Feminization of Poverty: Only in America?* New York: Praeger.

Goldman, Wendy. 1996. "Industrial Politics, Peasant Rebellion, and the Death of the Proletarian Women's Movement in the USSR." *Slavic Review* 55(1):46–77.

Gordon, Linda. 1990. "The New Feminist Scholarship on the Welfare State." Pp. 9–35 in *Women, the State, and Welfare,* ed. Linda Gordon. Madison: University of Wisconsin Press.

______. 1991. *Black and White Visions of Welfare: Women's Welfare Activism, 1890–1945.* Madison, WI: Institute for Research on Poverty.

Grewal, Inderpal. 1994. "Autobiographic Subjects and Diasporic Locations: 'Meatless Days' and 'Borderlands.'" Pp. 67–86 in *Scattered Hegemonies: Postmodernity and Transnational Feminist Practices,* ed. Inderpal Grewal and Caren Kaplan. Minneapolis: University of Minnesota Press.

______. 1999. "On the New Global Feminism and the Family of Nations: Dilemmas of Transnational Feminist Practice." Pp. 501–30 in *Talking Visions: Multicultural Feminism in a Transnational Age,* ed. Ella Shohat. Cambridge, MA: New Museum of Modern Art and MIT Press.

Grewal, Inderpal, and Caren Kaplan, eds. 1994. *Scattered Hegemonies: Postmodernity and Transnational Feminist Practices.* Minneapolis: University of Minneapolis Press.

Grimes, Kimberly M. 1998. *Crossing Borders: Changing Social Identities in Southern Mexico.* Tucson: University of Arizona Press.

Guarnizo, Luis Eduardo, and Michael Peter Smith. 1998. "The Locations of Transnationalism." Pp. 3–34 in *Transnationalism From Below*, ed. Michael Peter Smith and Luis Eduardo Guarnizo. New Brunswick, NJ: Transaction.

Guerrero, Marie Anna Jaimes. 1997. "Civil Rights versus Sovereignty: Native American Women in Life and Land Struggles." Pp. 101–21 in *Feminist Genealogies, Colonial Legacies, Democratic Futures*, ed. M. Jacqui Alexander and Chandra Talpade Mohanty. New York: Routledge.

Haas, Peter. 1992. "Introduction: Epistemic Communities and International Policy Coordination." *International Organization* 46:1–35.

Hall, Stuart. 1991. "The Local and the Global: Globalization and Ethnicity." In *Culture, Globalization, and the World System*, ed. Anthony King. London: Macmillan.

Harison, Bennett. 1994. *Lean and Mean: The Changing Landscape of Corporate Power in the Age of Flexibility*. New York: Basic Books.

Hartsock, Nancy C. 1996. "Theoretical Bases for Coalition Building: An Assessment of Postmodernism." Pp. 256–74 in *Feminism and Social Change: Bridging Theory and Practice*, ed. Heidi Gottfried. Urbana: University of Illinois Press.

Harvey, David. 1999. "What's Green and Makes the Environment Go Round?" Pp. 327–55 in *The Cultures of Globalization*, ed. Fredric Jameson and Masao Miyoshi. Durham, NC: Duke University Press.

Held, David, Anthony McGrew, David Glodblatt, and Jonathan Perraton. 1999. *Global Transformations: Politics, Economics, and Culture*. Stanford, CA: Stanford University Press.

Herrera-Sobek, Maria. 1990. *The Mexican Corrido*. Bloomington: Indiana University Press.

Herzog, Lawrence. 1990. *Where North Meets South*. Austin: University of Texas Press.

Hintzen, Percy C. 1985. "Ethnicity, Class, and International Capitalist Penetration in Guyana and Trinidad." *Social and Economic Studies* 343:107–63.

Hirasawa, Yasumasa. 2000. "Globalization of Human Rights Issues." *The Journal of Educational Sociology* 66:57–65.

Hochschild, Arlie. 2000. "Global Care Chain and Emotional Surplus Value." Pp. 130–46 in *Global Capitalism*, ed. Will Hutton and Anthony Giddens. New York: New Press.

Hosaka, Hiroshi. 1999. *Beikoku ga Mita Koza/Koza Riots: December 20, 1970*. Okinawa Shiyakusho Okinawa City Hall: Bodo Publishers.

Hoskyns, Catharine. 1986. "Women, European Law and Transnational Politics." *International Journal of the Sociology of Law* 14:299–315.

______. 1996. *Integrating Gender*. London: Verso.

______. 1999. "Gender and Transnational Democracy: The Case of the European Union." Pp. 72–87 in *Gender Politics in Global Governance*, ed. Mary K. Meyer and Elisabeth Prügl. Lanham, MD: Rowman & Littlefield.

Howard, Rhoda E. 1992. "Dignity, Community, and Human Rights." Pp. 100–137 in *Human Rights in Cross-Cultural Perspectives*, ed. Abdullahi A. An-Na'im. Philadelphia: University of Pennsylvania Press.

Hoyt, Katherine. 1997. *The Many Faces of Sandinista Democracy*. Athens: Ohio University Center for International Studies.

Hubbard, Dianne, and Colette Solomon. 1995. "The Many Faces of Feminism in Namibia." Pp. 163–86 in *Women's Movements in Global Perspective*, ed. Amrita Basu. Boulder, CO: Westview.

Human Rights Watch. 1992. "Hidden Victims: Women in Post-Communist Poland." *Human Rights Watch Women's Rights Project* 4(5):1–11.

______. 1995a. "Abuses against Women Workers." *Human Rights Watch Global Report on Women's Human Rights*. New York: Human Rights Watch.

______. 1995b. "Russia: Neither Jobs nor Justice: State Discrimination against Women in Russia." *Human Rights Watch Women's Rights Project* 7(5):1–30.

______. 1997. "Russia: Too Little, Too Late: State Response to Violence against Women." *Human Rights Watch Women's Rights Project* 9(13):1–51.

Hurtado, Aida. 1996. *The Color of Privelege: Three Blasphemies on Race and Feminism*. Ann Arbor: University of Michigan Press.

Hutchison, Gail, and Joanne Nelson. 1999. "Microenterprise Project Brings Farmers Together." *Women, Food and Agriculture Newsletter* 2(2):7.

Hutton, Will, and Anthony Giddens, eds. 2000. *Global Capitalism*. New York: New Press

Hyde, Lily. 1998. "Ukraine: New Anti-Trafficking Laws Set to Protect Women and Children." *RFE/RL Report*, April 15.

IAWS (India Association of Women's Studies). 1995. *The State and the Women's Movement in India: A Report*. New Delhi: Systems Vision.

ICGARDE (International Consortium on Gender, Agriculture, Rural Development, and Environment), 1999. Summary description.

Institute for Public Accuracy. 1999. "WTO Rules: The Record." Washington, D.C. http://www.accuracy.org.

Itokazu, Keiko. 1996. "The World Can Learn from Our History." Pp. 10–17 in *Okinawa Dreams O.K.*, ed. Tony Barell and Rick Tanaka. Berlin: Zehdenicker Strase.

Jad, Islah. 1995. "Claiming Feminism, Claiming Nationalism: Women's Activism in the Occupied Territories." Pp. 226–47 in *Women's Movements in Global Perspective*, ed. Amrita Basu. Boulder, CO: Westview.

Jameson, Fredric, and Masao Miyoshi, eds. 1998. *The Cultures of Globalization*. Durham, NC: Duke University Press.

Jancar, Barbara Wolfe. 1978. *Women under Communism*. Baltimore: Johns Hopkins University Press.

Jaquette, Jane, ed. 1994. *The Women's Movement in Latin America: Participation and Democracy*. San Francisco: Westview.

Jayawardena, Kumari. 1995. *The White Woman's Other Burden: Western Women and South Asia during British Rule*. London: Routledge.

Jelin, Elizabeth, ed. 1994. *Women and Social Change in Latin America*. New Jersey: Zed.

Jenson, Jane, and Boaventura de Sousa Santos. 2000. *Globalizating Institutions: Case Studies in Regulation and Innovation*. Burlington, VT: Ashgate.

Jessop, Bob. 1990. *State Theory. Putting Capitalist States in Their Place*. Oxford: Polity.

Johnson, Chalmers. 1996. "Go-Banken-Sama, GO HOME!" *Bulletin of Atomic Scientists*, July/August.

______. 1999. "The 1995 Rape Incident and the Rekindling of Okinawan Protest against the American Bases." In *Okinawa: Cold War Island*, ed. Chalmers Johnson. Cardiff, CA: Japan Pacific Resource Institute.

Johnston, Hank. 1994. "New Social Movements and Old Regional Nationalism." Pp. 267–86 in *New Social Movements*, ed. Enrique Larana, Hank Johnston, and Joseph Gusfield. Philadelphia: Temple University Press.

Johnston, Hank, and Bert Klandermas, eds. 1995. *Social Movements and Culture*. Minneapolis: University of Minnesota Press.

Jorio, Rosa de. 1997. "Female Elites, Women's Formal Associations, and Political Practices in Urban Mali (West Africa)." Ph.D. dissertation. University of Illinois.

Kabeer, Naila. 1999. *Reversed Realities: Gender Hierarchies in Development Thought*. London: Verso.

Kalb, Don, Marco van der Land, Richard Staring, Bart van Steenbergen, and Nico Wilterdink, eds. 2000. *The Ends of Globalization: Bringing Society Back In*. Lanham, Maryland: Rowman & Littlefield.

Kannabiran, Vasanth, and Kalpana Kannabiran. 1997. "Looking at Ourselves: The Women's Movement in Hyderabad." Pp. 259–79 in *Feminist Genealogies, Colonial Legacies, Democratic Futures*, ed. M. Jacqui Alexander and Chandra Talpade Mohanty. New York: Routledge.

Kante, M. 1987. 4e Congres ordinaire de l'UNFM. Debout sur tous les fronts du combat politique, economique, et social. L'Essor Hebdomadaire, 24–25 janvier: 2,3,4.

Kaplan, Caren. 1997. "The Politics of Location as Transnational Feminist Practice." Pp. 137–52 in *Scattered Hegemonies*, ed. Inderpal Grewal and Caren Kaplan. Minneapolis: University of Minnesota Press.

______. 2000. *Questions of Travel: Postmodern Discourses of Displacement*. Durham, NC: Duke University Press.

Kaplan, Caren, Norma Alarcón, and Minoo Moallem, eds. 1999. *Between Woman and Nation: Nationalisms, Transnational Feminisms, and the State*. Durham, NC: Duke University Press.

Kaplan, Temma. 1997. *Crazy for Democracy: Women in Grassroots Movements*. New York: Routledge.

Karabenta, Keita Djeneba. 1996. Report of the "Association des Juristes Maliennes (AJM) Clinique juridique mobile à Kayes," January 16–18.

Karlekar, Malavika. 1994. "Women's Nature and Access to Education in Bengal." In *Women, Education, and Family Structure in India*, ed. Carol Mukhopadhyay and Susan Seymour. Boulder, CO: Westview.

Katzenstein, Mary. 1995. "Discursive Politics and Feminist Activism in the Catholic Church." In *Feminist Organizations: Harvest of the New Women's Movement,* ed. Myra Marx Ferree and Patricia Yancey Martin. Philadelphia: Temple University Press.

______. 1998a. *Faithful and Fearless: Moving Feminist Protest inside the Church and Military.* Princeton, NJ: Princeton University Press.

______. 1998b. "Stepsisters: Feminist Activism in Different Institutional Spaces." In *The Social Movement Society,* ed. David Meyer and Sidney Tarrow. Lanham, MD: Rowman & Littlefield.

Katzenstein, Mary, and Carol McClurg Mueller, eds. 1987. *The Women's Movements of the United States and Western Europe: Consciousness, Political Opportunity, and Public Policy.* Philadelphia: Temple University Press.

Keck, Margaret E., and Kathryn Sikkink. 1998a. *Activists beyond Borders: Transnational Advocacy Networks in International Politics.* Ithaca, NY: Cornell University Press.

______. 1998b. "Transnational Advocacy Networks in the Movement Society." Pp. 217–38 in *The Social Movement Society,* ed. David Meyer and Sidney Tarrow. Lanham, MD: Rowman & Littlefield.

______. 1999. "Transnational Advocacy Networks in International and Regional Politics." *International Social Science Journal* 51:89–101.

Kelly, Rita Mae, Jane H. Bayes, Mary E. Hawkesworth, and Brigitte Young, eds. 2001. *Gender, Globalization, and Democratizaion.* Lanham, MD: Rowman & Littlefield.

Kelso, Ruth Ann. 2000. *Women of Okinawa.* Ithaca, NY: Cornell University Press.

Kendrick, Karen. 1998. "Producing the Battered Woman: Shelter Politics and the Power of the Feminist Voice." Pp. 151–74 in *Community Activism and Feminist Politics,* ed. Nancy A. Naples. New York: Routledge.

Kenney, Sally. 1992. *For Whose Protection? Reproductive Hazards and Exclusionary Policies in the United States and Britain.* Ann Arbor: University of Michigan Press.

______. 1996. "Pregnancy Discrimination: Toward Substantive Equality." *Wisconsin Women's Law Journal* 10:351–402.

Kerr, George H. [1958] 1975. *Okinawa: The History of an Island People.* Reprint, Rutland, VT: Charles E. Tuttle.

Kerr, Joanna, ed. 1993. *Ours By Right: Women's Rights as Human Rights.* London: Zed.

Kirk, Gwyn. 1997. "Standing on Solid Ground: A Materialist Ecological Feminism." Pp. 345–63 in *Materialist Feminism: A Reader in Class, Difference and Women's Lives,* ed. Rosemary Hennessy and Chrys Ingraham. New York: Routledge.

Kirk, Gwyn, Rachel Cornwell, and Margo Okazawa-Rey. 1999. "Women and the U.S. Military in East Asia." *Foreign Policy in Focus* 4(9). Interhemispheric Resource Center and the Institute for Policy Studies.

Kirk, Gwyn, and Carolyn Bowen Francis. 2000. "Redefining Security: Women Challenge U.S. Military Policy and Practice in East Asia." *Berkeley Women's Law Journal* 15. Berkeley: University of California Press.

Kirk, Gwyn, and Margo Okazawa-Rey. 1998. *Women's Lives: Multicultural Perspectives.* Mountain View, CA: Mayfield.

Kirmani, Mubina, and Dorothy Munyakho. 1996. "The Impact of Structural Adjustment Programs on Women and AIDS." Pp. 160–80 in *Women's Experiences with HIV/AIDS: An International Perspective,* ed. Lynellyn Long and E. Maxine Ankrah. New York: Columbia University Press.

Klapmeyer, Keith. 1998. Personal interview, November 19.

Klein, Ethel. 1984. *Gender Politics: From Consciousness to Mass Politics.* Cambridge, MA: Harvard University Press.

Klein, Naomi. 2000. *No Space, No Choice, No Jobs, No Logo: Taking Aim at the Brand Bullies.* New York: Picador USA.

Kligman, Gail. 1998. *The Politics of Duplicity: Controlling Reproduction in Ceausescu's Romania.* Berkeley: University of California Press.

Kole, Ellen S. 2001. "Appropriate Theorizing about African Women and the Internet." *International Feminist Journal of Politics* 3(2):155–79.

Kolence, Vic. 1999a. "Apparel Industry Was Precursor to Maquiladoras." *El Paso Times,* February 21.

______. 1999b. "El Paso's Unemployment Averages 10 percent in 1998." *El Paso Times,* January 22.

______. 1999c. "2 Call-Center Prospects Turn Down El Paso." *El Paso Times,* September: 10B.

Kopf, David. 1989. *The Brahmo Samaj and the Shaping of the Indian Mind.* Princeton, NJ: Princeton University Press.

Kornbluh, Peter. 1987. *Nicaragua, the Price of Intervention: Reagan's Wars against the Sandinistas.* Washington, DC: Institute for Policy Studies.

Krause, Jill. 1996. "Gender Inequalities and Feminist Politics in a Global Perspective. Pp. 225–37 in *Globalization: Theory and Practice,* ed. Eleanore Kofman and Gillian Youngs. New York: Pinter.

Kumar, Radha. 1993. *The History of Doing: An Illustrated Account of the Movements for Women's Rights and Feminism in India, 1800–1990.* London: Verso.

La Mujer Obrera. 1993. *Orientation Center La Mujer Obrera* El Paso, TX: La Mujer Obrera.

———. 1998. *Progress Report.* El Paso, TX: La Mujer Obrera.

______. 1999a. *Stop NAFTA's Violence against Women Workers.* El Paso, TX: La Mujer Obrera.

______. 1999b. *Women Working Together: Goals and Activities.* El Paso, TX: La Mujer Obrera.

Laclau, Ernesto. 1994. "Negotiating the Paradoxes of Contemporary Politics: An Interview." *Angelaki* 1(3):1–3, 43–50.

Laclau, Ernesto, and Chantal Mouffe. 1985. *Hegemony and Socialist Strategy: Towards a Radical Democratic Politics.* London: Verso.

Lang, Sabine. 1997. "The NGOization of Feminism: Institutionalization and Institution Building within the German Women's Movements." Pp. 101–120 in *Transitions, Environments, Translations: Feminisms in International Politics*, ed. Joan Wallace Scott, Cora Kaplan, and Debra Keates. New York: Routledge.

Lapidus, Gail. 1978. *Women in Soviet Society*. Berkeley: University of California Press.

______. 1995. "State and Society: Toward the Emergence of Civil Society." Pp. 125–46 in *The Soviet System: From Crisis to Coillapse*, ed. Alexander Dallin and Gail Lapidus. Boulder, CO: Westview.

Larudee, Mehrene. 1999. "NAFTA's Impact on U.S. Labor Markets, 1994–1997." Pp. 123–63 in *Pulling Apart: The Deterioration of Employment and Income in North America under Free Trade,* ed. Bruce Campbell, Maria Teresa Gutierrez Haces, Andrew Jackson, and Mehrene Larudee. Ottawa, Ontario: Canadian Center for Policy Alternatives.

Le Blanc, Ida. 1998. Interview conducted at NUDE's office, Tunapuna, Trinidad.

Lear, Arlene, ed. 1992. *A New Era for Development: Time for a Paradigm Shift. Ukraine and Russia.* Report of the Volunteer Executive Service Team (VEST) Initiative. Washington, DC: USAID.

Lebra, William P. 1966. *Okinawan Religion, Belief, Ritual, and Social Structure*. Honolulu: University of Hawaii Press.

Los Angeles Times. 2000. "Extensive Pollution Stalls Base Conversions." *Los Angeles Times,* May 1, part A, page 1.

Loseke, Donileen. 1992. *The Battered Woman and Shelters: The Social Construction of Wife Abuse*. Albany: State University of New York Press.

Lovenduski, Joni. 1997. "Sex Equality and the Rules of the Game." Pp. 91–108 in *Sex Equality Policy in Western Europe*, ed. Frances Gardiner. London: Routledge.

Lowe, Lisa. 1996. *Immigrant Acts: On Asian American Cultural Politics*. Durham, NC: Duke University Press.

Lowe, Lisa, and David Lloyd. 1997. Introduction to *The Politics of Culture in the Shadow of Capital,* ed. Lisa Lowe and David Lloyd. Durham, NC: Duke University Press.

Lycette, Margaret A. 1999. "History and Current Challenges in USAID's Approach to Addressing Gender in Development." Washington, DC: Office of Women in Development, USAID.

Macdonald, Laura. 1997. *Supporting Civil Society: The Political Role of Non-Governmental Organizations in Central America*. New York: St. Martin's.

Mackie, Vera. 2001. "The Language of Globalization, Transnationality and Feminism." *International Feminist Journal of Politics* 3(2):180–206.

Mahler, Sarah J. 1998. "Theoretical and Empirical Contributions toward a Research Agenda for Transnationalism." Pp. 64–100 in *Transnationalism from Below*, ed. Michael Peter Smith and Luis Eduardo Guarnizo. New Brunswick, NJ: Transaction.

Malkki, Liisa. 1994. "Citizens of Humanity: Internationalism and the Imagined Community of Nations." *Diaspora* 3(1):41–68.

Mangaliso, Zengie A. 1997. "Gender and Nation-Building in South Africa." In *Feminist Nationalism*, ed. Lois A. West. London: Routledge.

Mansbridge, Jane. 1986. *Why We Lost the ERA*. Chicago: University of Chicago Press.

Manuh, Takyiwaa. 1997. "Ghana: Women in the Public and Informal Sectors under the Economic Recovery Programme." Pp. 267–76 in The Women, Gender, and Development Reader, ed. Nalini Visvanathan, Lynn Duggan, Laurie Nisonoff, and Nan Wiegersma. London: Zed.

Maran, Rita. 2000. "International Human Rights in the U.S.: A Critique." *Social Justice* 26(1):49–71.

Marchand, Marianne H. 1996. "Selling NAFTA: Gendered Metaphors and Silenced Gender Implications." Pp. 253–70 in *Globalization Theory and Practice*, ed. Eleanore Kofman and Gillian Youngs. New York: Pinter.

Marsh, Rosalind, ed. 1996. *Women in Russia and Ukraine*. New York: Cambridge University Press.

Marshall, Thomas Humphrey. 1965. *Class, Citizenship, and Social Development*. Garden City, NY: Doubleday.

Martinez, Oscar. 1994. *Border People: Life and Society in the U.S.-Mexico Borderlands*. Tucson: University of Arizona Press.

Matthews, Nancy A. 1994. *Confronting Rape: The Feminist Anti-Rape Movement and the State*. London: Routledge.

______. 1995. "Feminist Clashes with the State: Tactical Choices by State-Funded Rape Crisis Centers." Pp. 291–305 in *Feminist Organizations: Harvest of the New Women's Movement*, ed. Myra Marx Ferree and Patricia Yancey Martin. Philadelphia: Temple University Press.

Matsui, Yayori. 1996. *Women in the New Asia*. Trans. Noriko Toyokawa and Carolyn Francis. New York: Zed.

______. 1998. "History Cannot Be Erased, Women Can No Longer be Silenced." *Women's Asia 21: Voices from Japan* no. 4. 26–32. Tokyo, Japan: Asia-Japan Women's Resource Center.

Matsuoka, Martha. 1999. "An Environmental Justice Framework for Base Conversion." Panel presentation to the International Grassroots Summit on Military Base Cleanup. Washington, DC: October 25–29.

Mayo, Katherine. 1926. *Mother India*. New York: Harcourt, Brace.

Mazey, Sonia. 1988. "European Community Action on Behalf of Women: The Limits of Legislation." *Journal of Common Market Studies* 27:63–84.

McBride Stetson, Dorothy and Mazur, Amy, eds. 1995. *Comparative State Feminism*. London: Sage.

McCormack, Gavan. 1998. "Okinawan Dilemmas: Coral Islands or Concrete Islands." Working Paper No. 45. The Japan Policy Research Institute, San Diego, California.

McCorquodale, Robert, and Richard Fairbrother. 1999. "Globalizing and Human Rights." *Human Rights Quarterly* 21:735–66.

McMichael, Philip. 2000. *Development and Social Change: A Global Perspective* 2nd ed. Thousand Oaks, CA: Pine Forge.

Meehan, Elizabeth, and Selma Sevenhuijsen, eds. 1990. *Equality Politics and Gender*. London: Sage.

Melucci, Alberto. 1989. *Nomads of the Present: Social Movements and Individual Needs in Contemporary Society*. Philadelphia: Temple University Press.

______. 1994. "A Strange Kind of Newness: What's 'New' in New Social Movements." Pp. 101–30 in *New Social Movements: From Ideology to Identity*, ed. Enrique Laraña, Hank Johnson, and Joseph R. Gusfield. Philadelphia: Temple University Press.

______. 1995. "The Global Planet and the Internal Planet: New Frontiers." Pp. 287–98 in *Cultural Politics and Social Movements*, ed. Marcy Darnovsky, Barbara Epstein, and Richard Flacks. Philadelphia: Temple University Press.

Menon, Nivedita, ed. 1999. *Gender and Politics in India*. Delhi: Oxford University Press.

Mercier, Rick. 1996. "The Peace Movement in Okinawa: The Continuing Pattern of Violence by U.S. Personnel." *Z Magazine*, February.

Metoyer, Cynthia Chavez. 1997. "Nicaragua's Transition of State Power: Through Feminist Lenses." Pp. 114–40 in *The Undermining of the Sandinista Revolution*, ed. Gary Prevost and Harry E. Vanden. New York: St. Martin's.

Meyer, Mary K. 1999. "Negotiating International Norms: The Inter-American Commission of Women and the Convention on Violence against Women." Pp. 58–71 in *Gender Politics in Global Governance*, ed. Mary K. Meyer and Elisabeth Prügl. Lanham, MD: Rowman & Littlefield.

Meyer, Mary K., and Elisabeth Prügl, eds. 1999. *Gender Politics in Global Governance*. Lanham, MD: Rowman & Littlefield.

Microcredit Summit Council. 2001. "Countdown 2005: The Newsletter of the Microcredit Summit Campaign." http://www.microcreditsummit.org/newsletter/action8.htm.

Mies, Maria, and Vandana Shiva. 1993. *Ecofeminism*. London: Zed.

Miles, Angela. 1996. *Integrative Feminisms: Building Global Visions, 1960s–1990s*. New York: Routledge.

Miller, Alice M. 1999. "Realizing Women's Human Rights: Nongovernmental Organizations and the UN Treaty Bodies." Pp. 161–76 in *Gender Politics in Global Governance*, ed. Mary K. Meyer and Elisabeth Prügl. Lanham, MD: Rowman & Littlefield.

Mills, Suzanne. 1995. "Rebel with a Cause: If You Want to Count Our Votes, Count Our Work." *Newsday*, October 1.

Mindry, Deborah. 2001. "NGOs, 'Grassroots,' and the Politics of Virtue." *Signs* 26(4):1187–1211.

Minimum Wage Board. 1998. *National Review of Employment*. Port of Spain, Trinidad: Ministry of Labor.

Ministry of Economic Forecasting and Planning. 1998. *The Socioeconomic Condition of Women in Morocco (Condition Socio-Economic de la Femme au Maroc).* Rabat: Kingdom of Morocco.

Ministry of Employment and Social Affairs. 1995. *Research for the Establishment of a Female Development Action Strategy.* Rabat, Morocco: EDESA.

Ministry of Employment Prevision and Planning, 1998. The Socio-Economic Condition of Women in Morocco (La Condition Socio-Economic de la Femme au Maroc), Vol. 1. Rabat: Government of Morocco.

Ministry of Social Development and Solidarity, Morocco, and the World Bank. 1999. *Plan of Action for Integrating Women into Development.* Rabat: Department in Charge of Social Protection, Family, and Childhood.

Ministry of Trade. 1997. *Creating a Nation of Entrepreneurs.* Port of Spain, Trinidad: Ministry of Trade.

Mink, Gwendolyn. 1995. *The Wages of Motherhood: Inequality in the Welfare State, 1917–1942.* Ithaca, NY: Cornell University Press.

Minkoff, Debra C. 1995. *Organizing for Equality: The Evolution of Women's and Racial-Ethnic Organizations in America, 1955–1985.* ASA Rose Book Series. New Brunswick, NJ: Rutgers University Press.

______. 1997. "Producing Social Capital: National Social Movements and Civil Society." *American Behavioral Scientist* 40(5):606–19.

Moffet, Julie. 1997. "Russia: Solving the Problem of Trafficking in Women." *RFE/RL Report,* July 4.

Moghadam, Valentine M. 1998. "Gender and Globalization: Female Labor and Women's Mobilizations." Presented at the Annual Meeting of the International Sociological Association. August 14–18. San Francisco, California.

______. 2000. "Transnational Feminist Networks: Collective Action in an Era of Globalization." *International Sociology* 15(1):57–85.

Mohanty, Chandra Talpade. 1991a. "Catographies of Struggle: Third World Women and the Politics of Feminism." Pp. 1–47 i n*Third World Women and the Politics of Feminism,* ed. Chandra Talpade Mohanty, Ann Russo, and Lourdes Torres. Bloomington: Indiana University Press.

______. 1991b. "Under Western Eyes: Feminist Scholarship and Colonial Discourses." Pp. 51–80 in *Third World Women and the Politics of Feminism*, ed. Chandra Talpade Mohanty. Bloomington: Indiana University Press.

______. 1994. "Under Western Eyes: Feminist Scholarship and Colonial Discourses." Pp. 196–220 in *Colonial Discourse and Post-Colonial Theory*, ed. Patrick Williams and Laura Chrisman. New York: Columbia University Press.

______. 1997. "Women Workers and Capitalist Scripts: Ideologies of Domination, Common Interests, and the Politics of Solidarity." Pp. 3–29 in *Feminist Genealogies,*

Colonial Legacies, Democratic Futures, eds. M. Jacqui Alexander and Chandra Talpade Mohanty. New York: Routledge.

______. 1998. "Crafting Feminist Genealogies: On the Geography and Politics of Home, Nation, and Community." Pp. 485–500 in *Talking Visions: Multicultural Feminism in a Transnational Age*, ed. Ella Shohat. Cambridge, MA: Massachusettes Institute of Technology.

Mohanty, Chandra Talpade, Ann Russo, and Lourdes Torres, eds. 1991. *Third World Women and the Politics of Feminism*. Bloomington: Indiana University Press.

Molyneux, Maxine. 1986. "Mobilization without Emancipation? Women's Interests, State, and Revolution in Nicaragua." Pp. 280–302 in *Transition and Development: Problems of Third World Socialism*, ed. Richard R. Fagen, Carmen Diana Deere, and Jose Luis Coraggio. New York: Monthly Review Press and Center of the Study of the Americas.

Moner Report. 1999. "Impact of Transition on Women in Eastern Europe." New York: UNICEF.

Montoya, Irma. 1999. Personal interview, February 24.

Montoya, Lisa, Carol Hardy-Fanta, and Sonia Garcia. 2000. "Latina Politics: Gender, Participation, and Leadership." *Political Science and Politics* 33(3).

Moon, Katharine H. S. 1997. *Sex among Allies: Military Prostitution in U.S.-Korea Relations*. New York: Columbia University Press.

Moravcsik, Andrew. 1993. "Preferences and Power in the European Community: A Liberal Intergovernmentalist Approach." *Journal of Common Market Studies* 31:473–524.

Moravcsik, Andrew. 1998. "The Choice for Europe: Social Purpose and State Power from Messina to Maastricht." Ithaca, NY: Cornell University Press.

Morgan, Patricia. 1981. "From Battered Wife to Program Client: The State's Shaping of Social Problems." *Kapitalistate* 9:17–39.

Morgan, Robin. 1984. *Sisterhood Is Global. The International Women's Movement Anthology*. Garden City, NY: Anchor.

Mormont, Marc. 1983. "The Emergence of Rural Struggles and Their Ideological Effects." *International Journal of Urban and Regional Research* 7(4):559–74.

______. 1990. "Who Is Rural? or, How to Be Rural: Towards a Sociology of the Rural." Pp. 21–44 in *Rural Restructuring: Global Processes and Their Responses*, ed. Terry Marsden, Philip Lowe, and Sarah Whitmore. London: David Fulton.

Mosley, Hugh G. 1990. "The Social Dimension of European Integration." *International Labour Review* 129:147–64.

Mouffe, Chantal. 1993. *The Return of the Political*. London: Verso.

Moulay, R'chid Abderazak. 1991. *Woman and Law in Morocco (La Femme et La Loi au Maroc)*. Casablanca, Morocco: Le Fennec.

Mullings, Leith. 1994. "Images, Ideology and Women of Color." Pp. 265–90 in *Women of Color in U.S. Society*, ed. Maxine Baca Zinn and Bonnie Thornton Dill. Philadelphia: Temple University Press.

Muzyria, Aleksandra Alekseevna. 1989. *Zhensovet: Opht, problemy, perspektivy.* Moscow: Izdatel'stvo politichnoi literatury.

Myerson, Alan. 1998. "Borderline Working Class: Texas Labor Is Feeling Trade Pact's Pinch." *New York Times,* May 8.

Nagel, Joanne. 1994. "Constructing Ethnicity: Creating and Recreating Ethnic Identity and Culture." *Social Problems* 41:152–76.

Nandy, Ashis. 1995. *The Savage Freud and Other Essays on Possible and Retrievable Selves.* Princeton, NJ: Princeton University Press.

Naples, Nancy A. 1997. "The 'New Consensus' on the Gendered Social Contract: The 1987–1988 US Congressional Hearings on Welfare Reform." *Signs: Journal of Women in Culture and Society* 22(4):907–45.

______. ed. 1998a. *Community Activism and Feminist Politics: Organizing across Race, Class and Gender.* New York: Routledge.

______. 1998b. "Conclusion: Women's Community Activism: Exploring the Dynamics of Politicization and Diversity." Pp. 327–49 in *Community Activism and Feminist Politics: Organizing across Gender, Race and Class,* ed. Nancy A. Naples. New York: Routledge.

______. 1998c. *Grassroots Warriors: Activist Mothering, Community Work, and the War on Poverty.* New York: Routledge.

Naples, Nancy A., and Marnie Dobson. 2000. "Feminist Praxis and the Welfare State: Aboriginal Health Care Workers and U.S. Community Workers of Color." Paper presented at the conference "Carework: Research, Theory, and Advocacy." Washington, D.C., Howard University.

Narayan, Uma. 1997. *Dislocating Cultures: Identities, Traditions, and Third World Feminism.* New York: Routledge.

Nash, June, and Maria Patricia Fernandez-Kelly, eds. 1983. *Women, Men, and the International Division of Labor.* Albany: State University of New York Press.

National Labor Committee. 1999. "Help End the Race to the Bottom." New York: National Labor Committee.

National Union of Domestic Employees. 1998. "A Women's Work Is Also in the Home." Speech delivered at the Toco Convocation. *Trinidad Guardian,* May 4.

Neft, Naomi and Ann Levine. 1997. *Where Women Stand: An International Report on the Status of Women in 140 Countries 1997–1998.* New York: Random House.

Nelson, Barbara J. 1990. "The Origins of the Two-Channel Welfare State: Workman's Compensation and Mothers' Aid." Pp. 123–51 in *Women, the State, and Welfare,* ed. Linda Gordon. Madison: University of Wisconsin Press.

Nelson, Paul J. 1997. "Conflict, Legitimacy, and Effectiveness: Who Speaks for Whom in Transnational NGO Networks Lobbying the World Bank?" *Nonprofit and Voluntary Sector Quarterly* 26(4):421–41.

Newsday. 1999. "NUDE Stripped of Voice at Vital Voice." September 30.

Noonan, Norma C. 1995. "Gender Politics and Post-Communism: Reflections from Eastern Europe and the Former Soviet Union." *Slavic Review* 54(1):152–54.

Nzomo, Maria 1994. "The Impact of Structured Adjustment Programmes on Women's Participation in Decision-Making." Unpublished paper.

O'Brien, Denise. 2001. "Three Interns Work on Local Farms." *Women, Food and Agriculture Newsletter* 4(3):1,4.

ODEF (Observatoire des droits de la femmes et de l'enfant). 1995. "Rapport de Mission, décembre 19, 1995." Bamako, Mali: ODEF.

______. 1996. "Rapport de Mission à Ségou, avril 1996." Bamako, Mali: ODEF.

______. 1997. "Rapport d'activités du 1ère décembre 1996 au 31 mars 1997." Bamako, Mali: ODEF.

Okin, Susan. 1998. "Feminism, Women's Human Rights, and Cultural Differences." *Hypatia* 13:32–52.

Okinawa Prefectural Government, Military Base Affairs Office. 1998. "A Message from Okinawa: U.S. Military Bases in Okinawa." Retrieved March 1999, http:// www.pref.okinawa.jp.

Okinawa Women Act against Military Violence. 1998. "Okinawa Women's American Peace Caravan." Pamphlet.

______. 1997. "Postwar U.S. Military Crimes against Women in Okinawa." Pamphlet.

______. 1996. "Okinawa Women's American Peace Caravan." Pamphlet.

Okinawa Women's Delegation to Beijing. 1995. "Military Violence and Women in Okinawa." Pamphlet.

Olvera, Joe. 1990. "Hunger Strikers Face New Battle on Home Front." *El Paso Times*, September 2, p. A12.

Ong, Aihwa. 1987. *Spirits of Resistance and Capitalist Discipline: Factory Women in Malaysia.* Albany: State University of New York Press.

______. 1999. *Flexible Citizenship: The Cultural Logics of Transnationality.* Durham, NC: Duke University Press.

Onna Village Committee to Oppose the Special Forces Training Facility Construction and Live Artillery Drills. 1992. "Risking Body and Soul to Prevent U.S. Military Drills: The Citizens' Struggle to Protect Onna Village." Naha City, Okinawa: Jono.

Orquiz, Paz. 1999. Personal interview, January 20.

Ortega, Roy. 2000. "Trade Soars Both Ways after NAFTA. " *El Paso Times*, July 9, pp. E1–2.

Osirim, Mary. 1996. "The Dilemmas of Modern Development: Structural Adjustment and Women Microentrepreneurs in Nigeria and Zimbabwe." Pp. in *The Gendered New World Order: Militarism, Development, and the Environment*, ed. Jennifer Turpin and Lois Lorentzen. New York: Routledge.

Ota, Masahide. 1999. "Re-examining the History of the Battle of Okinawa" Pp. 13–38 in *Okinawa: Cold War Island.* Cardiff, CA: Japan Pacific Resource Institute.

Otto, Dianne. 1996. "Nongovernmental Organizations in the United Nations System: The

Emerging Role of International Civil Society." *Human Rights Quarterly* 18(1):107–41.

Ownby, John. 1999. Personal interview, September 1.

Pantin, Dennis A. 1993. "Long Waves and Caribbean Development." *Social and Economic Studies* 36:1–20.

Pardo, Mary. 1995. "Doing It for the Kids: Mexican American Community Activists, Border Feminists." Pp. 356–71 in *Feminist Organizations: Harvest of the New Women's Movement*, ed. Myra Marx Ferree and Patricia Yancey Martin. Philadelphia: Temple University Press.

______. 1998. *Mexican American Women Activists*. Philadelphia: Temple University Press.

Pateman, Carole. 1988. *The Sexual Contract*. Stanford, CA: Stanford University Press.

______. 1989. *The Disorder of Women*. Stanford, CA: Stanford University Press.

______. 1994. "Three Questions about Womanhood Suffrage." Pp. 331–48 in *Suffrage and Beyond: International Feminist Perspectives*, ed. Caroline Daley and Melanie Nolan. Auckland, New Zealand: Auckland University Press.

Perry, Sylvia. 1995. "The Impact of Information Technology on Women as Partners in the Development Process and in the UN System." Pp. 43–49 in *Women and the United Nations*, ed. Filomina Chioma Steady and Remie Toure. Rochester, VT: Schenkman.

Peters, Julie, and Andrea Wolper, eds. 1995. *Women's Rights Human Rights: International Feminist Perspectives*. New York: Routledge.

Peterson, V. Spike. 1992. "Transgressing Boundaries: Theories of Knowledge, Gender, and International Relations." *Millennium: Journal of International Studies* 21(2).

Peterson, V. Spike, and Anne S. Runyan. [1993] 1999. *Global Gender Issues*. Boulder, CO: Westview.

Pfeil, Fred. 1994. "No Basta Teorizar." Pp. 225–26 in *Scattered Hegemonies: Postmodernity and Transnational Feminist Practices*, ed. Inderpal Grewal and Caren Kaplan. Minneapolis: University of Minnesota Press.

Pieper, Charles, and Neil E. Harl. 2000. "Iowa Farmland Ownership and Tenure, 1982–1997: A Fifteen Year Perspective." Unpublished paper. Iowa State University.

Pietilä, Hilkka, and Jeanne Vickers. 1994. *Making Women Matter: The Role of the United Nations*. London: Zed.

Pilkington, Hilary. 1996. *Gender, Generation, and Identity in Contemporary Russia*. London: Routledge.

Pillinger, Jane. 1992. *Feminising the Market*. London: Macmillan.

Piven, Frances Fox. 1986. "Women and the State: Ideology, Power, and Welfare." Pp. 326–40 in *For Crying Out Loud: Women and Poverty in the United States*, ed. Rochelle Lefkowitz and Ann Withorn. New York: Pilgrim.

Piven, Frances Fox, and Richard A. Cloward. 1977. *Poor People's Movements: Why They Succeed, How They Fail*. New York: Vintage.

PlaNet. 2001. "PlaNet Finance: Internet for the Development." http://www.planetfinance.org/en/rating/enligne/alamana.htm.

Plant, Judith. 1990. "Revaluing Home: Feminism and Bioregionalism." Pp. 21–23 in *Home! A Bioregional Reader*, ed. Van Andruss, Christopher Plant, Judith Plant, and E. Wright. Philadelphia: New Society.

Portes, Alejandro, Manuel Castells, and Lauren Benton. 1989. *The Informal Economy: Studies in Advanced and Less Developed Countries*. Baltimore: Johns Hopkins University Press.

Posadskaya, Anastasia, ed. 1994. *Women in Russia: A New Era in Russian Feminism*. Trans. Kate Clark. London: Verso.

Prashad, Vijay. 2000. *The Karma of Brown Folk*. Minneapolis: University of Minnesota Press.

Pratt, Geraldine, and Susan Hanson. 1994. "Geography and the Construction of Difference." *Gender, Place, and Culture* 1(1):5–29.

Prechal, Sacha, and Burrows, Noreen. 1990. *Gender Discrimination Law of the European Community*. Brookfield, VT: Gower.

Prevost, Gary. 1997. "The Status of the Sandinista Revolutionary Project." Pp. 9–44 in *The Undermining of the Sandinista Revolution*, ed. Gary Prevost and Harry E. Vanden. New York: St. Martin's.

Probyn, Elspeth. 1990. "Travels in the Postmodern: Making Sense of the Local." Pp. 176–89 in *Feminism/Postmodernism*, ed. Linda J. Nicholson. New York: Routledge

Prügl, Elisabeth. 1996. "Home-Based Producers in Development Discourse." Pp. 39–59 in *Homeworkers in Global Perspective: Invisible No More*, ed. Eileen Borris and Elizabeth Prügl. New York: Routledge.

______. 1999. "What Is a Worker? Gender, Global Restructuring, and the ILO Convention on Homework." Pp. 197–209 in *Gender Politics in Global Governance,* ed. Mary K. Meyer and Elisabeth Prügl. Lanham, MD: Rowman & Littlefield.

Pulido, Laura. 1998. *Environmental and Economic Justice.* Tucson: University of Arizona Press.

Purkayastha, Bandana. 1999. *Asian Indians in Connecticut*. Storrs, CT: Asian American Studies Institute.

Purkayastha, Bandana, Shyamala Raman, and Kshiteeja Bhide. 1997. "Empowering Women: Sneha and Multifacted Activism." Pp. 100–107 in *Dragon Ladies: Asian American Feminists Breathe Fire*, ed. Sonia Shah. Boston: South End.

Quandt, Midge. 1995. "Unbinding the Ties that Bind: The FSLN and the Popular Organizations." Pp. 265–81 in *The New Politics of Survival: Grassroots Movements in Central America*, ed. Minor Sinclair. New York: Monthly Review Press.

Rabson, Steve. 1999. "Assimilation Policy in Okinawa: Promotion, Resistance, and 'Reconstruction.'" In *Okinawa: Cold War Island*, ed. Chalmers Johnson. Cardiff, CA: Japan Pacific Resource Institute.

Racioppi, Linda, and Katherine O'Sullivan See. 1997. *Women's Activism in Contemporary Russia*. Philadelphia: Temple University Press.

Radcliffe, Sarah A., and Sallie Westwood, eds. 1993. *Viva: Women and Popular Protest in Latin America*. London: Routledge.

Radhakrishnan, Manju. 1999. "Ethnicity, Gender and Class; Personal Histories and Multifaceted Activism of Sneha Members." Master's thesis, University of Connecticut.

Radice, William, ed. 1998. *Swami Vivekananda and the Modernization of Hinduism*. Delhi: Oxford University Press.

Rai, Shirin. 1996. "Women and the State in the Third World." Pp. 25–47 in *Women and Politics in the Third World*, ed. Helen Afshar. New York: Routledge.

Rai, Shirin, Hilary Pilkington, and Annie Phizacklea, eds. 1992. *Women in the Face of Change*. London: Routledge.

Rajan, Rejeswari Sunder. 1993. *Real and Imagined Women: Gender, Culture and Postcolonialism*. New York: Routledge.

Rakowski, Cathy. 1994. *Contrapunto: The Informal Sector Debate in Latin America*. Albany: State University of New York Press.

Ramée, Pierre M. La, and Erica G. Polakoff. 1997. "The Evolution of the Popular Organizations in Nicaragua." Pp. 141–206 in *The Undermining of the Sandinista Revolution*, ed. Gary Prevost and Harry E. Vanden. New York: Monthly Review Press.

Randall, Margaret. 1992. *Gathering Rage: The Failure of the Twentieth Century Revolutions to Develop a Feminist Agenda*. New York: Monthly Review Press.

Rania, Queen (of Jordan). 1999. Keynote address. Presented at international women's conference "Lessons without Borders," June 3, Chicago. Available at http://www.usinfo.state.gov/usa/womenusa/nania.htm.

Ray, Raka. 1999. "Fields of Protest: Women's Movements in India." Minneapolis: University of Minnesota Press.

Reardon, Betty A. 1998. "Gender and Global Security: A Feminist Challenge to the United Nations and Peace Research." *Journal of International Cooperation Studies*. 6(1) 1–28.

Red Centroamericana de Mujeres en Solidaridad con las Trabajadoras de la Maquila. 1997. "Acta de Conformacion de The Network." *Nuestra Ruta* 1: unpaginated.

Reddock, Rhoda E. 1994. *Women, Labor, and Politics in Trinidad and Tobago*. London: Zed.

Reich, Jennifer Ann, and Michael Alan Sacks. 2000. "Globalizing Representations of Human Rights Violations: A Constructionist Approach." Presented at the annual meeting of the American Sociological Association, August 12–16. Washington D.C.

Reyes, Lorenza. 1999. Personal interview, January 13.

Riain, Sean. 2000. "States and Markets in an Era of Globalization." *Annual Review of Sociology* 26:187–213.

Rich, Adrienne. 1986. *Blood, Bread, and Poetry: Selected Prose, 1979–1985*. New York: Norton.

Richardson, Jeremy. 1996. "Policy-making in the EU: Interests, Ideas, and Garbage Cans of Primeval Soup." Pp. 3–26 in *European Union: Power and Policy-making*, ed. Jeremy Richardson. London: Routledge.

Roberts, Timmons J. 1996. "Predicting Participation in Environmental Treaties: A World-System Analysis." *Sociological Inquiry* 66:38–57.

Robinson, James C. 1969. *Okinawa: A People and Their Gods*. Rutland, VT: Charles E. Tuttle.

Rodriquez, Jeanette. 1994. *Our Lady of Guadalupe: Faith among Mexican-American Women.* Austin: University of Texas Press.

Rossilli, Mariagrazia. 1997. "The European Community's Policy on the Equality of Women. *The European Journal of Women's Studies* 4:63–82.

Rothermund, Dietmar. 1993. *An Economic History of India: From Pre-Colonial Times to 1991*. London: Routledge.

Rouse, Roger. 1995. "Thinking through Transnationalism: Notes on the Cultural Politics of Class Relations in the Contemporary United States." *Public Culture* 7:353–402.

Rowbotham, Sheila and Swasti Mitter, eds. 1994. *Dignity and Daily Bread.* London: Routledge.

Roy, Ratha. Personal correspondence.

Runyan, Anne Sisson. 1996. "The Places of Women in Trading Places: Gendered Global/Regional Regimes and Inter-nationalized Feminist Resistance. Pp. 238–52 in *Globalization: Theory and Practice,* ed. Eleanore Kofman and Gillian Youngs. New York: Pinter.

______. 1999. "Women in the Neoliberal 'Frame'." Pp. 210–20 in *Gender Politics in Global Governance,* ed. Mary K. Meyer and Elisabeth Prügl. Lanham, MD: Rowman & Littlefield.

Rupp, Leila J. 1997. *Worlds of Women: The Making of an International Women's Movement.* Princeton, NJ: Princeton University Press.

Rural Women's Workshop Statement for Action. 1996. "Rural Women's Workshop Highlights: From the fields of home to the city of Rome." P. 14 in the highlights of the Rural Women's Workshop, November 6–9, Rome, Italy, in preparation for the NGO Forum and World Food Summit, November 11–16.

Ryukyu Shimpo. 1989. As cited by the Okinawa Heiwa Center. October 9.

Sachs, Wolfgang. 1992. "Environment." Pp. 26–37 in *The Development Dictionary: A Guide to Knowledge as Power*. London: Zed.

Sacks, Karen. 1988. "Gender and Grassroots Leadership." Pp. 77–94 in *Women and the Politics of Empowerment,* ed. Ann Bookman and Sandra Morgan. Philadelphia: Temple University Press.

Safa, Helen. 1981. "Runaway Shops and Female Employment: The Search For Cheap Labor." *Signs* 7(2):418–33.

______. 1987. "Urbanization, the Informal Economy, and State Policy in Latin America." Pp. 252–74 in *The Capitalist City: Global Restructuring and Community Politics*, ed. Joe R. Feagin and Michael P. Smith. New York: Basil Blackwell.

______. 1995. "Economic Restructuring and Gender Subordination." *Latin America Perspectives.* 22:32–50.

Salahdine, Mohamed. 1992. "International Nongovernmental Organizations in Morocco" (Les Organizations Internationales Non-Gouvernmentales en Moroc). Pp. 229–45 in *Civil Society in Morocco*, ed. N. El Aoufi. Rabat, Morocco: SMER.

Sandberg, Eve. 1998. "Multilateral Women's Conferences: The Domestic Political Organization of Zambian Women." Contemporary Politics 4(3):271–83.

Sandholtz, Wayne, and Alec Stone Sweet, eds. 1998. *European Integration and Supranational Governance*. Oxford: Oxford University Press.

Sandoval, Chela. 1991. "U.S. Third World Feminism: The Theory and Method of Oppositional Consciousness in the Postmodern World." *Genders* 10 (spring):1–24.

Santos, Boaventura de Sousa. 2001. "Can Law Be Emancipation?" Presented at the annual meetings of the Law and Society Association, July 4–6, Budapest, Hungary.

Sanyal, Bishwapriya. 1991. "Organizing the Self-Employed: The Politics of the Urban Informal Sector." *International Labour Review* 130:39–56.

Sassen, Saskia. 1993. "Economic Globalization: A New Geography, Composition, and Institutional Framework." Pp. 61–66 in *Global Visions: Beyond the New World Order*, ed. Jeremy Brecher, John Brown Childs, and Jill Cutler. Boston: South End.

______. 1994. *Cities in a World Economy*. Thousand Oaks, CA: Pine Forge.

______. 1996. "Cities and Communities in the Global Economy." *American Behavioral Scientists* 39(5): 629–39.

______. 1998. "The Transnationalization of Immigration Policy." Pp. 53–67 in *Borderless Borders: U.S. Latinos, Latin Americans, and the Paradox of Interdependence*, ed. Frank Bonilla, Edwin Meléndez, Rebecca Morales, and María de los Angeles Tores. Philadelphia: Temple University Press.

______. 1999. *Globalization and Its Discontents: Essays on the New Mobility of People and Money*. New York: New Press.

Schaeffer, Robert K. 1997. *Understanding Globalization: The Social Construction of Political, Economic, and Environmental Change*. Lanham, Maryland: Rowman & Littlefield.

Schlesinger, Philip. 1987. "On National Identity: Some Conceptions and Misconceptions." *Social Science Information* 26(2):219–64.

Schneider, Annie L. and Helen Ingram. 1990. "Behavioral Assumptions of Policy Tools." *Journal of Politics* 52:510–29.

______. 1997. *Policy Design for Democracy*. Lawrence: University Press of Kansas.

Scott, Alan. 1990. *Ideology and the New Social Movements*. London: Unwin Hyman.

Scott, Joan W. 1992. "Experience." Pp. 22–40 in *Feminists Theorize the Political*, ed. Judith Butler and Joan Scott. New York: Routledge.

Seager, Joni. 1993. *Earth Follies: Coming to Feminist Terms with the Global Environmental Crisis*. New York: Routledge.

______. 1997. *The State of Women in the World Atlas*. London: Penguin Reference.

Seidman, Gay. 2000. "Gendered Politics in Transition: South Africa's Democratic Transitions in the Context of Global Feminism." Pp. 121–44 in *Globalizating Institutions: Case*

Studies in Regulation and Innovation, ed. Jane Jenson and Boaventura de Sousa Santos. Burlington, VT: Ashgate.

Sen, Amartya. 1999. *Development as Freedom*. New York: Knopf.

Sen, Gita. 2000. "Promises to Keep: Beijing and Beyond." Interview by Mary Thom. Special *Ford Fo*undation Report issue, "Women: Now It's a Global Movement." 31(1):30–33. New York: Ford Foundation.

Sen, Gita, and Caren Grown. 1987. *Development, Crises, and Alternative Visions: Third World Women's Perspective*. New York: Monthly Review Press.

Sen, Samita. 1999. *Women and Labour in Late Colonial India*. Cambridge: Cambridge University Press.

SEWA. 1998. Annual Report. Ahmedabad, India.

Shah, Purvi. 1997. "Redefining the Home: How Community Elites Silence Feminist Activism." Pp. 46–56 in *Dragon Ladies: Asian American Feminists Breathe Fire*, ed. Sonia Shah. Boston: South End.

Sharpe, Jenny. 1994. "The Unspeakable Limits of Rape: Colonial Violence and Counter-Insurgency." Pp. 221–44 in *Colonial Discourse and Post-Colonial Theory*, eds. Patrick Williams and Laura Chrisman. New York: Columbia University Press.

Shiva, Vandana. 1987. *Staying Alive*. London: Zed Books.

______. 1997. "Democracy in the Age of Globalization." Pp. 34–45 in *Women, Empowerment and Political Participation*, ed. Veena Poonacha. Bombay, India: Research Center for Women's Studies, S.N.D.T. Women's University.

______. 2000, *Stolen Harvest: The Hijacking of the Global Food Supply*. Cambridge, MA: South End.

Shukla, Sandhya. 1999. "New Immigrants, New Forms of Transnational Community: Post-1965 Indian Migrations." *Amerasia* 25:19–38.

Shuman, Michale, and Jayne Williams. 1986. *Having International Affairs Your Way: A Five Step Briefing Manual for Citizen Diplomats*. Irvine, CA: Center for Innovative Diplomacy.

Sikkink, Kathryn. 1993. "Human Rights, Principled Issue-Networks, and Sovereignty in Latin America," *International Organization* 47(3):411–40.

______. 1996. "The Emergence, Evolution, and Effectiveness of the Latin American Human Rights Network." Pp. 59–84 in *Constructing Democracy: Human Rights, Citizenship, and Society in Latin America*, ed. Elizabeth Jelin and Eric Hershberg. Boulder, CO: Westview.

Silbey, Susan S. 1996. "'Let Them Eat Cake': Globalization, Postmodern Colonialism, and the Possibilities of Justice." *Law & Society Review* 31(2):207–35.

Sinha, Mrinalini, ed. 1998. *Selections from Mother India*. New Delhi: Kali for Women.

Sklair, Leslie, ed. 1988. *Maquiladoras: Annotated Bibliography and Research Guide to Mexico's In-Bond Industry, 1980–1988*. Monograph Series 24. San Diego: Center for U.S.-Mexico Studies, University of California.

______. 1991. *Sociology of the Global System*. Baltimore: Johns Hopkins University Press.

______. 1995. *Sociology of the Global System*. 2d ed. Baltimore, MA: John Hopkins University Press.

______. 1999. "Social Movements and Global Capitalism." Pp. 291–311 in *The Cultures of Globalization,* ed. Fredric Jameson and Masao Miyoshi. Durham, NC: Duke University Press.

Slater, David. 1998. "Rethinking the Spatialities of Social Movements: Questions of (B)orders, Culture, and Politics in Global Times." Pp. 380–401 in *Culture of Politics, Politics of Cultures: Re-visioning Latin American Social Movements*, ed. Sonia E. Alvarez, Evelina Dagnino, and Arturo Escobar. Boulder, CO: Westview.

Smith, Dorothy E. 1987. *The Everyday World as Problematic.* Toronto: University of Toronto Press.

Smith, Dorothy E. 1990. *The Conceptual Practices of Power: A Feminist Sociology of Knowledge*. Boston: Northeastern University Press.

Smith, Jackie. 1998. "Global Civil Society?" *American Behavioral Scientists* 42(1):93–107.

______. 2001. "Globalizing Resistance: The Battle of Seattle and the Future of Social Movements." *Mobilization* 6(1):1–20.

Smith, Jackie, Charles Chatfield, and Ron Pagnucco, eds. 1997. *Transnational Social Movements and World Politics: Solidarity Beyond the State*. Syracuse, NY: Syracuse University Press.

Smith, Jackie, and Ron Pagnucco with George A. Lopez. 1998. "Globalizing Human Rights: The Work of Transnational Human Rights NGOs in the 1990s." *Human Rights Quarterly* 20(2):379–412.

Smith, Michael Peter. 1992. "Postmodernism, Urban Ethnography, and the New Social Space of Ethnic Identity." *Theory and Socitey* 2:493–531.

______. 1994. "Can You Imagine? Transnational Migration and the Globalization of Grassroots Politics." *Social Text* 12:15–33.

Smith, Michael Peter, and Luis Eduardo Guarnizo, eds. 1998. *Transnationalism from Below*. New Brunswick, NJ: Transaction.

Smith, Steven and Ingram, Helen. 1993. "Public Policy and Democracy." In *Public Policy for Democracy*, ed. Steven Smith and Helen Ingram. Washington, DC: Brookings Institution.

Snow, David, and Robert Benford. 1988. "Ideology, Frame Resonance and Participant Mobilization." *International Social Movement Research* 1:197–217.

______. 1992. "Master Frames and Cycles of Protest." Pp. 135–55 in *Frontiers in Social Movement Theory*, ed. Aldon Morris and Carol McClurg Mueller. New Haven, CT: Yale University Press.

So, Alvin Y. 1990. *Social Change and Development*. Newbury Park, CA: Sage.

Social Justice. 2000. Special issue, "Neoliberalism, Militarism, and Armed Conflict." *Social Justice* 27(4):154–57.

Social Politics. 1994. Special Issue, "Gender, Transitions to Democracy and Citizenship." *Social Politics* 1(3).

Sohrab, Julia. 1996. *Sexing the Benefit: Women, Social Security, and Financial Independence in EC Sex Equality Law*. Brookfield, VT: Dartmouth.

Soumaré, Aminata Maiga. 1995. "Factors that Affect Girls' Access to and Retention in School in Mali, 1965–1992." Ph.D. dissertation, University of Illinois.

Sparks, Holloway. 1997. "Dissident Citizenship: Democratic Theory, Political Courage, and Activist Women." *Hypatia* 12:74–110.

Spelman, Elizabeth V. 1988. *Inessential Woman: Problems of Exclusion in Feminist Thought*. Boston: Beacon.

Spender, Dale. 1988. *Man Made Language*. 2nd ed. New York: Pandora.

Sperling, Valerie. 1997. "Engendering Transition: The Women's Movement in Contemporary Russia." Ph.D. dissertation, Department of Political Science, University of California, Berkeley.

______. 1999. *Organizing Women in Contemporary Russia*. New York: Cambridge University Press.

Spivak, Gayatri Chakravorty. 1987. *In Other Worlds: Essays in Cultural Politics*. New York: Methuen.

______. 1996. "'Women' as Theatre: United Nations Conference on Women, Beijing, 1995. *Radical Philosophy* 75:2–4.

Spivak, Guattari H. 1988. "Subaltern Studies: Deconstructing Historiography." Pp. 3–44 in *Selected Subaltern Studies*, ed. R. Guha and G. C. Spivak. New York: Oxford University Press.

Sreberny, Annabelle. 2000. "Globalization." Pp. 930–34 in *International Encyclopedia of Women: Global Women's Issues and Knowledge*, ed. Chris Kramarae and Dale Spender. New York: Routledge.

Staggenborg, Suzanne. 1986. "Coalition Work in the Pro-Choice Movement." *Social Problems* 33:374–90.

______. 1991. *The Pro-Choice Movement: Organization and Activism in the Abortion Conflict*. New York: Oxford University Press.

Staples, Steven. 2000. "The Relationship between Globalization and Militarism." *Social Justice* 27(4):18–23.

Staudt, Kathleen, ed. 1990. *Women, International Development, and Politics: The Bureaucratic Mire*. Philadelphia: Temple University Press.

Steady, Filomina Chioma, and Remie Toure, eds. 1995. *Women and the United Nations*. Rochester, VT: Schenkman.

Stearns, Jill. 1998. *Gender and International Relations: An Introduction*. New Brunswick, NJ: Rutgers University Press.

Stienstra, Deborah. 1999. "Of Roots, Leaves, and Trees: Gender, Social Movements, and

Global Governance." Pp. 260–72 in *Politics in Global Governance,* ed. Mary K. Meyer and Elisabeth Prügl. Lanham, MD: Rowman & Littlefield.

Stites, Richard. 1978. *The Women's Liberation Movement in Russia: Feminism, Nihilism, and Bolshevism, 1860–1930.* Princeton, NJ: Princeton University Press.

Stone Sweet, Alec, and Jane Caporaso. 1998. "From Free Trade to Supranational Polity: The European Court and Integration." In *European Integration and Supranational Governance,* ed. Wayne Sandholtz and Alec Stone Sweet. Oxford: Oxford University Press.

Sturgeon, Noël. 1995. "Theorizing Movements: Direct Action and Direct Theory." Pp. 35–51 in *Cultural Politics and Social Movements,* ed. Marcy Darnovsky, Barbara Epstein, and Richard Flacks. Philadelphia: Temple University Press.

______. 1997. *Ecofeminist Natures: Race, Gender, Feminist Theory, and Political Action.* New York: Routledge.

Sullivan, Gail. 1982. "Cooptation of Alternative Services: The Battered Women's Movement as a Case Study." *Catalyst* 14:39–56.

Suny, Ronald. [1990] 1995. "State, Civil Society, and Ethnic Cultural Consolidation in the USSR: The Roots of the National Question." Pp. 351–64 in *The Soviet System: From Crisis to Collapse.* Boulder, CO: Westview.

Swidler, Ann 1985. Cultural Power and Social Movements. Pp. 25–40 in *Social Movements and Culture,* ed. Hank Johnston and Bert Klandermans. Minneapolis: University of Minnesota Press.

Tabb, William K. 2001. *The Amoral Elephant: Globalization and the Struggle for Social Justice in the Twenty-First Century.* New York: Monthly Review Press.

Taira, Koji. 1997. "Troubled National Identity: The Ryukyuans/Okinawans." Pp. 160–77 in *Japan's Minorities: The Illusion of Homogeneity,* ed. Michael Weiner. New York: Routledge.

Takaki, Ronald. 1993. *A Different Mirror: A History of Multicultural America.* Boston: Little, Brown.

Takazato, Suzuyo. 1995. "Testimony: An Okinawa Swallowed Up by the Bases." *Asia-Japan Women's Resource Center* (August 20–25).

______. 1996. *Women in Okinawa: Women's Human Rights and Military Bases* (*Okinawa no Onna Tachi: Josei no jinken to kichi, guntai*). Tokyo: Akashi Shoten.

______. 1997a. "The Military Mechanism: Systemic Violence and Women." Okinawa Country Report to the International Conference on Violence against Women in War and Armed Conflict Situations, October 30–November 3, Tokyo.

______. 1997b. "Okinawa Women, Fight Back the U.S. Military Base!" *Voices from Japan, Women's Asia* (October). Asian-Japan Women's Resource Center.

______. 1999. Personal interview. July 24.

______. 2000. "Report from Okinawa: Long-Term U.S. Military Presence and Violence against Women." Special issue, "Women in Conflict Zones." *Canadian Woman Studies* 19(4).

Tamamori, Terunobu, and John James. 1999. "A Minute Guide to Okinawa: Society and Economy." Bank of the Ryukyus International Foundation.

Tamboura, Sékou. 1997. "Les femmes deputés: quelle défense pour quelles armes?" *Nyéléni Magazine* 16:4,10.

Tarrow, Sidney. 1998. *Power in Movement: Social Movements and Contentious Politics*. 2nd ed. New York: Cambridge University Press.

Taylor, Verta, and Whittier, Nancy. 1992. "Collective Identity in Social Movement Communities: Lesbian Feminist Mobilization." Pp. 104–30 in *Frontiers of Social Movement Theory*, ed. Aldon Morris and Carol Mueller. New Haven, CT: Yale University Press.

Templin, Neal. 2000. "Anatomy of a Jobs Program That Went Awry." *Wall Street Journal*, February 11.

Tesoka, Sabrina. 1999. "The Differential Impact of Judicial Politics in the Field of Gender Equality. Three National Cases under Scrutiny." *RSC Working Paper* No. 99/18. Florence: European University Institute.

Thayer, Millie. 2001. "Joan Scott in the Sertao: Rural Brazilian Women and Transnational Feminism." *Ethnography* 2(2):243–72.

Tiano, Susan. 1990. "Maquiladora Women: A New Category of Workers?" in *Women Workers and Global Restructuring*, ed. Kathy Ward. Ithaca, NY: Cornell University Press.

______. 1994. *Patriarchy on the Line: Labor, Gender, and Ideology in the Mexican Maquila Industry*. Philadelphia: Temple University Press.

Tinker, Irene. 1997. "The Making of a Field: Advocates, Practitioners, and Scholars." Pp. 33–41 in *The Women, Gender, and Development Reader*, ed. N. Visvanathan, L. Dagan, L. Nisonoff, and N. Wiegersma. London: Zed.

______. 1999a. "Nongovernmental Organizations: An Alternative Power Base for Women?" Pp. 88–106 in *Gender Politics in Global Governance*, ed. Mary K. Meyer and Elizabeth Prügl. Lanham, MD: Rowman & Littlefield.

______. ed. 1990/1999b. *Persistent Inequalities: Women and World Development*. New York: Oxford University Press.

Tolentino, Richard. 1996. "Bodies, Letters, Catalogs: Filipinas in Transnational Space." *Social Text* 48:50–76.

Traoré, Maïmouna. 1997. "Femmes et institutions: enfin le bout du tunnel," *Nyéléni Magazine* 4(16):3.

Trinh, T. Minh-ha. 1989. *Woman Native Other: Writing Postcoloniality and Feminism*. Bloomington: Indiana University Press.

Tully, James. 1995. *Strange Multiplicity: Constitutionalism in an Age of Diversity*. Cambridge: Cambridge University Press.

Turshen, Meredeth. 1994. "The Impact of Economic Reforms on Women's Health and Health Care in Sub-Saharan Africa." Pp. 77–95 in *Women in the Age of Economic Transformation*, ed. Nahid Aslanbeigui, Steven Pressman, and Gale Summerfield. London: Routledge.

Ueunten, Wesley. 1997. "In the Shadow of Domination: The Asian American and Okinawan Movements." Unpublished manuscript, Department of Ethnic Studies, University of California-Berkeley.

United Nations. 1985. "The Nairobi Forward Looking Strategies." Department of Public Information. United Nations, New York.

______. 1995. "The Beijing Declaration and The Platform for Action." New York: Department of Public Information, United Nations.

______. 1997. "The United Nations and the Advancement of Women 1945–1996." New York: United Nations.

United Nations Commission on Crime Prevention and Criminal Justice. 1996. "Implementation of the Naples Political Declaration and Global Action Plan against Organized Transnational Crime Report of the Secretary-General." Fifth session, Vienna, May 21–31. Retrieved January 13, 1999, http://www.uncjin.org/Documents/5comm/2e.htm.

United Nations Development Programme. 1997. *Human Development Report 1997*. New York: Oxford University Press.

United Nations Gender in Development Bureau. 1999. *Gender Analysis of Ukrainian Society*. Kyiv: United Nations Gender in Development Bureau.

UNICEF and the Republic of Mali. 1998. "Programme de cooperation Mali-UNICEF 1998–2002." Bamako: UNICEF.

UNIFEM. 2000. "Progress of the World's Women." Biennial report, United Nations Development Fund for Women.

USAID. 1982. "A.I.D. Policy Paper: Women in Development." Bureau for Program and Policy Coordination.

______. 1998. "USAID Congressional Presentation." United States Agency for International Development website http://www.info.usaid.gov/countries/ua/: Ukraine Country Report on Human Rights.

______. 1999. "Addressing Gender Concerns: The Success of the USAID Gender Plan of Action and USAID Country Programs."

______. N.d.-a. "Lessons without Borders: Local Problems, Global Solutions."

______. N.d.-b. "Lessons without Borders: USAID Shares Microenterprise Experience."

______. N.d.-c. "The USAID Fact Sheet."

U.S. Department of Justice. 2001. United States Immigration and Naturalization History. Available at: http://www.ins.usdoj.gov/graphics/aboutins/statistics/legishist/index.htm.

U.S. Department of State. 1994. "Ukraine Human Rights Practices, 1993." U.S. Department of State website http://www.state.gov/www/global/human_rights/hrp_reports_mainhp.html: Ukraine Country Report on Human Rights Practices for 1993. Released by the Bureau of Democracy, Human Rights, and Labor, January 30, 1997.

______. 1997. "Ukraine Human Rights Practices, 1996." U.S. Department of State website http://www.state.gov/www/global/human_rights/hrp_reports_mainhp.html: Ukraine Country Report on Human Rights Practices for 1996. Released by the Bureau of

Democracy, Human Rights, and Labor, January 30, 1997.

Verdery, Katherine. 1994. "From Parent-State to Family Patriarchs: Gender and Nation in Contemporary East Europe." *Eastern European Politics and Societies* 8(2):225–55.

______. 1996. *What Was Socialism, and What Comes Next?* Princeton, NJ: Princeton University Press.

Veseth, Michael. 1998. *Selling Globalization: The Myth of the Global Economy*. Boulder, CO: Rienner.

Vickers, Jeanne. 1991. *Women and the World Economic Crisis*. London: Zed.

Visvanathan, Nalini, Lynne Dagan, Laurie Nisonoff, and Nalini Wiegersma, eds. 1997. *The Women, Gender, and Development Reader.* London: Zed.

Volunteers in Technical Assistance. 2001. "Morocco: Microenterprise Finance Activity." http://www.vita.org/projects/moroc.htm.

Wachtel, Howard. 2001. "Tax Distortion in the Global Economy." Paper presented at the Global Tensions Conference, March 10, 2001, Cornell University, Ithaca, New York.

Walcott, Clotil. 1993. "Sexism Reigns with Trio of Evils." *Sunday Express Independence Supplement,* August 29.

______. 1997. "Look at the Poor Workers." *Newsday,* December 16.

______. 1998. Interview conducted at NUDE's offices.

______. 2000. Interview conducted at NUDE's offices.

Walker, Thomas W. 1997. "Introduction: Historical Setting and Important Issues." Pp. 1–20 in *Nicaragua without Illusions: Regime Transition and Structural Adjustment in the 1990s,* ed. Thomas W. Walker. Wilmington, DE: Scholarly Resources.

Wapner, Paul. 1995. "Politics beyond the State: Environmental Activism and World Civic Politics." *World Politics* 47(3):311–40.

Ward, Kathy, ed. 1990. *Women Workers and Global Restructuring.* Ithaca, NY: Cornell University Press.

Warkentin, Craig. 2001. *Reshaping World Politics: NGOs, the Internet, and Global Civil Society.* New York: Rowman & Littlefield.

Warner, Harriet. 1984. "EC Social Policy in Practice: Community Action on Behalf of Women and Its Impact in the Member States." *Journal of Common Market Studies* 23:141–67.

Warren, Karen J. 1991. Introduction to *Hypatia* 6(1):1–2.

______, ed. 1994. *Ecological Feminism*. New York: Routledge.

Waterman, Peter. 1998. *Globalization, Social Movements, and the New Internationalisms.* London: Mansell.

Wisconsin Coordination Council on Nicaragua (WCCN). 1995. "Nicaraguan Women's U.S. Tour." Madison: WCCN.

Webb, Yvonne. 1999. "NUDE Calls for Equal Treatment for Low Income Workers—Calls on Govt to Honour Commitment to Beijing Platform." *Trinidad Guardian* April 6.

Weber, Clare. 1992. "The Peace Commissions of Nueva Guinea." Masters Thesis. Latin

American Studies. California State University, Los Angeles.

Weiss, Meredith L. 1999. "Democracy at the Margins: NGOs and Women's 'Unofficial' Political Participation in Singapore." Pp. 67–92 in *Democratization and Women's Grassroots Movements*, ed. Jill M. Bystydzienski and Joti Sekhon. Bloomington, Indiana: Indiana University Press.

Wekker, Gloria. 1997. "One Finger Does Not Drink Okra Soup: Afro-Surinamese Women and Critical Agency." Pp. 330–52 in *Feminist Genealogies, Colonial Legacies, Democratic Futures*, ed. M. J. Alexander and C. T. Mohanty. New York: Routledge.

Wellman, Barry, and B. Leighton, 1979. "Networks, Neighborhoods and Communities." *Urban Affairs Quarterly* 14:363–90.

Wells, Betty L., and Shelly Gradwell. 2000. "CSA: Woman Friendly Enterprise." *Women, Food and Agriculture Network Newsletter* 3(2): June, pp. 1, 6, 7.

Wells, Betty L., and Bonnie O. Tanner. 1994. "The Organizational Potential of Women in Agriculture to Sustain Rural Communities." *Journal of the Community Development Society* 5(2):246–58.

West, Guida and Rhoda Lois Blumberg, eds. 1990. *Women and Social Protest*. New York: Oxford University Press.

West, Lois A. 1997. "Introduction: Feminism Constructs Nationalism." In *Feminist Nationalism*, ed. Lois A. West. London: Routledge.

______. 1999. "The United Nations Women's Conferences and Feminist Politics." Pp. 177–193 in *Gender Politics in Global Governance,* ed. Mary K. Meyer and Elisabeth Prügl. Lanham, MD: Rowman & Littlefield.

Westra, Laura, and Peter Wenz, eds. 1995. *Faces of Environmental Racism: Confronting Issues of Global Justice*. London: Rowman & Littlefield.

White, Nijole. 1977. "Women in Changing Societies: Latvia and Lithuania." Pp. 203–18 in *Post-Soviet Women: From the Baltic to Central Asia,* ed. May Buckley. New York: Cambridge University Press.

White, Sarah C. 2000. "Men, Masculinities, and the Politics of Development." Pp. 205–11 in *Perspectives: Gender Studies*, eds. Renae Moore Bredin and Ana Louise Keating. Bellevue: Coursewise.

White, Stephen K. 1998. *The Recent Work of Jürgen Habermas: Reason, Justice, and Modernity*. Cambridge: Cambridge University Press.

Wiegersma, Nan. 1997. Introduction to Part 4 of *The Women, Gender, and Development Reader*, ed. N. Visvanathan, L. Dagan, L. Nisonoff, and N. Wiegersma. London: Zed.

Wignaraja, Ponna, ed. 1993. *New Social Movements in the South*. London: Zed.

Williams, Fiona. 1995. "Race/Ethnicity, Gender, and Class in Welfare States: A Framework for Comparative Analysis." *Social Politics* 2(2):127–59.

Williams, Patrick, and Laura Chrisman. *Colonial Discourse and Post-Colonial Theory: A Reader.* New York: Columbia University Press.

Wirth, Danielle M. 1996. "Environmental Ethics Made Explicit through Situated Narrative: Implications for Agriculture and Environmental Education." Ph.D. dissertation, Iowa State University, Ames.

Wirth, Danielle, and Gail Hutchison. 1999. "Detroit and the National Town Meeting." *Women, Food, and Agriculture Network Newsletter,* August 2, p. 7.

Women's Affairs Division. 1995. *National Report on the Status of Women in Trinidad and Tobago.* Prepared for the Fourth World Conference on Women, Beijing, China.

Women's Information Consultative Center. 1996. *Directory of Women's Organizations and Initiatives in Ukraine.* Kiev: Women's Information Consultative Center.

Women's Technical Exchange. 1995. "Report of Women's Technical Exchange." Madison: Wisconsin Coordinating Council on Nicaragua.

Woo, Deborah. 2000. *Glass ceilings and Asian Americans.* Walnut Creek, CA: AltaMira.

Wood, Elizabeth. 1997. *The Baba and the Comrade: Gender and Politics in Revolutionary Russia.* Bloomington: University of Indiana Press.

World Bank. 1995. "Trinidad and Tobago: Poverty and Unemployment in an Oil Based Economy." Report Number 14382-TR. Washington, DC: World Bank, Caribbean Division.

______. 1996. *From Plan to Market.* New York: Oxford University Press.

______. 2000 *Advancing Gender Equality: World Bank Action Since Beijing.* Washington DC: World Bank.

Young, Iris Marion. 1990. *Justice and the Politics of Difference.* Princeton, NJ: Princeton University Press.

Youngs, Gillian. 1996. "Dangers of Discourse: The Case of Globalization." Pp. 58–71 in *Globalization: Theory and Practice,* ed. Eleanore Kofman and Gillian Youngs. New York: Pinter.

______. 1999. *International Relations in a Global Age: A Conceptual Challenge.* Malden, MA: Blackwell.

Youngs, Gillian, Kathleen B. Jones, and Jan Jindy Pettman. 1999. "New Spaces, New Politics." *International Feminist Journal of Politics* 1(1):1–13.

Yuval-Davis, Nira. 1999. The Multi-Layered Citizen: Citizenship in the Age of Globalization. *International Feminist Journal of Politics* 1:141–36.

Zinn, Maxine Baca, and Bonnie Thornton Dill. 1996. "Theorizing Difference from Multiracial Feminism." *Feminist Studies* 22(2):321–31.

Zukin, Sharon. 1995. *The Cultures of Cities.* London: Blackwell.

Contributors

RACHEL A. CICHOWSKI is an assistant professor of political science at the University of Washington. Her visiting research appointments include Visiting Research Fellow at the European University Institute, Florence, Italy (1998–99) and Visiting Fellow at the Max Planck Institute, Bonn, Germany (2000). Her research interests include comparative judicial politics and political participation, with particular emphasis on the empowering effects of international and supranational courts. Her current research focuses on the role of the European Court of Justice and transnational activism in European integration in the environmental and social policy areas. Her research has appeared in edited volumes and has been published in numerous journals, including *Comparative Political Studies*, *Journal of European Public Policy*, and *Women & Politics*.

MANISHA DESAI is chair of the Department of Sociology and Anthropology at Hobart and William Smith Colleges and a member of the Women's Studies Program. Her main area of research is social movements, in particular the women's movement in India and the international women's movements. She also contributes to analyses of international development and human rights. Her work has been published in various journals and edited volumes. She is completing a book on three generations of women's rights activists in India. She has been invited to present her work in international forums in Norway, Israel, India, and Canada, among others.

YOKO FUKUMURA is a doctoral student in the Department of History at UC-Santa Cruz. She is a member of Okinawa Women Act against Militarism (OWAAMV) and a founding member of the Okinawa Peace Network and the East Asia-U.S. Women's Network against Militarism. Her field of research focuses on the modern history of Okinawa with perspectives of Japanese colonialism and nationalism (late nineteenth century to early twentieth century) and post–World War II Okinawa.

ALEXANDRA HRYCAK is an assistant professor of sociology at Reed College in Portland, Oregon. Her current work focuses on rivalries between feminist and nationalist women's organizations in Ukraine, and, more broadly, on the role that women's NGOs have played in the creation of post-Soviet publics. She has contributed articles on culture and identity to the *American Journal of Sociology*, the *Encyclopedia of Nationalism*, and *Harvard Ukrainian Studies*. She is also working on a book on theatergoing and the creation of public spheres in Ukraine.

MARINA KARIDES is an assistant professor at Florida Atlantic University. Her research interests are race, class, and gender inequalities and globalization. Her current work focuses on the implications of microenterprise development policies in Trinidad and the Caribbean.

MARTHA MATSUOKA is a doctoral student in urban planning at University of California, Los Angeles. She is a founding member of the Okinawa Peace Network and the East Asia–U.S. Women's Network against Militarism. Her research in neighborhood and metropolitan development focuses on organizing and planning as strategies for neighborhood development and social change. Her dissertation focuses on neighborhood-based organizing for the redevelopment of brownfields and the restoration of contaminated lands in low-income neighborhoods of people of color in Los Angeles County. Earlier research on Okinawa includes an assessment of community-based economic development strategies in Onna Village.

JENNIFER BICKHAM MENDEZ is an assistant professor of sociology at the College of William and Mary. Her research interests include gender and globalization, social movements, and transnational studies. She is the author of the forthcoming book entitled *The Global Here and Now: Gender and the Politics of Transnationalism in Nicaragua*. Her manuscript, "Creating Alternatives for Resistance: Gender and the Politics of Transnationalism in Nicaragua" is under review for publication. She is currently conducting research on Nicaraguan transmigrants in Miami, Florida.

NANCY A. NAPLES is author of *Grassroots Warriors: Activist Mothering, Community Work, and the War on Poverty* (Routledge, 1988), which was a finalist for the C. Wright Mills Award of the Society for the Study of Social Problems. She is also editor of *Community Activism and Feminist Politics: Organizing across Gender, Race, and Class* (forthcoming, Routledge). She currently holds a joint appointment in sociology and women's studies at the University of Connecticut. Her main research interests center on exploring the development of women's political consciousness and activism; the role of the state in reproducing or challenging inequality; and how differing community contexts influence women's resistance and political activism.

SHARON ANN NAVARRO is minority scholar-in-residence post-doctoral fellow in the department of political science at Carleton College. She has co-authored a book (with C. Richard Bath) titled *Elections and Party Politics in the State of Chihuahua: 1982–1994.* Her article "Las Voces de Esperanza (The Voices of Hope): La Mujer Obrera" is forthcoming in *Globalization on the Line: Gender, Nation, and Capital at U.S. Border*, ed. Claudia Sadowski-Smith and James D. Lilley. She is the recipient of the Ford Dissertation Fellowship for the academic year 2000–2001 by the National Academies of Science and the Chicana Dissertation Fellowship by the University of California-Santa Barbara. Her dissertation research focuses on Latinas, identity politics, and cross-border mobilization at the U.S.-Mexico border.

WINIFRED POSTER is an assistant professor of sociology at the University of Illinois, Urbana-Champaign. Her area of interest is gender and globalization. She has written on feminist activism, both in the California Bay Area (regarding class and race divisions among women's organizations), and transnationally in the United States and Morocco (through inter- and nongovernmental organizations). She is also interested in employment issues in the global economy, and is currently working on a book on which examines transnational configurations of gender in high-tech multinational corporations in the United States and India. Additional projects address corporate responsibility, international labor standards, and work-family policies in mulitnationals. Her research has appeared in the *Journal of Developing Societies*, *Gender & Society*, the *American Sociological Review*, and in a book with Stanford University Press.

BANDANA PURKAYASTHA holds a joint appointment in sociology and Asian-American studies at the University of Connecticut. Her current research is on women's earnings in global cities and the persistence of ethnic vitality. She is also working on a book looking at the experiences of second-generation nonwhite youths and a transnational model of ethnicity. She grew up in a family of activists, and she volunteers for Sneha in Connecticut and Vivekananda Nisdhi in Calcutta.

ZAKIA SALIME is an assistant professor at Ecole Normale Superieure in Fes, Morocco, and a Ph.D. student in sociology at the University of Illinois, Urbana-Champaign. She has published many articles on women and political participation, microenterprises, and structural adjustment in Morocco. Since 1994, she has been the head of a nongovernmental organization for women's microbusiness in Fes, and through this has taken part in several United Nations Conferences on women. Her current research is on women's movements in North Africa and the Arab world.

CLARE WEBER has a Ph.D. in social relations from the University of California, Irvine. She worked for many years as a human rights and community activist in Central America and Los Angeles. Her publications include "Latino Street Vendors in Los Angeles: Heterogeneous Alliances, Community-Based Activism and the State," in *Asian and Latino Immigrants in a Restructuring Economy: The Metamorphous of Southern California*, ed. Marta Lopez-Garza and David R. Diaz (2001). Her latest feminist and sociological research focuses on transnational activist responses to global economic processes and human rights with a focus on North-to-South activist dynamics.

BETTY L. WELLS is a professor of sociology at Iowa State University. She is a rural community development practitioner whose work focuses on local responses to rural restructuring, especially its gendered aspects, including the development of local food systems and rural women's networks and activism. Her current research focuses on the relationship between gender and land tenure in a participatory research project with women farmland owners in southwestern Iowa.

SUSANNA D. WING is a lecturer in the Department of Political Science and the International Development Studies Program at the University of California, Los Angeles. She has lived and conducted research in Mali, Nigeria, and France. Her current research focuses on democracy, women's rights, and legal pluralism in West Africa.

Index